GLOBAL AUCTION OF PUBLIC ASSETS

Global Auction of Public Assets

*Public Sector Alternatives
to the Infrastructure Market
and Public Private Partnerships*

Dexter Whitfield

SPOKESMAN

First published in 2010 by
Spokesman
Russell House, Bulwell Lane
Nottingham
NG6 0BT, England
Phone 0115 9708381   Fax 0115 9420433
e-mail elfeuro@compuserve.com
www.spokesmanbooks.com

© Dexter Whitfield

All rights reserved. No part of this publication may be reproduced, stored in a retrieval system or transmitted in any form or by means, electronic, mechanical, photocopying, recording or otherwise, without prior permission of the publishers.

ISBN 978 0 85124 773 1

A CIP Catalogue is available from the British Library

Printed by the Russell Press Ltd. (www.russellpress.com)

Contents

Preface

1. **Global crisis and the new infrastructure agenda**   20
   New challenges for infrastructure
   Changing context
   Fiscal crisis of the state
   Public provision of public goods

2. **The political economy of infrastructure**   40
   Definitions of infrastructure
   Privatisation and partnership models
   Infrastructure contributes to economic growth
      and community well-being
   Infrastructure expenditure and deficits

3. **Transformation and globalisation of infrastructure**   66
   Neoliberal transformation
   Political economy of public infrastructure
   Development bank infrastucture plans
   Resurgence of development banks
   PPPs as instruments of foreign policy

4. **Infrastructure – the new global wealth machine**   91
   A new asset class
   Types of infrastructure funds
   How privatisation and PPPs are financed
   Financial engineering

5. **Growth of the global infrastructure investment market**   114
   Money machines – the major investors
   Private infrastructure investment
   Infrastructure corporate interests

6. **The global spread of privatisation and PPPs**   142
   Key regional variations
   Country analysis
   United Kingdom   France
   Ireland   Germany
   USA   Canada
   Russia   Australia

    China   India
    Brazil   South Africa

7. **Trading portfolios of schools, hospitals and prisons**   183
    Growth of a secondary market
    Refinancing PPP projects
    Sale of PPP project equity/assets
    Sale of secondary market funds
    The next generation of PPPs

8. **Abandoned and terminated projects**   216

9. **Impacts of infrastructure PPPs and privatisation**   235
    Value-for-Money and the Public Sector Comparator
    Design, innovation and vision
    Affordability and cost
    Quality of service
    Governance and accountability
    Economic and social impact
    Social justice
    Quality of employment
    Public sector capability and planning

10. **Strategies for public investment**   284
    A vision for an infrastructure strategy with new priorities
    Financing public investment
    New global policies and regulations
    Revitalising the role for government
    A new evaluation framework
    PPP Infrastructure Stress Test

11. **Strengthening strategic alliances for the future**   320
    National and international alliances
    Blueprints and worker/community plans
    Organising and action
    Early intervention in planning and procurement

Conclusion   328

References   330

Index   367

Figures

1. General government gross fixed capital formation as a percentage of total government outlays, 1990-2005
2. Neoliberal approach to public sector reform
3. The PPP model in private provision
4. Infrastructure funds rise and fall, 2001-2008
5. Variations in infrastructure 'market maturity' across global markets
6. The growth wedge
7. Private infrastructure investment in developing countries 1990-2007

Tables

1. Eleven types of public infrastructure
2. Public Private Partnership (PPP) models
3. Infrastructure investment in G20 fiscal stimulus strategies
4. Political economy of public infrastructure
5. Illustrative investment returns
6. PPP assets located in tax havens
7. Global listed infrastructure market
8. Capital available in the top 10 infrastructure funds
9. Value of assets under global fund management
10. Ten largest Sovereign Wealth Funds in 2008
11. Infrastructure interests of the Macquarie Group
12. Who owns schools and hospitals?
13. Largest Transnationals in infrastructure industries
14. Top 20 transportation developers (2008)
15. International Major Projects Survey 1985-2008
16. PPPs in Europe 2000-2008
17. Infrastructure private investment in developing countries by region 1990-2007
18. Top 10 countries share of investment 1990-2007
19. Signed private finance initiative projects in the UK
20. US PPP programme 1985 – 2008
21. Asset monetisation in the US
22. Signed PPP contracts in Canada
23. Signed and planned PPPs in Australia
24. Sharing of gains on refinancing PPP/PFI projects
25. John Laing Investments
26. Macquarie European Infrastructure Fund assets
27. Annual rate of PPP equity trading by British PPP companies
28. PPP equity sales in Britain 1998-2008
29. Analysis of profits from 10 PPP equity sales
30. Sale of PPP teams and PPP contractors
31. Sale of Secondary Market Investment Funds
32. Summary of PPP and privatisation failures
33. Projects Cancelled or distressed by region 1990-2007
34. Projects Cancelled or distressed by sector 1990-2007
35. Summary of key PPP failures – Europe, North America and Australia
36. Failed privatised and PPP water projects

37. Risk allocation
38. The use of risk transfer
39. Projected dividends in six PPP projects
40. Assessing governance and accountability
41. The case against PPPs and privatisation
42. Potential savings in the UK
43. Progressive Public Service Renewal
44. Infrastructure Investment Evaluation Framework
45. Infrastructure Stress Test

Abbreviations

ABP	Associated British Ports
ADB	Asian Development Bank
AFA	Alternative Funds Advisory
AfDB	African Development Bank
AFP	Alternative Financing Procurement
AIG	America Insurance Group
AISR	Australian Institute for Social Research
ALMO	Arms Length Management Organisation
APRR	Autoroutes Paris-Rein-Rhone
ARH	Auckland Regional Holdings
ARRP	American Recovery & Reinvestment Plan
ASF	Autoroutes du Sud de la France
BBO	Buy, Build, Operate
BDES	Brazilian Development Bank
BDO	Build, Develop, Operate
BLOT	Build-Lease-Operate-Transfer
BOO	Build, Own, Operate
BOOT	Build, Own, Operate, Transfer
BOT	Build, Operate and Transfer
BROT	Build-Rent-Own-Transfer
BSA	Building Services Association
BSF	Building Schools for the Future
BTO	Build-Transfer-Operate
BTR	Brisbane Toll Road
CABE	Commission for Architecture and the Built Environment
CalPERS	California Public Employees Retirement System
CBI	Confederation of British Industry
CBO	Congressional Budget Office
CCT	Cross City Tunnel
CCM	Cross City Motorway Consortium
CDC	Community Development Corporations
CDO	Collateralised Debt Obligations
CDS	Credit Default Swaps
CEDB	Council of Europe Development Bank
CFIUS	Committee on Foreign Investment in the US
CHP	Community Health Partnerships
CMR	Construction Management at Risk
COAG	Council of Australian Governments
COFOG	UN Classification of the Functions of Government

CUPE	Canadian Union of Public Employees
DBFO	Design, Build, Finance and Operate
DCLG	Department for Communities and Local Government
DCMF	Design, Construct, Manage, Finance
DCSF	Department for Children, Schools and Families
DfT	Department for Transport
DH	Department of Health
DoE	Department of the Environment
DPW	Dubai World Ports
DSA	Driver Standards Agency
DSO	Direct Service Organisation
DVLA	Driver and Vehicle Licensing Authority
DWP	Department for Work and Pensions
EBRD	European Bank for Reconstruction & Development
EDS	Electronic Data Service
EIB	European Investment Bank
EIC	European International Contractors
EPB	Economic Prosperity Boards
EPI	Economic Policy Institute
EPEC	European PPP Expertise Centre
EPPPC	European PPP Centre
EPSN	European Public Services Network
EPSU	European Public Service Unions
ESDP	European Spatial Development Perspective
ESF	European Social Forum
ESSU	European Services Strategy Unit
ETUC	European Trade Union Confederation
EU	European Union
EURODAD	European Network on Debt And Development
FDI	Foreign Direct Investment
FHA	Federal Highways Administration
FM	Facilities Management
FOI	Freedom of Information Act
GAO	General Accountability Office
GATS	General Agreement for Trade in Services
GCHQ	Government Communications Headquarters
GDP	Gross Domestic Product
GS	Goldman Sachs
GSL	Global Solutions
G20	Group of 20 Industrial and Emerging-Market Countries

HICL	HSBC Infrastructure Company Ltd
IAP	Infrastructure Action Plan
IBM	International Business Machines
IBRD	International Bank for Reconstruction and Development
ICA	Infrastructure Consortium for Africa
ICC	International Chamber of Commerce
ICSID	International Centre for the Settlement of Investment Disputes
ICT	Information and Communications Technology
IDB	Inter-American Development Bank
IEA	International Energy Agency
IFC	International Finance Corporation
IFDC	Infrastructure Finance Development Corporation
IFRS	International Financial Reporting Standard
IFSL	International Financial Services London
IIFCL	India Infrastructure Finance Company Ltd
IIG	Infrastructure Investment Group
IMF	International Monetary Fund
IRP	Independent Reconfiguration Panel
ISTC	Independent Sector Treatment Centre
JASPERS	Joint Assistance in Supporting Projects in European Regions
JESSICA	Joint European Support for Sustainable Investment in City Areas
JVC	Joint Venture Company
KIA	Kuwait Investment Authority
KKR	Kohlberg Kravis Roberts
LABV	Local Asset Backed Vehicles
LAC	Latin America and Caribbean Region
LDO	Lease, Develop, Operate
LEP	Local Education Partnership
LIFT	Local Improvement Finance Trust
LSP	Local Strategic Partnership
MAA	Multi-Area Agreements
MAP	Macquarie Airports
MCG	Macquarie Communications Infrastructure Group
MDG	Millennium Development Goals
METP	Marches d'Entreprises de Travaux Publics
MIG	Macquarie Infrastructure Group
MIGA	Multilateral Investment Guarantee Agency

MIIF	Macquarie International Infrastructure Fund
MoD	Ministry of Defence
MoDEL	Ministry of Defence Estate in London
MRG	Minimum Revenue Guarantee
NAO	National Audit Office
NATO	North Atlantic Treaty Organisation
NAFTA	North American Free Trade Agreement
NCPPP	National Council for Public Private Partnership
NGO	Non-Governmental Organisations
NHS	National Health Service
NPDO	Non-Profit Distribution Organisation
NPV	Net Present Value
NTTA	North Texas Tollway Authority
OBC	Outline Business Case
ODA	Official Development Assistance
OECD	Organisation for Economic Co-operation and Development
OGC	Office of Government Commerce
OJEU	Official Journal of the European Union
OMERS	Ontario Municipal Employees Retirement System
PCT	Primary Care Trust
PDO	Project Development Organisation
PFI	Private Finance Initiative
PfS	Partnerships for Schools
POAL	Ports of Auckland Ltd
PPC	Prime Plus Contacting
PPI	Private Participation in Infrastructure
PPIAF	Public Private Infrastructure Advisory Facility
PPP	Public Private Partnership
PRGF	Poverty Reduction and Growth Facility
PRSC	Poverty Reduction Support Credit
P3	Public Private Partnership
PSC	Public Sector Comparator
PwC	PricewaterhouseCoopers
RBS	Royal Bank of Scotland
RCE	Regional Centre of Excellence
REIT	Real Estate Investment Trust
ROSCO	Rolling Stock Company
SANEF	Societe des Autroutes de Nord et de l'Est de la France
SED	Strategic Estates Development

SIP	Strategic Infrastructure Partnerships
SMIF	Secondary Market Infrastructure Fund
SPB	Strategic Partnership Boards
SPP	Social Private Partnerships
SPV	Special Purpose Vehicle
SRA	Strategic Rail Authority
SSP	Strategic Service-delivery Partnership
STEPS	Strategic Transfer of the Estate to the Private Sector
SWF	Sovereign Wealth Fund
TARP	Troubled Asset Relief Programme
TABD	Transatlantic Business Dialogue
TEU	Twentyfoot Equivalent Units
TIFIA	Transportation Infrastructure Finance & Innovation Act 1998
TNC	Transnational Corporation/Companies
TRIPS	Trade-Related aspects of Intellectual Property Rights
TUPE	Transfer of Undertakings (Protection of Employment) Regulations 1981
UK	United Kingdom
UN	United Nations
UNDP	United Nations Development Programme
UNCTAD	United Nations Conference on Trade and Development
UNECE	United Nations Economic Commission for Europe
US	United States
VITA	Virginia Information Technologies Agency
VfM	Value-for-Money
WBG	World Bank Group
WEF	World Economic Forum
WTO	World Trade Organisation

Preface

The public infrastructure provides basic human needs – homes, water, energy for light, heat and cooking; the transport of people, raw materials and goods by road, rail, sea and air; hospitals, schools, sports and leisure and cultural facilities; communications networks; police stations, courts and prisons for the criminal justice system; and civic and governmental buildings for democratic governance, social and political activity.

As living standards rise, we rely more heavily on access to, for example, electricity for information and communications systems, air conditioning and consumer gadgets; land, sea and air transport for trade and travel. The quality and access to infrastructure determines community well-being, social justice, cultural life and governance. We expect public infrastructure to be safe, reliable, well designed, networked and democratically managed with reasonable prices or charges and progressive taxation.

Infrastructure has a vital role in achieving economic development and stability, growth and regeneration and eliminating poverty. But there can also be negative consequences – the upheaval of relocation of homes and livelihoods and the loss of jobs in the transfer from a fossil fuel-based energy sector to a low carbon economy.

The network industries (transport, energy, water, information and communications technology) are the prime focus of the World Bank and development agencies, but they are only part of public infrastructure. The health, education, housing, justice system, sport, cultural and governance infrastructure are equally important.

Infrastructure investment declined as a proportion of Gross Domestic Product (GDP) in most countries over the last thirty years as a result of public policy and fiscal decisions on taxation, user fees and spending priorities. Public infrastructure has been privatised to an unprecedented degree in the same period, although the extent and scale varies widely between countries and sectors.

The term Public Private Partnership (PPP) is used throughout this book to include the Private Finance Initiative, P3s (in USA and Canada), Strategic Service-delivery Partnerships, Build Operate Transfer (BOT) and similar types of partnerships. There are differences in the national legal, financial and political frameworks within which PPPs operate, and there are variant PPP models just as there are types of privatisation.

The objectives of this book
This book examines the emergence of a global infrastructure market driven by the privatisation of utilities, transportation and other public assets, together with the widening use of Public Private Partnerships. The infrastructure market and PPPs are essentially one and the same and should not be examined in isolation. Most studies of PPPs and privatisation pay scant regard to the growth and scale of the global infrastructure market, and, in particular, the competition for resources between infrastructure sectors, between construction and finance capital, and between them, the state and development banks. The assessment and evaluation of proposals and bids is usually less than comprehensive and frequently contrived. Equally, the long-term implications of infrastructure markets and PPP policies are frequently ignored.

What is at stake is far greater than any cost difference between public and private investment, obtaining new or improved buildings and networks and sustaining quality employment, important as these are. What also matters is social justice, the transition to a low carbon economy, sustainable economic and social development, the transformation of public services, the regulation and control of markets, and taxation/use of public resources.

I begin with an overview of the major challenges confronting future infrastructure investment – climate change, the new energy order, the growth of megacities, global trade, the water crisis and the digital economy – in the context of geo-political power shifts, the government debt crisis and the World Trade Organisation's (WTO) plan to extend the marketisation and privatisation of public services.

The public infrastructure provides the networks, buildings and facilities to power the economy and enable us to live our lives. It also creates employment in construction and maintenance and the services that operate within the buildings. Public infrastructure also supports jobs and businesses in the production and supply chains that deliver the materials, equipment, furniture and goods required to build and operate the facilities. The jobs in infrastructure and production and supply chain in turn support further employment through consumer spending in the local economy.

Public Private Partnerships are a product of neoliberal economic policy and public sector reform. Financialisation, commodification and marketisation are creating a global wealth machine to further exploit public needs and resources. Transnational construction, energy and service companies, banks, management consultants and law firms, aided and abetted by governments, are turning schools, hospitals, prisons and roads into commodities which are bought and sold globally. As PPPs and privatisation proliferate, more new infrastructure investment funds are set up, increasingly with the collusion of pension funds, to trade in this new 'asset class' (chapters 4-7). This is not an economic or social crusade to get 'additional investment', but has the objective of full privatisation of the public infrastructure and services, and consolidating the corporate empires to facilitate this process. PPPs are not just about buildings, they are increasingly focused on the 'whole service' concept.

Why the drive for Public Private Partnerships?
PPPs, or variations of the design, build, finance and operate model, initially allow governments to improve and expand the public infrastructure to a greater extent than the resources available from a low tax/balanced budget regime permits. However, this is short-lived and is flawed as a long-term strategy.

Firstly, a low taxation/low public spending regime does not provide sufficient resources to properly maintain the existing infrastructure and to build new facilities and networks required by economic growth and population increases. This results in governments switching to increase financial resources through indirect taxation by imposing charges, tolls and market tariffs on service users. But this has fundamental economic, equity, social justice and public interest problems. In other words, PPPs mask the fact that it is impossible to have a low taxation/low public spending model of government *and* provide comprehensive good quality public infrastructure to meet the economic and social needs of modern society (see chapter 10).

Secondly, PPPs manipulate public sector financial and accountancy rules to conceal public debt and the ownership of public assets. Off-balance sheet projects are structured on a 'build now, pay later' basis, and are in practice no different from the credit card consumerism boom that contributed to the global financial crisis. Project debt is securitised similar to mortgages. Furthermore, PPPs create the illusion of infrastructure being privately financed when, in fact, it is ultimately entirely financed by taxpayers and/or service users. Public debt is transferred to contract obligations under long-term leases, which require government to repay the private sector via a stream of revenue payments and/or future generations of service users are saddled with ever-increasing tolls and charges. Narrowly defined public sector comparators and value-for-money appraisal ensure that democratic accountability, economic development, sustainability, social justice and other public interest matters are marginal to the financial assessment of risk and 'whole life' costs.

Thirdly, the construction industry, financial institutions and consultants gain by having a larger workload than would otherwise be the case under a low taxation/low public expenditure regime. Having diversified into facilities management, construction subsidiaries frequently gain long-term operating and maintenance contracts. PPPs, in effect, commodify and privatise future efficiency gains so that they primarily benefit the private sector consortia rather than the public sector. There is nothing innovative about this, it is simply identifying the potential long-term gains in a 25-30 year contract and capturing them for private value.

Banks, private equity and infrastructure funds gain new opportunities for investment and accumulation, supported by government-backed security, designed to maximise their profits and minimise risk. The full extent of government guarantees, subsidies and tax concessions are rarely disclosed. Private architects, lawyers, engineers and management consultants gain new commissions, and advisers benefit in direct proportion to the increasing financial and legal complexity of PPPs.

Fourthly, PPPs transfer some risks to the private sector but at a price. Contractors and financial institutions charge a premium for taking on risks, which, in other circumstances, they would be responsible for, but would have other methods of avoiding, mitigating or eliminating. PPPs place certain responsibility for construction and operational risks on contractors, who, on payment of the risk premium, can now build on time and within budget!

Fifthly, work and jobs are reorganised to maximise productivity. Public sector workers are made redundant, transferred or seconded to a private contractor with more extensive use of cheaper migrant labour on construction sites, with poor work conditions.

Finally, the refinancing of projects and sale of equity has resulted in the growth of a secondary market, in which schools and hospitals are sold like commodities to infrastructure and private equity funds and companies. They manage ever larger bundles of assets to extract further profit.

In 2001, I concluded in *Public Services or Corporate Welfare* that the

PPP model is '... *a new development paradigm and raises key questions of who will own and control cities/regions in the future. It is rooted in capital accumulation, marketisation of the state, private land and property ownership and corporate governance in the developmental, regeneration and urbanisation processes*' (Whitfield, 2001). This prediction, unfortunately, remains relevant today as PPPs emerge beyond the global financial crisis.

The World Bank, global management consultancies and lawyers glowingly report the 'successful' implementation of PPPs and privatisation. There are project finance handbooks and journals for both PPPs and the project finance industry. The PPP and privatisation 'industry' has a strong propensity to focus on individual projects, the PPP process, deal flow, procurement, legislation and project finance. This effectively limits, either by design or default, debate and analysis of broader public policy issues and the longer-term implications.

The provision of public infrastructure and the role of public investment, PPPs and privatisation raise many profound financial, technical and legal issues, but public policy cannot be limited to technical debates within the PPP industry. Decisions on infrastructure investment must be part of a wider democratic and participatory decision-making process.

The implications of the continued growth and spread of PPPs and privatisation are far-reaching for democratic governance, social justice, jobs and the quality of public services. Despite the introspection and gloss of the PPP lobby, it is evident that the PPP model is fundamentally flawed (chapters 8 and 9), as evidenced by the abandoned and terminated projects and the contrived assessment of 'value for money'.

There is a robust and clear alternative. New infrastructure priorities, public investment and new public sector management, coupled with radical reform of global and nation state financial markets and regulatory frameworks could chart a new era for public infrastructure.

The widespread opposition to PPPs and privatisation must be harnessed and mobilised by trade union, community and civil society organisations.

The scale of UK privatisation since 1979 and PPPs since 1992 is unprecedented. The UK also embarked on a neoliberal public sector reform programme, which created an operational and ideological framework (competition, choice, commissioning, contestability, consumerism) and in turn fuelled more PPPs and privatisation. The UK provides an important evidence base and lessons for other countries. The Department for International Development has systematically promoted PPPs and privatisation in overseas aid programmes and provided over £200m over an eight-year period through the Private Sector Development Infrastructure Department (Department for International Development, 2007). The Treasury has advised over 70 countries likewise.

This book draws on a wide range of sources including public policy research and analysis, academic, trade union, private sector and PPP industry sources in many countries. It is important to avoid the silos in which academics search solely for academically sourced evidence or show misplaced confidence in economic modelling despite the caveats, assumptions and limited evidence base. It develops the analysis of the commodification and marketisation of public services in *New Labour's Attack on Public Services*, 2006, which explained how neoliberalism has driven commissioning, outsourcing, developing markets and other forms of privatisation under the umbrella of new public management.

The internationalisation of privatisation, private cross-border flows of infrastructure investment and the spread of the PPP model, the price of neoliberal modernisation, the emerging corporate welfare complex were discussed in *Public Services or Corporate Welfare: Rethinking the Nation State in the Global Economy*, 2001. It also proposed a framework for a new public order and public service management, and established a typology of privatisation and marketisation, which identified the increasingly wider forms and variants promoted by finance and service capital, global chains of consultants and lawyers, right-wing academics and business organisations.

Two earlier books, *The Welfare State: Privatisation, Deregulation & Commercialisation*, 1992; and *Making it Public: Evidence and Action Against Privatisation*, 1983, detailed the privatisation process and performance, the cost and consequences for the state, services, users and staff, and proposed strategies of resistance and public sector alternatives. Both these books argued that 1980s style privatisation, with its emphasis on stock market flotation of state owned corporations, would be the precursor to the deepening and widening of privatisation across the public sector and the welfare state.

This book draws on more than three decades of research, policy analysis and the development of action strategies with public bodies, trade unions and community organisations to improve public services and oppose marketisation and privatisation. A commitment to public service principles and values underpins this work, together with the belief that government, at all levels, must have the capability and resources to provide public infrastructure and public services.

Acknowledgements
I inevitably draw on the experience and ideas of many people from public bodies, trade unions and community organisations with whom I have worked through the European Services Strategy Unit, previously the Centre for Public Services. They are too numerous to mention.

I am indebted to many people who have contributed to the research and writing of this book. I extend specific thanks to Andy Mott (US), Raymond Leger and Keith Reynolds (CUPE, Canada), John Quiggin and John Spoehr (Australia), Karen Escott, Keith Hayman, Steve Machin, Kenny Bell, John Burgess and John Shutt (UK). The Australian Institute for Social Research, University of Adelaide, provided valuable support. Particular thanks to Tony Simpson of Spokesman Books for his commitment to this project.

I sincerely thank Dorothy Calvert for her love, solidarity, support and her editorial skills.

CHAPTER 1
Global crisis and the new infrastructure agenda

Public infrastructure in the 21st century is confronted with new challenges – adapting to climate change, meeting the economic, energy, water, transportation and social infrastructure needs of megacities in Asia, megaregions in North America and European city regions. Continued urbanisation and demographic change – population increases, migration and ageing of the population – create new pressures. New technology enables smarter, self-monitoring infrastructure but smart cars, new energy breakthroughs and nanotechnology will impose new demands on cyberspace and require faster networks.

This chapter discusses the major challenges confronting public infrastructure and the fiscal crisis of the state. Public infrastructure investment declined long before the 2009 financial crisis and global recession. Bridge collapses, the failure of the New Orleans levees and mounting maintenance backlogs are examples of a decline in the condition of public infrastructure, which is essential for economic activity and community well being.

Public Private Partnerships (PPPs) and privatisation have spread around the world, financed by new infrastructure funds using pension fund, private equity and hedge fund investment. Meanwhile, transnational construction companies, financial institutions, management consultants, law firms and facilities management companies clamoured to consolidate new markets for their services.

Infrastructure requires long-term planning, it is costly and is, thus, virtually always in catch-up mode. Financial and economic crises lead to further delays and deficits and reduce the ability of the state and economies to finance new facilities and maintain the existing stock and networks.

So how do we pay for public infrastructure, particularly in a financial crisis and recession when there are competing demands for current spending on services, welfare benefits and investment in infrastructure. Decisions on the scope, content and size of fiscal stimulus policies illustrate the difficult choices. However, it is not just about money. The future of public infrastructure will be shaped by the transformation of public services and how they are managed in a democratic, accountable, equitable and sustainable way and by the extent to which the growing global infrastructure market can be constrained and controlled.

There is a high degree of consensus that the global financial crisis was caused by systemic failure of financial markets with subprime mortgage debt accelerating the consequences (Wade, 2009). The problem was, and is, not simply a failure to regulate, monitor and supervise the financial markets and corporate sector, but the deliberate deregulation and removal of capital controls between countries, markets and companies. Light and self-regulation led to weak and inadequate controls and under-resourced regulatory bodies. Lax control of financial products, banks, private equity and hedge funds by governments and central banks was also mirrored in the public sector, where private contractors were regarded as 'partners' and allowed to self-monitor to save client costs.

The increased concentration of private wealth in the last decade led to large flows of money across borders. High levels of consumption in the US, Britain and other developed countries, which had prolonged low savings ratios, led to an unsustainable meteoric rise in debt. Surplus savings in China, Germany, Japan, and the oil exporting countries and emerging economies, created imbalances in global markets and a concentration of funds in US financial markets. The current account surpluses of these countries increased six-fold between 2001-2007 (Colonial First State, 2008).

In the blind pursuit of bigger speculative profits, mortgages, consumer and corporate debts were financialised and securitised, combined with insurance against their default. Financial 'innovation' had little to do with providing new financial services and products for the public. Instead, the proliferation of new asset-backed securitised products, such as collateralised debt obligations (CDOs) and credit default swaps (CDSs) made possible by complex computer programmes, enabled financiers to search for new ways of profiteering in poorly regulated financial markets.

However, this system and the complex software programmes used in securitisation, concealed high risks and toxic loans. US mortgage and credit card debt totalled US$13 trillion, or 123% of after-tax income compared to 83% of income in 1995 (Wall Street Journal, 2009). The Federal Reserve Banks flow of funds for the first quarter in 2009 revealed an 18% or US$11 trillion fall in the net worth of US households, the biggest loss since records began after the second world war (Federal Reserve Bank, 2009).

We are at an important juncture, where the remedy for getting out of recession and creating a new framework for the future of the global economy is more and better regulation, economic collaboration, elimination of tax havens and tax avoidance scams and increased transparency and disclosure.

Yet the neoliberal model of public service transformation, adopted most fervently in Britain, of commissioning, outsourcing, contestable markets, private finance and partnerships, are precisely the policies and practices that led to the crisis. In particular, Public Private Partnerships are designed with special purpose companies, off-balance sheet accounting, securitisation, outsourcing, secondary market refinancing and commercial confidentiality.

The partnership ideology is largely a sham. PPPs are financed by public money, with minimal risk transfer, contrived comparators, high transaction costs and value for money, which cannot be proven for 25-35 years. The financialisation and marketisation of infrastructure creates a new asset class through PPPs and privatisation and further consolidates the power of banks and investment funds in the economy.

Governments are a driving force behind PPPs alongside the World Bank, IMF and regional development banks, trade and business organisations together with banks, private equity and infrastructure funds, transnational construction and operating companies and management consultants. They are supported by an increasingly globalised network of national PPP units, agencies, and news and research intelligence services.

New challenges for infrastructure

The built infrastructure has to weather and adapt to climate change, withstand escalating demands from the rapid growth of megacities and megaregions, surging demand for energy supply and distribution, extremes of water shortages and flooding and continuing innovation in information and communications technology.

Adapting to climate change
Temperature increases and heat waves, increased rainfall, rising sea levels, more intense cyclone activity and increase in the areas affected by drought will have mainly negative impacts on natural and human environments (Inter-Governmental Panel on Climate Change, 2007). Warmer weather will reduce energy demand for heating, although increase it for cooling, and reduce disruption due to snow and ice.

Heat waves are likely to reduce the quality of life in warm areas whilst increasing demand for water. Heavier rainfall will cause flooding, contaminate water supply and increase disruption to transport. High winds will threaten power supplies and disruption to water supplies.

It is estimated that 1.8 billion people will face water stress by 2080, particularly in South Asia and northern China, 600m will face malnutrition as a result of drought and rising temperatures, up to 400m more people will face the risk of malaria, and up to 330m face displacement from flooding in coastal and low-lying areas such as Bangladesh and Vietnam (United Nations Development Programme, 2006). Rising sea levels threaten coastal areas, for example 53% of the US population live in counties with coastal regions, seven of the largest US ports (traffic volume) and significant oil and gas production facilities are located on the vulnerable Gulf Coast (Transportation Research Board, 2008). Coastal counties generate almost half the US gross domestic product (United States Commission on Ocean Policy, 2004). An increase in drought areas will mean water and food shortages and potential population migration.

These impacts have health consequences. Warmer weather will reduce human mortality from cold exposure but most of the other impacts are negative – heat-related mortality, increased risk of death, injuries, infectious diseases and malnutrition. These changes will affect both existing and planned water, power, telecommunications and transport infrastructure. Heat waves can cause thermal expansion of paved surfaces and track deformation. Higher rainfall levels, rising sea levels and storm surges cause flooding, landslides, erosion and inundation of roads, rail tracks, tunnels and runways. Ports and harbours have to accommodate high tides and storm surges. Services are likely to suffer from more frequent delays, interruptions and restrictions. *'Improving the resilience of existing transport infrastructure and energy networks requires a common and coordinated approach for assessing the vulnerability of critical infrastructure to extreme weather events. This provides a basis for strategic choices regarding networks, back-ups and energy security, and for maintaining stable transport networks and services'* (European Union White Paper, 2009).

The effects will vary across the world's regions. Asian megacities in the South, East and Southeast delta regions will be at greatest risk of flooding, disease and food shortages. Africa faces the risk of reduced agricultural production and low-lying coastal areas with large populations affected by rising sea levels. Water and food shortages will increase disease and malnutrition. The thawing permafrost in northern Canada threatens pipeline, road, rail, airport, water and sewage instability (Infrastructure Canada, 2006). In Australia, '... *coastal and offshore gas, oil and electricity infrastructure is potentially at risk of significant damage and increased shut-down periods from increases in storm surge, wind, flooding and wave events, especially when combined with sea level rise*' (Commonwealth Scientific and Industrial Research Organisation, 2006). The benefit of reduced demand for heating in Northern Europe may be outweighed by more frequent floods and heat waves in Southern, Central and Eastern Europe causing water shortages and forest fires (European Commission, 2009). One in six properties are at risk of flooding from rivers or the sea in England. National infrastructure assets in flood risk areas include 28% of gas infrastructure, electricity (14%), railways (20%), major roads (10%), hospitals, schools and day nurseries (7%) (Environment Agency, 2009).

Public infrastructure will have to withstand cyclones, hurricanes and floods. Infrastructure adaption and mitigation of climate change will drive investment in solar projects, wind farms, waste minimisation and recycling, water conservation, desalination and irrigation projects.

The carbon trading and offset system is failing – no emissions reductions, no fundamental 'overhaul of energy systems', and offsets under the UN carbon market only reinforce fossil dependency in developing countries (Lohmann, 2009, Carbon Trade Watch, 2009). '... *instead of aiding a transition away from fossil fuel mining and use, which must be the overriding goal of any coherent climate policy (Lohmann, 2006), the market instruments at the centre of today's international climate change regime are designed in ways that actually entrench fossil fuel use and delay the changes that need to be initiated immediately*' (Lohmann, 2009). The European Union's emission trading scheme '... *is now witnessing the development of more complex carbon market products, which package together credits from several installations, then slice these up and resell them. In essence, this is the same structure that brought the derivatives market to its knees, and the same problem; carbon markets involve the selling of a product that has no clear underlying asset – fertile conditions for the creation of a new "bubble"*'' (Reyes, 2009).

The cost of inadequate action is likely to be enormous. Global insured and non-insured losses from natural disasters, an economic indicator of the impact, have increased from US$53.6bn between 1950-59 to almost US$778.3bn in the 1990-99 period and likely to be exceeded in the current decade (Wharton Risk Management and Decision Processes Center, 2008).

Growth of megacities and megaregions
The rapid growth rates of megacities put severe strain on public infrastructure and services and widening class divisions between the wealthy and slum dwellers. There are twenty urban agglomerations of more than ten million people; twelve are in Asia, four in Latin America, two in North America and two in Africa. By 2035, it is expected that nearly two-thirds of the world's population will live in cities (Deutsche Research, 2008). London, New York and Paris have less than 10m population but remain global cities because of their economic, political and cultural influence.

Private investment in urban infrastructure in developing countries has played a relatively minor role in the overall flow of PPP projects, even during the peak period in the mid-1990s according to World Bank research (Annez, 2006). Urban infrastructure (water supply and sanitation and transport) accounted for just 10% of PPP projects between 1983-2004 and a quarter of those were cancelled, distressed or otherwise compromised (ibid). PPPs addressed only a fraction of the needs of urban areas and megacities and were '... *a fairly unpredictable source of finance, given the number of problems encountered with even the relatively limited number of transactions completed. Those local governments strapped for funding and keen to expand their investments would be wise to recognise these limitations ... Private finance cannot be a substitute for sound public finance in developing country cities*' (ibid).

The fiscal impact of ageing in Korea, Spain and Canada is forecast to require increased GDP of 13.4%, 8.8% and 7.7% respectively by 2050 for additional pension, health and long-term care costs. Most other developed countries will require a 3% increase in GDP, for example the EU25 will require an average increase of 3.4% of GDP (International Monetary Fund, 2009).

The US population is forecast to increase by over 40% to 420m by 2050, with more than two-thirds of economic growth concentrated in ten emerging megaregions such as the Northeast, Midwest, Texas Triangle, Arizona Sun Corridor, Cascadia, Northern and Southern California (Todorvich, 2009). The megaregions encompass major cities, suburbs and rural areas in networks of metropolitan areas and thus differ from the Asian single megacities. Despite the problem of fragmented governance, the megaregions have enormous potential for integrated transportation, environmental protection and economic development.

The ageing of the US population will impact in the old US suburbs.

They have the highest proportion of elderly and concentrations of high-need groups that are nearly twice those for new and rural suburbs. The old suburbs experienced rapid growth decades ago, driven largely by an influx of baby-boomers' parents, who have now aged. '... *the demand for services and infrastructure tends to be greatest in those parts of upstate New York that are already experiencing fiscal stress because of rising expenditures and eroding tax bases – its large cities, the inner ring suburbs, and the large urban counties that contain them*' (Deitz and Garcia, 2007).

Population growth, fertility rates and dependency ratios plus the shift from rural to urban living and ageing of the population (particularly acute in Japan, Germany, US and Canada) have an impact on the basic needs for health, housing, water, heat, light, food and transport and communications. The type, planning, provision and control of power stations, other utilities and water supply are, therefore, central: for example, more local health centres with a wider range of services and mobile services. The development of telemedicine, and the ICT infrastructure to support it, could have an important role in future care systems.

Population ageing will put increased pressure on publicly funded services and reduce the ability of central government to finance infrastructure. '*This will encourage government to favour full cost pricing business models and to push financing to the local level whenever it is feasible to do so*' (Organisation for Economic Co-operation and Development (OECD), 2007). However, high user charges, marketised health, social care, transport, leisure and culture services, combined with the dwindling value of pensions, signal a frugal future for the elderly.

Global trade
The current recession has inevitably led to a decrease in global freight flows after a decade of rapid growth. The evolution of global trade routes relies heavily not just on ports and terminals but also on the hinterland transportation infrastructure to transport minerals and raw materials and to distribute manufactured products. Container cargo, major bulk (coal, iron ore, grain), liquid bulk and minor bulk (agricultural and forest products, steel) have different trade routes determined by economic growth, the shift of manufacturing production to Asia, energy consumption and the source of minerals and raw materials. The Panama Canal upgrade completion in 2014 will significantly increase shipping capacity by accommodating 12,500 TEU (Twentyfoot Equivalent Units) container ships, nearly three times

current capacity. In early 2009 there were nearly 300 containers ships on order with over 8,000 TEU capacity (RREEF, Deutsche Bank, 2009).

The increasingly globalised supply network has led to fierce competition between ports, many of which have major expansion plans for new terminals and inter-modal truck-train terminals integrated into rail and road networks such as the Trans-European Transport Network. East and West coast ports are competing to become the key North American gateways, alongside new container ports in Mexico, but '... *while many ports in the region have improved their hinterland infrastructure over time, the pace of development has not matched the pace of growth in ship size*' (ibid). Port trucking in the US carries 80% of the shipping containers between ports and warehouses or distribution centres, but deregulation has resulted in the growth of a low paid, 'independent contractor' truck industry that has externalised health, environmental and pension costs to the public (Bensman, 2009).

The US$184bn Trans-Texas Corridor was planned to transport freight from Mexico into several US megaregions, but has been significantly scaled back (Texas Department of Transportation, 2009). The 1,200 foot-wide corridor would have incorporated roads, high speed freight and commuter rail, oil and gas pipelines, water, electricity and telecommunications, but will now be a series of individual projects.

Few countries have fully privatised ports, although there are a wide range of leases, joint ventures and PPPs with shipping lines, global port operators such as Hutchison Port Holdings, APM Terminals, PSA International and Dubai Ports World, financed by infrastructure funds such as Macquarie, Borealis, Ontario Teachers Pension Plan and Deutsche Bank. The UK privatised its major ports in the early 1980s and they are now owned by a consortia consisting of Singapore's Sovereign Wealth Fund, Goldman Sachs, Prudential and Ontario Municipal Pension Fund from the Jersey tax haven.

New energy order

A new international energy order has developed in the search to procure energy supplies. International energy demand is expected to increase by 57% over the next twenty-five years (Klare, 2008). Government-owned national oil companies own 81% of known petroleum reserves, hence energy security is a key foreign policy. For example, Russia has been renationalising its energy infrastructure following the disastrous privatisation in the early 1990s to own or control a growing energy network supplying Europe and Asia.

Two issues dominate, the '... *fear that global energy supplies will fall short of anticipated demand and that the rising industrial powers of the developing world – with their booming economies, surging middle classes, and new automotive cultures – will trigger a brutal struggle for whatever energy there is*' (Klare, 2008). This is a zero-sum contest, which could lead to conflict in which 'energy-intensive, high-tech weaponry' consumes even greater energy supplies. '*NATO will engage in ... supporting the protection of critical energy infrastructure. The Alliance will continue to consult on the most immediate risks in the field of energy security*' (North Atlantic Treaty Organisation (NATO), 2008).

The Middle East has 60% of the proven global oil reserves and 40% of the gas reserves – three countries – Iran, Qatar and Russia have 56% of proven global reserves (Klare, 2008). Eastern and Central Europe, Africa and Central and South America each have 10% of oil reserves. Eastern and Central Europe also has 30% of the global proven natural gas reserves followed by Africa and Asia and Oceania each with 8% (ibid). Within these regional shares, individual countries dominate supplies. For example, four Middle East countries – Saudi Arabia (20%) and Iraq, Iran, Kuwait and United Arab Emirates (10% each) account for global oil reserves (ibid). The potential oil supply from vast oil sands and oil shale deposits is twice those of conventional oil reserves but greenhouse gases are produced in its extraction and conversion (Spiegel et al, 2009). Environmental degradation and the high cost are further potential obstacles.

More oil and gas pipelines are planned across Central Asia to serve Europe and Pakistan and India. Turkmenistan and other former USSR states have vast gas reserves they want to sell to Pakistan, India and China. Afghanistan is an energy '... *bridge connecting land-locked, energy-rich Central Asia to energy-deficient South Asia*' and whether Iran will be able to export its large oil and gas resources (Canadian Centre for Policy Alternatives, 2008). There is intense commercial and political rivalry between pipelines with the US and Russia supporting different routes.

China has the third largest coal reserves after the US and Russia but increasing energy demand by China could lead to it accounting for half of world coal consumption. The renewed drive for nuclear power is driving competition for uranium mines in Australia, Canada, Namibia, Niger, South Africa, US, Russia and the former Soviet Union states of Kazakhstan, Kyrgyzstan and Uzbekistan.

Water crisis

In 2004, some 1.1bn people in developing countries had inadequate access to clean water and 2.6bn lacked basic sanitation (United Nations Development Programme, 2006). Deprivation in water and sanitation produces a series of human development costs – 1.8m child deaths, loss of 443m school days annually from water related illness and health problems caused by water and sanitation deficits. There are local/regional water shortages but there is sufficient global supply of water for domestic, agriculture and industrial use. The problem is that '*... scarcity is manufactured through political processes and institutions*' and '*... the poor get less, pay more and bear the brunt of the human development costs associated with scarcity*' (ibid). The Millennium Development Goals (MDG) aim to halve the proportion of people without sustainable access to safe drinking water and basic sanitation by 2015.

The OECD estimate that by 2025 two-thirds of the world's population could be living in water stressed areas, which will affect local and regional economies and potentially cause conflicts. Industrialised countries will bear the impact of climate change too – a study of US, Canada, UK and Finland identified the threat of floods, drought, insufficient water, changes in snowmelt water supply and saltwater intrusion (Levina and Adams, 2006).

Water from the Himalayas and Tibetan plateau flows into the great river deltas, the Yellow, the Yangzi, Salween, Irrawaddy, Brahmaputra, Ganges, Sutlej and Indus, providing resources and livelihoods for nearly half the world's population. A series of mega dam projects is under construction or planned to harness water resources, and in the case of China to divert 45bn cubic metres of water per annum to the north and north west of the country, and to generate energy. They are '*... the largest series of construction projects in human history. Looked at individually, some of these carry enormous risks and, even if they work as planned, will hurt large numbers of people while helping others. Looked at collectively – as overlapping, sometimes contradictory demands on environments that will also feel some of the sharpest effects of global warming over the next several decades – their interactions will be extraordinarily complex and their possible implications are devastating*' (Pomeranz, 2009). With all but the Ganges sourced in Tibet, which also has the greatest descent of water to generate hydro-power, China is in a unique position, particularly given its dam-building experience and financial resources (ibid).

Biodiversity is also threatened by changes in water supply – wetlands, forests and upland areas being at risk. Water conflicts, if not wars, over access to river basins, diversions and dams are inevitable, just as widespread drought can set '... *neighbour against neighbour in a desperate fight for survival*' as witnessed in Northern India in the water shortages and rationing in 2009 (Chamberlain, 2009).

The global water justice movement regards water not just as a human right but a public trust and demands the democratisation of water, public investment and the end of water privatisation and PPPs (Barlow, 2007).

The UNDP identify two key roles for public sector water provision – over 90% of water is publicly provided in developing countries. *'First, the water sector has many of the characteristics of a natural monopoly. In the absence of a strong regulatory capacity to protect the public interest through the rules on pricing and investment, there are dangers of monopolistic abuse. Second, in countries with high levels of poverty among unserved populations, public finance is a requirement for extended access regardless of whether the provider is public or private'* (United Nations Development Programme, 2006). However, the World Bank and International Finance Corporation/Multilateral Investment Guarantee Agency (IFC/MIGA) promote the privatisation and commercialisation of water despite the record of failures and contract terminations in water and wastewater projects (Reclaiming Public Water, 2005, Public Services International Research Unit, 2005, Norwegian Forum for Environment and Development, 2006). *'The possibility of bulk water transfers has caused concern in water-abundant regions that a global water-trading regime might lead to the requirement that abundant resources be tapped to provide fresh water for the rest of the world, at the expense of local environment and people'* (Wolf, 2007).

Cyberspace and the digital economy
Access to information and communications infrastructure and broadband infrastructure is essential for economic activity. E-government has increased access to public services and improved the delivery and management of many services. E-democracy can facilitate new methods of democratic accountability and enhance participation in civil society and political life. But ICT can be used to charge for virtually everything and to further marketise and privatise life. The pan-European electronic road use-charging framework for 'seamless travel on Europe's tolled road network' is underway. Satellite systems to track vehicles could also be used in a nation-wide congestion-charging scheme and monitoring of compliance with speed limits. This raises important civil liberty implications. Local authority contact

centres are potential databanks to extend the marketisation of services, for example, in supporting school choice, individual budgets, vouchers and payment schemes for welfare state and public services.

Other technological advances such as nanotechnology, the art and science of manipulating matter at the nanoscale (down to 1/100,000 the width of a human hair) could lead to '... *new medical treatments and tools; more efficient energy production, storage and transmission; better access to clean water; more effective pollution reduction and prevention; and stronger, lighter materials*' (Project on Emerging Nanotechnologies, 2009).

Security of critical infrastructure
Critical infrastructure, the systems and assets, physical and virtual, which we depend on for economic security, public health and safety, includes energy, water, telecoms, transportation, information and communications, hospitals, banking and finance, defence, police and emergency services. US and European Critical Infrastructure Protection programmes constantly assess vulnerability to attacks and response capabilities.

New technology constantly increases the connectivity and inter-relationships between networks and systems. This has benefits for continuous real-time and autonomous sensing, tracking and warning systems to better monitor buildings (smart buildings which sense maintenance) and more automated transportation infrastructure. At the same time there is increasing interdependence between healthcare, biotechnology and cyber infrastructures. However, these developments create new risks and vulnerabilities.

Changing context

Geo-political power shifts
The control of resources – oil, water, food and other commodities and manufacturing centres – has led to a shift in economic and political power between nation states, from North America and Europe to the Middle East and Asia. There is evidence of a trend towards a multi-polar world (National Intelligence Council, 2008).

The geo-political power shifts impact on the provision of public infrastructure as networks of supply, particularly in oil, gas and electricity, increase international interdependence with individual countries becoming more reliant on the policies of their neighbours. This could lead to greater international cooperation in negotiating the extension of networks, global standards and responses to accidents, natural disasters or terrorist attacks.

Will the rapid expansion of sovereign wealth funds and private sector investment in public infrastructure cause a major global power shift in financial markets and political change? Will nation states, particularly the Middle East and South East Asia, increasingly own the North's infrastructure? The growth of portfolios of infrastructure assets by global investment funds could fundamentally erode democratic accountability and make localisation and participation a sham. Industrial capital has a vested interest in speeding up the flow of goods from manufacture to market, for example, accessible low cost ports, and good quality highways. However, it is finance capital, which is gaining increasing control of key economic and social infrastructure. Local public services cease to have full control of the building and facilities from which they operate, replaced by operational rules and charges imposed by national/international facilities management contractors and infrastructure funds.

The delivery of core public services is also under threat of marketisation under the World Trade Organisation's negotiations for a General Agreement for Trade in Services (GATS) (Kelsey, 2008). The commitment to global markets in services through four modes remains – cross border supply, consumption abroad, commercial presence and movement of labour – although agreement has not been reached on its scale and scope. The EU single market project, articulated in the Lisbon strategy and a series of directives on rail, telecoms, postal services and utilities, is developing markets and deregulation in the network industries (see chapter 3). The liberalisation agenda of deregulation, marketisation, PPPs and privatisation is also pursued by the World Bank, IMF and development banks and governments via multilateral and bilateral trade agreements, and public sector 'reform' programmes are a condition of financial aid.

Power shifts from the nation state to private capital as outsourcing, PPPs and privatisation escalate, further undermine democratic governance. At present there are different funding 'programmes' for services and buildings, but they are likely to merge into one as marketisation continues and consolidates. The provision of private services in public buildings is not tenable in the long term because capital will always seek to achieve economies of scale and efficiencies/higher profits by owning and managing buildings in addition to providing services. The private sector will want to control the design, planning and provision of new buildings for growth/regeneration. They will seek to lower rents, want to gain from land and property ownership, and want the freedom to trade other services and not be affected by public sector constraints. The commodification of labour, a key element in the marketisation of public services, involves the reorganisation of work, job design and working practices to maximise productivity, facilitate competitive procurement and the transfer of staff to another provider, and ultimately to the fragmentation and weakening of trade union organisation (Whitfield, 2006).

Development, social justice and labour
The recapitalisation of US and European banks, and financial bailouts of US$4.1trillion, is forty times the combined 2007 Official Development Assistance budget (US$90.7bn) committed to fight poverty and bilateral and multilateral climate change finance (US$13.1bn) in developing countries (Institute for Policy Studies, 2008).

Development banks and the OECD promote 'pro-poor PPPs' (that benefit the poor disproportionately and/or explicitly integrate their concerns and needs). The OECD's pro-poor infrastructure strategy claims that the private sector could deliver pro-poor growth if there are incentives for entrepreneurship and investment, increased productivity through competition and innovation, international economic linkages through trade and investment, improved market access and functioning, and reduced risk and vulnerability (OECD, 2006). The reality is best summarised in an Asian Development Bank report '... *governments need to first create the appropriate enabling environment for PPPs to work, and then take further steps to ensure pro-poor benefits of infrastructure provision*' (Panggabean, 2006).

However, the creation of infrastructure markets and PPPs are extremely unlikely to reduce poverty because marketisation and privatisation create new divisions, inequalities and are more likely to be a means of increasing corporate and financial power. PPPs contribute to the financialising and internationalising of developing economies, which benefit transnational companies. These companies operate in developing countries to increase market share and profits, not to reduce poverty or to promote social justice.

Furthermore, the continuing advocacy of PPPs and the privatisation of the public infrastructure and the parallel growth of the infrastructure market, has far-reaching generational consequences, global implications and maintains gender stereotypes.

Inter-generational issues, such as, the scale that the costs and benefits of making today's public infrastructure investment has for the next and future generations, is particularly important in a period of fiscal crisis. For example, the extent to which nation states invest to create a low carbon economy and curtail investment in fossil-fuels now, will have a significant impact on the quality of the environment for future generations. Similarly, current levels of debt are transferred to future generations unless action is taken to reduce them or inflation erodes the obligations. A public-, rather than a road-transport policy, has greater inter-generational benefit, particularly when demographic change is resulting in the ageing of the population. Similarly, intra-generational 'imposition' of North American/European infrastructure and PPP models in developing countries impacts on economic strategies, values and choices for current and future generations.

What gets built, where and for whom in neighbourhoods, cities and regions is being increasingly shaped by a *global* agenda as deregulation and liberalisation policies facilitate the flow of foreign investment around the world. 'Local' is being marginalised, although most projects are initiated locally, project finance, design and management are international, with the construction and operation of projects often carried out, or managed, by transnational companies. Interest in deal flows, risk profiles, revenue streams and profit margins dominate the agendas of developments banks, governments, banks, and infrastructure funds rather than local social needs.

It matters how infrastructure priorities are agreed and whose interests they serve. It matters how projects are funded and whether public money is siphoned off in profits and dividends. It matters who is forced to relocate by infrastructure projects and what assistance they are given. It matters that facilities are under democratic control. It matters that public infrastructure hosts public services and that user charges are affordable. It matters that local people have access to good quality construction and facilities management jobs. It matters that the production and supply of building materials and equipment benefits businesses and employment in the local/regional economy. And it matters who controls workers' pensions funds and the terms and conditions if they invest in infrastructure projects.

There is also a *gender* dimension. PPPs and privatisation are propelled not just by a neoliberal political ideology, but sustained by dominant male power relations within business and government. The lack of concern for inter/intra-generational issues and the belief in a global operating system are both rooted in attitudes, motives and practices that 'justify' disregard, sometimes in an aggressive and arrogant manner, of frontiers, boundaries and values in the relentless, and often ruthless, pursuit of business interests. It is also reflected in the rather macho bias towards economic infrastructure, the interest in mega projects such as roads and dams, the batching of projects and the upholding of traditional vested interests of the construction and project finance sectors.

Fiscal crisis of the state

Government debt has soared – the IMF has predicted a debt-to-GDP ratio for advanced economies in 2014 to be about 25% above the 2007 level (IMF, 2009). The ratio will increase for eight of the G20 group of countries – France, Germany, Italy, Japan, Mexico, Spain, UK and US – but decline for the majority. The G20 average is forecast to rise from 63.5% to 76.8% in the same period. The government debt/GDP ratio in the UK and US will rise from 44.0% and 63.1% in 2007 to 76.2% and 99.5% respectively in 2014 (ibid).

The forecasts are vulnerable to the effects of a longer recession and lower growth rates, and do not take into account further government support/guarantees, the cost of public support to provide fully-funded pension schemes or the impact of higher interest rates, all of which could increase government debt. Fiscal frameworks such as the Stability and Growth Pact 1997 and the Maastricht Treaty fiscal rules have been suspended. A return to a UK target of net public sector debt not exceeding 40% of national income is not forecast until the early 2030s and could continue rising to about 90% of national income until 2050 (Institute for Fiscal Studies, 2009).

'The rise in government debt observed so far in advanced countries, while sizeable, is not exceptional from a long-term perspective. Historically, large debt accumulations (bringing the debt to 100–200 percent of GDP) have resulted from war-related spending, prolonged recessions, or protracted fiscal problems' (International Monetary Fund, 2009).

The level of public sector net debt interest is a crucial factor. The lower the interest rate, the less it costs the government in annual interest charges on the debt and more of the principal can be paid off. In Britain, the government has in effect paid '*... a nominal interest rate between 4% and 5% on the public sector's net debt, compared with between 6% and 8% over most of the 1990s and between 8% and 11% over most of the 1980s. It has been relatively cheap for all industrial country governments to* borrow in recent years' (Institute for Fiscal Studies, 2009).

'If future borrowing costs are expected to remain at their current low levels, the burden on future taxpayers of additional borrowing in the short term is small. Conversely, if future borrowing costs are expected to be high – for example, if they returned to the levels seen in the mid 1990s – then future taxpayers would have to devote considerably more of their incomes to servicing the stock of debt that they inherit and further fiscal tightening may be required' (ibid).

The UK currently has the world's largest PPP programme and the debt associated with this programme, in the form of contractual payments from public sector revenue budgets, is part of the debt crisis (Institute for Fiscal Studies, 2008). Between 2008/09 and 2033/34 the public sector will have to pay £216.5bn to private companies on signed deals up to October 2008 – the £62.8bn signed deal figure only indicates the capital value (HM Treasury, 2009). Annual payments were forecast to peak at nearly £11bn in 2017/18, but this does not take account of the continuing stream of PPP deals. Only 13% of PPP projects, 43% by capital value, are included in the public sector balance sheet. The PPP commitments, particularly in a period of fiscal crisis and reductions in public expenditure, mean that cuts will be borne in service provision. PPP finance is not additional investment – it replaces public investment with frequently more expensive private investment built into contracts, that virtually guarantee long-term profits to contractors and banks.

Governments are addressing the fiscal crisis with a combination of higher tax revenues, cuts in public sector capital and revenue budgets, and assumptions about economic growth and income/household spending growing faster than public spending. Most fiscal stimulus policies are a combination of additional investment plus investment planned for future years brought forward, but this could create a period of declining investment in subsequent years. For example, the UK public sector capital expenditure is planned to fall from £44bn in 2009/2010 to £22bn by 2013/14.

A wave of asset monetisation could emerge in the US as states and cities rush to obtain immediate lump sum cash payments to deal with budget crises. A new privatisation drive in the UK could result in large sections of motorways being tolled, new PPP models, joint ventures and most services outsourced in the NHS and local government. Neoliberalism could be taken to new heights creating a new geography of public infrastructure with more private ownership and control, but with more significant implications for public finance, employment and public sector planning. Large chunks of revenue budgets would be committed to PPP payments, further constraining government's ability to take action.

PPPs suffer delays and withdrawals
Several high profile projects failed to reach financial agreement in 2008/09, including the leasing of the US$12.8bn Pennsylvania Turnpike and Chicago Midway Airport, Ireland's new Thornton Hall prison complex and five Dublin housing projects – whilst others failed to attract bids such as Florida's Alligator Alley highway. In other cases many bidders simply withdrew, for example, from the sale of the UK's Gatwick Airport. The part privatisation of German railways was postponed and a host of other projects were delayed as banks demanded higher margins with shorter-term syndicated loans. Plummeting property values and the big reduction in construction work has forced many contractors to rethink PPP plans.

Some banks withdrew from the PPP market, for example, a global leader in project finance, the Royal Bank of Scotland, withdrew from long-term project finance (Infrastructure Investor, 2009); HBOS sold a 49.9% stake in 47 PPP projects to four pension funds immediately prior to its takeover by Lloyds TSB in December 2008 (see chapter 7); and DEPFA bank, a major PPP funder, was nationalised when its parent, Hypo Real Estate, was bailed out by the German Financial Markets Stabilisation Fund.

The rate of new PPP project agreements in developing countries declined 15% in value between July 2008 and March 2009 – 147 projects were signed with investment of US$55bn in 46 countries (Public Private Infrastructure Advisory Facility (PPIAF), 2009). The PPIAF review revealed the slowdown in PPP projects with 14% of projects by investment, delayed or cancelled, with a further 8% at risk of delay if financing was not agreed shortly, and another 6% experienced delays in tenders. Transport and energy projects were most affected. A further 21% of projects were delayed or risked delay due to other factors, partially or unconnected, to the financial crisis (ibid). The review concluded '... *projects will face a challenging environment as net private capital flows to developing countries in 2009 are expected to decline substantially compared to the peak levels of 2007 and 2008, and to remain subdued for years as global deleveraging continues*' (ibid).

The signing of new PPPs slowed in developed countries in the 2008/09 period. For example, in the UK, lending did not stop and 'resumed' in May 2009 with funding of the £6bn M25 project and Building Schools for the Future (BSF) projects. *The credit crunch depending upon its length and severity may in our view accelerate the growth of hybrid PPP methods which retain many of the advantages of PFI* (Local Partnerships, 2008). In other words, the bailout is unlikely to be a short-term fix or a temporary and reversible measure. In fact, the slowdown could hasten the introduction of new PPP models, based on wider state involvement (see Chapter 7). Earlier predictions of the demise of PPPs were always illusory.

The French government launched a €18bn plan to sustain the flow of PPP projects in the recession. It provided €8bn to the Caisse des Depots (CDC), the public administrator of savings and retirement funds, which will co-fund PPPs with commercial banks. CDC provides long-term loans for transportation projects (high speed rail, freight and combined road/rail projects). The government also provided up to €10bn in guarantees for bank lending for 80% of private sector finance in PPP and concession projects.

The UK government established a £2bn bailout fund in March 2009 to assist up to 110 PFI projects with a capital value of £13bn to proceed to financial closure in the next two years. They include £3.1bn transport projects, £2.4bn of schools and £3.5bn waste treatment and environmental projects. The government *'will be prepared to lend to PFI projects alongside commercial lenders and the European Investment Bank – or where required may act as sole lender'* (HM Treasury, 2009). Projects will apply to the Treasury's new Private Finance Initiative (PFI) debt finance unit for loans on a 'co-lending' basis when they '... *cannot raise sufficient debt finance on acceptable terms*' (ibid). The government anticipates being able to sell on the loans at a later date. So where will the money come from? *'Funding will be provided from across Government, including initially unallocated funds and Departmental underspends on previous projects'* (ibid).

Pension funds in many countries have continued to invest in infrastructure and new commitments have continued despite the financial crisis. In April 2009, Goldman Sachs having reported first quarter profits of US$1.81bn, admitted it had US$164bn cash and liquid assets ready to buy up distressed securities and loans as companies offloaded debt and repaid the US$10bn Troubled Asset Relief Programme (TARP) funds so that it could return to paying bonuses, investing abroad and hiring foreign staff (Financial Times, 14 April 2009).

Public provision of public goods

Many parts of the public infrastructure are classified as public goods. Public goods have two key properties. They are non-excludable (users cannot be excluded from consuming the goods) and non-rival (consumption by one user does not reduce the supply available to others). Local or national public goods include defence, law and order, public health, macro-economic management, roads, parks and open spaces. Global public goods are those with benefits, which extend across borders, populations groups and generations (Kaul et al, 1999). The United Nations (UN) identified ten global public goods that are fundamental to the implementation of the UN Millennium Declaration. They include access to basic education and health care, for example, preventing the emergence and spread of infectious disease, the integration of communication and transportation systems across borders, a global public domain free from crime and violence, universal human rights, transparent and accountable governance, and harmonisation of technical standards (Kaul et al, 2003).

Privately provided public goods, services and activities carry social costs, subsidies, increased inequality, stringent regulations and collusion and corruption risk.

Positive and negative externalities arise from the activities of individuals, firms, organisations and states that result in benefits (education benefiting society) or damage (air or river pollution) but they do not bear the costs. The state plays a crucial role in minimising negative externalities and promoting positive externalities through taxation, regulation, monitoring and inspection, planning and the provision of activities and services. States have also acted to regulate monopolies and afford consumer protection in the provision of goods and services. There are two other key elements to public goods; they suffer from under-provision, and policy is mainly determined by the nation state.

This chapter has outlined the broad context of current and future challenges for public infrastructure. The next eight chapters focus on the parallel development, operation and impact of PPPs and privatisation and the growth of a global public infrastructure market. The final two chapters detail the opportunities, radical policy and organisational changes, and the strategies needed to ensure their implementation.

CHAPTER 2

The political economy of infrastructure

This chapter defines public infrastructure, surveys the different types of PPPs and summarises the evidence of the economic and social benefits of infrastructure investment. Public infrastructure has a key role in many fiscal stimulus strategies, particularly generating or sustaining employment. It concludes with an explanation of the relationship between infrastructure and the provision of core public services.

Definitions of infrastructure

'Infrastructure' is commonly defined as transport, energy, telecommunications, water and sewage, also known as the network industries. But this definition is limited to the needs of capital to produce and move goods and provide very basic community services. Network industries are essential, but they are only part of the infrastructure needed for economic, social and political activity. Housing, schools, hospitals and leisure facilities, town halls to host democratic governance and public administration, and the criminal justice infrastructure (police stations, courts and prisons) are also a basic part of the infrastructure required for economic and community well-being, and in the provision of a healthy and trained workforce.

Infrastructure is '... *at the very heart of economic and social development*' and provides '... *the foundations for virtually all modern-day economic activity, constitute a major economic sector in their own right, and contribute importantly to raising living standards and the quality of life*' (OECD, 2006). Infrastructure has a '*catalytic role*' in poverty reduction (World Bank, 2008). Yet infrastructure plans focus almost exclusively on the 'network industries' (ibid) and this avoids having to define infrastructure (Statistics Canada, 2008).

The matter is more complicated because the World Bank, IMF, development agencies and governments use different definitions of infrastructure for lending, economic analysis, taxation and policy reviews. Infrastructure Australia identified three main types of publicly, quasi-publicly owned, and privately owned infrastructure – physical, digital and collaborative, the latter including '... *communities, networks, regions, business groups learning networks, and competitive interactions between people, objects, and places*' (Infrastructure Australia,

40

2008). An eight-part Canadian classification by function omitted housing and the democratic and public administration infrastructure (Statistics Canada, 2008). The US National Infrastructure Plan lists 18 types of infrastructure categorised by government department rather than an infrastructure typology (Department of Homeland Security, 2009). The American Society of Civil Engineers Infrastructure Report Card has 15 types (American Society of Civil Engineers, 2009) whilst others simply divide economic and social infrastructure into hard and soft categories (Grimsey and Lewis, 2005).

The crude classification of 'economic' and 'social' infrastructure ignores the considerable direct and indirect economic benefits of health, education and housing infrastructure (Agenor and Moreno-Dodson, 2006). Most econometric modelling reinforces the crude division between economic and social infrastructure, because it relies on the charges and tolls, which are clearly evident for utility and transport projects but less so for social facilities. 'Social' infrastructure also has a higher service content, and thus employment, and supply chain linkages compared to most economic infrastructure. The user cost of utilities and other 'economic' infrastructure are frequently high in developing countries. But privatised health and education also imposes high costs to the poor. Some classifications isolate 'regulated assets' such as transmission, distribution and water and sewage assets and 'user pay assets' such as toll roads, rail and airports but they overlap with other categories. The public infrastructure has a key role in the provision of welfare state services ranging from health and social care, education, children's services, facilities and services for older people, social housing, employment and training services.

Another approach describes four interdependent 'lifeline systems' that provide the essential services of a modern society:

Water for a vast array of needs, including drinking, washing, cooking, fire-fighting, farming, and sanitation, as well as for manufacturing, industrial, and mining processes;

Power for numerous uses, including heat, light, refrigeration, cooking, food processing, and security purposes; the production of durable goods; and the operation of oil and gas refineries, the Internet, television, and appliances;

Mobility for people, materials, goods, and services to and from workplaces, markets, schools, recreational facilities, and other destinations;

Connectivity for purposes of communication, public safety, emergency services, financial transactions, and for the control and monitoring of other infrastructure components' (National Research Council, 2009).

I use the term 'public infrastructure' to identify the networks, buildings and equipment required to sustain and improve the economy and quality of life, distinct from corporate infrastructure in companies and industries, for example the facilities required for the production of goods and services, agriculture, mining. An eleven-part matrix, based on the UN Classification of the Functions of Government (COFOG), provides a comprehensive definition – see Table 1. This framework focuses on the physical infrastructure and I recognise that public infrastructure includes organisational structures, intellectual knowledge, a trained and skilled workforce and operational systems.

The three core elements of the welfare state infrastructure – education, health and housing – accounted for a third of PPP investment in the UK up to the end of 2008. The quality of networks of facilities and ICT has an important effect on the quality of, and access to, core services.

The Berlin and Jerusalem concrete walls are another form of infrastructure used to divide communities, impose security and expropriate land. The US-Mexico border fence/wall is intended to mitigate the flow of illegal border crossings.

The terms 'critical infrastructure' and 'mega-projects' must be clarified before examining the privatisation and PPP models.

The US, UK and European Union operate Critical Infrastructure Protection Programmes in case of natural disaster or major incident. The US define critical infrastructure as '... *systems and assets, whether physical or virtual, so vital to the United States that the incapacity or destruction of such systems and assets would have a debilitation impact on security, national economic security, national public health or safety, or any combination of those matters'* (Department for Homeland Security, 2007). Critical infrastructure usually covers transportation, economic affairs and digital, water supply, public health, security services (police, fire and rescue, military), food production and distribution, and financial services (banking).

The EU does not define particular types of infrastructure but refers to '... *critical infrastructures which are of the highest importance for the Community and, which, if disrupted or destroyed would affect two or more MS, or a single Member State if the critical infrastructure is located in another*

Table 1: *Eleven types of public infrastructure*

Transportation	Utilities and networks communications	Recreation and culture	Welfare state infrastructure Education
Roads, bridges and tunnels Motorways Railways Rapid transit systems Airports & air traffic control Sea ports & inland waterways Ferries	Electricity generation & distribution Gas distribution & storage Oil Coal Wind/solar power Water treatment & supply Information & communications networks Satellite systems Postal network	Libraries & art galleries Performing arts centres & theatres Museums Sports & leisure centres and gyms TV & radio	Creche and nursery schools Children's Centres Primary and secondary schools Learning Centres Further Education Colleges & training centres Universities Research & development centres
Public Safety	*Environmental protection*	*Defence*	*Health and social care*
Police stations Law courts Remand centres Prisons Fire & Rescue Services	Waste management Waste water management Environmental & flood protection Natural parks, reserves and botanical gardens	Defence facilities Equipment Accommodation	Hospitals & health centres Diagnostic centres Laboratories Care homes Day and activity centres Sheltered housing
General public service – Democratic & public administration		*Economic development*	*Housing and community amenities*
Town Halls and Civic Centres Offices for central and regional government departments and state agencies Depots and operational centres		Business start-up facilities Science parks and development zones	Council/public housing Hostels Community centres Parks & open spaces

Member State. This includes trans-boundary effects resulting from interdependencies between interconnected infrastructures across various sectors' (EU, 2006).

Mega-projects are large-scale investment projects, usually costing over US$1bn and the 'mega' classification indicates their scale and boldness. They include highways, bridges, tunnels, public buildings, transit systems, railways, airports, seaports, dams, power plants, oil and gas pipelines, ICT and defence equipment. A US study defined a mega-project as costing a minimum US$250m at 2002 prices (Altshuler and Luberoff, 2003). However, large national spending programmes such as National Health Service (NHS), Local Improvement Finance Trust (LIFT) and Building Schools for the Future (BSF) in the UK that consist of individual relatively small projects should not be classified as mega-projects. In addition, asset monetisation projects are usually multi-billion projects because of their very long-term scope but are not technically mega-projects, except in financial terms. New PPP models are likely to increase in value as they include more services and functions in their scope (see Chapter 7) and may also be mega only in terms of financial value.

Privatisation and partnership models

Partnership is used as a generic term to describe a wide variety of contracts, agreements and coalitions involving the public sector, private firms, voluntary organisations and non-governmental organisations. The term is frequently misused and abused primarily because it has such a broad meaning, which differs from country to country. Further ideological confusion is created by statements such as *'Private-Public Partnerships could help to reduce 90% of World Poverty'* (World Economic Forum, 2005), *'The role of the private sector is to create wealth, whereas the public sector's job is to create health. Where these two overlap is the PPP'* (ibid). The $85bn US nationalisation of American Insurance Group (AIG) in return for a 80% stake was claimed to be '... *a classic example of "public-private" partnership'* (Wall Street Journal, 2009).

The type of partnership is determined by four factors – obligations and responsibilities, voluntary or contractual relationships, governance and accountability, and sharing of risk.

The most common forms of privatisation and PPPs for infrastructure are:

Privatisation by flotation or trade sale – Infrastructure assets are sold in a public share offer on the stock exchange or sold via a bidding

Table 2: *Public Private Partnership models*

PPP models	
Description	Names of schemes
Building and operating new infrastructure	
The private sector designs, builds, finances and operates an asset and transfers it to the public sector when the operating contract ends, or at some other pre-specified time. The private sector partner may subsequently rent or lease the asset from the public sector.	Design, Build, Finance, Operate (DBFO) Build-operate-transfer (BOT) Build-own-operate-transfer (BOOT) Build-rent-own-transfer (BROT) Build-lease-operate-transfer (BLOT) Build-transfer-operate (BTO)
The private sector designs, builds, owns, develops and operates an asset with no obligation to transfer ownership to the public sector.	Build-own-operate (BOO) Build-develop-operate (BDO) Design-construct-manage-finance (DCMF)
Leasing or buying existing public assets	
The private sector leases an existing asset from the public sector; renovates, improves and/or expands it; and then operates the asset for a specific period.	Asset Monetisation
The private sector buys an existing asset from the public sector with no obligation to transfer ownership back to the public sector. Public sector then rents facilities from private sector.	Sale and leaseback Lease-develop-operate (LDO) Buy-build-operate (BBO)
Delivering services and infrastructure	
The private sector operates services and invests in new buildings and equipment under a 10-15 year contract. This may also involve establishing a Joint Venture Company (JVC) by the public and private sector.	Strategic Service-delivery Partnership (SSP) Independent Sector Treatment sector
Urban renewal and economic development	
Public and private sector land acquisition and development and provision if finance and/or infrastructure for economic development.	Local regeneration projects, local housing companies, economic development companies

Source: Developed from Public-Private Partnerships, Government Guarantees and Fiscal Risk, International Monetary Fund, 2006.

competition between private companies.

Public Private Partnership (PPP) – (includes Private Finance Initiative (PFI) in the UK, Korea and Japan) a long-term contractual relationship between a public body and private contractor or consortia via a Special Purpose Vehicle (company). The SPV is usually owned by the parent companies of the construction firm, banks and the facilities management company leading the consortia. Most SPVs are financed by 80% – 90% borrowing or debt and the remainder in equity divided between the consortia. A long-term contract, often between 25–50 years, will be awarded following a procurement process, that commits the private sector to design, build, finance and operate the facility. The payment mechanism requires the public body to pay a unitary charge to the SPV for the availability of facilities and performance-related service provision. The transfer of some risks, affordability and value for money are key issues.

This book focuses on the standard Design, Build, Finance and Operate (DBFO) facilities model (similar to Build-Operate-Transfer), although there are other PPP variants such as Build-Own-Operate-Transfer (BOOT) depending on the degree of state control of design, construction, finance, ownership and operation (International Monetary Fund, 2004). In the UK, PFI/PPP has accounted for about 10-15% of public sector capital investment since 1996 (International Financial Services London, 2008). Globally, PPPs account for about 4% of public investment (Siemens, 2007). However, these figures are deceptive, because they do not take account of the increasing rate of PPPs in many countries, nor do they take account of the very high use of PPPs in some services. PPPs accounted for 91.6% of major capital investment in the NHS between 1997-2008 – namely 102 projects with a capital value £11.5bn (Department of Health, 2008).

ICT projects have been excluded from the UK's Private Finance Initiative since July 2003 and a £20m minimum capital value applies. The minimum size of PPPs varies. A recent US study recommended that a PPP should only be considered for a large and complicated project (US$500 million or more in cost), which addresses significant transportation needs, has strong community support, and the public sector lacks the organisational or funding resources to deliver the project by conventional means. The project should have the potential of generating revenues (tolls, property development, and shadow payments) which could be captured to finance capital and operating expenses of the project; and a range of potential private sector competitors are capable, available, and interested in competing to deliver the project (Cambridge Systematics, 2009).

The PPP model is also used for the provision of services, the management and operation of facilities either through a management contract or lease, and concession, which gives the private sector exclusive rights to provide, operate and maintain facilities. The public sector usually retains ownership of assets.

Concession Agreement or Asset monetisation – the long-term leasing of existing public assets such as highways or other infrastructure, which already have tolls or where there is potential scope to introduce user charges. The leaseholder is responsible for maintenance and improvement work and upgrading tolling technology. The public sector receives a lump sum payment at the start of the contract. Concession agreements or leases are used worldwide in the construction of new highways but their use to privatise existing infrastructure assets in the US is recent (see chapter 4). International standards specify the terms of operating or financial leases depending on the level of government financing of the asset and length of contract relative to the economic life of the asset (International Monetary Fund, 2006).

Strategic Service-delivery Partnership **(SSP)** is a long-term (usually ten-year with option for further five years) multi-service, £50m-£600m contract between a public body and a private contractor. They are financed by local authority revenue budgets and the private sector may front load some investment. Between 50 – 1,000 staff transfer to a private contractor or a Joint Venture Company (JVC) established between the local authority and contractor, or staff may be seconded to a JVC. The range of services usually includes ICT, human resources, payroll, revenues and benefits, financial and legal services, property management and other professional services (highway management, technical services).

There are currently over 50 SSPs in the UK. Thirty-five provide ICT and corporate services with a total contract value of £7.5bn with over 15,000 staff transferred or seconded to private contractors or JVCs. Some SSPs involve private sector takeover of local authority maintenance departments.

Although strategic partnerships are medium-term contracts, they frequently have a significantly bigger impact than Private Finance Initiative, because the private sector is embedded more deeply in local government or public bodies. Strategic Partnership contracts allow the authority to bring additional services within scope through a change control mechanism in the contract. Strategic partnerships deliver a much wider, increasingly frontline, range of services, whereas PFI projects generally only provide buildings and facilities management services. The geography of strategic partnerships is significant. The sale of Direct Service Organisations, white collar services and large scale public housing transfers started mainly in district councils in the south of England and spread northwards, whereas SSPs started mainly in northern cities, a reflection of Labour-controlled councils adopting the New Labour agenda.

Independent Sector Treatment Centres (ISTCs) are another example of service-led health partnerships in the UK, which operate from either private facilities or use spare capacity in National Health Service hospitals. This is a £5bn programme, in which the private sector provides elective surgery and other clinical services.

Several international firms are seeking partnerships with universities to provide foreign language teaching centres and student accommodation. Academies are education PPPs in all but name – privately built and owned schools, which are privately run, employ their own staff (except where there is a predecessor school and TUPE (Transfer of Undertakings (Protections of Employment) Regulations) applies), appoint the majority of governors and determine ethos, specialism and much of the curriculum.

Asset Management/Property Partnerships (Sale/leaseback) Government departments and public bodies negotiate the long-term transfer of their estates to property management companies. Contracts normally include the purchase of the freehold premises, facilities management of the properties and services, letting vacant space and selling surplus property. At the end of the contract, departments/public bodies retain a right to occupy the buildings that they wish to remain in, with market leases.

Real Estate Investment Trusts (REITs) are also being considered as a PPP model. A Reit is a listed property company that usually does not pay tax on its earnings as long as these are mostly distributed to investors in the form of dividends. The rules vary between countries but usually a public corporation invests in property and is required to distribute 90% of their income to investors (see chapter 7).

Other PPP models
Projects are sometimes described as PPPs for political purposes. For

example, the UN has facilitated the formation of global public private partnerships in which transnational companies provide cash or in-kind donations (for example, HIV/Aids drugs, vaccines, computer equipment) linked to their production and marketing operations in developing countries. Some Non-Governmental Organisations (NGOs) are involved in order '... *to reduce political risks*' of nationalisation, confiscation and 'operational disturbances' (World Economic Forum, 2005). This can be classified as corporate philanthropy rather than a PPP.

In another twist, the US government plan to buy up US$1 trillion in toxic assets from banks and financial institutions – legacy mortgage loans and securities, was named the Public-Private Investment Programme (Wall Street Journal, 24 March 2009).

A new body of words and phrases has been developed to conceal real intentions, impose new business values in public sector transformation and to discipline public policy-making (Whitfield, 2006). The branding of outsourcing contracts as 'partnerships' and claims that a council-wide joint venture company responsible for a series of service delivery vehicles is 'not privatisation' are increasingly common (European Services Strategy Unit, 2008).

Even the evaluation of PPPs evidently requires a partnership. Statements such as '... *theoretically-informed, empirical studies*' in '... *partnership with the National Audit Offices around the world*' are required '... *before meaningful insights*' into such questions as '... *is PFI (PPP) a form of privatisation?*' can be answered (Broadbent and Laughlin, 2003), beggar belief. Much of the accounting research literature assesses PPPs within a contractual framework, for example, English and Baxter's (2008) analysis of risk allocation, specified service standards, payment and incentive mechanisms and management and control structures in five Australian prison contracts. This is undoubtedly informative but within the small PPP box.

Public investment in infrastructure is usually considered as 'sunk' investment – in other words it is money spent to gain a fixed asset, which adds to the stock of facilities or networks. Its value lies in meeting economic and social needs for the economy and society and becomes part of the public sector 'assets'. However, private investment in public infrastructure is traded. Investments can be bought and sold and money is made at different stages of the process, for example in sharing risk and then refinancing or selling equity in projects once the main risks have significantly declined and it is operational.

Infrastructure contributes to economic growth and community well-being

Studies in the last twenty years have used various techniques and models to quantify the impact of improved infrastructure on economic efficiency and labour productivity, but have not addressed social welfare benefits or differences between public and private sector investment.

The benefits are always 'potential' because one benefit may reduce or cancel out another; for example, construction of a new road will create employment but the benefits could be reduced if this is a toll road with high charges. The emphasis on the potential benefit is important because of the lack of evidence, the limitations of econometric modelling, different types of infrastructure and the range of local, regional and national contexts. The focus on economic affairs (transport, energy, telecommunications and water) has the effect of ignoring the socio-economic value of infrastructure and the policy issues of public or private provision. The key question is, what is the net effect of adding new infrastructure compared to the benefits achieved by alternative use of the same investment?

In other words, the benefits are relative to the alternative use of the same investment. They are also relative to the condition and extent of the existing infrastructure, for example, benefits of a new road or hospital in a developing country will usually be greater than those in an urban area of a developed country. In addition, infrastructure projects in an economic development zone or regeneration area may generate additional development in adjacent sites thus increasing the economic and employment benefits.

The economic benefits of infrastructure are, not surprisingly, likely to be larger in developing countries than industrialised economies. However, most of the empirical research on the growth benefits of public spending on infrastructure has been in OECD countries. *'These characteristics may limit the relevance of these results to emerging economies particularly the poorest Asian countries, where initial commitments to infrastructure have little private opportunity cost and can achieve dramatic gains in private output, income, and productivity growth. For these reasons, the results examined here probably represent very conservative indications of what responsibly targeted investments in infrastructure could accomplish in developing Asia'* (Roland-Holst, 2006).

The potential economic benefits of infrastructure investment are threefold – it can contribute to economic growth, it can contribute to improving the quality of life and it can contribute to poverty reduction.

Increased efficiency and productivity
Infrastructure has a key role in promoting economic growth, although it is difficult to identify the precise scale of economic benefits for different types of infrastructure in different regions and countries. Many studies have analysed the macroeconomic effects of infrastructure (Estache, 2006 refers to 'over 150 since late 1980s'). The findings vary depending on the type of infrastructure, sample, geographic scope, the data, time period, methodology and economic model used. They do not take account of how infrastructure is financed. Finally, '... *estimating the impact of infrastructure on growth is a complicated endeavour, and papers vary in how carefully they navigate the empirical and econometric pitfalls posed by network effects, endogeneity, heterogeneity and very poor quality data*' (Estache and Fay, 2007).

Infrastructure has several important attributes – they are long lasting immobile capital goods, which, in combination with labour, provide services that are usually consumed by both households and private industry (Prud'homme, 2004). The supply of infrastructure is also 'lumpy', meaning that it is intermittent rather than incremental because of the time taken in planning and construction, and the fact that partly completed projects have no use value. This makes it difficult to adjust the supply and demand of infrastructure.

Infrastructure investment may reduce the cost of production, for example, improving the quality of public roads, enhancing the longevity of trucks and transport used to move goods and workers, and access to electricity and telecommunications can increase productivity (for example, logistics costs as a percentage of the sale value of products, were between 18% – 32% in Latin America compared to an OECD average of 9% in 2001 (Gonzalez et al, 2007)). Infrastructure investment may also increase demand and employment in the construction and supply industries.

Early studies by Aschauer (1989) and Munnell (1990) reported that public infrastructure investment had a significant effect on private sector output. Aschauer's analysis of the relationship between investment in public infrastructure and economic performance in the US between 1949-85 indicated that a 1% increase in the stock of public sector capital could boost GDP by 0.38 to 0.56 percent annually

(Aschauer, 1989). Later studies concluded that the link between infrastructure investment and growth had been overstated (Canning and Bennathan, 2000, O'Fallon, 2003, OECD, 2003). A study of twenty-two OECD countries in the period 1960-2001 estimated a one-off sustained increase in GDP of 0.22 percent in a developed economy (Kamps, 2004). In other words, a 10% increase in public capital stock, increases GDP by about 2%. Another research review found increased output of between 0.20 to 0.51 for national studies and 0.12 to 0.17 in regional studies with road and rail infrastructure investment having the biggest impact (Infrastructure Canada, 2007).

An analysis of 77 studies concluded that most found that public capital had a positive impact on economic growth, although this was much lower than the Aschauer findings, and the effect of public investment differs across regions, countries and sectors (Romp and de Haan, 2007). Other studies and literature reviews have confirmed these findings (Brox, 2008, Roland-Holst, 2006, Straub, 2008). There is no guarantee that initial high returns from infrastructure investment will be maintained in additional investment – '... *once basic infrastructure is in place, adequate investment in maintenance might actually have a higher rate of return than new investment*' (Straub, 2008).

Most of the studies use five types of economic models (production function, cost function, growth, general-equilibrium and data-orientated models) and conclude '*the impact of infrastructure on output is likely to be higher at the national level than at the regional level. In addition, consensus exists around the notion that local infrastructure projects benefit local economies where projects are taking place, but spillover effects may negatively impact other neighbouring regions. This last observation is significant because financing public infrastructure projects should consider the cost and benefit to other regions or industries that are impacted even if they are not the recipients of the investments*' (Infrastructure Canada, 2007).

A study of twelve OECD countries found that the short- to medium-term rates of return on public and private investment in infrastructure are similar, but long-term rates of return for public investment are significantly higher (Demetriades and Mamuneas, 2000). Various studies found the implied rate of return on public capital to be higher than the rate of return on private capital, for example, 17% compared to 10% (Macdonald, 2008) or 20% compared to 13% (Demetriades and Mamuneas, 2000).

US highway investment is reported to have led to productivity growth, but initial gains were partially offset by subsequent increases in congestion in urban areas (Crafts and Leunig, 2005). They also point to the considerable effect of deregulation of the trucking industry and technological improvements in vehicles relative to the impact of new roads. The extent to which transport infrastructure investment can promote agglomeration – the general relationship between the density of a location and the productivity of firms – to obtain economies of scale, specialisation and how trade can be developed, relies on a number of area-specific factors such as employment density, industrial composition and gross domestic product (Gibbons and Machin, 2006).

Infrastructure enables the provision of activities and services, which, in turn, have different economic impacts. For example, the direct, indirect and induced economic effects of hospitals, schools, universities and child care in the US have an output multiplier of between 1.79 and 1.91, which are greater than retail and tourism multipliers of 1.60 – 1.71 (Warner, 2009).

A mix of infrastructure investment would create about 40,000 direct and indirect short-term jobs in Latin America per US$1bn expenditure (Tuck et al, 2009), based on a 'prototypical mix' of 50% transport (25% highways, 20% urban roads and 5% rural roads), 30% electricity (25% in generation and 5% rural electrification) and 20% in water and sanitation (15% in coverage expansion and 5% in treatment plants). The 2009 US$25bn fiscal stimulus programme in the LAC region is expected to generate about 2 million jobs based on an induced employment multiplier of 2.0 and no crowding out or substitution effect. Direct employment impacts ranged from 750 jobs per US$1bn for coal-fired generation to 100,000 jobs for water supply and sanitation network expansion (ibid).

Improving the quality of life
Infrastructure improves health outcomes in developing countries – access to clean water and sanitation helps to reduce infant mortality, electricity improves the functioning of hospitals and health services, reduces use of biomass fuels and thus air pollution and respiratory illness. *'Infrastructure raises the economy's ability to produce health services; in turn, greater access to health services enhances workers' productivity, and thus output'* (Agenor, 2006).

New schools can increase educational attainment by raising school attendance, improved accessibility helps to recruit teachers, and improved health contributes to positive education outcomes (Agenor and

Moreno-Dodson, 2006). Their study summarises recent evidence of the relationship between good health and labour productivity and economic growth. They also conclude that most studies do not identify the externalities associated with public infrastructure or their effect on health and education and, thus, underestimate its contribution to growth.

Infrastructure has a key role in the spatial planning of development and cities. Economic and social benefits that could be obtained by a more integrated public sector approach should include the composition, sequencing and efficiency of alternative infrastructure investment.

Regional and local economic development strategies
Cross-border infrastructure has an important role in reducing transport costs, building connectivity and enlarging markets and linking regional and global supply chains.

Public infrastructure has an important role in regional strategies, although there are often conflicting policies and interests. For example, North East England has traditionally prioritised public investment, but by March 2009 the region had 43 PFI projects with capital value of £1,845m. Seventeen were health projects with a capital value of £834m, thirteen education projects (£391m), a government office complex (£127m), and four street lighting projects (£127m) plus three strategic partnerships in Middlesbrough, South Tyneside and Redcar & Cleveland with £634m total project value. The in-house success story of Newcastle City Council's ICT project stands out like a beacon (Wainwright and Little, 2009).

Quite separately, the region's four public sector pension funds, Tyne and Wear, Teeside, Durham and Northumberland (covering local government, housing, police, probation, fire, further education and other related services with combined assets of £7.9bn) have increased their PFI infrastructure investment. The Tyne and Wear Pension Fund invested £15m in the Henderson PFI Secondary Fund II and £30m in the Infracapital fund, both invested in the UK and Europe. By March 2008 the total investment in infrastructure assets was valued at £49 million, representing 1.3% of the Fund. The investment strategy provides for up to 2.5% in infrastructure assets (Tyne and Wear Pension Fund, 2005). The Teeside Pension fund strategy allows up to 10% in alternative investments including infrastructure. These figures do not take account of other national pension schemes to which North East authorities and staff contribute.

The Northern Way has sought increased investment to close the prosperity gap between the northern regions (North East, North West and Yorkshire and Humberside) and the UK average. It's Private Investment Commission, headed by James Crosby, deputy chairperson of the Financial Services Authority 2004-09 and former chief executive of bailed-out HBOS bank, proposed the integration of public infrastructure programmes with regeneration funds to create '... *some form of social infrastructure PFI at an appropriate spatial level*', which would lever in private investment (Northern Way, 2009). The Commission revealed that the real agenda ultimately had little to do with regeneration and public needs but rather '... *the development of buildings for the public realm provide significantly attractive low risk, high profit development opportunities for the private sector*' (ibid).

The Commission's interim report concluded that the speculative 'dash for flats' and debt-financed investment was '... *driven by the need to make immediate returns for investors, rather than to meet the needs of occupiers*' (Northern Way, 2008). It resulted in a chronic over-supply of apartments in Manchester, Leeds and Sheffield central areas, which account for three of the five postcode areas with the largest annual fall in house prices to October 2008.

The Commission refers to '... *a smaller number of focused public private partnerships ... mutual public-private objectives that de-risk private parameters*' (ibid). It also refers to the '... *investment through a better understanding of public and private sector investment*' and specifically cites the Macquarie-owned M6 toll road in the West Midlands '... *road pricing helps to open up new opportunities for capital investment in transport infrastructure, and might in the longer-term be appropriate for some forms of investment; for example, to manage congestion on the highway network*' (ibid).

Meanwhile, the UK public sector transformation strategy of commissioning, contestability and creating new arms length companies for every economic development and regeneration function – Multi-Area Agreements (MAA), Economic Prosperity Boards (EPB), Community Development Corporations (CDC), Local Housing Companies and so on, fragments infrastructure needs, accountability, plans and capabilities.

In this scenario, it is increasingly difficult to protect jobs, terms and conditions of employment, including pensions and trade union organisation and to prevent low wage, market-driven employment conditions and labour market. The economic and social benefits of infrastructure investment, in particular local labour, good pay and conditions benefiting the local economy and labour market, are significantly reduced.

Crowding out
It is often claimed that public sector investment may displace or 'crowd out' private investment when it is financed through taxation, or borrowing, on domestic financial markets (Straub, 2008). High levels of public borrowing may also '... *raise concerns about the sustainability of public debt over time and strengthen expectations of a future increase in inflation or explicit taxation*' leading to a rise in interest rates, lower return on capital and private investors may scale down their investment plans (Agenor and Moreno-Dodson, 2006). However, the crowding out argument '... *only holds under a specific set of narrow economic circumstances*' when there is full employment, financial resources are fully used in financing productive investment, and new public investment makes no contribution to expanding economic capacity (Political Economy Research Institute, 2009).

The current situation is somewhat different. It can equally be argued that the multi-billion bail-out of private sector banks and financial companies has 'crowded out' the public sector. Recapitalisation and nationalisation of banks has massively increased public debt, resulting in very large cutbacks in public investment, notwithstanding the infrastructure content of many fiscal stimulus strategies.

Infrastructure expenditure and deficits

Public sector capital spending in OECD countries steadily declined as a percentage of total government spending since 1990, falling from 9.5% to 7.2% by 2005 (see Figure 1). The question is, to what extent this indicates an unwillingness, or an inability, to pay for infrastructure investment? Commentary on this evidence usually assumes that further decline is 'inevitable' and that the trend could or should not be reversed. This in turn fuels discussion of infrastructure gaps and deficits and is used to justify private sector investment. US spending will be less than 1% of GDP on infrastructure compared with China's 8% – 10% and India's 3.5%.

Infrastructure spending did not just 'fall' but was the result of public policy and fiscal decisions on taxation, user fees and spending priorities. Infrastructure expenditure was relatively easily delayed and/or budgets cut because it was 'hidden' in contrast to social spending, which had more immediate service and employment consequences.

Figure 1:
General government gross fixed capital formation as a percentage of total government outlays

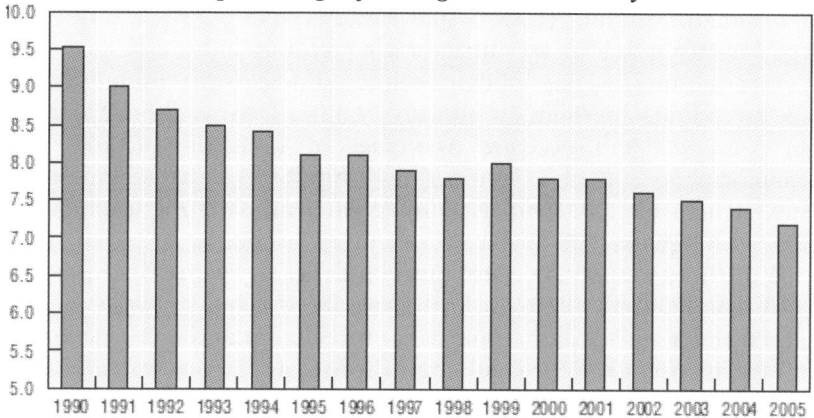

Note: Weighted average using government total outlays converted to USD using 2000 purchasing power parities for GDP.
Source: OECD (2006c), Economic Outlook No. 80 database, November, OECD, Paris.

World Bank infrastructure investment declined by 42% between 1993-2002 in the expectation of increased private sector investment. Although PPP investment peaked in 1997, private sector investment declined from US$128billion in 1997 to US$58billion in 2002 (World Bank, 2003). Multilateral and bilateral aid to infrastructure also suffered a 50% decline. The '... *infrastructure deficit has become the most glaring deficit that governments around the world have to deal with*' concluded an analysis of the challenges facing infrastructure development in South Asia (Nataraj, 2007). Development banks have since developed new infrastructure investment strategies.

The World Bank has estimated that, on average, '... *developing countries actually invest about 3–4% of their GDP on infrastructure annually, whereas that they should be spending about 7–9% on new investment projects and maintenance of existing infrastructure, if broader economic growth and poverty reduction goals are to be achieved*' (United Nations Conference on Trade and Development, 2008). About 70% of investment is publicly funded, private sector 20% and Official Development Assistance the remainder. '*In order to meet the shortfall, governments need to tap into all sources of investment funds, including transnational corporations*' (ibid).

There are no easy ways of identifying infrastructure needs. There are severe limitations in using gross domestic product growth models to identify investment needs and detailed sector studies may be little more than 'wish lists' (Estache and Fay, 2007).

Identifying deficits is important for planning but it also has a key role in monitoring rates of deterioration or improvement in the level of disrepair, changes in levels of use and need, the causes of changes in condition and potential remedies or mitigating action. The American Society of Civil Engineers grading of the condition of infrastructure in 2005 and 2009 is a good example (American Society of Civil Engineers, 2009).

But there are always infrastructure deficits – in provision, repair and maintenance, adaption to the impact of climate change and in green/renewable projects. The planning, design and construction of infrastructure projects is a lengthy process. Population increases, migration and rising living standards mean that infrastructure needs frequently outstrip the resources available and/or the ability to construct facilities when and where they are needed. There are also conflicts about the relative needs and priorities for different parts of the infrastructure network and the economic and social benefits of investment.

The OECD claims that closing the gap for new infrastructure and maintenance and upgrading of existing infrastructure *'... will be crucial to tap into the vast capital and expertise of the private sector through various forms of public-private partnerships. Both of these – PPPs and institutional funds – offer substantial scope for expanding the financial resources available for investment in infrastructures'* (OECD, 2007).

The claim that *'... the alternative to PPP is no project or at least no project within the foreseeable future, rather than a public-procurement project'* (European Investment Bank, 2005) helps to create the belief that there is no other option. The idea that 'more can be delivered earlier' might be appealing if there were not wider and long-term consequences, but these are systematically ignored by PPP vested interests (Whitfield, 2007).

The common approach is to refer to backlogs and multi-billion infrastructure plans, cite examples of government support for PPPs in other countries and extol their virtues. For example, California has a US$500bn infrastructure deficit and needs to examine all reasonable forms of financing in addition to bonds and sales tax revenue. PPPs in the UK were claimed to deliver *'... on time and on budget, procure and manage at lower cost, and lower risk to taxpayers'* and the provincial government PPP units of PartnershipsBC and Infrastructure Ontario were extolled (Crane, 2008). No other options were considered. The author is a special advisor to the Governor of California, prior to which he was a partner with infrastructure investment bank Babcock & Brown for 25 years.

Off or on balance sheet
In 2003, 57% of UK PPP investment was 'on balance sheet' although none of the PFI capital spending has been included in the Treasury's calculation of public sector net debt (Office of National Statistics quoted in IFS, 2006). The £42.7 billion capital spending on PPP/PFI deals signed by the end of 2004 would, if financed conventionally through the public sector, have increased national net debt by 3.4% that year (ibid).

The accounting treatment of PFI projects is complex. UK National Statistics revised public sector net debt by £4.5bn to £424.5bn in 2006 to take account of PFI finance lease liabilities (National Statistics, 2006). UK National Accounts do not include liabilities that are contingent on the completion of construction projects or delivery of services, thus the scope of liabilities and time of recording on balance sheets is different from overall PFI liabilities and the capital value of PFI projects. The adoption of International Financial Reporting Standards (IFRS) means that the majority of PPP assets will in future be on the public sector balance sheet, although some may not because of differing interpretations of contractual terms and conditions.

Strategic Service-delivery Partnerships (SSPs) are not off-balance sheet, because, they largely are funded by existing revenue budget allocations, for the services within scope.

Infrastructure and fiscal stimulus policies
Increased infrastructure spending has a key role in most of the G20 fiscal stimulus policies in response to the economic crisis, ranging from 90% in China's strategy to nil in the case of Russia and Brazil (see Table 3). The timeframe varies between one and five years with most being over two years. The impact on GDP is calculated using three multipliers for tax cuts, infrastructure investment and all other policies, arriving at a range of between 0.4% to 1.2% of GDP in 2009 and about 1.0% in 2010. In other words, GDP in these countries will be an average 0.8% higher than would otherwise be the case.

Table 3:
Infrastructure investment in G20 fiscal stimulus strategies (2009/2010)

Country	Total Cost USbn	Infrastructure investment USbn	% of total package	Impact on GDP	Type of infrastructure	No of jobs created
Argentina	4.1	3.1	75	1.3	Increase investment to 5% of GDP – transport, sanitation, housing, hospitals and schools	380,000
Australia	30.4	7.8	26	2.7 and 1.7	Accelerate 14 road projects, $1.2bn rail investment, $1bn universities, schools, housing	32,000
Brazil	8.1	0	0	0.3	n/a	
Canada	36.1	16.2	45	1.5 and 1.3	n/a	
China	586.0	195.4	42	2.0	Infrastructure $300bn, public housing $60bn, rural areas $51bn, earthquake areas $130bn	
France	35.8	9.0	25	0.7	n/a	
Germany	115.7	27.2	24	1.5 and 2.0	Infrastructure and transport	n/a
India	6.8	2.2	32	0.5	n/a	
Indonesia	9.8	0.9	9	1.3 and 0.6	n/a	
Italy	12.2	2.4	20	0.2 and 0.1	n/a	
Japan	97.8	23.3	24	1.4 and 0.4	n/a	
Mexico	14.1	5.4	38	1.5	n/a	
Russia	23.9	0	0	1.7	n/a	
Saudi Arabia	n/a	n/a	n/a	n/a	n/a	
South Africa	n/a	n/a	n/a	n/a	n/a	
South Korea	13.1	3.5	27	1.5 and 0.3	Cleaning 4 rivers and flood defences	190,000
Spain	34.4	11.2	33	2.3	n/a	
Turkey	n/a	n/a	n/a	n/a	n/a	
UK	27.5	1.1	4	1.4 and -0.1	n/a	
USA	540.5	78.8	15	2.0 and 1.8	n/a	

Sources: International Monetary Fund, 2009, Wall Street Journal, Financial Times, www.economist.com

However, using higher multipliers provides higher growth estimates but '... *anyway you slice the numbers, policymakers are falling short of real ambition in the face of the worst global downturn since the Great depression*' (Peterson Institute for International Economic, 2009).

The head of Macquarie Capital Funds in Asia, Nick van Gelder, believes that the next three years could turn out to be a '... *golden age for private equity.*' '*The capital that many government's consume over the next 24 months in economic recovery packages will leave them short of funding for infrastructure development and they will have no choice but to increase levels of private participation over time. Privatisation of stimulus projects in five to 10 years may offer another level of opportunity for the industry*' (Redrawing the Landscape, The Banker, April, 2009)

Employment impact
A stimulus package should generate growth and jobs to offset rising unemployment, take effect quickly, target unmet needs, be fair and raise current deficits but not affect the long-term budget outlook (Economic Policy Institute (EPI), 2008). Increased government spending can reduce unemployment and reduce unused productive capacity in the economy. Multipliers tend to vary between countries, tend to be larger for bigger economies and '... *may be decreasing over time as the marginal productivity of infrastructure falls with its expansion*' (International Monetary Fund, 2008). The importance of regulating, monitoring, reviewing and assessing, and if necessary, changing policies, to ensure objectives and benefits are achieved, cannot be understated.

A $1.00 increase in US infrastructure spending is estimated to result in $1.59 change in real GDP one year after the spending actually occurs (Zandi, 2008). Infrastructure spending has a bigger economic impact than the Bush income and corporate tax cuts, dividend and capital gains tax cuts or for temporary tax cuts and lump-sum rebates. Increasing unemployment benefit, food stamps and financial aid to state governments would have a similar impact to infrastructure spending (ibid).

The fiscal stimulus generated a wide range of estimates of the employment impact. Between 14,000 to 38,000 jobs are supported for every $1bn US public infrastructure expenditure taking account of direct, indirect (for example building materials industries) and induced (retail and service jobs created by construction jobs) effects (Economic Policy Institute, 2008, Political Economy Research

Institute, 2009). The employment impact varies depending on the type of infrastructure, for example, US$1bn expenditure on water systems is estimated to generate 19,769 jobs compared to fewer jobs in transport (18,930 jobs), school buildings (18,262) and energy (16,763). How expenditure is prioritised within each sector also has an impact, for example, transport spending on mass transit projects will generate 4,000 (21%) more jobs than the same expenditure on roads and bridges (Political Economy Research Institute, 2009).

Drinking water infrastructure investment is claimed to generate up to 57,400 jobs for $1bn investment (Massachusetts Infrastructure Investment Coalition, 2008). Highway operations such as traffic control, maintenance, and snow removal supported fewer jobs, 17,810 per US$1bn expenditure at 2000 prices (Federal Highways Administration, 2003). The speed of infrastructure implementation is important, for example, highway projects, excluding short-term resurfacing projects, spend an average 27% of a project budget in the first year (Federal Highways Administration, 2008).

Transit investment supports the largest number of jobs (and has the highest proportion of indirect employment) compared with construction spending and green investment. The percentage share of infrastructure expenditure which is spent in construction (53% for mass transit compared to 64% for general construction spending) has an impact on the gender ratio of jobs created, for example, the construction sector male/female ratio is 90%/10% compared to 63%/37% for indirect employment (Economic Policy Institute, 2009). Another analysis showed that two thirds of indirect jobs generated by construction spending are in manufacturing, retail, professional/scientific technical services and administration, waste management and remediation services (Irons, 2008).

In Canada an additional C$1bn infrastructure expenditure is estimated to support 11,500 jobs in 2008, declining annually to 7,200 jobs by 2012. There are marginal differences in the different types of infrastructure with transportation (11,900 jobs in 2008), building (11,800), waste management (11,200) and water (10,800) (Federation of Canadian Municipalities, 2008).

The relationship between infrastructure and services
The design and condition of buildings has a big influence on the provision of services with regard to their location space, functional suitability and availability of utilities and equipment.

Infrastructure PPPs are promoted as 'buying a service' rather than a building. The design, build, finance and operate or Build, Operate and Transfer (BOT) model has led to the outsourcing of these functions which results in increasing private sector markets for architectural, financial services and facilities management firms but a parallel decline in the workload for public sector architectural staff and in-house maintenance organisations.

Balfour Beatty recently promoted the use of PPPs schools in Florida – 'private solutions for public needs' – by highlighting the importance of indoor air quality, lighting, climate control and noise control to show how facilities effect student performance in US school buildings. They also compared international science and maths scores – *'our children are falling behind'* – and claimed that PPPs were not privatisation (Balfour Beatty, 2008).

There are no discernable boundaries between constructing and operating buildings and the provision of core services, such as teaching and clinical services, in those buildings, except for political/public acceptability and the ability of the private sector to deliver quality core services. The notion that capital is 'content' with the scope of PPPs or the private sector is 'not interested' in delivering core services is naive.

Public service outsourcing has enabled the private sector to gain an important share of related services, such as supply teacher agencies in education. Teaching in state schools in the UK is already encircled by privately controlled schools, PPPs, new markets, outsourcing of facilities management, ICT and educational support services (Whitfield, 2006). PPPs have provided new opportunities for private provision of core services ranging from the operation of new prisons, clinical services in treatment centres, the provision of ICT in Building Schools for the Future, a wide range of corporate services in Strategic Service-delivery Partnerships. Furthermore, PPP structures have emerged which provide opportunities for widening the scope of service delivery in new health centres and surgeries (NHS Local Improvement Finance Trust (LIFT) projects).

The launch of Independent Sector Treatment Centres (ISTCs) in the UK's health service in 2003 was a classic example where infrastructure and service delivery were one and the same. Treatment centres were part of commercialisation strategies which also included outsourcing support services and social care, the sale of residential homes, PPPs for hospitals and health centres and primary care commissioning (Ruane 2008, Pollock 2004).

The treatment centre programme had a key role in widening the role of the healthcare market. The £5.6bn programme was designed to carry out 1.3m procedures by harnessing the capacity of the private sector to reduce National Health Service (NHS) waiting times. Player and Leys (2008) and Pollock and Kirkwood (2009) comprehensively show how the procurement process, performance and finance of the centres was flawed and shrouded in secrecy. The government succeeded in the prime objectives of normalising the use of the private sector in healthcare delivery and restructuring the domestic private healthcare industry. At least a quarter of the work carried out by first wave ISTCs was not additional work but 'transferred activity' which would otherwise have been carried out by the NHS. By September 2007, only four centres were working at 100% of the value of the contract and four had fewer than 60% contract utilisation (end of September 2007). Yet ISTCs were given guaranteed contracts requiring the government to pay the full cost irrespective of how many patients are treated.

The extent to which services are commissioned and marketised influences the degree to which the private sector will seek to privatise public infrastructure. Co-location and various types of strategic partnerships create new opportunities for capital to acquire both physical and intellectual assets.

The question will be why should a 'strategic council' own buildings? Commissioning could simply involve the leasing of space in private buildings using property partnerships. There is, of course, another contestable market scenario – in order to maintain competition and keep the cost of market entry low and minimise the cost of infrastructure and equipment in relatively short-term contracts – schools, hospitals and other public infrastructure could be leased to the private sector to provide and manage services (Prowle, 2008). A right wing nirvana!

Changing role of the state
Neoliberal transformation of public services has required changes in the role of the state, moving to commissioning and directly providing fewer services, making and managing markets and creating new financial systems so that funding follows pupils and patients in a performance management system.

Governments in many countries have also transferred

responsibilities and functions to arms length companies, trusts and joint ventures. They have also promoted the idea that globalisation, outsourcing, offshoring and partnerships were 'inevitable'.

The roles and the responsibilities of the state have changed but do not radically reduce the cost of the services because they remain financed by the state. Despite these changes, government spending as a percentage of GDP in OECD member countries is expected to decline only fractionally to 40.8% between 1990-2009 (Plender, 2008). This also reflects the demand for public goods, rising expectations and demographic change. Commissioning, procurement, partnerships and contract management bring new responsibilities and staffing/resource requirements. Neoliberal public management and PPPs have reduced government in-house capability but the state has borne higher transaction costs employing lawyers and consultants to provide advice and guidance during the long procurement process.

The global financial crisis has required government intervention to recapitalise/nationalise banks, respond to market failures, reform financial markets and finance fiscal stimulus packages. This has been described as a return to the Keynesian economic model. However, this change of direction had yet to be reflected in public sector transformation policies in the UK in 2009.

CHAPTER 3

Transformation and globalisation of infrastructure

It is important to examine the rationale for PPPs in neoliberal economic policy and public sector reform based on mainstreaming commissioning, outsourcing, private finance and the transfer of functions to arms length companies. The World Bank and regional development banks have had a key role in implementing this agenda and promoting PPPs and privatisation.

Neoliberal transformation

Neoliberal ideology has dictated economic policy and public sector transformation over the last three decades. It is rooted in the belief that free trade and competition should determine the supply of goods and services and the superiority of markets to allocate resources and organise the economy. Minimum regulation of financial and supply markets should permit the free flow of capital, goods and services globally to create new opportunities for accumulation. Neoliberals want the state reconfigured so that it commodifies and outsources services, develops markets, and creates a pro-business climate and flexible labour market. This would include privatising publicly owned assets and transferring responsibility for service provision to the private and voluntary sectors. The state must also deepen business involvement in the public policy making and legislative process (Whitfield, 2006).

Financial markets, financial institutions, financial elites and financial values, have had an increasing influence over economic policy, accumulation and redistribution (Harvey 2005, Palley 2007, Crotty 2007). This has several dimensions. The financialisation of personal income – increasing penetration of formal finance into the transaction of ordinary life: housing, pensions, insurance, consumption and so on. The financial crisis also revealed the extent to which contemporary finance relies on drawing profits directly from the personal income of working people and others across society (Lapavitsas, 2008). Another aspect is the drive towards private investment in public infrastructure that requires financial markets to provide new loans, additional securitisation, new Special Purpose Vehicles (SPVs) and new opportunities for profit. Employees are being required to make their own pension provision through savings schemes, thus increasing the flow and stock of funds.

The process of financialisation and individualisation has effected important parts of daily life – tolls for roads, tunnels and bridges; tuition fees for college students; charges for television in hospitals; fees for homecare; charges for music and other 'non-core' activities in schools. This system of multi-tax collection is inefficient and masks the extraction of profit by an array of contractors and consultants delivering public services. It also breeds anti-collective attitudes – why should I pay for education when I don't have children? or why should I pay for motorways when I can't drive? Individualisation and personalisation should not be confused – the first focuses on the structure of services such as direct payments and individual budgets, whereas personalisation covers how users are treated in the design and delivery of services.

Financialisation and individualisation inevitably lead to commodification, marketisation and deregulation and ultimately to commercialisation and privatisation (see Figure 2).

Figure 2: *Neoliberal approach to public sector reform*

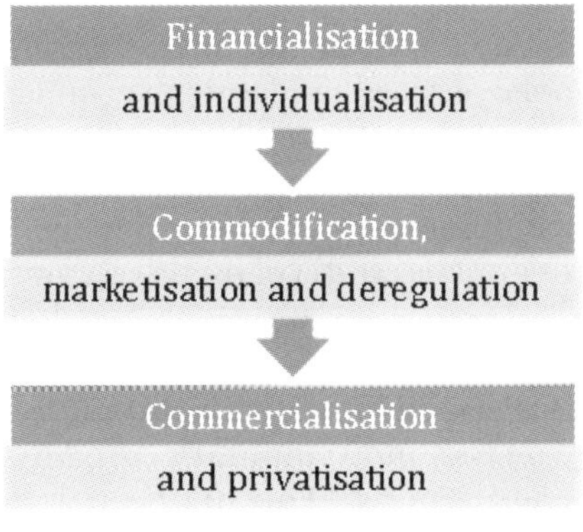

```
Financialisation
and individualisation
        ▼
Commodification,
marketisation and deregulation
        ▼
Commercialisation
and privatisation
```

Source: Whitfield, 2009.

The marketisation process requires the state to restructure for competition and market mechanisms. What were previously 'whole' coordinated systems or networks of schools, hospitals, and roads are divided into individual or group projects so that they can more easily be privately financed and operated. This aligns with the policy of consumerism, localism and reducing the power of local government to determine public policy. Marketisation has five elements:

Commodifying (commercialising) services – services are reorganised so that they can be specified and packaged in a contract, thus extending outsourcing and offshoring.

Commodifying (commercialising) labour – the reorganisation of work and jobs to maximise productivity and assist transfer to another employer.

Restructuring the state for competition and market mechanisms – schools, hospitals and other facilities are compelled to compete against each other, funding is changed to follow pupils and patients, public bodies are reduced to commissioning functions creating opportunities for private finance and so-called partnerships.

Restructuring democratic accountability and user involvement – service users are treated as consumers; services and functions are transferred to quangos, arms length companies and trusts each of which commissions consultants and contractors and has infrastructure responsibilities.

Embedding business interests and promoting liberalisation internationally – business is more involved in the public policy making process and promotes national, European and global liberalisation of public services (Whitfield, 2006).

The neoliberal agenda is designed to transform the organisation and provision of public services and local government, particularly by the creation of new 'partnerships'. New Labour's transformation required local authorities to become strategic leaders and 'place makers' by commissioning services and functions from a mixed economy of private, public and voluntary sector providers. Thus procurement, market making and outsourcing dominate a contract culture with a small 'strategic hub' retained for the commissioning role. Local Strategic Partnerships, an alliance of local council, other public bodies, business and voluntary organisations are now considered corporate 'partners'. This has been accompanied by the fragmentation of local government and public bodies by hiving off services, functions and assets to arms length companies, trusts, special purpose vehicles, and in some cases, full privatisation to private companies and voluntary organisations.

The broader use of private investment in the design, build, finance and operation of public infrastructure had four important roles in neoliberal public sector transformation strategy. Firstly, it widens the role of partnerships and private finance in infrastructure, which, in turn, produces a variety of special purpose and other arms length companies to manage and operate facilities. Secondly, it creates a mixed economy of providers and helps to establish commissioning, contestability and choice (although the imposition of PPPs reduce choice as 'the only show in town', reduces procurement options and make it more complex and confidential, and schools and hospitals have no choice, indeed are usually totally un-aware, when project equity is sold to infrastructure funds). Thirdly, it creates markets in the design, build, finance and operation of facilities, which runs in parallel with the marketisation of back office and frontline service delivery. Finally, it provides new opportunities for construction, financial and service companies to diversify (for example, Bertelsmann/Arvato) which, in turn, enables business interests to have a greater role in public policy making. It thus has an economic, political and ideological function.

Privatisation is '... *a comprehensive strategy for permanently restructuring the welfare state and public services in the interests of capital*' (Whitfield, 1983). By the late 1990s most of the state-owned industrial companies, utilities, oil, telecommunications and transport, a large part of the public infrastructure, had been privatised in the UK (Whitfield 1992, 2001 and 2002).

The privatisation of state owned corporations and property has evolved into the fracturing and fragmenting of public assets and services, governance and democracy and the public domain, in an attempt to marketise and privatise the welfare state and establish the universalisation of markets and individual access. The next stage was local government and the welfare state, which could not, at least politically, be privatised by flotation and trade sales. A different strategy was needed which required commodification, introduction of user charges and marketisation as the means of achieving privatisation. The UK's role in promoting and developing the PPP model was not accidental but grew out of its privatisation programme and neoliberal approach to public sector transformation.

The OECD's Global Infrastructure Needs study was completed before the economic crisis and exemplified a neoliberal approach to public infrastructure, although it only focused on energy, transport and water (OECD, 2007). The 500-page report made constant reference to 'business models', to the 'public monolith model, and appeared reluctant to recognise that water is a public good. Its first three recommendations were to '*1. Encourage public-private partnerships (PPPs) as a means of raising additional financing for infrastructure* investment and diversifying business models. 2. Encourage the investment of pension funds and other large institutional investors in infrastructures. 3. Make greater use of user charges for funding infrastructures ...' (ibid).

The OECD study was constructed around a series of assumptions about a limited role of the state, public sector performance and the benefits of markets. It argued for the separation of ownership and operation to inject competition into the design and provision of infrastructure, or where competition is not possible, '... *competition for the market through the use of PPPs*' (ibid). It did not assess the consequences of expanding the infrastructure market. A very brief section dealing with labour relations issues referred only to limiting the right to strike!

PPPs are privatisation
Elected members, managers, consultants and contractors often claim that PPPs are 'not privatisation' because they are not buying an asset but a stream of services via a partnership (Grimsey and Lewis, 2004). This issue must be addressed firstly by defining 'privatisation' and then 'partnership'.

Privatisation includes the transfer of responsibility and control from the public sector to the private sector – corporate and voluntary sectors or to families and individuals. Those who cling to the Thatcherite definition of privatisation as meaning only the sale of state-owned corporations do so because it enables them to ignore the different ways in which privatisation has mutated in the past thirty years. Privatisation is not confined to transacting a sale of assets, but a process beginning with financialisation and commodification through to marketisation and commercialisation and concluding with different forms and degrees of privatisation. This is fully described in the four-part typology embracing the marketisation and privatisation of global public goods; the marketisation and privatisation of assets and services; the privatisation of governance and democracy and the privatisation of the public domain (Whitfield, 2001 and 2007).

'Partnership' is a grossly misused term. PPPs are a principal-agent relationship in which one party, the principal (government) has a contract with another party, the agent (private contractor or consortia) to provide goods and/or services. The extent to which a design, build, finance and operate PPP is a genuine 'partnership' is a matter of debate. The public sector effectively outsources these responsibilities to the private sector in long-term contracts. The extent to which risks are shared and jointly managed is questionable because a clear division of labour or separation of client/contractor responsibility determines relations between the public sector and the Special Purpose Vehicle. Refinancing gains are shared but profits from the sale of equity in PPPs are not (see Chapter 7). The degree of 'joint' and 'shared' responsibilities evident in a genuine partnership are absent.

PPPs allow governments and business to avoid/dampen the debate about levels of taxation and to conceal the true public cost of new infrastructure. PPPs conceal the fact that they are fully funded by government and/or user charges. The private sector charges for the risks for which it takes responsibility. Off balance sheet private finance is not a solution but a means of widening the trade in services and marketising the public infrastructure. The claim that PPPs represent 'only' 10%-15% of infrastructure investment, so are therefore relatively unimportant, is deception.

Local Education Partnerships (LEPs) established in Building Schools for the Future (BSF) projects in the UK have more partnership attributes, but they are usually 80% controlled by the private sector. New PPP models extend and deepen private sector involvement in procurement and service provision thus further embedding control and longer term opportunities for asset ownership (see Chapter 7).

Political economy of public infrastructure

There are ten elements to the political economy of public infrastructure – economic, social, public health, finance, climate change, environmental, sustainable development, social justice/poverty reduction, employment and operational management (see Table 4).

Theory of PPPs
The right's case for private provision and PPPs/privatisation rests on the theory of competition, increased efficiency and innovation with additionality, partnership and risk transfer, providing value for money. These are claimed to outweigh the imperfections associated with contractual relations and the mediation of public and private interests.

The idea that PPPs are '... *a way of protecting existing and future taxpayers, reducing the overall tax burden, spreading risk, reducing "bureaucracy" and increasing the effectiveness of delivery of many public sector*

Table 4: *Political economy of public infrastructure*

Elements	Description
Economic	Supporting economic activity, reducing costs and improving productivity
Social needs	Meeting human needs, reducing inequalities
Public health	Extent to which infrastructure improves external/internal conditions and supports other community well being initiatives
Finance	Cost to the public purse, charges and tolls for users.
Climate change	Contribution to energy efficiency and low carbon economy and mitigating effects of climate change
Environmental	Improves living and working environment
Sustainability	Provides for future generations and construction/operation supports local production and supply chains.
Social justice and poverty reduction	Access, reduction in inequalities, achievement of development goals
Employment	Providing quality jobs
Operational management	How facilities are managed in the public interest.

Source: Whitfield, 2009.

"*responsibilities*'" (Adams et al, 2006) is economic deception.

Private provision model

Competition in the provision of public infrastructure and services is claimed to lead to better quality services at lower cost. Competition in the construction of public infrastructure is not new – it has generally

Figure 3: *The PPP model in private provision*

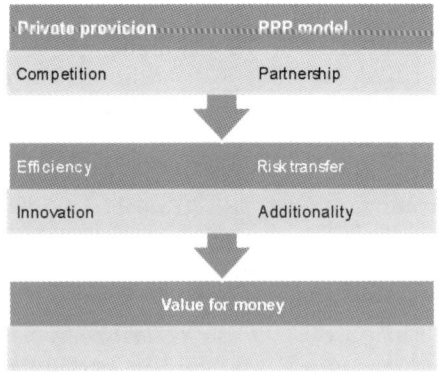

Source: Whitfield, 2009.

been carried out by the private sector, except in a few cases state owned construction companies. PPPs and privatisation are no different, except, that they enable the private sector to supply and distribute energy and water, operate telecommunications services, to deliver education, health and environmental services and to operate corporate services for the public sector.

Detailed government and independent research have demolished claims of 20%-25% savings from competitive tendering in the UK, which reveal that savings are minimal (Escott & Whitfield, 1995, European Services Strategy Unit, 2006). The degree of competition for PPP contracts is very variable due to the high tendering costs. Many contracts have been awarded after contractors have withdrawn from the procurement process leaving only one bidder.

Efficiency and a narrow definition of value-for-money are the prime focus of public sector transformation and PPP decision-making. Comparative efficiency compares the historic public sector performance with future private sector performance, an approach with fundamental flaws. Effectiveness and equity are equally important, plus, there are inevitably trade-offs between costs and benefits.

The exclusive focus on efficiency crowds out the important values and criteria, which are essential in public policy decision-making. It assumes that comparisons can readily be carried out and ignores major methodological problems, for example comparing the performance of new private prisons with publicly operated old prisons. It encourages everything to be reduced to money such as the 'high cost of democracy'.

Comparisons of privatised services/companies (which have been subjected to investment and a change of managerial control) are made with continuing public sector services/companies, which generally have not had the benefit of additional investment and/or improved management or operational systems. Even longitudinal studies, examining performance over five years, do not take the potential for public sector improvement into account. It limits discussion to current arrangements and systems, when, in fact, both public and private provision may be inadequate in meeting social needs, social justice and community aspirations.

Competition also legitimatises the extraction of profit from education, medical care, social services and prison services. It also legitimates the exploitation of private sector employees once they are outside the better conditions and more organised public sector because this 'reduces taxes' and supports the idea that terms and conditions should vary according to local labour market conditions (Dolovich, 2005).

UK government studies purport to compare PFI with traditional procurement to demonstrate that PPPs deliver assets on time and on budget (see chapter 9). However, the government has made no attempt to take account of the benefits gained by reforming and improving public sector capacity to manage and control the procurement and construction process. This could eliminate delays and cost overruns in public sector construction projects carried out by the same PPP contractors. The claim that PPPs speed up the delivery of schools and hospitals does not take account of the long and complex procurement process and the abandonment of some projects resulting in even longer delays.

PPPs have led to 'whole life' costing of the operation, maintenance and renewal of infrastructure, but this is limited to the length of a contract, not the life of a building. The period of handover of facilities at the end of PPP contracts has yet to occur and is almost certain to raise some major issues and legal disputes over the condition of buildings.

Value-for-money is claimed for every PPP project proposed to ensure it would proceed. However, it is frequently contrived by comparing the private sector in the future with the public sectors historic track record in which the same construction companies were culpable for delays and cost overruns. Furthermore, it is only a forecast, not a guarantee, because no one can be certain of value for money at the start of a long-term contract. The figures are likely to tell a different story at the end of a 25-30 year contract, although the original decision-makers will have long moved on or been replaced.

The International Monetary Fund concluded that, *'Much of the case for public private partnerships rests on the relative efficiency of the private sector. Whilst there is an extensive literature on this subject, the theory is ambiguous and the empirical evidence is mixed'* (International Monetary Fund, 2004).

Debt write-offs, capital restructuring, rationalisation, land and property deals, use of pension fund surpluses and accounting changes undertaken by the government *before* privatisation in the 1980s laid the ground for the early post-privatisation efficiency and productivity increases (Whitfield, 1992).

A comprehensive review of post-privatisation performance was

'... unable to find sufficient statistical macro or micro evidence that output, labour, capital, and TFP productivity in the United Kingdom increased substantially as a consequence of ownership change at privatisation compared to the long-term trend' (Florio, 2004).

Innovation: Access to expertise and innovation, not otherwise available in the public sector, is another frequently claimed advantage. But good design in a handful of PPP projects does little to alter the fact that there has been no step-change in innovation and design in the UK. In fact the standard of civic design has been eroded.

Strategic Service-delivery Partnerships (SSPs) have focused on e-government but contributed little, if anything, to e-democracy and e-citizenship. A lack of confidence in internal capability and intellectual knowledge and a belief that only the private sector can achieve the required level of budget savings are commonly used to justify Strategic Service-delivery Partnerships (SSPs). It is claimed that ICT technologies can transform corporate services and with customer contact centres can create 'world class' services. Yet the evidence is weak. One in ten projects has been terminated. One local authority chief executive arrogantly claimed on television that his authority would be '... beyond excellence' if the contract succeeded, but then referred to the potential of 'risk and chaos' associated with innovation (Jones, 2008). Regeneration and new jobs are part of the rationale for SSPs but the pitiful record of job creation reinforces the conclusion that the promise of 'social transformation' is used as just another 'sweetener' to justify the project.

Privatisation and PPPs have spurned a plethora of new companies such as Special Purpose Vehicles (SPVs), Joint Venture Companies (JVCs) and Local Education Partnerships (LEPs). These are innovative in the extent to which they are new companies operating within the public sector, but they are designed to achieve financial engineering objectives rather than the interests of service users. This increases rather than decreases risk, irrespective of who bears that risk. There are also negative consequences for public sector capability (see chapter 9).

PPP model
Additionality: Public Private Partnerships are claimed to 'accelerate infrastructure provision' because of faster procurement within budget. Off-balance sheet treatment avoids public finance constraints, thus providing infrastructure more quickly than traditional public

procurement. The PPP lobby also promote the concept as 'buying a service' rather than a building, which is also said to avoid the cyclical problem of cuts in maintenance budgets because the maintenance budget is, in effect, ring-fenced within the contract payment.

Governments promote Public Private Partnerships because capital investment can often be classified off balance sheet thus public debt is not increased. Analysis of 621 contracts in the UK signed by 2007 show that just 80 (13%) were on balance sheet but they accounted for 43% of the capital value of all projects (Public Private Finance, 2007). Project finance may remain within externally imposed fiscal frameworks such as the EU Maastricht criteria but the long-term stream of monthly payments to the contractor is accounted for in public sector revenue expenditure. These payments are contractual commitments, which inevitably imposes pressure on other services and functions, particularly when cuts are imposed in revenue budgets. Claims to 'reduce the burden' on taxpayers are false. In most cases the private sector make no financial contribution to creating infrastructure assets and is repaid in full for financing the construction and operation for the contract period.

Additionality, cash payments or reducing public subsidies are a major feature in urban renewal and asset monetisation PPPs. For example, in Ireland, Dublin City Council turned to PPPs for housing renewal in an attempt to leverage private capital to provide public and affordable housing in return for land and development rights to build private housing. It was a total failure (see chapter 6).

Privately financed toll roads, energy and water projects are the exception where tolls and charges repay the debt and/or equity used to finance projects. However, they have other financial concerns with regard to the level of tolls, equity issues and the use of public subsidies to offset market prices.

Partnership: A contractual partnership between the public sector and a private sector consortia assumes that there is a commonality of interest and that any divergence of interests can be mediated within the partnership. In practice, everything is determined and defined by contractual relations, yet a complete or perfect contract does not exist, any more than perfect competition in procurement. In practice, a contract culture is more prevalent in PPPs than the notion of partnership.

It is most likely that PPP infrastructure will not return to the public sector at the end of long-term contracts, because public bodies may have reduced capability to manage and operate them as a result of being asset stripped by other neoliberal policies. For example, Sheffield City Council was one of the first embryo SSP contracts in 1998, which was recently retendered rather than returned to in-house provision. Secondary market infrastructure funds have a vested interest in pressing for PPP renewal.

Risk transfer: The public sector only pays for facilities when they are available for use and only pays for services when they meet acceptable standards. Non-availability of rooms and/or poor standard of service, results in financial deductions from the unitary payment. This ensures high quality facilities and services.

Value-for-money: This is often dominated by financial issues and, particularly where a Public Sector Comparator (PSC) is used, may be contrived – see Chapter 9.

The fable of the mixed economy
The neoliberal transformation model creates a three-part market structure, with the state financing capacity building of the voluntary/social enterprise sector so that it can 'compete' with the public and private sectors. This structure is unlikely to be sustainable because the private sector will seek to become the dominant contractor and the state will be unable to maintain this mixed economy with measures, which will not distort the very market it is seeking to protect! The level of service and quality will ultimately be shaped by market forces.

This model also assumes that the state will be able to retain its capability to research social needs, develop innovative approaches, manage markets, undertake options appraisal and procurement without outsourcing this work to the private sector, thus contributing to a spiral of decreasing capability and privately controlled commissioning *and* provision.

Also it is based on the belief that there is perfect competition – alternative suppliers, ease of entry and exit, full information and that contractors will not use gaming tactics – low bids, parking of 'difficult' clients and so on – on a scale which does not distort the market.

It assumes that the quality of employment, labour standards and workers rights can be protected in this market system. This relies on the state being able to monitor performance *and* management practice when current practice is, at best, inconsistent and less than rigorous. In reality public bodies and ruling political parties are usually committed to contracts being successful and generally minimize the disclosure of poor performance and collude with contractors to 'fix' the problem. Level of non-compliance usually has to be severe before contract termination is even considered.

There is also an assumption that private investment will spur economic development and create new jobs more successfully than the public sector. However, evidence of job creation by private companies in Strategic Service-delivery Partnerships in the UK and the economic impact of US rural towns with private prisons are equally poor (Whitfield, 2008).

If the service is commodified and delivered through competition between other providers, this also means that the relationship between service users and between service users and staff are defined by competition and affordability; although in some cases there is no choice i.e. which prison or which hospital people are sent to in an accident or emergency. Service users are empowered in this system but are individual consumers with limited choice and influence. The social relations between service users and staff delivering the service are constrained by commercial ideology. Despite their claim of 'world class commissioning' no one is able to claim a 'world class contract'!

The 'transformation' of the National Health Service (NHS) and social care in the UK illustrates the point. Privatisation began in non-clinical support services and the building of new hospitals and health centres. Meanwhile the public provision of long-term nursing and residential care was reversed to create a predominately private/voluntary dominated sector. Exactly the same happened to home care services provided by local authorities. Subsequently the objective of a quasi-internal market became the creation of a mixed economy in health care (Pollock, 2004). This required restructuring financial systems, so that money followed patients and also the pricing of every treatment.

The private sector gained further foothold in the provision of clinical services with the £5.6bn diagnostic and treatment centre programme carried out in private hospitals, new private centres or utilising 'spare capacity' in NHS hospitals. Commissioning was extended to primary care in 2009 with the separation of commissioning and provision, mainstreaming procurement and a contract culture, and pressure to consider 'whole estate solutions' through Strategic Estates Development models, another PPP model (see chapter 8). The mixed economy was now 'plurality in provision' to be achieved by increased commissioning and contestability, with new regional commercial support units following the abolition of the NHS Purchasing and Supply Agency. A new Procurement, Investment and Commercial Division (PICD) includes PFI and a new Strategic Market Development Unit (SMDU) supports market analysis and market-making (Department of Health, 2009).

Future generations
Investment in public infrastructure not only addresses deficits and current needs but also provides for future generations. We currently benefit from the foresight of previous design and of engineering foresight (Rohatyn, 2009) but are also suffering the consequences of the more recent failure to maintain investment levels and/or increase charges and tolls in line with inflation.

PPPs and privatisation impose conditions and constraints on future generations that they may consider to be unwanted burdens. Long-term contracts, particularly those with non-compete clauses and punitive termination costs, may reduce flexibility and constrain future spending priorities (see chapter 9). Whether the large hospital developments built under PFI in the UK will reflect health infrastructure needs 25 years hence is questionable.

PPPs and privatisation also will change the nature of public goods. Although individual projects are unlikely to have an impact, the accumulation of projects accompanied by a more influential and powerful infrastructure market, is likely to change values, priorities and the scope of public infrastructure for future generations.

Not a single market
Although reference is often made to an infrastructure market there are, in fact, a number of distinct sub-markets, for example in energy, ICT and health, which are at different stages of development from country to country. Firms also compete for construction and equipment supply contracts. The demand for new infrastructure is driven by a number of factors; access to mineral mining drives road, rail and port facilities; energy supply generates demand for oil and gas pipelines and distribution grids; and improving rail networks creates demand for line upgrades and extensions.

Concept of market power
Control over sections of the public infrastructure provides the private

sector with a degree of market power. This is relevant to long-term toll road concessions, particularly where there are no viable alternative routes that provide comparative speed and cost. Non-compete contract clauses that limit the improvement of adjacent roads to funnel traffic into the concessionaire's toll road are another aspect of market power.

Globalisation of services and the General Agreement for Trade in Services (GATS)/EU single market
The EU Services Directive is vague, applies to all services not specifically excluded from it, and the European Court of Justice will have wide powers for discretionary judgments which will determine the exact content to continue liberalization. A Norwegian Study on Power and Democracy has described this as *'judicialisation'* which *'... implies that larger areas and more detailed elements in society are being regulated by laws and directives, that the decision-making competence of the courts and other judicial institutions is increasing at the expense of political and administrative bodies, and that interests are increasingly being formulated as legal requirements'* (Norwegian Union of Municipal and General Employees, 2008). Although education, healthcare, social care, police, prisons and courts, postal services, certain services in the gas and electricity sector, waste treatment and water supply and most transport services are currently excluded they could be re-classified at a later date. Many of the above are already subject to specific EU Directives to increase competition and liberalisation.

Crucially, the country of origin proposals were claimed to have been removed, but in fact remain. *'As a result, service providers will know that they will not be subject to the legislation of the receiving Member State except where its application is justified for the four reasons set out in Article 16(1) and 16(3) – public policy, public security, public health and environmental protection – (or the legislation in question is covered by a derogation provided for in Article 17)'* (European Commission, 2007).

PPPs are part of the marketisation process creating markets in schools and hospitals, and are linked to EU/World Trade Organisation attempts to create global markets in services, part of creating global markets in agriculture and trade, trading schools and hospitals are part of the same system.

It is currently unclear how different types of PPPs will be affected by the GATS proposals. *'The primary contract might be catorgised as government procurement under Article XIII, but only for those services that do not involve commercial re-sale. The exemption does not apply for those governments that made government procurement commitments in their accession packages or in bilateral agreements. It is also unclear how far down the PFI chain the definition of government procurement would apply, because the GATS does not define procurement'* (Kelsey, 2008). In the case of Public-Public Partnerships (PUPs), the public body '*... remains the service authority, responsible for regulation, setting tariffs, planning and monitoring. Trade in services commitments have the potential to prevent governments from adopting either stronger regulation or PUPs, even when PFI privatisations go wrong'* (ibid).

OECD infrastructure market
The OECD's two year Global Infrastructure Needs: Prospects and Implications for Public and Private Actors forecast needs to 2030 for electricity, water, surface transport (rail freight and road) and telecommunications (OECD, 2007). But the OECD approach to closing the infrastructure gap is basically more of the same. '*Since the 1980s more than USD 1 trillion of assets has been privatised in OECD countries. Infrastructures have consistently been on centre stage. Averaged out over the 1990-2006 period, almost two-thirds of all privatisations in the OECD area have concerned utilities, transport, telecommunications and oil facilities.*

Elsewhere, too, privatisation activity has been vigorous. Over roughly the same period, some USD 400 billion of state-owned assets were sold in non-OECD countries, of which about half were accounted for by infrastructures.

New business models with private sector participation, notably variants of public-private partnership models (PPPs) that are being increasingly used particularly in OECD countries, offer further scope for unlocking private sector capital and expertise. So too do the huge pools of private sector capital managed by pension funds and insurance companies. Infrastructures, with their low-risk and steady-return profile, are of considerable potential interest to such funds' (ibid).

Millennium Development Goals and poverty reduction
Globally, more than 1 billion people have no access to roads, 1.2 billion do not have safe drinking water, 2.3 billion lack reliable sources of energy, 2.4 billion have no sanitation facilities and 4 billion no modern communication services. In the absence of accessible transport, energy and water, the poor pay heavily in time, money and health. The infrastructure gap is huge. Despite its clear benefits for

growth and poverty reduction, infrastructure spending is far below what is truly needed. Moreover, that gap widens as country incomes fall. World output is projected to decline by 1.3% in 2009 and to recover only gradually in 2010, growing by 1.9% (International Monetary Fund, 2009). The impact, based on experience of earlier crises, is likely to be long-lasting as welfare losses continue, together with lower productive activity and the effects of defensive action taken to protect living standards (Ravallion, 2008).

Whilst the number of people living in extreme poverty declined to 1.4bn in 2005, there are wide regional differences. Most of the improvement in Asia was a result of China's economic expansion that lifted 475m people above the $1.25 a day poverty line (United Nations, 2009). The number in extreme poverty in Sub-Saharan Africa increased by 100m in the 1990-2005 period. The global recession is expected to push another 90m into poverty and *Africa will not meet many of the targets for 2015, and, in most countries, health and education goals have been harder to achieve than those for income. Even if all the goals were to be met, as much as half the abject poverty found in 1990 would still remain*' (Department for International Development, 2009).

The role of the private sector in the provision of infrastructure must be kept in perspective. *'Only about a third of developing countries can count on private sector operators for the delivery of electricity, water or railway services'* with about sixty percent of countries having private telecoms providers (Estache and Fay, 2007).

Infrastructure is not directly included in the Millennium Development Goals (MDGs), which focus on reducing poverty and hunger, increasing education and gender equality, reducing mortality and disease and improving environmental protection.

The ideology under-pinning the World Bank approach to pro-poor PPPs is standard business practice, *'... only if a project benefited the poor disproportionately and or explicitly integrates the concerns and needs of the poor into it'. 'The way in which PPPs are financed, and the manner in which risks are allocated between government and private participants, has an important bearing on the degree to which such initiatives will benefit the poor. If a PPP is adequately capitalised, competitively financed and has made adequate provisions to manage political, market, financial, institutional, and external risks, then it is likely to provide services at a competitive price to all consumers, including the poor'* (Panggabean, 2006). So the claim to be 'pro-poor' is deceptive.

Not surprisingly, the reasons given for why the poor have not always benefited from infrastructure investment were hardly revealing and did not address the fundamental design, finance, operation or management of PPPs. Six main reasons were cited: *'(i) when tariffs were redesigned to be more efficient, they sometimes became less progressive or more regressive (or both) than before the reform (such as when countries eliminated cross subsidies); (ii) major increases in indirect tax rates – which tend to be more regressive – were applied to reformed infrastructure sectors to allow the state to capture part of the rent generated by efficiency gains; (iii) operators increased enforcement of revenue collections; (iv) Increases in quality made services unaffordable for some users; (v) cream-skimming in the design of restructuring eliminated cross-regional subsidies and thus slowed investment programs in the poorest regions when governments could not compensate through increased subsidies; and, (vi) failures to alleviate credit rationing added to the difficulties of financing poor users' expansion needs'* (Estache, 2006).

In some cases the level of infrastructure investment in fiscal stimulus policies is additional investment but, in others, it merely brings forward planned investment and is followed by a period of cuts in capital spending, which would likely exceed the investment brought forward. Since the welfare state infrastructure is likely to face the brunt of cuts, this further reduces progress in reducing inequalities and poverty.

Water privatisation has failed to deliver to the poor, undermined the human right to water, and has taken place at the expense of democratic principles, with minimal accountability to local citizens and led to foreign control and monopoly (Norway Forum for Environment and Development, 2006).

Development bank infrastructure plans

The World Bank Group's (WBG) (World Bank, International Finance Corporation (IFC) and Multilateral Investment Guarantee Agency (MIGA) Sustainable Infrastructure Action Plan for 2008-11 is reliant on 'crowding in' the private sector by expanding PPPs (World Bank, 2008). The WBGs continued commitment to privatisation is highlighted in the annexe on core sector strategies. In water, the '... *WBG will actively pursue effective PPPs in this area, particularly with an emerging set of potential sponsors including central governments, municipals, consortia led by financial institutions, local construction companies and industrial operators from developing countries. IFC has an unprecedented opportunity to take a leadership position in enabling private investment into the global water sector'*; and in transport *'... encourage successful private sector participation in competitive markets for transport and logistics services'* whilst the IFC will *'... build on its successful experiences in advising countries on successful preparation of private transactions for large transport investments in ports and airports'* (ibid). So the Bank has not fundamentally changed its privatisation and liberalisation objectives, only the speed and means by which they will be achieved.

The World Bank Group's infrastructure plan, launched in July 2008, identifies expenditure of between US$59bn – US$72bn with a further US$109bn – US$149bn leveraged in Official Development Assistance. The Plan will focus on transport, energy, water and ICT and cross-sectoral issues, such as, the role of infrastructure in climate change adaption, the role of PPPs in the provision of infrastructure services and support for rural-urban integration. The Action Plan contrasts with the US$41bn programme for 2004-07 period which leveraged US$70bn.

The OECD and World Bank forecasts were made before the global economic crisis and many national infrastructure programmes have changed as a result of fiscal stimulus strategies, which have brought forward, and undoubtedly increased, infrastructure investment programmes. In addition, the OECD forecast excludes the social, public transport, airports and seaports and criminal justice infrastructure.

The Bank's strategy *'... shifted from a focus on transfer of infrastructure assets from the public to the private sector to a flexible range of PPPs'* (ibid). The new Plan *'... recognizes the need for ongoing government support, considering the political sensitivity of certain public services, greater attention to adequate risk assessments, establishing a market environment to attract private sector participation, operating environment conducive to the full range of private sector competition and participation, and increasing awareness of the limits to achieving cost reflective tariffs, with more explicit use of government subsidies for financing services to the poor'* (ibid).

The Plan is heavily dependent on government creating policies and institutional arrangements to encourage private sector participation and competition; *'... establishing sound legal and regulatory frameworks that provide clarity and predictability to private investors and consumers'* (ibid); improving public sector capacity to develop new approaches for PPPs and to more explicit use of government subsidies for financing services for the poor (this puts all responsibility for providing cost effectives services to the poor onto the government); and to strengthening the public sector so that it '... *understands the commitments entered in the partnerships with the private sector*' (presumably to minimise termination of contracts).

The plan to leverage between US$109bn – US$149bn through PPPs, managing risks for public finance, mobilising aid and partnership resources is almost certainly not now achievable. For example, the International Finance Corporation's plan to leverage investment through financial intermediaries '... *by enabling infrastructure fund vehicles to access international capital markets and thereby mobilize long-term debt and equity for underlying infrastructure investments*' (ibid) will be more costly, with more lengthy negotiations and due diligence.

The International Finance Corporation's key role in privatisation
Addressing constraints to private sector growth in infrastructure, health and education is one of five priorities of the International Finance Corporation (IFC), part of the World Bank Group. It is the largest source of private sector finance of the development institutions and looks for 'ways to unlock new markets and extend the pipeline of bankable projects' in frontier markets. '*Public-private partnerships will continue to afford new opportunities in all infrastructure sectors – especially in IDA (International Development Association) countries – where traditional concession or privatization approaches cannot be relied on*' (International Finance Corporation, 2008).

The IFC's Road Map 2009-11 states that infrastructure business provides additionality through the development of innovative projects and public-private partnerships in difficult markets and sub-sectors, providing risk mitigation, and leveraging specialized financial structuring, policy, environmental, and social capabilities. IFC's InfraVentures is a US$100m fund to '... *play a key role in the early development of private and public-private partnership infrastructure projects in the power, transport, and utilities sectors of IDA countries. IFC is engaging early with private infrastructure companies, working with project developers, and helping governments introduce private participation and structure partnerships*' (International Finance Corporation, 2009).

The IFC and MIGA want to improve the creditworthiness of public support to PPPs by providing supplemental subsidies and minimum revenue guarantees to increase investor confidence, increase competition and reduce the cost of debt and equity. They will partner emerging investors, and leverage investment through financial intermediaries and partial risk guarantees.

Resurgence of development banks

There has been a resurgence in the role of multilateral banks and export credit agencies following the liquidity problems of banks and the withdrawal or reduction in project funding of banks such as Royal Bank of Scotland (RBS), Dexia and Depfra. The economic crisis has led to the effective freezing of new lending and the reduced liquidity of banks meaning that they are less able to syndicate loans and provide long-term funding. The downgrading of the credit rating of monoline insurers (who guaranteed the repayments to bond holders in return for a fee, thus reducing project costs) led to their virtual disappearance in 2008/09. The crisis in some key infrastructure funds, Macquarie and Babcock & Brown in particular, contributed to the difficulties in arranging deals and the higher cost of project finance (Moody's Global Infrastructure, 2009).

The IFC launched an Infrastructure Crisis Facility with US$300m funding to bridge the PPP funding gap in developing countries. It estimated in December 2008 that US$110bn of new projects could be delayed or postponed and about US$70bn of existing projects faced financing or refinancing risk (International Finance Corporation, 2008). The IFC reported that investors were demanding higher returns, hedge funds were rapidly scaling back investment, private equity funds were hoarding capital, Asian and Middle Eastern sovereign wealth funds were likely to focus investment in the regions and poorer developing countries were being crowded out as private investors focused on the larger emerging markets (ibid).

The higher cost of financing and the effect on demand and users' ability to pay were the prime reasons for the slowdown in PPP projects in developing countries (Public Private Infrastructure Advisory Facility, 2009). Although project closures were just 15% lower in the August-December 2008 period than the previous year, projects worth US$81bn, primarily in transport and energy sectors, were delayed or at risk of being delayed. Reduced economic activity and demand, for example reduced traffic flows (highways, airports, ports) and, therefore, lower toll income and lower energy usage, was imposing financial pressures on contracts. Banks were opting for club deals where debt was shared, instead of the traditional lead-arranger model. These deals required more complex negotiations, longer procurement times and higher transaction costs.

Multilateral and national development banks also increased funding of PPP projects. The Brazilian Development Bank (BNDES) secured US$42.6bn additional government funding in January 2009 to increase financing of private energy, transport and telecoms infrastructure projects. In Europe the European Investment Bank (EIB) and European Bank for Reconstruction and Development (EBRD) played an important role by increasing their liquidity and maintaining infrastructure investment. EIB loans of £182m and £200m respectively for the Greater Manchester Waste and M25 motorway widening projects, helped to close the PPPs at a crucial stage in 2009.

Multilateral development banks are driving the PPP agenda. The EIB had funded over 120 PPP projects by late 2008 with €25bn finance, including PPPs and aid in the transition economies of Eastern Europe. Transport accounts for about 80% of projects, the remainder being in health, education, energy, water and wastewater treatment. The UK accounts for a third of EIB PPP projects with Spain, Portugal and Greece each accounting for 15%. The EIB reports that France, Germany, Italy, Poland and Turkey '... *have ambitious programmes to increase the proportion of public investment financed by PPP*' (European Investment Bank, 2008). EIB and the European Commission set up the European PPP Expertise Centre (EPEC) in 2008 to enable EU public authorities to '... *become more effective participants in PPP transactions*' by providing expertise and sharing experience and knowledge (ibid).

The EBRD financed 11 water, waste water, urban transport, district heating and solid waste PPP projects between 1993-2006 providing €658m of the total €1,385m cost and 12 transport projects – motorways, railway stations, ports and airports – with €564m finance of total project cost of €2,578m (EBRD, 2007). EIB capital investment increased to €60 – 65bn per annum from 2009 (compared to €40bn plus in 2008) to help boost the European economy – adding to existing funding of fossil fuel projects, support for roads and airports and large PPPs in Central and Eastern Europe.

PPPs as instruments of foreign policy

Privatisation, deregulation and marketisation are frequently part of bilateral and multilateral trade agreements under the guise of 'public sector reform'. In addition, finance and technical support for PPP projects such as dams, highways, and pipelines are common in foreign policy formulation.

Some 1,500 multilateral and bilateral free trade and investment agreements in the last twelve years included *'... the right for private foreign investors to bypass domestic courts to sue governments in international tribunals, a ban on capital controls which imposing restrict the flow of capital, a ban on local economic development conditions such as local content and technology transfer, restrictions on 'indirect' expropriation such as claiming damages where regulations reduce the value of foreign investment, treat domestic and foreign investors alike (national treatment and most favoured nation treatment) but policies and regulations which have a disproportionate impact on foreign investors could be targeted as violations'* (Institute for Policy Studies, 2007).

For example, in parallel to the EU draft Migrant Return Directive, the European Union was trying to convince the Andean Community (Bolivia, Colombia, Ecuador and Peru) to sign an 'Association Agreement' which includes a Free Trade Agreement as its third pillar.

'We are under intense pressure from the European Commission to accept profoundly liberalized conditions for trade, financial services, intellectual property or our public services. Furthermore, under the heading of legal protection, we are being pressured over our process of nationalization of water, gas and telecommunications, as realized on International Workers Day. I ask, in this case, where is the "legal security" for our women, adolescents, children and workers who seek better horizons in Europe?' (Evo Morales, President of Bolivia, June 2008).

In addition to United Nation agencies, business-led public private partnerships, such as UNDP's (United Nations Development Programme) Growing Sustainable Business, the US, UK and Germany and other countries have development aid programmes and trust funds, which promote and finance PPPs. These initiatives perpetrate belief in the superiority of private investment and provision (Altenberg, 2005). They also facilitate company access to 'emerging markets'. The United Nations Economic and Social Commission for Asia and the Pacific (UNESCAP) lamented that *'The poor are often excluded from PPPs because of institutional constrains that prevent the development of an attractive market for private investors that involves the poor'* (United Nations Economic and Social Commission for Asia and the Pacific, 2004).

Aid-supported infrastructure has reinforced privatisation and PPPs in developing countries, for example, by the transfer of public management 'reform' policies from developed to developing countries. The UK's Selling into Wider Markets policy and the remit of PartnershipsUK ensured that privatisation and PPPs have been heavily promoted overseas. This has provided a conduit to open up foreign business opportunities, particularly for consultants, lawyers and advisers.

The World Bank and the IMF have consistently used conditionality in structural adjustment and Poverty Reduction Support Credits to enforce privatisation and liberalisation in developing countries, as a requirement for financial aid. In response to criticism, the Bank introduced new Good Practice Principles in 2005 – ownership, harmonisation, customisation, criticality and transparency and predictability – in the use of conditions. Studies have shown that there are fewer privatisation and liberalisation conditions imposed than in the past, however, a review of 40 Poverty Reduction and Growth Facility projects revealed that privatisation is a condition in over half (Bull et al, 2006). A European Network on Debt & Development (EURODAD) study, using the World Bank database, found that although the Bank was reducing the number of conditions, over seventy percent of loans and grants from the Bank's International Development Association (IDA) have sensitive policy reform conditions, the majority of which were privatisation related (European Network on Debt & Development, 2008).

Furthermore, the Bank was using conditions such as *'public sector governance reform'*, *'encourage the participation of non-state establishments in the delivery of public services'*, *'public procurement reform'* and *'international best practice'* to continue the privatisation and liberalisation agenda (ibid). The appointment of the 'appropriate' consultants and advisers is another way of driving this agenda.

Shock treatment
Neoliberalism promotes a ruthless approach in war, disaster and economic crisis scenarios. World Bank and IMF aid has almost universally required deep revenue and capital public spending cuts and privatisation of utilities and transportation as an integral part of 'shock doctrine' tactics. Infrastructure investment is frequently delayed or postponed with maintenance programmes cut, leading to further longer-term deterioration.

Infrastructure privatisation has been a key policy in the restructuring and shock therapy for developing countries. The enforced sale of public infrastructure assets is often accompanied by radical change in service provision. For example, Hurricane Katrina was used by the Bush Administration and right wing organisations to takeover the New Orleans public school system and imposed charter and private schools (Center for Community Change, 2006). Peck describes the 'management' of the disaster by conservative and free-market think tanks as '... *a programme of contracted-out urban structural adjustment, designed in Washington and New York*' (Peck, 2006). PPPs are also a feature of the Iraq and Afghanistan War Reconstruction programmes.

CHAPTER 4

Infrastructure –
the new global wealth machine

Why has public infrastructure become a new target for private investment? This chapter explains the growth of a 'new asset class', how PPP projects are funded and the financial engineering utilised by many financial institutions.

Private infrastructure investment accelerated from 2000 with the formation of new European and global infrastructure investment trusts, private equity investment companies extending into infrastructure investment and increased flow of pension funds into infrastructure. Some investment funds target toll roads or airports, others are geographically focused in Europe, Africa or North America. Some fund new projects (primary funds), others fund secondary market investments (operational projects) or both.

A new asset class

Private infrastructure investment is often referred to as 'alternative investment', which includes private equity, hedge funds, real estate and speculation in physical commodities, currencies, interest rates and natural resources. Infrastructure is referred to as a 'new asset class', which refers to it becoming a profitable source of private investment with a range of competing investment funds providing good returns relative to other types of investment.

PPPs involve international, if not global, financing, international construction companies, transnational management consultancies and legal firms. They originate in different ways depending on national legislative frameworks but the common element is the 'big business' or international scope of the main participants.

The rationale for private sector investment in the design, build, finance and operation of public infrastructure is summarised as low risk, long-term inflation-protected earnings, and high demand often with monopoly position. One Australian bank regards public infrastructure as '... *an attractive investment opportunity. Payments by the public sector are agreed up-front and mainly based on availability payment streams where the payment is linked to the physical availability of the asset (e.g. school or hospital) rather than the level of demand or usage of the asset. This results in predictable returns and low volatility for public infrastructure*

investors' (Babcock & Brown, 2008). Public infrastructure attracts private investment because it is claimed to have:
● A long asset life with fixed-term contracts or concessions usually 25–40 years (or 50 – 99 years in the case of US asset monetisation).
● Large investment scale but with low operating costs.
● Inflation-linked relatively stable cash flows that are predictable (often linked to inflation via a regulated return framework or a contracted rate of return) from users who regard the service as a necessity and often have no alternative service.
● Government-backed with legally binding contracts.
● Limited regulatory regimes confined to certain performance objectives but allow the private sector maximum flexibility on financial policies, ownership, control of profits and the management of assets.
● Many infrastructure facilities are natural monopolies or have high barriers of entry that restrict other providers from entering the market, for example, roads and power stations are difficult to duplicate due to their scale and cost.
● Availability of surplus or development land or access rights which may be under-valued and therefore provide scope for additional commercial development and profit.

The PPP industry believes that public infrastructure has additional attributes such as the ability to transfer project related risks, including construction and operational risks to subcontractors, majority ownership of most assets ensures *'... a high degree of control over asset operations'*, *'... opportunities to enhance income through active management, e.g. client variations, third party income, refinancing, and portfolio synergies'* and *'... solid growth potential of the asset class as government entities procure more assets through PPP/PFI type procurement and/or sell interests in public infrastructure assets'* (Babcock & Brown, 2008).

Infrastructure investment usually generates predictable, stable and sustainable cash flows over an extended period and is, thus, attractive to pension funds which have long-term liabilities and to other financial institutions wishing to spread risk. It also has high earnings potential because most infrastructure assets require high, up-front, capital but with relatively low levels of continuing operating costs. *'This allows infrastructure to produce relatively high earnings before interest, tax and depreciation'* (AMP Capital, 2007). However, infrastructure is not risk-free. High levels of borrowing make projects vulnerable to movement in real interest rates (exceeding increases in inflation), changes in regulatory regimes and/or public policy, fluctuation in currency exchange rates and external shock from terrorist attacks affecting performance and viability.

A study of US electricity, natural gas, water and sewage companies, toll roads, airports and seaports found that cash flows of infrastructure assets grow faster than the Consumer Price Index, the volatility of infrastructure cash flows is materially lower than those of equities and real estate, and that '... *diversification opportunities exist within the infrastructure asset class itself*' (JPMorgan, 2008).

Macquarie Infrastructure Company succinctly describes their justification for infrastructure investment: '*The prices charged for the use of infrastructure assets that are our focus can also generally be expected to keep pace with inflation due to the pricing power generally enjoyed by "user pays" assets, the contractual terms of contracted assets, and for regulated assets the regulatory process that determines revenues and typically provides for an inflation adjustment.*

Infrastructure assets, especially newly constructed assets, tend to be long-lived, require predictable and manageable maintenance capital expenditure and are generally not subject to major technological change or rapid physical deterioration. This generally means that significant cash flow is often available from infrastructure businesses to service debt, make distributions to shareholders and retain and expand the business.

The sustainable and growing long-term cash flows of infrastructure assets mean that infrastructure assets can typically support more debt than other businesses, which can increase returns to shareholders. This indicates the importance of financial structuring and capital optimization in enhancing shareholder returns to owners of infrastructure assets'. (www.macquarie.com/mic/aboutus/intro_infrastructure.htm)

This is further evidence of the cynical wealth creation machine and level of financial engineering used to gain control of, and extract, profit from public infrastructure assets.

The Standard & Poor Global Infrastructure Index is based on 75 infrastructure companies from around the world. This index has balanced weights across three distinct infrastructure clusters – utilities (40%), transportation (40%) and energy (20%). Returns before the credit crunch and economic recession averaged 12.7% over a ten-year period and exceeded that of hedge funds, public equity and fixed income. Other analyses of infrastructure investment returns ranged from 14.1% per annum (based on 19 unlisted Australian funds) and 13.5% per annum for a portfolio of diversified Australian funds (Deutsche Bank Group, 2007).

Table 5: *Illustrative investment returns**

Asset	Risk	Average cash yield (years 1 – 5)**	Average leveraged IRR***	Capital appreciation potential
Toll roads (operating)	Low	4-9%	8-12%	Limited
Private Finance Initiative	Low-Medium	6-12%	9-11%	Extremely Limited
Regulated assets	Low-Medium	6-10%	10-15%	Limited
Rail	Medium	8-12%	14-18%	Yes
Airports/seaports	Medium	5-10%	15-18%	Yes
Toll roads (development)	Medium-High	3-5%	12-20%	Yes
Communications networks	Medium-High	8-10%	15-20%	Yes
Power generation	High	4-12%	12-25%	Yes

Notes: *The returns are estimates calculated from market information available to JPMorgan in 2007. ** Cash contribution to equity holders as a percentage of equity investment. *** Assumes debt of 50% to 85% and investment periods of not less than five to seven years.
Source: JPMorgan presentation, Chartered Institute for Public Finance and Accountancy Scotland Asset Management Workshop: Investing in Infrastructure, March 2007.

The main global infrastructure indices operated by Standard & Poor's and Macquarie Bank illustrate the rapid growth of infrastructure profits between 2001 – 2007 followed by a steep decline as the financial and economic crisis deepened – see Figure 4.

Financial analysts are predicting that investors will, in future, favour 'real assets' such as infrastructure and property as opposed to financially engineered products. Similarly, '... *there will be a re-emphasis on active funds management to deliver out-performance, instead of a reliance on general market momentum driven by capital flows*' (Colonial First State, 2008). The trend towards tangible, inflation-hedging assets and simpler, more transparent products, is expected to make infrastructure fund investment more attractive. So, far from curtailing the global infrastructure market, the financial crisis is likely to spur its expansion in the longer term.

The change in the risks is summed up:

'As an infrastructure business matures and its income flow becomes reliable,

Figure 4: **Infrastructure companies: growth and decline**

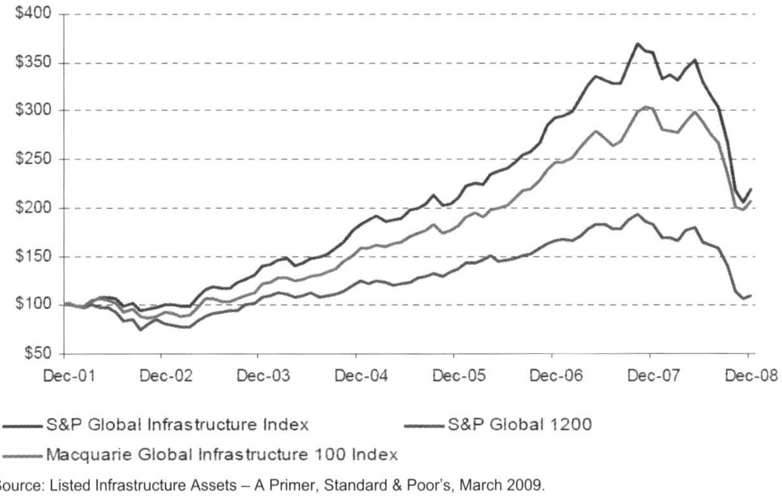

- S&P Global Infrastructure Index
- S&P Global 1200
- Macquarie Global Infrastructure 100 Index

Source: Listed Infrastructure Assets – A Primer, Standard & Poor's, March 2009.

Source: Standard & Poor's, SSGA, FTSE. Cluster Weights are as of 12/31/2008.

the perceived risks of the business decrease. The resulting decrease in the equity risk premium can increase the implied equity value of the business. With original debt levels remaining unchanged and the enterprise value increasing, the gearing ratio falls. Once the major operational risks have been managed, this offers the opportunity for re-gearing the business and may allow for the return of some capital to shareholders' (Deutsche Bank Group, 2005).

Most developed countries have a large backlog or infrastructure deficit in the maintenance and improvement of transport, social and other parts of the public infrastructure. Global population growth and the creation of mega-cities, is creating additional demand for public infrastructure to meet basic social needs such as housing and social facilities, improving information and communications technology, transportation and the provision of utilities. So the demand for public infrastructure is growing.

Private infrastructure ownership unfortunately opens opportunities to new multi-billion markets in the provision of core public services such as health and education. The development of project finance and derivatives of the PPP model creates a new tertiary market in PPP financial and legal advice, refinancing and equity sales, insurance, project management and facilities management. Many countries allow foreign ownership of public infrastructure following financial deregulations and the growth of global financial markets.

The Hypo Real Estate Holding AG (Germany) €5.7bn takeover of DEPFA Bank plc in 2007 combined international commercial real estate financing with public sector and infrastructure project finance. *'The current public sector budgetary situation, the continued rise of Public Private Partnership initiatives and the global demand for inflation-linked structured finance investments will create significant opportunities for a specialist in the Public Sector, Infrastructure and Commercial Real Estate Finance.'* (Recommended Offer document, www.depfa.com/press/1840.html).

According to a mature, maturing and emerging categorisation of infrastructure markets, Australia and the UK are 'mature' with other major developed countries in the 'maturing' category – see Figure 5.

Figure 5: *Variations in infrastructure 'market' maturity*

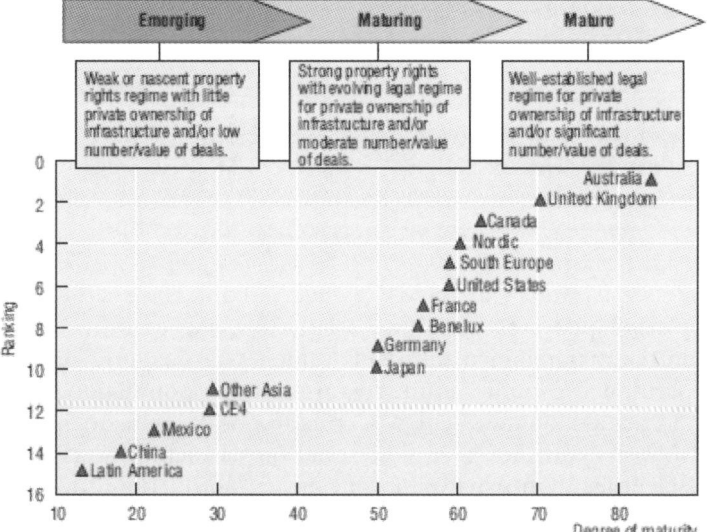

Note: This figure developed by RREEF infrastructure ranks countries by maturity based on country risk (including legal and regulatory risk along with political, economical and financial risk) to gether with the value of completed deals in the last 24 monts as a percentage of GDP (reflecting a country's experience with private involvement in infrastructure projects). CEA are Poland, Hungary, the Czech Republic and the Slovak Republic.
Source: Löwik and Hobbs (2006) of RREEF Infrastructure, using data and analysis from IMF (April 2006), Thomson Financial (11 April 2006), Euromoney (March 2006).

China, Latin America, South Asia and Central and Eastern Europe are in the 'emerging' category.

Hypo described the economic advantages and opportunities as being able to '... *offer larger and more complex financing on a global scale*' and '... *to take advantage of previously unavailable growth opportunities with extremely attractive margins, particularly with regard to financing real estate for the public sector and infrastructure financing*' (ibid).

Governments promote private finance for infrastructure
Development banks and nation states promote, organise, facilitate and finance PPPs. They also legislate to provide financial, legal and procurement frameworks for contracts, long-term public spending commitments, accepted demand risk and absorbed high transaction costs. Governments have also contrived Public Sector Comparators, limited audits by National Audit Offices and commissioned consultants reports that purport to 'prove' value-for-money.

Many governments have provided revenue or exchange rate guarantees to the private sector. Spain, Chile, Columbia, South Africa, Malaysia and Republic of Korea have given toll road guarantees and Chile and Columbia revenue guarantee for airports. These guarantees proved very costly in Spain and Chile. Korea, Chile and Malaysia provided exchange rate guarantees in contrast to Argentina where privatised utility prices were set in US dollars, thus forcing service users to bear unacceptable exchange-rate risk (Irwin, 2007).

Most governments have provided political and financial support for central and departmental PPP units, which offer technical advice to project teams. They have also facilitated industry-based PPP organisations to promote private investment in infrastructure. Both the UK and Germany encouraged PPPs in their respective overseas aid programmes, claiming that pro-poor PPPs will reduce poverty. Government infrastructure funds such as Infrastructure Australia and Build Canada also promote PPPs.

The UK's New Labour government developed new PPP models such as BSF and NHS LIFT, which created large, national, long-term, funding programmes and broadened the scope of the private sector in infrastructure and service delivery. This has run parallel with the marketisation and privatisation of local government services, for example, Developing the Local Government Services Market reports commissioned from consultants (Department of Communities and Local Government, 2006-07).

PPPs are frequently described as 'additional' or 'new' investment and the lack of clarity is exploited by the pro-PPP lobby. In Ireland, the Dail Eireann Committee of Public Accounts puts the record straight by describing PPP as '... *a means of substituting public sector investment (and hence debt) for private sector investment (and hence debt) in a manner that is still directed by central government*' (Dail Eireann, 2007). The private debt is paid off by monthly payments from public sector revenue accounts.

Types of infrastructure funds

There are basically four ways in which the private sector invests in privatisation and PPPs, and in energy, water, telecom and healthcare companies. Financial institutions manage funds which pool money from individual and corporate investors to buy shares, bonds and securities in companies and projects. The investment fund or portfolio manager charges an annual fee and individual investors share the collective gains or losses.

Listed infrastructure funds, or publicly traded infrastructure companies, have a portfolio of existing infrastructure facilities such as toll roads, airports and energy companies, usually spread across different countries. Investors can readily buy and sell shares in these companies but they are subject to stock market volatility, for example, Babcock & Brown shares plummeted 90% in less than a year in 2008.

Unlisted infrastructure funds invest directly in a range of infrastructure projects and are usually only open to institutional investors. Some funds are open-ended, whilst others require investment for a given period, resulting in less flexibility or liquidity due to the long-term nature of projects. The average size of unlisted funds increased significantly from $159 million in 2003 to $3.3 billion in 2008 (Private Equity Intelligence, 2008). These funds usually have complex organisational, debt and equity structures. Morgan Stanley closed a new US$4bn Infrastructure Partners fund in May 2008 having raised capital from pension funds, insurance companies and wealthy individuals in North America, Europe, the Middle East, Asia and Australia. '*Infrastructure is now an important component of any asset allocation strategy; it offers portfolio diversification and the ability to invest in 'real' assets, with uncorrelated investment returns relative to other asset classes*' stated James Gorman, Co-President of Morgan Stanley (Press Release, 12 May 2008).

Direct infrastructure investment enables pension funds, banks and financial companies to acquire infrastructure assets outright or as a member of syndicate, for example the acquisition of Associated British Ports by Singapore's Sovereign Wealth Fund, Goldman Sachs, Prudential and Ontario Municipal pension fund. Ontario Teachers Pension Plan and Morgan Stanley Infrastructure jointly acquired SAESA Group, one of Chile's largest electric generation, transmission and distribution companies in a US$870m deal in 2008.

Indirect infrastructure company investment involves buying shares in publicly traded construction and Facilities Management (FM) companies engaged in PPPs or in privatised energy and water companies.

The 'Macquarie Model' is a way of '... *financing the purchase and development of public infrastructure, often through public private partnerships (PPPs) with a leveraged structure of debt and equity, where the infrastructure asset is used as a basis on which a public investment fund can be launched on the Australian Stock Exchange (ASX) to attract investment. The asset is sold to the fund upon its launch and the fund is managed by Macquarie Bank, which collects management and performance fees from the new satellite fund. The range of transactions in this process, all performed in-house by the Bank for a fee to the fund'* (Jefferis and Stilwell, 2006).

Infrastructure funds are usually launched or 'opened' to corporate and individual investors to commit an amount of money to the fund which will be 'closed' once the target investment level has been achieved.

How privatisation and PPPs are financed

Financing privatisation
Public assets are sold via a public share sale or a trade sale to a new or existing company (Whitfield, 1992). Companies in trade or negotiated sales will usually borrow from banks and other financial companies issue additional shares to finance the deal.

The UK's privatised assets are being acquired by infrastructure funds and private equity groups. Many privatised assets sold via share flotation in the 1980s and 1990s, particularly in the utility and water sector, were subsequently acquired by European and US energy companies. Some of these assets are now being acquired by infrastructure investment trusts/banks, with assets transferring from the utility sector to ownership by financial institutions. For example, Thames Water was acquired by Macquarie for £8bn in 2006 from German utility company RWE and Anglian Water by Osprey Acquisitions, a consortium of financial investors comprising Canadian pension fund Canada Pension Plan Investment Board, Commonwealth Bank of Australia investment arm Colonial First State, UK private equity house 3i and Australian pension fund manager Industry Funds Management in a £2.2bn deal in 2007.

Between 1998 and 2006 emerging market investors and operators funded 44% of the total investment in PPP projects that achieved financial closure (von Klaudy et al, 2008). The remainder was financed by investors and companies in developed countries. There were differences between sectors with local investment accounting for 58% in transport projects,, 40% in water and 34% in energy which '... *remains dominated by large utility firms from developed countries, while the emerging market players that have emerged tend to secure contracts for relatively small power systems*' (Ibid).

Financing PPPs
A new company (Special Purpose Vehicle – SPV) is set up for each project by the lead contractor. The capital structure of the company will be a mix of debt (borrowing) and equity (shares) divided between members of the project consortia, usually the construction company, the lead bank and the facilities management contractor. In the past this has usually been on a 90/10 ratio but moved to a 75/25 ratio during the credit crunch.

The bulk of the finance for the project comes by borrowing from banks and financial companies via commercial loans, bonds or subordinated loans. Commercial loans, usually securitised by the projects assets and dependent on the financial strength of the borrower, are classified as 'senior debt' and have priority access to assets in the event of default.

Bonds are long-term interest-bearing debt instruments, purchased by institutional investors (investment funds, insurance companies, pension funds) either through public capital markets or through private placement. Until recently, credit risk insurance was available for asset-backed bonds, mainly in the US and the UK. Monoline insurance companies with triple A rating, in effect, wrap their own credit rating around a bond and guarantee payment of interest and principal for a fee. These bonds provide a higher rate of return. Monoline wrapped bonds were only available for projects with robust and predictable cash flows and subjected to due diligence by the insurers. In January 2008, Fitch Ratings downgraded Ambac, one of the three leading monoline insurers, sending shock waves through the market. The rating agencies had repeatedly revised their loss assumptions and capital requirements and Ambac was unable to raise about US$1bn additional capital (Euromoney, 1 February 2008).

In the latter part of 2008 the monoline wrapped bond market in the UK was effectively closed to new transactions, increasing reliance on the banking market. *The combination of capital adequacy requirements, reduced liquidity and higher funding costs has increased the strain on the project finance banking model*' stated Andy Ross, PartnershipUK's Executive Director, in November 2008.

Subordinated loans have priority over equity holders in the event of default, but are secondary to commercial loans, hence have a higher level of risk and a higher rate of return.

The public sector will not begin paying the unitary charge until the building or facility is completed and operational. The land is usually retained in public ownership.

Risk mitigation instruments have a key role in the financing of PPPs in developing countries. They transfer some risks to a third party, frequently multilateral or bilateral development agencies, that the private sector is unable or unwilling to take. Risks covered include credit guarantees and export credit guarantees or insurance to cover losses in the event of a debt default, changes in regulations and political risk insurance to cover losses incurred as a result of devaluation, foreign exchange or transfer problems, nationalisation, war and civil disturbance or breach of contract.

Developing countries are therefore able to '... *mobilize private capital to supplement limited public resources; (b) enable private lenders and investors to participate when risks beyond their control or perceived excessive are transferred; (c) enable governments to share the risks of public projects with private sector financiers; upgrade governments' credit and in turn lower financing costs; (e) allow official agencies to leverage their financial resources; and (f) facilitate the development of commercial and sustainable financing mechanisms for infrastructure development*' (Matsukawa and Habeck, 2007).

Strategic partnerships (SSPs) are primarily service contracts with a relatively small level of construction, so there is usually little or no borrowing. Monthly contractual payments to the contractor from public sector revenue accounts begin when the project commences. The private sector may frontload some investment, which they will finance and this will be reflected in the monthly payments.

PPPs create new markets in project finance and arrangement fees, insurance and securitisation. New markets have also emerged in the provision of technical and legal advice, contracts and the due diligence process. A PPP information and conference industry has mushroomed. A secondary market in refinancing of debt and sale of equity in PPP projects is presented as 'recycling investment' but is essentially about extracting market value/profit created by public expenditure via PPPs (see chapter 5)

Company/consortia mechanism in PPPs ensures private equity has increasing value as the project reaches completion and operational stage begins. This is part of the commodification and financialisation of infrastructure. It is also a means by which private capital captures the developmental gains from public investment – in other words the private sector puts up the money to finance the building, charges a higher price for building the infrastructure asset, captures the developmental gains, and then the public sector pays for the cost of building and renting the building for 25 – 35 years or longer.

PPPs are part of the financialisation process (Leyshon and Thrift, 2007). The process of securitisation in the last two decades has driven the search for new asset streams (mortgages, car loans, credit card debt, rents from student halls of residence) which, suitably bundled, can be turned into predictable income streams through speculation.

'Whereas the assets produced through securitization were once backed by projected future incomes and revenues from large corporations and governments, now financial companies are chasing new, more closely de?ned asset classes, and especially classes like 'infrastructure': highways, streets, roads and bridges; mass transit; airports and airways; water supply and water resources; wastewater management; solid-waste treatment and disposal; electrical power generation and transmission; telecommunications; and hazardous waste management – and the combined systems that these elements comprise. This particular asset class is now perceived as much more exciting and valuable than was once thought to be the case, not least because it yields predictable and secure income streams over long time periods and because the supply of most infrastructure tends to depend upon a quasi-monopolistic relationship with its customers. Yet, complicating this new gold rush is the fact that, even after the waves of privatization of the 1980s and 1990s, large amounts of infrastructure still have a close relationship with the state, whether that is in the form of contracts or regulation' (ibid).

There are spatial consequences of financialisation, for example, where investment takes place, which type of projects are prioritised according to their attractiveness to global investors, and on whose terms, has a big impact on local economies. More distant non-accountable control means that operational assets can be sweated more easily.

It ultimately means, '... *long-range investments in public goods become subordinated to international financial imperatives*' (Leyshon and Thrift, 2007). The spoils of speculation are shared out via major financial cities or in offshore tax havens such as the Cayman Islands, or Jersey.

Financialisation inevitably leads to changes in economic and social relations as a result of the values and management ethos, which determine how assets are managed and operated, the attitude to accountability and disclosure, employment policies and social justice.

PPPs provide an opportunity for serial speculation and exploitation. Profit is extracted at three stages. Firstly, in the provision of design, finance, construction, operation and consultancy/advice for PPP projects. Secondly, in refinancing the project when it is operational to take advantage of lower interest rates. Thirdly, from the sale of equity in the Special Purpose Vehicle to another infrastructure investor who will manage and operate the facility and have the opportunity to 'sweat the assets' to recoup its investment and increase profits.

Concessions and asset monetisation – the economics of long-term leases
A new form of privatisation has emerged in the US – the long-term leasing of existing public infrastructure assets to PPPs. This is a new paradigm to extract value from existing assets through user fees and monetising future growth to provide a lump sum payment to revenue starved states and cities.

'Asset monetization is the raising of capital today by increasing rates in the future and then pledging those revenues to the people providing the capital' (NW Financial Group, 2006). The state is in fact selling the private sector the right to obtain increasing toll charges/user payments for up to 99 years in return for a lump sum today.

In other words, tolls or user fees are increased to a level over and above the amount needed to pay off the public debt incurred in building the road and maintaining it for public use. The additional money collected pays for the transaction costs of negotiating the deal, operating the facility, collecting tolls, profit for the new owner/manager. In return, governments receive a lump sum, which they can use to reduce debt, invest in new infrastructure or improve the maintenance of existing roads and facilities. The private sector accepts some risks but takes on facilities with little or no competition,

Figure 6: *The growth wedge*

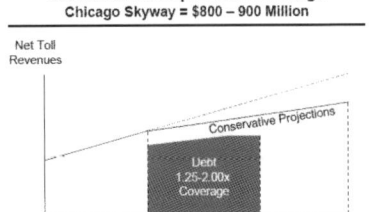 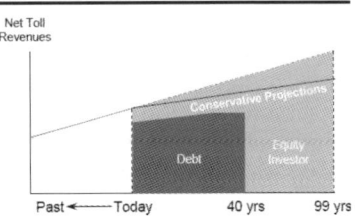

Source: Ma and Pineiro, 2006.

negotiates a contract, which usually prohibits expansion/improvement of similar facilities within its proximity and obtains a potential cash cow.

Growth wedge
The public sector generally uses the capital and operating cost of a facility and historical revenues obtained from tolls and user charges to set future charges in the context of public policy. It takes a medium term perspective. The private sector on the other hand continually seeks to maximise growth to maximise profits. The value of the facility is its market value, which is determined by the potential level of return, which can be extracted from a long-term agreement, which guarantees annual price hikes. Their interest in the wider planning and development of communities, economic growth and employment increases use of 'their' facility to ensure that it does not impact negatively.

For example, the Chicago Skyway and Indiana Toll Road have the same toll escalation regime, which allow toll increases at the highest of three factors, 2% per annum, increase in the Consumer Price Index or increase in nominal Gross Domestic Product per capita. These constant toll increases coupled with traffic forecasts provide revenue, profit and risk scenarios, coupled with operational and maintenance costs, determine the bid price.

The growth wedge in Figure 6 illustrates the additional long-term growth in toll or fee income that can be obtained from an asset.

The finance of asset monetisation projects is similar to a PPP with a percentage of equity from the partners in the consortia with bank loans to finance the bulk of the deal. Asset monetisation has certain key characteristics and contract clauses. They usually have non-compete clauses, which prohibit or constrain improvements, which can be made to improve or amend feeder and local roads in order to maximise traffic and tolls on motorways. They often require the city government to impose restrictions on neighbouring roads to prevent users diverting to other parts of the network to avoid tolls. For example, in the Indiana Toll Road agreement the state '... *agreed not to build any road twenty miles in length and within ten miles of the new toll road for fifty-five years. The agreement also stipulated that US-20, which runs east to west through the state, is not a competing highway, but will be considered one if the state expands or improves it, and it comes within ten miles of the toll road. Therefore, if Indiana needs to do repairs or adjust the road because of congestion problems, they would be in breach of the contract*' (Farber, 2008).

California's State Route 91 non-compete clause '... *prevented the increase of highway capacity within a one and a half mile area along the side of the toll road, but the state wanted to add merging lanes between the free lanes and the toll lanes to improve traffic safety. The non-compete clause allowed this, but the toll road company disputed the state's safety analysis. In the end, the state was forced to buy the road back for $207.5 million*' (ibid)

Operators favour projects where there is a mixture of local and regional/national users to avoid reliance on a high level of local usage and hence avoid local political power to effect change. But there are consequences and public interest conflicts arising from the impact of a market-based system of tolled motorways on a parallel system of publicly owned regional and local roads.

Deal flow

The World Bank's Public Private Infrastructure Advisory Facility (PPIAF) reports that '... *bond markets are inactive, the syndication market has collapsed, and the cost of financing is unpredecentedly high*' (World Bank, 2008). It reported that the rate of PPP projects being developed, tendered and signed was 40% lower in 2008 than the August-November period a year ago. The Bank also predicted a 'flight to quality' by banks and other financial companies '... *the likely impact will be more stringent financial conditions, not only via higher cost of financing but also with lower debt/equity ratios and more conservative structures. The expected economic downturn in developed and developing countries is also likely to reduce demand levels and have a significant impact on project revenues, and consequently on projects' financial viability*' (ibid).

However, the same organisation issues a reminder that '... *the PPP model remains robust and an attractive asset class for banks due to the Government backed cash flows*' (ibid). There are changes in the financing of PPPs '... *there is a strong trend away from the traditional lead arranger model where one bank does the deal, underwrites the whole debt and then syndicates part of the debt to other banks to reduce their project risk. Many banks are refusing to accept syndicated debt at the moment due to a lack of confidence in each other and, where transactions can be done, there is a trend towards 'club' deals. Club deals are where groups of banks club together to do the deal and spread the debt between them (typically £25 million to £50 million each)'* (Local Partnerships, 2008).

Many government and public sector bodies are likely to relaunch PPPs as soon as financial and economic conditions improve, anticipating that a recovery will be firmly established by the time facilities are completed and the payment mechanism becomes operative.

Financial engineering

This takes a number of forms, such as securitisation, refinancing, insurance and organisational structures which facilitate the extraction of management fees.

It became standard practice for financial institutions to seek to spread the risk of investments. In effect they transfer the risks associated with the loans/investments to other financial institutions. This can be done in two ways. 'Asset backed securitisation' which involves placing the assets in a special purpose company *'in order to capture incremental benefits derived from the lower probability of loss associated with a mixed pool of loan assets rather than an individual loan.'* 'Synthetic securitisation' entails transferring the credit risk on the loans but retaining the assets.

The prominent role of securitisation, the packaging and repackaging of debts/loans to other financial bodies is a derivative of the pass the parcel game except that when the music stops all the participants are affected, not just the one holding the parcel. Banks used to hold loans on their balance sheet until they were repaid, with only some loans being sold on. Then US mortgage companies and Wall Street started issuing bonds '... *with payments tied to the cash flows from large pools of loans.'* This practice has mushroomed in the last decade and '... *global private-debt securities are now far bigger than stock markets'* (McKinsey, 2007).

Banks are keen to securitise mortgages and loans because they are moved off-balance sheet, which improves the return on income and equity and they obtain fees in the process. However, although banks sell many loans, they usually retain the most risky tranche, often referred to as 'toxic loans'. The new instruments or derivatives can then be traded providing new avenues of accumulation for capital. Hedging is the purchase of insurance against default in the credit derivatives market. Derivatives are financial engineering with development of new financial instruments. Instruments are derived from underlying cash assets that can be bought, sold and traded in a similar way to shares or any other financial instrument. The pricing and performance of derivatives such as futures, options and swaps is largely based on the underlying asset. In practice, derivatives often drive the underlying market and the volume traded in certain futures and options contracts can outstrip the underlying cash market. Derivatives can be traded on an investment exchange, or directly by telephone or computer in an over-the-counter (OTC) market. The revolution in information and communications technology has led to the simultaneous growth and complexity of the derivative market and the globalisation of financial markets.

For example, in 1999 Newcastle United became the first football club to securitise the revenue stream from future ticket sales and corporate hospitality to finance the reconstruction of St James Park stadium with a £40m loan via a 17-year fixed interest bond repayable in annual instalments. Property rents generally can also be securitised by packaging and swapping the rental income stream for a lump sum, which can then be used for improvements. The root of securitisation is the transfer and under-pricing of risk.

'*One fundamental reality of credit derivatives is that they do not eliminate credit risk. They merely shift it around. As a result, when the credit cycle turns and default rates rise, someone, somewhere, will lose money*' (Gibson, 2007). Furthermore, there is the risk that a counterparty to a credit derivative contract will default, the risk of flaws in the complex models used for valuation and hedging of credit derivatives, the risk that rating agency assessments are not sensitive to the different types of risks, and the risk that defaults are not settled within the fixed time period.

In addition, new risks emerge. Asset price inflation, non-economic motives of state investors, credit risk from private equity and systemic risk from hedge funds arise from changes in investment flows (McKinsey, 2007). '*The enormous size, high leverage and increasingly illiquid investments of hedge funds raise their potential to create contagion across unrelated asset classes, or trigger the failure of some of the large investment banks that lend to them*' (ibid).

DEPFA Bank created a precedent in 2004 when it purchased credit protection from the German KfW Bankengruppe for 24 PFI loans totalling £355.7m for schools, hospitals, roads, police stations, court buildings and other facilities. Three-quarters of the loans were accommodation projects and considered at the lower end of the risk spectrum. KfW in turn purchased credit protection from a number of banks and institutional investors. The credit protection cost £32.05m via a special purpose company, Essential Public Infrastructure Capital plc. The PFI loans remain on DEPFA's balance sheet.

As a result of this transaction DEPFA has reduced the amount of regulatory capital required to support the loans, thereby materially improving the return on equity of its infrastructure financing activities. The transaction will reduce the risk-weighted assets of the Group by ca. EUR 500 million. This transaction will therefore enable DEPFA to increase its already substantial involvement in the public infrastructure market on a competitive footing. The know-how gained from this initial transaction will also smooth the way for DEPFA to channel more infrastructure assets into the secondary markets in the future. Additionally, institutional investors and banks now have an additional way of gaining exposure to the UK infrastructure market and it is likely that other major PFI lenders will follow DEPFA's lead in due course.' (www.depfa.com/press/732.html)

In the UK, *'The Treasury has accepted that since such securitisations are external to the PFI contracts and at a lender's corporate level, they are not to be included in the gain sharing arrangements'* (National Audit Office, 2006).

Securitisation did not isolate banks, because of the wide use of bank-owned structured investment companies to hold derivatives for which they were ultimately still responsible, but rather the increased opaqueness made matters worse. Most structured instruments are rarely traded and their valuations are based on complex theoretical models rather than market prices. Valuations were over-optimistic and the complexity concealed the real level of risk. The Bank of International Settlements described the worrying situation:

'Assuming that the big banks have managed to distribute more widely the risks inherent in the loans they have made, who now holds these risks, and can they manage them adequately? The honest answer is that we do not know. Much of the risk is embodied in various forms of asset-backed securities of growing complexity and opacity. They have been purchased by a wide range of small banks, pension funds, insurance companies, hedge funds, other funds and even individuals, who have been encouraged to invest by the generally high ratings given to these instruments. Unfortunately, the ratings reflect only expected credit losses, and not the unusually high probability of tail events that could have large effects on market values' (Bank for International

Settlements, 2007).

This state of affairs breeds complexity, uncertainty, confusion, fragments responsibility and lowers credit standards. The packaging of loans into securities severs the relationship between lenders and borrowers, which makes renegotiating loans less likely and foreclosure more likely and may accentuate market swings as holders of structured instruments sell assets during periods of market turmoil.

Asian central banks, hedge funds, private equity and petrodollar investors '... *are collectively pushing outward the risk-return frontier. They are also beginning to cross into each other's investment territory. Hedge funds are buying up companies, while private equity firms are branching out to other types of investment funds. Asian central banks are starting to replicate the sovereign wealth funds of oil exporters, while oil exporters are creating more sophisticated investment vehicles, such as private equity funds*' (ibid).

The global credit crisis serves to highlight the systemic aversion to risk. The argument that PPPs transfer risk to the private sector must be explored in this context. The level of risk transferred is frequently greatly exaggerated because some risks cannot be transferred, they remain with government whatever happens.

The financial assets of private equity funds, hedge funds and Sovereign Wealth Funds have soared. So too have pension funds and insurance company investment, fuelled by the personalisation of pensions. The rapid growth of private equity funds fuelled a surge in buy-outs and delisting of companies. Private short-term ownership led to changes in corporate governance of companies with the single objective of restructuring and managing assets to extract profit and quick disposal.

Financial markets also depend on state intervention when the inevitable crisis occurs. The role of central banks, for example the Federal Reserve Bank in the US was to lower interest rates and arrange the 'cannibalisation' of Bear Stearns by JP Morgan and the Bank of England's bail out of Northern Rock bank and many others besides (Lapavitsas, 2008, Elliott and Atkinson, 2008).

The legitimation of greed and the search for higher and higher profits, which fuels speculation and large-scale fraud, collusion and theft (Enron, World Com) are just higher profile examples.

How the funds operate

Investment funds and financial companies frequently create a spider's web of subsidiary companies in different countries taking advantage of different tax, disclosure and regulatory frameworks. Assets, investment funds, fees, charges and staff can be traded between these companies with different degrees of transparency. The system allows financially complex company arrangements and trading of assets between funds.

An analysis of Macquarie Capital funds by New York financial analysts, RiskMetrics, reveals many of the complex arrangements (RiskMetrics, 2008a).

Multiple company structure: A separate company is usually established for each infrastructure fund, resulting in the larger banks having a labyrinth of principle and secondary subsidiary companies. In some cases, companies are set up in overseas tax havens or where company law provides fewer regulatory controls. Australian company law permits the 'stapling' of a listed investment trust with a management company. Investors receive a unit of the trust and a share in the company, which cannot be traded separately. Some Macquarie and Babcock & Brown funds are structured with trusts registered in Australia and the 'stapled' management company registered in Bermuda. In some cases there is a third company holding the assets which leases the assets to the management company (Davis, 2008 and RiskMetrics, 2008b).

Securitisation: An investment fund may securitise part of its future toll road income by selling entitlement to future cash flows to another investment fund or bank in return for immediate cash.

Internal and external fees and charges: It is common practice for parent banks to charge fees to their subsidiaries for management of assets, financial services, performance fees, advisory, underwriting, debt management and other bank fees. The percentage fees applied may range from 0.5% to 10% or more and run into millions because of the large sums involved. For example, the fee income for Babcock & Brown Infrastructure was A$86.4m and A$157.5m for Macquarie Infrastructure group in 2006 (RiskMetrics, 2008). Babcock & Brown charged Babcock & Brown Power A$106m in fees in 2008, which exceeded the fund's current market value (Financial Times, 4 Sept 2008). It comprised a management fee of A$22.4m plus A$83.4m for advice and services for deals concluded during the year. A Credit Suisse analysis revealed that some of the fees were 'excessive' and related to transactions that later had to be unwound to reduce debt in the financial crisis (Business Spectator, 4 Sept 2008).

Management contracts require payment of significant fees, irrespective of the investment funds cash flow. In '... *nine out of 15* funds (Australia) for which data was available, the manager's fees were a double-digit percentage of operating cash flow; and were above 20 per cent in six of those nine funds. In another fund, cash flow was negative' (RiskMetrics, 2008a).

Many of the fees are not contestable, because infrastructure funds are locked into fee arrangements set by parent companies, and may be front-loaded for newly established funds. Some investment banks appoint a subsidiary to provide advice under an 'Asset Advisory Agreement' which is an additional lock-in of fee income.

Revaluing assets: Unlisted infrastructure funds will usually revalue assets annually relating to a market valuation based on current and future cash flow projections. 'The gains from revaluation can be material. In 2005, MIG's revenue from revaluing unlisted securities in companies and trusts was $786 million, representing 57 per cent of total revenue for the year. In 2006, revaluation revenue for unlisted holdings was $425 million, representing 40 per cent of total revenue' (RiskMetrics, 2008a).

Complex agreements, pre-emptive rights and protocols: Protective agreements often lie undisclosed behind listed funds in order to change the manager of assets, and hence cutting the source of fees. These include pre-emptive rights (in cases where assets are co-owned), debt covenants (which trigger mandatory repayment of debt), fee structure and management agreements (which include costly winding up or performance fees to the departing management company) and priority protocols (giving rights to the purchase of assets to other subsidiaries which acts as a impediment to other bidders) (RiskMetrics, 2008b).

Refinancing: Funds will refinance project debt in order to lower costs and increase profits (see Chapter 7).

Acquisition and sale of assets: Once a fund has built up a portfolio of assets, it may sell some assets to raise cash to finance the repayment of debt due on other assets. For example, Macquarie Infrastructure Group originally acquired an interest in 28 toll roads in eight countries but by early 2009 this had reduced to nine in six countries.

Accounting practices: The whole system is reliant on having accounting systems which only measure money, accommodating accountants and accounting standards that audit individual companies and take a selective view of wider corporate impacts and ignore wider economic, community and environmental impacts.

Tax havens: A growing number of PPP projects and privatisation assets are controlled by companies in offshore tax havens, which

Table 6: PPP assets located in tax havens

Company	Tax haven	No of PPP assets	Type of projects
HSBC Infrastructure	Jersey	27	Substantial stakes in hospitals, schools, police stations, Home Office Headquarters, London, and Dutch High Speed Rail
3i Infrastructure	Jersey	Part ownership 123 projects	9% stake in Anglian Water ownedby a private consortium, Osprey; 31% of Infrastructure Investors secondary fund of 120 projects, 26% of Norfolk & Norwich University Hospital, 50% of Alpha schools, Scotland.
Babcock & Brown Public Partnerships	Guernsey	50	59% in UK, 18% in Australia. 100% interest in Tower Hamlets, Northants, Derbyshire and Calderdale schools, 4 health centres in London, 2 children centres Wolverhampton, 3 police stations, Dublin courts, 75% Alberta schools, Canada;
Mapeley	Bermuda	1	Mapeley is owned by Fortress Investment Group, USA, Soros Real Estate, Netherlands and Delancy East Ltd, UK. £3.6bn PPP project – 700 buildings of the Inland Revenue, HM Customs and Excise, and the Valuation Office Agency in Strategic Transfer of the Estate to the Private Sector (STEPS) project.
Associated British Ports	Jersey	1	Owned by GIC, Singapore's Sovereign Wealth Fund (33.3%), Borealis (infrastructure manager of Ontario Municipal Employees Retirement System 33.3%), Goldman Sachs (23.3%) and Prudential (10%)
Excelcare Holdings PLC	Jersey	3	Owns and operates care homes in Essex, Milton Keynes, Cambridge and health centres, South Derbyshire LIFT

Company	Tax haven	No of PPP assets	Type of projects
Roadbridge Ltd, Ireland	Jersey	3	20% stake in €660m Limerick tunnel and ring road, 20% in €295m Fermoy bypass, Cork and €434m Cashel toll road.
West African Gas Pipeline, Nigeria-Ghana and Tenke Fungurume copper/cobalt mine, Democratic Republic of Congo	Bermuda	2	WAPCo sponsor and Tenke Holding/Lundin Holding, receive EIB funding of €75m and €100m respectively.
Mopani Copper Project, Zambia	British Virgin Islands	1	Majority owned by Carlisa Investments Corporation, €48m EIB funding.
Bujagali Hydrelectric Dam project, Uganda	Cayman Islands	1	Part owned by Blackstone SGP Capital Partners, €136m EIB funding
Macquarie Group	Bermuda	n/a	Various Macquarie infrastructure funds use offshore tax havens.

Source: HSBC plc, 3i Infrastructure, Babcock Brown Public Partnerships websites, accessed May 2009, European Services Strategy Unit, 2008.

provides the companies with tax-free or low tax for the length of the contract. Table 6 provides evidence of nearly 200, primarily British, PPP projects either fully or partially owned by companies located in tax havens. Tax havens such as Jersey, Guernsey, Bermuda and the Cayman Islands have no or very low corporate taxation, no taxes on profits, dividends, capital gains and no sales or value-added taxes (HM Treasury, 2009).

CHAPTER 5

Growth of the global infrastructure investment market

The recession has merely tempered the surge of investment money, from sovereign wealth funds, pension funds, private equity and hedge funds into infrastructure funds and financing of PPPs and privatisation. This chapter maps the key financial institutions in the rapidly expending infrastructure investment market and charts the power and influence of key corporate interests.

The global infrastructure stock, both publicly and privately owned, is estimated to be US$20.5 trillion. North America has 32%, Asia Pacific 29%, Western Europe 27% with South America, Central and Eastern Europe and the Middle East and Africa each having 4%. The global market in listed infrastructure securities on the public market was estimated to be valued at US$155.3bn at the end of 2007 with Europe accounting for 61.5%, Americas 20.3% and AsiaPacific 18.2% (Deutsche Bank Group, 2008).

Private sector infrastructure investment continued to grow in 2008 with European and UK deals rising to $91bn compared to $77bn in 2007. However, the debt/equity ratio has changed markedly from the 90/10 ratio in 2006 to 74/26 in 2008 (Financial Times, 2008). *As reduced leverage causes returns for private investors to fall, governments should look for ways to sweeten the terms of deals struck with private companies*

Table 7: *Global Listed infrastructure market (2008)*

UBS Region	Shares (US$bn)	% of total
Europe	95.5	61.5
Europe (ex UK)	90.6	58.4
North America	31.6	20.3
USA	30.6	19.7
Asia Pacific	28.2	18.2
Australia	22.9	14.8
Asia Pacific (ex Japan and Australia)	5.3	3.4
UK	4.9	3.1
Global	**155.3**	**100.0**

Source: UBS (Switzerland), in Infrastructure Goes Global, RREEF Research, Deutsche Bank, October 2008.

to build hospitals or operate toll roads – or prepare to do more of the digging themselves' (ibid).

Some US$260 billion was invested globally, mainly Europe, Australia and Canada, by the private sector in PPPs between January 1994 and September 2005 (PricewaterhouseCoopers, 2005). Projects in Europe in this period were valued at one billion Euros, with the United Kingdom accounting for two thirds of deals, and Spain and Portugal accounting for 9% – 10% each.

Infrastructure finance is only a small part of the activities of financial centres such as London, New York and Paris. Financial services accounted for 7.6% of GDP in the UK in 2007, 54.4% concentrated in London and the South East, and employing just over a million people (June 2008). Financial and business services generated £36.9bn and £17.9bn trade surpluses in 2007, helping to offset the large deficits in goods and services (International Financial Services London, 2009).

Take the UK's railway system, privatised in 1996, as an example. It was split into three parts – rail infrastructure (track, signalling and stations), 25 train operating companies and three rolling stock companies (ROSCOs). The corporate history of the three rolling stock companies illustrates the growing global infrastructure market. The short-term nature of operating franchises meant that train operators would not purchase their own rolling stock but lease it through one of the ROSCOs. Since each ROSCO provides a specific type of rolling stock '... *train operators had virtually no choice in selecting which ROSCO would supply it. The net effect was the ROSCOs were very secure businesses and faced very little threat to their revenue streams*' (McCartney and Stittle, 2008).

Angel Trains Contracts Ltd was sold to GRS Holding Company (Nomura, Babcock & Brown and others) for £696m. A year later Angel was sold to the Royal Bank of Scotland for £1,085m, a 56% gain. In June 2008, RBS sold the company to an Australian consortium of Babcock & Brown European Infrastructure Fund, Babcock & Brown Public Partnerships, AMP Capital Investors, Statewide Superannuation Pty Ltd (South Australia's largest private sector fund) and the Public Sector Pension Investment Board (Canada) for £3.6bn, including debt.

Porterbrook Leasing Ltd was sold to a management buyout for £528m but within months was acquired by Stagecoach for £826m, a 56% increase on the sale price. Porterbrook was sold by Stagecoach to

Abbey National in 2000, which was itself taken over by the Spanish bank Banco Santander in 2004. A consortium led by BNP Paribas (Antin Infrastructure Fund), Deutsche Bank and Lloyds TSB acquired Porterbrook for £1.4bn in autumn 2008.

Eversholt Leasing Ltd was sold to a management buyout for £518m and a year later was sold to HSBC Holdings for £726m, a 40% increase.

In just over a decade, the rolling stock companies are now owned by financial institutions, ownership has been internationalised and the value of the assets soared 200%. In the meantime, Railtrack went bust and many maintenance contracts had to be returned to in-house provision by its successor, Network Rail, and some operating franchises have been terminated. A privatisation that beggars belief!

Surge of investment money

The amount of money available for investment has surged in the last decade, having four main sources. Firstly, from oil production and other commodities leading to the formation of new investment companies i.e. sovereign wealth funds. Secondly, from the switch of manufacturing to China, India and Asia resulting in the accumulation of foreign reserves. Thirdly, as a result of reduction of pension provision by the private sector, the realisation that future state provision alone will be inadequate, coupled with the ageing of the population, has led to the growth of private pension funds. Finally, it has come through the growth of the world economy and increasing corporate and personal wealth.

Goldman Sachs (USA) first infrastructure fund, Goldman Sachs Infrastructure Partners, closed in early 2007, with $6.5 billion in committed capital. Goldman Sachs (GS) has also financed or advised a number of major PPP projects such as the €10.3 billion acquisition financing of Autostrade, the £2 billion refinancing of Tube Lines, the £1.4 billion refinancing of the Skynet 5 PFI project for the UK Ministry of Defence and the €14.8 billion sell-off of the French motorway companies.

There has been a rapid growth of infrastructure funds with over 25 new unlisted funds set up between 2004-06 with an average fund of US$700m. Infrastructure fundraising rapidly increased from US$2.4bn in 2004 to US$34.3bn in 2007 and even as the financial crisis accelerated in 2008, a further US$24.7bn was raised that year. New funds were launched in 2009 such as the UBS Alternative Funds

Advisory (AFA) Global Infrastructure Multi-Manager Fund (initial target US$200m to invest in 'mature' PPP projects and utilities) (Prequin, 2009).

However, the number of PPP projects funded fell 43% to US$40.4bn in the first quarter of 2009 compared to the same period in 2008. This affected all regions except Latin America where two large hydroelectric projects distorted the overall decline, which was most severe in Eastern Europe with a 95% decline (Project Finance, 2009).

Globally some 87% of 341 public and private infrastructure rated transactions in power, industrial, transportation, public and social infrastructure and PFI/PPP projects were considered not to have any exposure to credit or interest rate risks in November 2007 (Fitch Ratings, 2007). Sixty-one deals were exposed to base interest rate risk (mainly oil and gas projects, water utilities and toll roads). Some transactions had a refinance risk but over half were after 2011 and comprised mainly of the corporate debt structures of UK water distribution companies and transportation projects (ibid). They concluded '... *inherent strengths allow many infrastructure projects to weather the usage and revenue effects of economic cycles, as well as the*

Table 8: *Capital available in the top 10 infrastructure funds*

Firm	Location	Total Funds Raised US$m	Available Capital US$m
Macquarie Funds Group	Australia	17,218	6,119
Global Infrastructure Partners	US	5,640	4,337
Morgan Stanley Infrastructure	US	4,000	3,186
Alinda Capital Partners	US	6,000	2,918
F2i – Fondi Italiani per le infrastrutture	Italy	2,822	2,615
Babcock & Brown – Infrastructure	Australia	5,082	2,303
American International Group – Infrastructure Investments	US	5,231	2,173
Goldman Sachs Infrastructure Investment Group	US	6,500	2,153
Innisfree	UK	3,514	1,813
Tenaska Capital Management	US	3,238	1,656

Source: Prequin.com – accessed 9 March 2009.

financial market uncertainties of debt refinancing' (Fitch Ratings, 2008).
  'The proliferation of infrastructure funds, the powerful appetite of commercial banks to lend (especially in Asia) in recent years and growth in global pension savings suggest that the financial table for infrastructure investment has been set. On the other hand, the menu so far has been skewed, since the funds seemed busy chasing (and sometimes overpricing) a small universe of established utilities, airports and publicly transferred toll roads, and in pumping extraordinary amounts of equity into companies that develop or finance infrastructure projects. These easy avenues for infrastructure investment seem heavily exploited, and with the exception of equity investments in the companies that build and finance projects, they have added very little so far to the funding of new infrastructure' (ibid).

The same pressures are likely to encourage more refinancing and PPP equity sales once projects are operational. Lower interest rates and more construction company/financial institution partnerships will facilitate the continued growth of PPPs. In addition, economic conditions are likely to lead to pressures/reductions in public spending with the likelihood that governments increase their reliance on the PPP model in order to maintain current levels of investment and to meet commitments. Forecasts of fee income from tolls and charges are likely to be more conservative, at least in the early years of concession, due to reduced levels of economic activity.

Money machines – the major investors

Global fund management is dominated by pension fund, mutual fund and insurance company investment, which account for 82% of the total assets (see Table 9). The investment activities of private equity and hedge funds receive a degree of attention exceeding their asset value of 2% and 1% of global assets. However, hedge and private equity short-term high-risk investment strategies and the fear of state-backed sovereign wealth funds have an influence in money markets well beyond the relative value of their assets.

New power brokers – Sovereign Wealth Funds
State-owned investment funds are powerful investors in the global economy and have a key role in the acquisition of infrastructure assets. Surging oil and commodity prices created huge windfalls, particularly for oil producing nations, and created new power brokers in the global economy. This is '... *a paradigmatic change from a world in which private investors from wealthy industrialised countries used to invest*

Table 9: Value of assets under global fund management

Rank	Type of Fund	Assets US$ billion	%
1	Pension Funds	25,000	32
2	Investment/Mutual & Managed Funds	22,000	28
3	Insurance Companies	17,000	22
4	Foreign Exchange Reserves	7,400	9
5	Sovereign Wealth Funds	3,900	5
6	Hedge Funds	1,700	2
7	Private Equity Funds	700	1
8	Real Estate Investment Trusts	700	1
	Total	**78,400**	**100.0**

Source: International Financial Services London 2009, Sovereign Wealth Fund Institute, 2009.

around the globe to one in which emerging market governments become major shareholders in Western companies' (Deutsche Research, 2007). These funds are also investing in public and private debt securities, equity, private equity and real estate leading to ownership or major stakes in manufacturing and financial companies and the public infrastructure. The implications of the realignment of financial and political power and the almost total lack of transparency for multilateral surveillance are discussed in Chapter 6.

There are different types of state-owned investment funds. Firstly, central banks hold foreign currency and gold reserves to help stabilise its currency from excessive volatility. These reserves must be invested in highly liquid and marketable securities, usually government bonds.

Secondly, commodity Sovereign Wealth Funds (SWFs) are predominately funded by oil and mineral exports that are owned or taxed by governments. Non-commodity SWFs are funded by the transfers from official foreign exchange reserves, pension reserves and privatisation revenue. These funds have long-term objectives to accumulate national wealth to protect against the extinction of natural resources such as oil and the erosion of reserves by changes in the international industrial competitiveness. Sovereign Wealth Funds are *'... state-owned investment funds composed of financial assets such as stocks, bonds, real estate, or other financial instruments funded by foreign exchange assets. SWFs can be structured as a fund or as a reserve investment corporation. Some funds also invest indirectly in domestic state owned* enterprises. *In addition, they tend to prefer returns over liquidity, thus they have a higher risk tolerance than traditional foreign exchange reserves.*' (Sovereign Wealth Fund Institute, 2008).

Thirdly, state-owned sovereign investment vehicles, such as a Reserve Investment Corporation, Pension Reserve Fund, Development Fund or state owned companies, are used to channel investment of reserves.

Finally, the same countries have many very wealthy individuals and private companies who also invest in foreign assets. Wealthy private investors in the Gulf States are estimated to hold about US$600bn foreign assets in 2006 with the top ten individuals/families having US$124.6bn worth of foreign assets (McKinsey, 2008).

Sovereign wealth funds are not new. One of the oldest, the Kuwait Investment Office, founded in the 1950s, was the centre of the debacle in the sale of a 31.6% share stake in BP (Whitfield, 1992). But the rapid growth, an estimated £500bn annually, of these funds, in deregulated financial markets, is new. SWF forecast to be '*... sources of 'high octane' cross-border flows that are very large in size and relatively proactive in nature; these SWFs are likely to lead, rather than follow, private investors*' (Jen, 2008).

Since 2001, the US has been the world's largest net *consumer* of foreign capital because it has invested and consumed more than it has produced. The net capital inflow was US$597bn between 2001-2006 compared to the UK's US$34bn. China, Germany, Japan, and Saudi Arabia were the largest net *providers* of capital.

Total assets under management could reach US$12 trillion by 2015 and could surpass the world's official reserves by 2011 (Morgan Stanley, 2007). Sovereign Wealth Funds are reported to take controlling stakes in companies in about half of their investments, despite the general impression of being a passive investor (Wall Street Journal, 6 June 2008). Some sovereign wealth funds have suffered big losses in the recession, for example, Temasek Holdings suffered a US$39.9bn loss in the eight months between March and November 2008 due to the fall in share prices in Singapore controlled companies such as Singapore Telecommunications and its stakeholding in Bank of America (Wall Street Journal, 2009).

Other such funds include the Australian Future Fund with US$58.5bn assets and Ireland's National Pension Reserve Fund (US$30.8bn). A proposal to get the latter to finance Dublin's five failed housing PPPs did not gain momentum but within months, the fund had underwritten the bailout of three Irish banks to the tune of €9bn! The government then agreed a €90bn bank bailout, establishing the National Asset Management Agency to takeover land and development loans from banks.

Sovereign Wealth Funds already have significant infrastructure assets and bailed out several banks in the subprime credit crisis. Citigroup, UBS and Barclays were among several banks and financial companies bailed out by US$60.5bn from SWFs between March 2007 and October 2008. Singapore's Temasek Holdings owns or has major stakes in infrastructure assets in energy, telecom and transportation. China State Investment Corporation also acquired a 10% stake in the Blackstone private equity group with a US$3bn investment in May 2007. SWFs have between US$120bn – US$150bn investment in private equity firms – about 10% of global capital available to the sector (Private Equity Intelligence, 2008). Many private equity firms

Table 10: *Ten largest Sovereign Wealth Funds in 2008*

Country	Fund	Assets US$bn	Inception	Origin
UAE – Abu Dhabi	Abu Dhabi Investment Authority	875	1976	Oil
Saudi Arabia	SAMA Foreign Holdings	433	n/a	Oil
Singapore	Government of Singapore Investment Corporation	330	1981	Non-Commodity
China	SAFE Investment Company	312		Non Commodity
Norway	Government Pension Fund – Global	301	1990	Oil
Kuwait	Kuwait Investment Authority	265	1953	Oil
Russia	National Welfare Fund*	225	2008	Oil
China	China Investment Corporation	200	2007	Non-Commodity
China – Hong Kong	Hong Kong Monetary Authority Investment Portfolio	173	1998	Non-Commodity
Singapore	Temasek Holdings (Singapore)	134	1974	Non-Commodity

Source: SWF Institute website, October 2008. *This includes the oil stabilization fund of Russia.

have substantial infrastructure investments, for example, in 2007 alone, the Carlyle Group acquired Kinder Morgan (owns and operates 26,000 miles of oil pipelines in the US), ARINC (aerospace and military communications networks with a US$15bn Federal contract) and Manor Care (37,000 nursing home beds) (Service Employees International Union, 2008).

Many developed countries have investment in infrastructure in developing countries, for example, the UK's Commonwealth Development Corporation is a government owned fund with net assets of £2.7bn invested primarily in Africa and South Asia. Infrastructure accounts for 18% of investment, which include Compania Boliviana de Energia Electrica, supplies one third of Boliva's power supply and a US$100m investment in Suntech Power Holdings, a solar energy company in Wuxi, China (Commonwealth Development Corporation, 2008).

The acquisition of US port operations by the Dubai Ports World (DPW), a United Arab Emirates government company, in 2006, caused a wave of protest that foreign ownership threatened national security. The fact that DPW was acquiring the assets from another foreign company, P&O Steam Navigation, was ignored. The acquisition led to scrutiny of the Committee on Foreign Investment in the United States (CFIUS) and the National Security Foreign Investment Reform and Strengthened Transparency Act of 2006. CFIUS reviews between 40-65 transactions out of over 1,000 annual foreign acquisitions. The Exon-Florio Amendment in the Omnibus Trade Act of 1988 gives the US President wide powers, without Congress approval, to block a proposed private sector acquisition.

The post 9/11 national security concerns and '... *the reliance of the United States on capital inflows and the growing capital surpluses of China and countries in the Persian Gulf – not previously major investors in the United States – have combined to create a volatile mix of politics surrounding*' acquisition of US assets, particularly transportation and energy (Council on Foreign Relations, 2006). There is particular concern that many companies from China, Asia and Europe are government owned and controlled! The solution was: '*The United States should continue to press for privatization of state-owned companies on both economic and national security grounds*' (ibid).

Pension investments in public infrastructure
Pension funds began direct investment, or via private equity, in

privatised infrastructure and PPPs in the last decade, having previously acquired shares in utilities and transportation companies or property portfolios. Public sector pension funds have had share stakes in private contractors bidding for local authority and NHS contracts since the Thatcher Government began competitive tendering in 1980 (Whitfield, 1983).

The US accounts for nearly 65% of global pension assets followed by the UK with 11%, Canada 5% and the Netherlands, Australia and Japan each with 3%. Global pension assets reached US$30 trillion in 2007 only to lose 18% of their value (US$5 trillion) in the 2008 financial crisis (International Financial Services London, 2009). Pension funds traditionally primarily invested in shares (40% – 65%) and bonds (20% – 40%) and about 10% invested in property and other assets. These figures vary between countries, funds and financial markets. Australian, US and Canadian pension funds were the first to invest in infrastructure funds in the mid-1990s and later followed by European pension schemes. Globally, pension funds are estimated to have about US$400bn in listed infrastructure shares (OECD, 2009). European pension funds have about 2%-3% of their funds invested in infrastructure funds. Pension funds account for 52% of investors in unlisted infrastructure funds with public pension funds accounting for 31% of the total number of investors, private sector pension funds 11% and superannuation schemes 10% (Prequin, 2008).

The Ontario Municipal Employees Retirement System (OMERS) led the way into pension fund infrastructure investment in 1998 establishing Borealis Infrastructure Management ($5.6 billion infrastructure investments). The US$234bn California Public Employees' Retirement System (CalPERS) launched a new infrastructure investment policy in 2008 allocating US$7.2bn (3%) to infrastructure investment in transportation, energy, natural resources, utilities, water, communications, and other social support services. It aims to achieve an average annual investment return of 5% over the rate of inflation. The CalPERS Responsible Contractor Program secures agreements from investment vehicle manager's guidelines for fair labour practices and to minimize potential adverse impacts to public employee jobs in the development and operation of infrastructure projects.

Other pension funds with defined benefits in infrastructure include Teamsters, Western Conf. ($637m with JP Morgan), Illinois State Board ($225m Alinda and Macquarie) and Washington State Board

($167m Alinda) (Pensions & Investments, 2009). State pension reserve plans such as the Canadian Pension Plan and the Irish National Pension Reserve Fund have begun investing in infrastructure, the latter agreed in 2008 to invest €200m (1% of assets) in domestic public sector infrastructure projects (OECD, 2009).

Examples of UK pension fund infrastructure investment include the West Midlands Pension Fund which has investments in the Barclay's European Infrastructure Fund (£10.0m), Henderson PFI Secondary Fund (£17.5m), ABN AMRO Infrastructure Capital Equity Fund (€20.0m) and Goldman Sachs Infrastructure Fund 1 (US$25.0m). The Universities Superannuation Fund has substantial investments in such as Goldman Sachs International Infrastructure (£162.7m) plus Babcock & Brown Public Partnership, Henderson PFI Secondary Fund, HSBC Infrastructure and several Macquarie funds in addition to infrastructure contractors such as Cintra Concesiones, Veolia Environment and Accenture. See discussion of pension fund investment and local economy in chapter 3.

Other examples include Europe's largest pension fund, Stichting Pensioenfonds ABP for the Dutch public sector, which has invested €3bn in infrastructure since 2004 with a target of 3% of the €173bn fund in 2009. It currently invests in ten infrastructure funds including Macquarie European (Infrastructure Investor, 2009).

Pension funds increasingly appear to know no boundaries other than financial risk and rate of return! For example, Canadian pension funds investing in Chilean and UK assets, Australian investment funds financing PPPs in the UK, UK construction companies in other European countries and vice versa, German and UK construction companies in Canada, and other examples in energy, water, transport and postal services. Global investment funds own or finance local (and in some cases national) infrastructure assets and extract profit to share with other global investors with whom they have shared a degree of risk.

Australian pension funds have allocated a percentage of their total assets for infrastructure investment (see chapter 4). However, funds remain under pressure – the top 100 US corporate pension funds had a US$198.9bn funding deficit in 2008, a 30% decline and reversal of surpluses in previous years (Pensions & Investments, June 2009). Ontario Municipal Employees Retirement System suffered a C$8bn (15.3%) loss in 2008 (Infrastructure Investor, 2009).

The structure of pension funds means that they must seek a return on their investment to meet the needs of their members and to avoid the erosion of the value of funds through inflation. On the other hand, banks and financial markets view pension funds as allies with large accessible assets ready for investment. This is resulting in contradictory and conflicting interests. For example, Canadian public sector pension funds are acquiring privatised public infrastructure assets in the UK, operated from an offshore tax haven.

Banks and investment funds poured money into infrastructure
Macquarie Bank (Australia) is the largest private manager of infrastructure funds with over 60 listed and unlisted infrastructure investment funds, mostly global in scope, although some are country specific. Many are registered in Bermuda. Macquarie's Capital and Funds Management division jointly finances and manages the group's infrastructure assets. The Macquarie model was described in chapter 4. A summary of the main funds, are described in Table 11.

Macquarie's half-year profits plummeted by 43% in 2008, and it was forced to write down the value of its assets by A$684m (Infrastructure Investor, 2008). It made a significant move away from the 'Macquarie model' in July 2009 when Macquarie Airports (major stakes in Sydney, Brussels, Copenhagen) transferred to in-house fund management replacing Macquarie Group management. In return for giving up the lucrative flow of fees, Macquarie Group received A$345m new shares in the Airport fund (Wall Street Journal, 2009). Macquarie's lock-in of investors, described in chapter 4, is beginning to be prised open.

A month earlier Macquarie Leisure Trust Group also transferred to in-house fund management. Macquarie Group has also sold assets such as Macquarie Communications Infrastructure Group in a C$1.64bn deal with Canada Pension Plan, a 19.9% stake in Japan Airport Terminal Company, and suffered a US$1bn loss in the 2009 sale of Macquarie CountryWide Trust 75% stake in a portfolio of 85 US shopping centres to a joint venture between CalPERS and First Washington Reality Inc. Despite the crisis and a 43% drop in its share price in 2008, Macquarie had nearly A$250bn assets under management (Macquarie, 2009).

The financial power of investment banks was demonstrated by Macquarie's acquisition of American Consolidated Media (ACM) in the middle of the bidding for Highway 121 concession and the development of the Trans Texas Corridor (TTC) (see chapter 6). The

Table 11: Infrastructure interests of Macquarie Group

Company	Infrastructure assets
Listed infrastructure vehicles	
Macquarie Infrastructure Group (MIG)	One of the largest developers of toll roads in the world.
Macquarie Airports (MAP)	Specialist airport investment vehicle, A$4.4bn assets.
Macquarie Communications Infrastructure Group (MCG)	Specialist communications infrastructure fund (acquired by Canadian Pension Plan Investment Board in 2009 for A$1.64bn)
Macquarie Power & -Infrastructure Income Fund (MPT)	Invests in North American infrastructure assets with emphasis on power infrastructure.
Macquarie Infrastructure Company (MIC)	Owns, operates and invests in an infrastructure businesses in the US and other developed countries, A$2.8bn assets 2007.
Macquarie Airports Reset Exchange Securities Trust (MAZPA)	A registered management investment scheme issuing hybrid securities.
Macquarie Capital Alliance Group (MCQ)	A broad global investment mandate to invest in any industry sector (except property)
Macquarie International Infrastructure Fund	Formed to own, operate and invest in infrastructure businesses around the world, S$1,641m Asian fund.
Macquarie Media Group (MMG)	Invests in media assets globally.
Macquarie Korea Infrastructure Fund	Provides Korean institutional investors opportunity to invest in local infrastructure assets.
Unlisted infrastructure funds	
Macquarie Airports Group Limited (MAG)	A global private equity fund which has invested in airports and associated infrastructure.
Global Infrastructure Fund (GIF)	A 10-year closed end fund focusing on infrastructure investments in OECD countries.
Global Infrastructure Fund II (GIF II)	A 10-year closed end fund focusing on infrastructure investments outside of Australia
Macquarie Essential Assets Partnership (MEAP)	Canada's first fund focusing on essential infrastructure assets

Unlisted infrastructure funds	Infrastructure assets
African Infrastructure Funds	Two closed end infrastructure funds investing predominantly in South African infrastructure projects.
Macquarie European Infrastructure Fund (MEIF)	A wholesale fund focusing on investments in infrastructure and related assets located in EU, A$313m assets 2008.
Macquarie European Infrastructure Fund II (MEIF II)	Invests in infrastructure businesses located in EU member states plus Norway and Switzerland
ZonesCorp Infrastructure Fund (ZIF)	75/25 equity joint venture with Abu Dhabi Commercial Bank, US$272n industrial and commercial infrastructure.

Source: Macquarie Group, 2008.

ACM deal cost Macquarie US$102m but it nevertheless gained control of about 40 local community newspapers, primarily in small-to-medium towns in Texas and Oklahoma, some of the same papers that have expressed strong opposition to the US$185 billion TTC. The Sydney Morning Herald reported the takeover as just another Macquarie business deal. Macquarie Media managing director Alex Harvey said the acquisition was part of a broader strategy to acquire and grow a portfolio of community newspaper businesses in the US (Sydney Morning Herald, 2007).

Deutsche Bank (Germany): launched a €2bn European Infrastructure Fund in 2006 and its RREEF Infrastructure division has €5.2bn investments in transport, communications, utilities and social infrastructure in Europe and Australia.

Barclays Bank (UK): raised over A$2.6bn (£1bn) for two European infrastructure funds, a student accommodation fund and the Infrastructure Investors fund to invest in operational PPP/PFI projects.

HSBC Infrastructure Company Ltd (HICL): has a £445.7m portfolio of 27 PPP assets including the Home Office headquarters and several NHS hospitals (see chapter 7). Operational profits in 2008 soared 35% to £20.4m but the recession reduced the valuation of its assets leading to an overall loss before tax of £22m.

JPMorgan Infrastructure Investment Group (IIG): this New York-based fund made a number of significant investments since it was founded in 2006, including energy and water companies in the US (Southwest Generation, Southern Missouri Gas, Summit Utilities) and the UK (Zephyr portfolio of wind farms, Electricity North West). The group

Table 12: Who owns schools and hospitals?

	Schools & colleges	Hospitals & health centres	Highways	Transport	Other	Total capital value*
HSBC Infrastructure Co Ltd						
UK	21	6			12	£2.0bn
Rest of Europe				1		£625m
Innisfree Ltd						
UK	280	26				£8.1bn
Canada		1				£150m
John Laing plc						
UK	101	17	5	5	21	£7.6bn
Rest of Europe			6		2	£2.3bn
Canada		3				£440m
Australia				1		n/a

Source: Company websites accessed 3 September 2009. *Equity share varies between 30% – 100% of projects.

led a consortium, which paid the Royal Bank of Scotland £4.2bn for Southern Water in 2007. JPMorgan has a 32% stake, UBS and Access Capital Partners both 18%, and Australia's Challenger Infrastructure Fund a 27% stake. Another Australian fund, Hastings Funds Management, acquired South East Water in a £665m deal in 2006.

Prior to its takeover by Lloyds Bank, HBOS plc had arranged over £8bn of senior debt in over 100 PPP projects and invested in over 60 PPPs with over £200m committed risk capital. This includes 30 education projects and 27 hospitals providing 10,000 hospital beds.

Infracapital Partners, Prudential (UK) was established to make investments in 'cash generative infrastructure assets', including electricity and gas transmission and distribution networks, water and sewerage companies, and transport infrastructure including ports.

Innisfree: Has three primary funds investing in PPP projects in UK (60%), Europe (15%), USA (17%), Canada (6%) and Japan (2%). Investors are mainly pension funds and insurance companies.

The downfall of Babcock & Brown

Babcock & Brown Ltd grew rapidly from a US leasing company into a global infrastructure company between 1977 and 2008 and finally into administration in 2009. It was structured around listed, unlisted and private equity funds. The listed funds on the Australian, London, New York and Singapore stock exchanges included B&B Infrastructure, B&B Power, B&B Public Partnerships and B&B Air, which were valued at A$30bn in June 2008. The unlisted funds owned and managed infrastructure assets in Asia, Europe and North America had a 2008 book value over A$12bn. However, Babcock was heavily in-debted, particularly after it acquired the Alinta energy after a bidding war against Macquarie in 2007, which deteriorated as the credit crisis worsened.

The B&B model had a three-tier structure, similar to Macquarie, with the group holding between 8%-10% stake in subsidiary companies together with long-term management and advisory agreements and debt. This structure provided each fund with an '... *escape hatch in case the mother ship ever went under*' (Podkul, 2009). '*Babcock is free to sell its equity stake as it see fit to repay its senior lenders. The management agreements can be sold back to the satellites (subsidiaries) to raise cash. And the satellites can do their own asset sales to pay back their loans to Babcock*' (ibid).

The collapse of Babcock & Brown Limited '... *is not expected to have any material impact on Babcock & Brown International Pty Ltd (BBIPL) the main operating and asset owning entity of the Babcock & Brown Group. BBIPL will continue to operate and will proceed with the orderly realisation of assets over an approximate 2-3 year time horizon to reduce debt*' (Babcock & Brown, 2009).

B&B Public Partnerships was acquired by a £430m management buy-out in 2009 and renamed International Public Partnerships Limited. This was followed by the sale of Babcock & Brown Infrastructure Fund North America to John Hancock Life Insurance and renamed SteelRiver Infrastructure. Babcock & Brown had earlier sold a controlling interest in seven LIFT projects in the UK for £14m to Ashley House PLC, a primary care infrastructure provider with over thirty primary care centres.

Private Equity Funds
Private equity funds are raised mainly from pension and mutual funds and usually acquire outright ownership of companies using high levels of debt. The buyout funds are locked into the private ownership of companies, which are subjected to new management, financial engineering and asset stripping to increase productivity and profits. Job losses, a lack of transparency and a short-term perspective

are common features of private equity fund investments (Froud and Willismas, 2007). Funds obtain a return on investments through floating the company on the stock exchange, sale or merger, or the restructuring of companies. Currently there are 1,700 private equity funds globally with a target US$900bn fundraising (Prequin, 2009).

Some private equity funds have dedicated infrastructure funds, whilst others organise in business sectors, for example, Apax Partners has £20bn invested in five sectors: technology and telecommunications, retail and consumer, media, healthcare and financial & business services. The healthcare sector includes ownership of Capio hospitals and diagnostic centres in Europe, General Healthcare Group (largest private hospital operator in the UK), and Apollo, one of India's largest hospital chain, plus several laboratory and pharmaceutical companies.

There are often conflicts between the short-term priorities of private equity funds and the long-term development focus of infrastructure operators. For example, private equity funds are likely to maximise their discretion to minimise expenditure on service delivery fulfilment of public service responsibilities; the long-term investment strategy of infrastructure operators conflicts with the short-term pricing and cash generating strategy of private equity funds who are also more likely to minimise resources for research and development and staffing/training, compared with traditional infrastructure operators' long-term development programmes.

The ten largest private equity firms headquartered in the US and the UK, including the Carlyle Group, Goldman Sachs, TPG, Kohlberg Kravis Roberts (KKR) and CVC Capital Partners, raised US$365bn between 1 January 2003 and 15 April 2008 (Private Equity International, 2008).

Despite the credit crunch, a number of new infrastructure funds were set up in 2008 including Morgan Stanley's US$4bn and Global Infrastructure Partner's (General Electric and Credit Suisse) US$5.6bn funds. Henry R. Kravis and George R. Roberts, Co-Founders of Kohlberg Kravis Roberts (KKR) launching their global infrastructure fund said: *'Infrastructure is a multi-trillion dollar global marketplace with enormous need for private investment. KKR recognizes the important role infrastructure investing plays in the growth of both developed and developing economies'* (KKR Press Release, 16 May 2008). KKR already owns Energy Future Holdings and ITC Holdings Corp, major US energy firms, the Hospital Corporation of America, Laureate

Education Inc, Northgate Information Systems, TDC Telecoms and has sponsored and managed 14 private equity funds with US$60bn capital commitments todate.

Other key private equity groups established infrastructure funds in 2007 – Carlyle Group (US$1.2bn), North American fund, CVC Capital Partners (US$2.0bn) and AIG Highstar (US$3.5bn). Goldman Sachs Infrastructure Partners raised US$6.5bn for toll roads, airports and ports, regulated gas, water and electrical utility investment.

Hedge funds
Hedge Funds are private investment funds with restricted membership, which invest in complex and often high-risk investments using futures, swaps and other derivatives and leverage. They are exempt from mutual and investment fund regulation and operate with very limited transparency. Hedge funds suffered volatile performance in 2008 and overall assets shrunk. However, Credit Suisse and Barclays Bank surveys suggest that hedge funds will begin to attract further investment in 2009 whilst Citigroup reported hedge funds were hoarding US$294bn in cash (BNET, 2009). The three main investors in hedge funds are US pension funds (US$306bn), US private banks (US$216bn) and European private banks (US$177bn) (Barclays Capital, 2009).

The Children's Investment Fund (TCI) (sic) is an aggressive and interventionist hedge fund with key infrastructure investments. It attempted to double its 9.9% stake in J-Power, Japan's largest electricity wholesaler, but was thwarted by the Japanese government, which considered TCI's proposal against 'public order' and the national interest. In 2007 TCI sought to get J-Power to increase its dividend but failed. The fear is that higher dividends demanded by TCI could result in underinvestment in infrastructure. J-Power is currently building a nuclear power plant and other Japanese power plants are relying on the supply of plutonium from a reprocessing plant.

TCI also has a 4.2% stake in CSX, the fourth largest US rail operator by revenue. TCI challenged CSX investment strategies and nominated five new directors to the 12-member board. TCI levelled allegation of insider trading against the CSX board in spring 2008 with CSX filing claims that TCI and 3G Capital partners had violated disclosure laws in building stakes in the company. CSX also lobbied Congress that TCI's aggressive tactics threatened future railroad investment.

Global Auction of Public Assets

TCI allocates a percentage of its profits to the Children's Investment Fund Foundation, run by the TCI founder's wife, which funds children's projects in developing countries. TCI operates from London and the Cayman Islands tax haven.

Hedge fund managers also personified the greed machine gorging on super profits in the boom years, for example, five US Hedge Fund managers personally earned between US$3.7bn and US$1.5bn in 2007 alone. It '... *may well prove to be the greatest display of individual wealth creation in any year in the modern history of finance*' (Alpha Magazine, 15 April 2008). The top 25 managers in the list earned an average US$892m in 2007.

Merrill Lynch & Co. had a net loss of US$27.6bn in 2008 but secretly awarded 39,000 employees US$3.6bn bonuses prior to its take over on 1ˢᵗ January 2009 by the Bank of America Corporation. A New York Attorney General investigation revealed that four senior executives shared US$121m bonuses with another 149 executives receiving a total of US$858m and 696 employees each receiving a bonus of over US$1m (New York Attorney General, 2009).

BrisConnections – an Australian PPP saga
Here is a story of a project financing which went horribly wrong for investors and banks. It involved Leighton Holdings, Australia's largest construction contractor with 55% owned by Hochtief (Germany) in which ACS of Spain had a major stake, Macquarie Bank and Deutsche Bank. Queensland awarded the BrisConnections consortia in May 2008 a 45-year A$4.8bn Brisbane airport link toll road, Northern Busway (Windsor to Kedron) and Airport Roundabout Upgrade projects. This is Australia's largest road infrastructure project to date.

The equity-financing element of the deal was to be raised by 390m units @ A$3 each with A$1 paid in July 2008 and two further instalment payments of A$1 in April 2009 and January 2010. BrisConnections promised to pay the unit holders 5.95 cents before the April 2009 instalment but later slashed this to just 0.05cent and postponed until after the second instalment was due. The equity deal was underwritten jointly by Macquarie Bank and Deutsche Bank, which meant the two banks would be liable for any payments not made by the unit holders. The issue was undersubscribed, leaving the two banks holding a large number of shares. Queensland Investment Corporation, the state pension fund (10%) and Capital Group (7%), had significant share stakes. The US-based New Hampton Distressed Asset fund owns 15.2% of BrisConnections via Brisbane Toll Road Link (BTR), and has sought to remove its management, replacing it with Armstrong Corporate Capital Ltd. BTR launched a A$1.3bn class action in late April 2009 on behalf of past and present shareholders. This was thrown out of court because of defects and costs were awarded against BTR.

The shares opened at 65 cents but fell to 41cents on the first day of trading and then to 1 cent by September 2008. About 70% of the shareholders were individuals, many of whom evidently did not realise that shares required two additional A$1 payments. A speculator built up a 19.8% stake in BrisConnection in an attempt to 'green mail' the company to negotiate with him and to extract some value from this shareholding. He forced a shareholders' meeting in April 2009 to vote on a series of resolutions, which could have led to the winding up of the company. However, he secretly sold his voting rights for A$4.5m to a subsidiary of Leighton Holdings, which then voted against the resolutions.

In April 2009 the Victoria Supreme Court granted the Australian Securities and Investments Commission a court order to prevent BrisConnections telephoning shareholders before the special meeting on the grounds of '... *inadequate and deficient*' statements to shareholders. An auction of partly paid units, representing over 70% of its share capital, failed with no sales.

Macquarie wrote-down its BrisConnections holding by A$27m in 2008 but it was also exposed to a A$325m bridging loan via its banking subsidiary, plus A$390 underwriting obligations and it acquired an 8.1% share stake in March 2009 after dumping 60m shares retained at the original flotation. In a further twist, two weeks before the first instalment was due, Macquarie offered investors with less than 50,000 shares to take over their shares and the A$2 per share instalment obligation without payment. The bank made A$110m fees from the share flotation including A$56.1m advisers' fees, underwriting fees of A$42.2m, a A$12.5m sponsor development fee, plus a ten-year commission as BrisConnections exclusive financial adviser (The Age, 2009).

BrisConnections half-year financial report revealed that its decision to hedge interest rates using interest rates swap derivatives had caused a A$476m black hole (The Age, 2009). By August 2009, Macquarie and Deutsche Bank had been compelled to fund the

A$270m shortfall on the second instalment and BrisConnections was taking legal action against 135 individuals and companies who had defaulted on the second instalment (Sydney Morning Herald, 2009).

Private infrastructure investment

Foreign Direct Investment
'The share of construction has declined, but FDI in infrastructure services as a group has risen in both absolute and relative terms. As infrastructure development requires vast amounts of financing, it is almost impossible to meet such requirement from public sources alone in particular in developing countries. TNCs have therefore been increasingly involved in infrastructure development through FDI (both greenfield investments and M&As) as well as through non-equity forms of participation (such as build-operate-transfer and other modalities). For example, infrastructure-related industries accounted for 22% of worldwide cross-border M&As in 2006, and for 30% in the developing and transition economies – with both sets of shares rising recently. Private equity firms are also entering this market, and accounted for more than half of the worldwide M&A deals (both domestic and cross-border) in infrastructure in 2006, compared with only 2% in 1998' (UNCTAD, 2007).

Five developed countries are estimated to account for the largest share of global Foreign Direct Investment (FDI) stock in infrastructure, led by the UK with US$206,196m (2006), France US$99,524m (2005), Spain US$89,325m (cumulative 1992-2006), US US$49,120m (2006) and Canada US$41,610m (2006). However, the share of developing and transition economies in FDI in electricity, gas and water had reached 7% and in transport 9% by 2006 (UNCTAD, 2008).

Energy and telecommunications accounted for 41.1% and 38% respectively of foreign investment commitments in developing and transition economies between 1996-2006. Transport accounted for 16.9% and water and sewage 4% (UNCTAD, 2008). Concession contracts accounted for between 62% – 86% of investment in energy, water and transport in contrast to the 67% for Greenfield FDI investment in telecoms. Management and lease investment accounted for 25% of investment in water, but was relatively smaller in other sectors. Privatisation FDI accounted for 26% of energy investment with telecoms, transport and water accounting for 16%, 7% and 5% respectively (UNCTAD, 2008).

The stock of FDI in infrastructure in developing countries, as a measure of Trans-National Corporation (TNC) involvement, increased 29-fold in the 1990-2006 period. TNC involvement remains 'small compared to the overall investment needs' (World Bank, 2008).

'Asia accounted for about 47% of the total stock of infrastructure FDI in developing countries in 2006, with Latin America and the Caribbean accounting for 46% and Africa for about 7%.'

'The group of LDCs has remained by and large marginalized in the process of globalization of infrastructure investment, accounting for about 2% of the stock of infrastructure-related FDI in developing countries in 2006. Given the scale of the infrastructure gap faced by these countries, an important question is the degree to which TNCs can help in financing the gap, and what this participation entails in the wider context of sources of finance. In some LDCs, firms from other developing countries are prominent investors in infrastructure, especially in telecommunications and transport' (ibid).

A UK Trade and Investment analysis of transportation business opportunities, India's 'sunrise sector', explained the advantageous policy and regulatory regime. 100% Foreign Direct Investment is allowed for construction and maintenance of highways, bridges and toll roads; a new DBFO Model Concession Agreement has replaced the earlier BOT model with the concession period extended to 30 years; the government has committed '*... to carry out all preparatory work including land acquisition and utility removal before granting the project. Right of Way (ROW) to be made available to concessionaires free from all encumbrances*' (UK Trade & Investment, 2009). In addition, the Indian government and National Highways Authority of India will, if necessary, provide gap funding up to 40% of the project cost.

The UK government Minister launching the report highlighted India's plans to spend £27bn upgrading roads, £6.3bn on 276 port projects and £4.6bn on upgrading 25 airports. He extolled British expertise in PPPs: '*Over 70 countries have come to the UK seeking advice on PPP. For example, we have helped Singapore develop its PPP model, and it is now taking forward projects in education and sports infrastructure development. The UK is India's natural partner of choice as the Indian people enjoy the reality of a step change in infrastructure investment*' (UK Trade and Investment, 2009).

Infrastructure corporate interests

There are large and powerful transnational companies, global chains of management consultants and lawyers, global and national business organisations and political interests promoting and defending PPPs and privatisation.

Claims of a 'public service industry' in the UK (Julius, 2008) are theoretically and ideologically little more than a thinly veiled attempt to justify the growth of outsourcing. And the main trade union response (UNISON, 2008) compiled significant evidence on the negative impact of outsourcing and partnerships but failed to acknowledge that the New Labour government was primarily responsible for the rapid growth of this so-called 'industry' since 1997 due to its fixation with the marketisation and privatisation of public services (Whitfield, 2001 and 2006). The 'industry' was not simply an outcome of economic growth but was designed and financed by the state. The review was commissioned by the Department of Business Enterprise & Regulatory Reform, obviously wanting to promote the government's achievements.

The definition of a 'public services industry' is fundamentally flawed because it excludes water, transport, telecoms and energy services, presumably because they have largely been privatised in the UK and are, therefore, considered private services. It also excludes the financial institutions funding PPP projects. Furthermore, the Julius review evidence base is partial and selective.

Whilst there are organisations specifically established to promote PPPs and privatisation, they should not be considered separately from the national and global business organisations, which advocate a much wider role for the private sector in the public infrastructure, public services and the welfare state.

Finance interest – the City
The global financial centres of London and New York have a key role in providing financial services for public investment, PPPs and privatisation, although they face increasing competition from emerging regional centres in Asia and the Gulf, strong niche centres such as Geneva and Chicago, and national centres such as Frankfurt, Paris, Toronto and Sydney. The globalisation of markets, the growth of emerging economies and demographic change '... *will deeply influence how cash and capital flows are channelled around the world*' (HM Treasury, 2009).

Over £10trillion investment flows in and out of London annually, through UK and foreign-owned financial institutions. Four international banks (HSBC, Barclays, Standard Chartered and Royal Bank of Scotland) are headquartered in London and UK banks account for 8% and 9% of project and asset finance respectively (ibid). London also has an important role in the growth areas of carbon trading, Islamic finance and sovereign wealth funds. More rapid and cheaper funding of infrastructure projects is cited as one of London's potential innovations. Financial services account for about 8% of UK output and employs over one million people. There are, thus, powerful corporate interests in banking, asset management, insurance and pensions and in related services such as law and accountancy.

Transnational companies (TNCs)
There have been significant changes in the structure of transnational companies. Whilst TNCs in telecoms and utilities have consolidated within these sectors, those in construction have diversified into arranging finance, facilities management and operating concessions. Although some of this has been achieved by organic growth, most growth has been achieved through large takeovers and mergers. TNCs have extended their reach with many of the major companies bidding for PPPs and operating concessions in Europe, Latin America, North America and Asia Pacific. Some developing country TNCs, particularly in telecoms and transport, have become important companies.

Some major infrastructure companies are state-owned enterprises or are indirectly state-owned via sovereign wealth funds or financial bailouts.

'Looking to the future, infrastructure TNCs as a whole, including those in the UNCTAD survey, appear to be very optimistic about the global outlook for infrastructure in general, and prospects in developing countries in particular. Apart from the major recipient host countries of recent years (e.g. Brazil, China, India and South Africa), many other economies are being targeted by infrastructure TNCs, including some LDCs.' (United Nations Conference on Trade and Development, 2008).

Construction companies have diversified and internationalised their operations to take advantage of the growth of PPPs (see Table 14). Several major construction companies have formed partnerships with financial institutions to fund PPP projects. This enables companies to retain primary investments after the construction phase is completed. Bovis Lend Lease and the Bank of Scotland (Catalyst Investment Holdings) have a 50/50 joint venture that merged equity interests in 11 PPP projects including Newcastle and Lincoln schools, Cork Maritime College, and Calderdale, Leeds, Hexham, Worcester and Burnley hospitals. Balfour Beatty Capital Projects and the Royal Bank of Scotland; Skanska Infrastructure Developments with Innisfree Company Ltd; and Hochtief PPP Schools Capital Ltd holds assets of operational schools and sold 49% stake to PFI Co Ltd (later

Global Auction of Public Assets

Table 13: *Largest Transnationals in infrastructure industries, ranked by foreign assets, 2006*

Rank	Electricity	Telecoms	Transport	Water/ sewage	Natural gas	More than 1 infrastructure industry
1	Electricite de France (France)	Vodafone Group (UK)	Grupo Ferrovial	Veolia (France)	Gaz de France (France)	Suez (France)
2	E.ON (Germany)	Telefonica (Spain)	Albertis (Spain)	Grupo Agbar (Spain)	Spectra Energy Corp. (US)	Hutchison Whampoa (Hong Kong, China)
3	Endessa (Spain)	Deutsche Telekom (Germany)	AP Moller-Maersk	Waste Management Inc (USA)	Centrica (UK)	RWE Group (Germany)
4	Vattenfall (Sweden)	France Telecom (France)	DP World (UAR)	Shanks Group (UK)	Gas Natural (Spain)	Bouygues (France)
5	National Grid (UK)	Vivendi (France)	China Ocean Shipping (China)	Waste Services Inc (US)	Transcanada Corp (Canada)	YTL Power (Malaysia)

Source: United Nations Conference on Trade and Development 2008

acquired by Infrastructure Investors). Investment companies such as Balfour Beatty Capital are part of the group structure.

In the UK, strategic service delivery partnerships sometimes have a prime and secondary contractor, for example IBM/Mouchel in Somerset, Mouchel/Agilysis in Rochdale and Oldham. Capita Group is an example of an ICT managed services provider, which has diversified, mainly by acquisitions, into design and technical construction services.

Marketisation and privatisation also provide new opportunities for the growth of relatively small companies. For example, Ashley House PLC, a primary care infrastructure company with £20m annual turnover, recently expanded into National Health Service Local Improvement Finance Trust (LIFT) projects, and established a clinical services subsidiary, Ashley Novoe, to assist the creation of social enterprises and community ventures under the NHS transforming primary care programme.

Global consultancies
The big four global accountants and management consultancies (Pricewaterhouse Coopers, KPMG, Deloitte, Ernst & Young) have been joined by the global banks such Goldman Sachs, JP Morgan and

Table 14: *Top 20 transportation developers (2008)*

Company	Concessions/PPP Projects	
	Construction/ Operating	Active Proposals
ACS/Iridium (Spain)	57	27
Macquarie group (Australia)	44	18
Sacyr/Itinere (Spain)*	40	22
Ferrovial-Cintra (Spain)	38	30
Global Via (FCC-Caja Madrid) (Spain)	33	17
Abertis (Spain) 32 7 OHL (Spain)	28	33
NWS Holdings (China)	24	2
Hochtief (Germany)	23	11
Vinci/Cofiroute (France)	22	23
Road King (China)	22	0
Acciona/Necso (Spain)	19	22
Bouygues (France)	17	16
EGIS Projects (France)	16	18
Alstom (France)	15	11
Cheung Kong Infrastructure (China)	15	9
Bilfinger Berger (Germany)	13	9
BRISA (Portugal)	9	7
John Laing (UK)	9	4
Transurban (Australia)	9	4

Source: Public Works Financing, October 2008. *Itinere acquired by Citigroup in 2008.

Citigroup offering financial advice and bidding for PPP contracts. They in turn bring global law firms in to advise on possible legislative solutions to benefit the private sector and carry out due diligence during procurement, and in the sale of PPP equity and refinancing. PPPs and privatisation also increase the transfer of planning, design, engineering and project management functions to private sector management consultants. This leads to the run-down of public sector design and technical services.

Development banks collusion
Regional bodies ranging from Asian Development Bank, European Investment Bank to global bodies such as UN Agencies, World Bank

and the International Monetary Fund supply financial aid through loans in addition to policy and technical support. The drive for free markets in investment, services and trade is orchestrated by a combination of the US, EU and developed countries, the World Bank and many other international and global organisations, banks and investment funds, construction companies and PPP trade bodies, and global consultancies.

The fourth annual meeting of the Infrastructure Consortium for Africa (ICA), also attended by senior representatives of G8 ministries and multilateral agencies, heard that ICA will continue to advocate for increased private sector participation in infrastructure at the highest levels in African governments. It worked with the US Treasury on an African Ministers' meeting on PPPs in late 2008. ICA supports cross-border projects, particularly regional power grids, road corridors and investment in the water sector. ICA members' infrastructure investment increased 20% in 2007 to US$10bn compared to 2006 together with increased support from the World Bank, African Development Bank, European Investment Bank and European Commission together with increased funding from the US, France and Japan.

International and global business organisations
Each service industry or sector has its own international organisations, such as the International Bridge, Tunnel and Turnpike Association, the International Project Finance Association, plus those that operate on a regional or world-wide basis such as the European International Contractors (EIC), Transatlantic Business Dialogue (TABD) and the International Chamber of Commerce (ICC). The European PPP Center (EPPPC) was created in 2006, by mainly Hungarian PPP advisers, to promote PPPs in Eastern and Central Europe.

National PPP lobbyists and allies
Infrastructure Partnerships Australia has prioritized several initiatives to inject greater urgency with federal, state and local governments to reform relevant regulation, taxation, intellectual property rights, and bid cost issues and higher investment in infrastructure using both public and private finance. It has also promoted streamlined planning legislation for critical infrastructure and encouraged the private sector to have more equitably shared political risk in projects. Membership is limited to chief executives of Australia's leading public and private infrastructure organisations in four sectors: property,

transport, social infrastructure and utilities.

The National PPP Forum in Australia formed in 2004 with members from all States, Territories and the Federal Government, *'is designed to deliver improved project and related service outcomes through harmonising policies and processes, and encouraging better coordination and information sharing among Australian governments'* (www.pppforum.gov.au). National Council for Public Private Partnerships (NCPPP), Canadian Council for Public-Private Partnerships, and the Czech Republic Public Private Partnerships Association are examples of national PPP lobby organisations.

The PPP Forum in the UK (sponsored by 33 major contractors, 44 financial institutions and 35 consultancies/advisors) is dedicated to defending and promoting the PPP model. Infrastructure Partnerships Australia performs a similar role in Australia.

Allies and participants in the PPP lobby include national business organisations such as the Confederation of British Industry's (CBI) Public Services Strategy Board (80% of the non-CBI executives represent major PPP interests) and assorted academics who either produce papers promoting PPPs or focus exclusively on attempting to model obscure theories of contracting.

PPP lobbyists play a major role in maintaining a high profile case for PPPs and 'partnerships' and create the illusion that there is no alternative. One New York consultant advised US firms to '... *think like an owner, not like a contractor*' (sic) (Construction, 2006).

CHAPTER 6

The global spread of privatisation and PPPs

Public private partnerships have spread to all continents and many countries in the last two decades, although there are big differences in government support, legal frameworks and levels of investment. This chapter charts the geography of PPPs, highlighting regional variations, and examines their role in the UK, France, Ireland, Germany, US, Canada, Russia, Australia, China, India, Brazil and South Africa.

The development of privatisation and PPPs of the public infrastructure has been uneven and conflict striven in virtually all countries. It has developed in phases, depending on the clarity of legislation, the establishment of PPP units in government departments, financial and construction companies perspective on the market potential and government commitment, the willingness of public bodies to initiate projects, the quality of projects and the level of political opposition. Although the UK had over 900 PPPs in 2009, the first decade of the PFI programme from its launch in 1992, the private sector manoeuvred to shift the balance of the programme to its terms.

Figure 7: *PPP investment in developing countries 1990-2007*

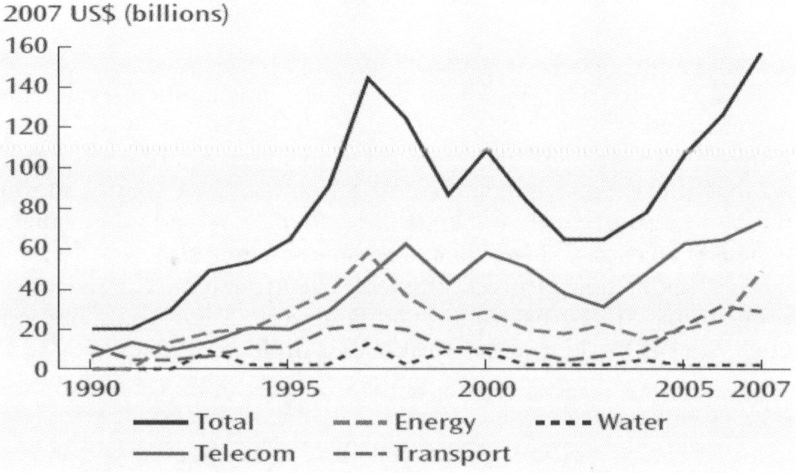

Source: Global Monitoring Report, 2009, World Bank.

PPP investment grew rapidly before reaching a peak in the mid 1990s and only surpassed that level again in 2007, prior to the financial and economic crisis. This is illustrated in Figure 7 which shows the relatively high level of investment in telecoms and energy and the comparatively low level of investment in water.

Key regional variations

In Europe, the Lisbon strategy for growth and employment proposed '... *more targeted investment in infrastructure coupled with more effective competition in areas like electronic communications, energy and transport to drive down costs for businesses wherever they are located*' (EU, 2004). The Kok report on the Treaty called for '*Public–private partnerships should be facilitated and encouraged as a means of boosting investment*' to strengthen the science base (Kok, 2004).

European Investment Bank, the European business lobby and the PPP/PFI 'industry' have contributed to the creation of a 'European market' with similar legislative frameworks, financial mechanisms, project design and operating practices, although there are wide differences in the number and type of projects across Europe.

'*PPPs are not a first step towards the privatisation of public tasks*' stated a text adopted by the European Parliament in October 2006. It called for PPP/PFI projects at European level, for example, to implement the trans-European transport networks (European Parliament, 2006). It referred to PPP/PFI as an '... *alternative to privatisation in times of scarce budgetary funding and help public administrations to modernise by acquiring know-how from the private sector*' (ibid). It also called on Member States to '... *create transparent mechanisms guaranteeing that private investor's legal and financial interests are protected during the whole lifetime of a contract*' (ibid).

Table 15: *International Major Projects Survey 1985-2008*

Sector	Total planned and funded since 1985		Funded by October 2008	
	No of projects	Cost US$m	No of projects	Cost US$m
Roads	1,046	580,265	500	265,177
Rail	311	342,190	145	144,089
Water	767	146,351	469	90,729
Buildings	582	119,648	410	85,381
Total	**2,706**	**1,188,454**	**1,524**	**585,376**

Source: Public Works Financing, 2008.

Europe already has a framework for charging heavy goods vehicles on motorways and roads. The Eurovignette Directive (2006/38/EC) allows countries to charge vehicles of more than 3.5 tonnes and can integrate the external costs into toll prices, for example congestion costs, environmental pollution, noise pollution, landscape damage, social costs such as health, and indirect accident costs not covered by insurance. The Directive requires toll revenue to be used for maintenance of the road infrastructure or to cross-finance the transport sector as a whole. It also allows authorities to levy an additional 15% charge to finance new alternative transport infrastructure projects and they can exempt isolated areas and economically weak regions from tolls or user charges and can issue rebates for frequent users. From 2010, countries that already apply tolls or user charges must vary prices according to vehicle pollution standards. Germany and Switzerland already have a national electronic truck charging scheme with the Netherlands, Sweden, Poland, Hungary and the Czech Republic developing similar systems and advancing '... seamless travel on Europe's tolled road network' (Bell, 2006).

There are many European Union programmes promoting and supporting PPPs. The Joint Assistance in Supporting Projects in European Regions (JASPERS) provides free expertise and support in the development of large projects supported by EU funds in Member States covered by the new Convergence Objective for the period 2007-2013. JASPERS is a partnership between the European Commission, the European Investment Bank and the European Bank for Reconstruction and Development.

Another form of support is the Community Realisation European Aid Masterplan. CREAM Europe PPP Alliance is an EU body, dedicated to the promotion of public-private partnerships. It commenced in 2001 to accelerate the implementation of the European Spatial Development Perspective (ESDP) and EU policy in the candidate countries within the framework of the EU pre-accession process. 'EuroPPP and MasterPPPlan: Building Europe Together with Public Private Partnerships' promotes the use of PPPs for urban and regional development projects, transport and public building construction projects. The Alliance provides a range of PPP services to network partners in Central and Eastern Europe including training, project management, evaluation, the formation of consortia and lobbying.

The Joint European Support for Sustainable Investment in City

Areas (JESSICA) is also a partnership between the European Commission and the European Investment Bank (EIB) with the Council of Europe Development Bank (CEDB), providing expertise and access to loan capital from the EIB, international financial institutions, private banks and investors to fund growth and jobs in Europe's urban areas.

Table 16: *PPPs in Europe 2000-2008*

Country	2001-04 m	2005 m	2006 m	2007 m	2008 m	Total	No of signed deals 2001-08	Projects being deals procured Jan 2007
UK	21,849	6,237	14,111	10,698	8,236	61,131	536	
Spain	1,000	1,154	1,664	309	–	4,127	38	*2,931*
France	0	1,788	735	329	1,241	4,093	34	*3,964*
Italy	890	2,179	439	55	–	3,563	20	*29,799*
Ireland	720	121	623	1,489	300	3,253	19	–
Greece	0	798	1,600	3,885	1,000	2,398	8	*6,270*
Germany	440	830	177	465	117	2,029	40	*9,495*
Belgium	1,300	480	–	300	680	1,780	6	*3,635*
Netherlands	1,302	–	431	–	1,020	1,733	9	*1,211*
Poland	1,520	–	–	–	–	1,520	2	*1,317*
Austria	49	0	850	–	–	899	6	*20*
Finland	0	700	–	–	–	700	1	–
Bulgaria	0	366	288	366	–	654	6	*2,202*
Hungary	0	0	38	15	500	556	11	*264*
Cyprus	0	500	–	–	–	500	1	–
Portugal	278	–	32	140	–	450	7	*1,515*
Other countries	485	2	490	15		977	7	*4,957*
Total	**29,836**	**15,155**	**21,478**	**18,051**	**13,194**	**97,714**	**751**	***67,580***

Source: Public Private Finance, DLA Piper.

The EIB estimated that the essential infrastructure investment needs, the 'catch-up' expenditure of €500bn, in the Central and Eastern Europe (CEE) until 2010, were water (36%), energy (22%), environment (14%), telecoms (125), roads (9%) and railways (7%). Yet by 2008, the 'major infrastructure opportunities' were dominated by 22 road and 16 airport projects valued at about €14bn compared to twelve health and leisure projects valued at about €500m (PwC, 2008). Only one water and one power project were signed.

Developing countries

The World Bank's Private Participation in Infrastructure Database is based on signed energy, telecoms, transport, water and sewerage projects in East Asia and Pacific, Europe and Central Asia, Latin America and the Caribbean, Middle East and North Africa, South Asia and Sub-Saharan Africa. It covers projects only in low and middle-income countries, for example the Europe and Central Asia category and excludes western European countries. The database divides projects into divestiture (full or partial privatisation) and greenfield projects that account for over 90% of the projects, plus concession and management/lease contracts. The greenfield and concession contracts embrace a variety of PPP models.

However, the database excludes health, education and other social infrastructure, criminal justice, environment and democratic/public administration infrastructure sectors (see Chapter 1) and the energy sector is limited to electricity, gas and telecoms and excludes other information and communications technology projects. The database should not be mistaken for a 'world' or global perspective on private sector infrastructure investment, because developed countries that have a high level of privatization and PPPs, are excluded. Similarly, the privatization and PPP totals for sectors, regions and countries should be treated separately, because they identify two distinct types of private sector investment and ownership.

Three regions, East Asia and Pacific, Latin America and the

Table 17: *Infrastructure private investment in developing countries by region 1990-2007 (US billion)*

Region	Energy	Telecom	Transport	Water/sewage	Total
Europe* & Central Asia	56.7	150.6	18.3	4.8	230.4
East Asia & Pacific	100.7	77.1	70.6	27.2	275.6
Latin America & Caribbean	142.1	224.2	85.4	22.9	474.6
Middle East & North Africa	19.5	40.3	5.4	1.1	66.3
South Asia	43.6	63.2	20.4	0.2	127.4
Sub-Saharan Africa	8.8	49.4	10.2	0.3	68.7
Total	**371.5**	**604.8**	**210.3**	**56.5**	**1243.0**

Source: World Bank Private Participation in Infrastructure Database, November 2008.
* Low and middle income countries only

Caribbean and Europe and Central Asia accounted for 79% of projects (see Table 17). PPP/concession projects accounted for 80% of the projects in the 1990-2006 period, 82% by value. Telecoms accounted for 48.6% of the total public private investment, energy projects accounted for nearly a third (29.9%), followed by transport with 16.9%, and water/sewage projects a mere 4.5%.

Ten countries accounted for 63% of private sector investment in infrastructure in developing and transition economies between 1990-2006 (see Table 18), clear evidence that '... *private investors in infrastructure have tended to be directed to a small group of developing countries: the ones with relatively large, rich or fast-growing markets*' (Pessoa, 2007).

'*South Asia has seen a recent surge in investment commitments to infrastructure projects with private participation. Indeed, of total commitments in 1990–2006, almost half came in the last three years of the period. Moreover, South Asia is receiving a greater share of the investment commitments going to all developing countries. While it attracted only 5 percent of the total in 1995–2000, its share grew to 13 percent in 2001–06. In 2006 its share was 19 percent*' (PPIAF, 2009).

The financial crisis has led to delays in PPP project signings in developing countries as a result of '... *the rapid scaling back of hedge funds, private equity funds are holding back capital, currency devaluation making foreign debt more expensive, investors are demanding higher returns. Private investors focusing on largest markets, good policy frameworks,*

Table 18: *Top 10 countries share of investment 1990-2007 (US$bn)*

Country	Project Investment US$bn	% of total investment
Brazil	196.2	15.8
China	99.6	8.0
India	96.1	7.7
Mexico	86.1	6.9
Argentina	78.4	6.3
Russian Federation	61.1	4.9
Malaysia	50.2	4.0
Philippines	42.2	3.4
Indonesia	40.7	3.3
Turkey	36.8	3.0
Total		**63.3**

Source: World Bank Private Participation in Infrastructure Database, November 2008.

developing countries may get crowded out' (Public Private Infrastructure Advisory Facility, 2009).

Some 48% of the US$786bn global private infrastructure investment, between 1990-2003, went to Latin America. Yet 75% of the population expressed discontent with privatisation in 2004, up from 40% in 1998 (Fay and Morrison 2005). This is hardly surprising – there were twelve casualties in Arequipa, Peru, during protests against planned privatised electricity price rises in 2002; there were fifty casualties in protests in the same year against blackouts and price increases in the Dominican Republic, which resulted in the bailout of the utility company. Civil disturbances in Ecuador and Paraguay resulted in energy and telecom privatisations respectively being abandoned. These events followed the Cochabamba, Bolivia, protests of two years earlier, which had 130 casualties and led to the cancellation of the water concession (Andres et al, 2008). The high level of failed and renegotiated contracts is examined in Chapter 8.

Privatisation accounted for 22% of projects, but 54% of the total amount of private finance raised in developing countries. Concessions and greenfield projects accounted for 31% and 44% of projects and 17% and 29% of the total amount of private finance raised. Six countries – Argentina, Brazil, Chile, Columbia, Peru and Mexico – accounted for 93% of Latin America's PPP projects. Nearly half (46%) of Latin America's projects were telecoms followed by energy (32%), transport (17%) and water (5%). There was a surge of projects in 1997/98 but subsequently declined back to the 1990 level by 2003.

New private prisons have been built in Chile, Mexico and Peru using the PPP model. Between 2001 and 2003, three concession contracts, worth some US$200 million, were awarded for a total of eight new prisons. Vinci won three Chilean prison PPP contracts in 2004. Another three prisons were built by a Torno/Sodexho/Besalco consortium but the consortia withdrew from another two-prison contract following a dispute over the terms of the concession (Business Chile, 2009).

The Columbia government provided substantial guarantees for private sector participation in electricity (US$3.0bn), tolls roads (US$450m) and telecoms (US$936m) projects. They were eventually called and accounted for 54% of private investment (Andries et al, 2008). Similar guarantees for the 1997 Mexican toll road bailout cost between US$7bn – US$12bn representing between 1% and 1.7% of Mexico's Gross Domestic Product (Guasch et al, 2005).

Governments in Bolivia, Venezuela and Argentina have

renationalised privatised infrastructure assets to achieve political objectives, but also due to exploitative prices and the failure of private companies. However, in other countries most renationalisation was forced on governments because projects failed or governments refused further concessions in renegotiating contracts.

Mexico has three public private partnership models – highway concessions, private service contracts in highways (PPPs) and asset utilisation to invest in infrastructure. It is using this approach for health (hospitals), education (technical colleges) and transport (roads). Mexico's first PPP toll road programme was financially disastrous. Thirty-four projects were signed between 1987-95 with US$9.9bn private investment. However, construction costs overruns averaged 25% and toll revenues were about 30% below forecast. Average tolls increased sevenfold. The government had to takeover 23 projects and paid US$5bn outstanding debt to Mexican banks and US$2.6bn to construction companies (Cuttaree, 2008). Brazil has over 9,000km of private sector operated tolled highways in 36 concession agreements.

China has a key role in financing and building infrastructure projects in over 35 African countries, particularly Nigeria, Angola, Sudan and Ethiopia (Public Private Infrastructure Advisory Facility (PPIAF), World Bank, 2008). Chinese financial commitments rose sevenfold from US$1bn in 2001 to 2006 and then reducing to US$4.5bn in 2007. At the end of this period, China was financing ten major hydropower projects and constructing 1,600km, and rehabilitating a further, 1,350km of railways. It has also invested in telecoms, water and road projects.

China has many mineral projects in Africa but only 7% of infrastructure finance is directly linked to facilitating the export of copper, bauxite and iron. Africa supplies about 30% of China's oil imports but this accounts for only 16% of African exports in 2006, the bulk going to the US and Europe. Chinese infrastructure finance is channelled through the China Export-Import Bank, with terms and conditions negotiated on a bilateral basis, including an average grant element of about 36% compared to the 66% grant in Overseas Development Assistance to Africa.

Country analysis

United Kingdom
The UK leads the world in the privatisation of public services and use of PPPs for infrastructure. It has also led the development of the PPP model, developed a secondary market in refinancing and PPP equity

sales (see chapter 7), facilitated the internationalisation of PPP finance and construction, and developed a well-oiled corporate lobbying machine promoting privatisation and PPPs (Whitfield 1992 and 2001).

Privatisation of utilities, water, telecoms, public transport, ports and airports and state-owned corporations between 1980-1997 was such that much of the infrastructure was owned and operated by the private sector. This accounts for the absence of PPPs in these sectors.

UK PPP investment exceeded levels for the rest of Europe with over 900 projects with a capital value of over £70bn – see Table 19, nearly 40 Strategic Service-delivery Partnerships (SSPs) valued at over £8bn plus a variety of other PPP projects (ESSU, 2009). The breadth of the PPP programme is significant because it extends across the social welfare infrastructure, such as schools and hospitals, the criminal justice system through police, court and prison PPPs and defence with military equipment and accommodation projects. The largest PPP contracts are for the London Underground, but there has been only one toll road project to date, in sharp contrast with other major European countries.

Table 19: **Signed private finance initiative projects in the UK**

Service	No of projects	Capital Value of projects (£m)
Education	225	9,925
Health	279	13,650
Housing	26	1,665
Transport	66	26,079
Regeneration	2	610
Leisure	14	252
Property	7	315
Information and Communications Technology	83	3,412
Equipment (defence, vehicles)	36	4,782
Environment (waste, water, energy)	57	3,816
Prisons and Detention Centres	16	564
Other accommodation (barracks, police, courts, libraries and offices)	99	6,705
Total	**910**	**71,775**

Source: PartnershipsUK database accessed 8 June 2009.

The UK is unique in the extent to which it has used PPPs in the defence sector with 57 projects with a capital value of £22.5bn (June 2009). Over half were military equipment projects, accounting for 75% of the capital value, followed by accommodation, IT/communications and training college projects. Two new PPP models were launched in 2001 and 2004 for health centres and secondary schools respectively in England.

National Health Service Local Improvement Finance Trust (LIFT): LIFT is a £1bn programme to renew the primary care and social services infrastructure such as GP surgeries, health centres and one-stop-centres in inner cities. It has a different structure from 'normal' private finance initiative schemes. Originally the Department of Health and Partnerships UK (part-owned by the private sector) established a national joint venture company, Partnership for Health, to operate the programme, which later became Community Health Partnerships (CHP), wholly owned by the Department of Health.

The programme establishes local joint ventures (LIFTCo's), in which the PPP contractor has a 60% stake with Community Health Partnerships and local stakeholders (usually Primary Care Trusts) each having a 20% stake. LIFTCo builds and refurbishes premises, which it leases to primary care trusts, general practitioners, dentists, pharmacists and social care/voluntary organisations. LIFTCo batches projects in an area in order to meet the minimum £20m capital cost imposed on private finance initiative projects, with an exclusivity agreement for future projects over the 20-25 year contract,

By summer 2008, Community Health Partnerships had developed 48 LIFTCos, covering half of England's population, and with £1.4bn investment. An Express LIFT programme extending LIFT to the remaining areas of England was launched via a framework agreement in 2008 which will have between six and ten PPP consortia from which Primary Care Trusts (PCTs) will select.

The LIFT rate of return – 14.3% to 15.9% – is higher than that obtained by other similar-sized private finance initiative projects (12.5% to 15.0%) (National Audit Office, 2005). This study was '... *fundamentally flawed*' because it was based on surveys of participants with a vested interest in LIFT schemes, and did not include comparisons with other financing methods, risk transfer, affordability or governance issues (Centre for International Public Health Policy, 2005).

Building Schools for the Future (BSF): a £2.2bn PPP programme to renew the secondary school infrastructure in England and deliver the 400 Academies programme. Local authorities use public and/or private finance. A Local Education Partnership (LEP), 80% controlled by the private sector, with the local authority and Partnership for Schools (a new Department for Education and Skills quango) each with a 10% stake, is at the core of Building Schools for the Future. Of 19 signed projects in summer 2008, 11 had established LEPs which design, build, finance and operate new and refurbished schools.

But Building Schools for the Future is not just about the provision of new schools. The local education authority must fully review its educational vision, develop a strategy for educational provision, which integrates the building programme with service delivery, a new information and communications technology infrastructure, teaching, school management and community use. The local educational partnership will not only deliver facilities management but also provide other services such as educational support services and school transport.

There are a few joint PPP projects, for example, three NHS Trusts in Peterborough and Cambridgeshire combined to build a 612-bed acute hospital, a 102-bed mental health unit and an integrated care centre. The £335m project with Progress Health was signed in 2007. There are two joint projects in North East England – the Newcastle/North Tyneside street lighting and Gateshead/South Tyneside schools projects.

A new London-West Midlands High Speed rail line is under investigation in addition to the new east-west £15.9bn Crossrail line through central London and to link to the Channel Tunnel Rail Link. Rail travel has grown rapidly in the past decade with a 50% increase in passenger numbers and a 40% increase in rail freight (Department for Transport, 2009). High Occupancy Tolled (HOT) lanes are being examined to '... *better manage motorway capacity*' and discussions are taking place with potential operators and financiers (Department for Transport, 2008).

The sale and transfer of public housing over the last 30 years foreshadowed what was to befall other services. We accurately forecast in *The Great Sales Robbery*, 1980, the outcome of selling individual homes that quickly developed into estate sales and then stock transfers to housing associations. Investment in the remaining stock was conditional for many authorities on stock transfer or the establishment of an arms length management organisation (Centre for Public Services, 2004). PPPs are used for housing improvement with 26 PPP projects with a capital value of £1.66bn. The Defend Council Housing campaign was ultimately successful in pressing New Labour to reverse previous policies and to committing to a council house-building programme in 2009.

The UK has a well-oiled corporate PPP promotion industry, ranging from industry bodies such as the PPP Forum, Confederation of British Industry, the Serco Institute, the global management consultants, law firms, 'think tanks', plus government bodies such as the National Audit Office, Audit Commission and Local Partnerships.

France
Concessions supply 71% of water and 73% of urban waste via about 12,000 contracts, about 75% of the 10,000km motorway network and 99% of energy in France. The privatisation of state-owned utilities, transport, financial institutions and industrial companies commenced in the mid 1980s and included full or partial share sales, mergers and disposal of stakes in listed companies. Asset sales totalled €65.8bn between 1988 and July 2003 of which €50.5bn was allocated to the firms as equity injection (Minefi, quoted in Berne and Pogorel, 2004).

The METP (marches d'entreprises de travaux publics) was used for school building projects in the 1980s-1990s until it was banned following a series of political scandals. Construction companies had long-term contracts to construct and maintain buildings using private finance and were remunerated by public bodies. As with PPPs, the model avoided the initial capital cost for the public sector but led to '... *local authorities paying for expensive private sector financings*' (Linklaters, 2006). In addition, the METP did not have a defined legal framework. The Ministry for Justice was the first department to adopt the PPP model in 2002 following a general enabling act for PPPs in 2003; a government order in 2004 introduced the concept of 'partnership contracts'. The first school PPP under the new legal framework, a secondary school for 550 students, was awarded to Vinci in 2006 by Loiret council.

The French government part-privatised the three toll road operators Autoroutes du Sud de la France (ASF), Societe des Autoroutes du Nord et de l'Est de la France (SANEF) and Autoroutes Paris-Rhin-Rhone (APRR) between 2002-04 followed by a sale of the remaining government-owned stakes the following year, raising €14.8bn. Vinci already held a 23% stake in the (ASF) and was the sole bidder for the government's 50.4% stake. Albertis, Spain, won the (SANEF) network. A joint Eiffage/Macquarie bid won the (APRR) network, the second largest in France with 28% of the network, over a higher bid from the Spanish construction group Cintra. Another large French contractor, Bouygues, pulled out of the bidding.

Societe Generale reported that French PPPs increased 140% in volume between 2006-08 with €4bn capital value of projects at the tender stage and a further €7bn planned over the next three years (Societe Generale, 2008).

The fifty-year 50km Perpiguan-Figueras freight/high speed rail link concession between France and Spain was signed in 2005 with ACS-Eiffage. Both governments funded 57% of the €1bn construction costs. A Global System for Mobile Communications €900m rail project and €6.5bn Tours-Bordeaux 302km high-speed rail link concession are also planned. Light rail projects are in procurement for Reims and Lyon.

The Ministry of Justice launched a €1.4bn plan for 18 new prisons providing 11,000 places in 2004. The first tranche of four prisons was awarded to Eiffage with a second group of three prisons at Le Mans, Le Havre and Poitiers awarded in 2008. A third tranche of three prisons will include facilities management services.

Thirty-five health PPP projects with a total capital value of €1.4bn range from new hospitals, such as the €330m Sud Francilien, to specialist units and treatment centres. Thirteen major PPP road projects with a total capital cost of over €5bn were at the planning, procurement, construction or operational phase (DLA Piper, 2007). The Millau Viaduct, a suspension bridge over the Tarn River, is a tolled section of the A75 motorway between Clermont-Ferrand and Beziers and has won many design accolades since it opened in 2004. Designed by Norman Foster and built by Eiffage in three years, the bridge is one of the longest and highest of its kind in the world. Other planned projects include a €3bn 182km rail link between Connerre and Rennes and the relocation of the Ministry of Defence in Paris.

Ireland
An eight project pilot PPP programme costing €762m was launched in 1999 following '... *sustained lobbying by the Irish Business Employers Confederation and the Construction Industry Federation*' (Hurst and Reeves, 2004). The incoming Fianna Fail/Progressive Democrat government commissioned financial consultants/accountants Farrell

Grant Sparks, together with Goodbody's Economic Consultants and Chesterton Consulting, to examine the potential use of PPPs in Ireland. Their recommendations were predictable and Farrell Grant Sparks became the lead adviser on the first PPP project, i.e. five new second level schools. It has since advised on many more PPP projects.

The National Development Finance Agency assumed responsibility for the procurement of major PPP projects in 2005. By mid 2009, Ireland's PPP programme had 32 signed major projects (projects over €20m) primarily roads, schools and water and drainage schemes. A further major 38 projects for schools, roads, social housing, prisons, water and four major public transport projects were at the planning and procurement stages. It includes three bundles of higher education projects – three university libraries, and new facilities at six other colleges and universities. The Macquarie Partnerships For Ireland consortia is building four new schools in the first part of the 23 school PPP programme.

The National Development Plan 2007-2013 anticipates PPPs accounting for 17.3% and 7.6% respectively for economic and social infrastructure investment (Government of Ireland, 2007). However, Ireland's emergency budget in April 2009 revealed a €4.8bn gap in the government's planned €31.4bn five year infrastructure investment programme. It is reported that the government is looking to increase the proportion of PPPs and seeking a €3bn pensions fund initiative to support publicly funded projects (Infrastructure Investor, 2009).

The €250m – €500m health PPP programme is still at the planning stage based on the National Network for Radiation Oncology with centres in Dublin, Cork and Galway and satellite centres in Waterford and Limerick. Government plans for co-location of private hospitals next to existing public hospitals have ground to a virtual halt.

The first schools' PPP turned into a saga. The Department of Education concluded that the €283m project PPP would achieve 6% savings, even though new schools were 15% because of new circulation space requirements, but the Auditor General estimated the actual cost was between 8% and 13%, more expensive than conventional procurement (Comptroller and Auditor General, 2005). An additional €3.3m was paid to Jarvis for additional site costs. The Department had paid for site tests, which were supplied to each bidder but the foot and mouth disease crisis prevented further detailed site visits. And in another twist of fate, Farrell Grant Sparks acquired the Northern Ireland branch of Chesterton, which was also advising the Department of Education, but key PPP financial evaluation documents were lost in the process of separating Chesterton's Belfast office from its British operations (Committee of Public Accounts, 2005).

In February 2003, the first schools PPP was 50% refinanced by the European Investment Bank, with the proceeds shared 75/25 between the Department and Jarvis. This reduced the NPV by 1.5% although the Department incurred €236,000 legal and financial costs negotiating the refinancing (Comptroller and Auditor General, 2004). The remaining 50% commercial debt was later refinanced by Barclays Bank and the proceeds shared 50/50. Jarvis had severe financial problems and the schools project was acquired by Hochtief, the German construction company in 2005. Two years later Hochtief PPP Schools Capital Ltd sold a 49% shareholding to the PFI Infrastructure Company, which was in turn acquired by Infrastructure Investors in May 2007. Two years later Barclay Private Equity Integrated Infrastructure Fund bought out the Societe Generale, 3i and Fleming stakes in a £558.6m deal for the 84 project portfolio (see chapter 7).

Dublin's housing renewal strategy for inner city estates was intended to be financially neutral for the government and city council by using PPPs to build a mixture of public, affordable and private housing.

A McNamara/Castlehorn consortia was appointed to redevelop three inner city estates, St Michael's in Inchicore, O'Devaney Gardens and Dominick Street and to build new housing on two city council sites. However, in May 2008 the developer withdrew from five social housing PPPs in Dublin blaming 'adversely changed circumstances' in the housing market. The withdrawal from the five €900m projects happened on the same day as the government announced that it had rejected 130 objections to the new 2,200 inmate Thornton Hall prison complex in North Dublin where the McNamara/Barclays Private Equity/GSL consortia was the preferred bidder!

However, a year later, the government withdrew from the prison project claiming it was now 'unaffordable'. The government acquired the Thornton Hall site in a secret €30m deal in 2005, paying twice the price of comparable land purchases in the area and has spent over €10m on preliminary site work (Irish Examiner, 2009).

Housing and property development are at the core of the fiscal crisis in Ireland – residential investment accounted for 13% of GDP (compared to 6% in UK) and capital gain tax and stamp duty accounted for 13% of tax revenues (compared to 4% in UK) and property development accounts for the bulk of bank losses.

The Dublin social housing PPPs demonstrate the dangers of relying on market forces for the provision of public housing. When the private housing market hits crisis, which it does on a regular basis, social housing is stopped because developers do not want an over-supply of private housing. There are other implications such as the marginalisation of public housing because private housing provision determines not only the number of public and affordable units built but also the social and community facilities. Furthermore, there is a danger that private housing gets prime access to transport and other facilities. Higher densities mean the loss of houses and concentration of apartments. The original St Michaels estate plan in 2001 had 320 dwellings in 53%, 25%, 22% ratio of public, affordable and private but the PPP plan increased the dwellings to 575 in a 26%, 12%, 62% ratio (Bisset, 2008).

Unfortunately, the Irish Congress of Trade Unions signed up to Social Partnership Agreements that specifically sought to develop PPPs and to the National Framework Agreement on PPPs without challenging the use of PPPs (Hearne, 2004).

Germany
By June 2009, Germany had over 130 PPP projects including seven transport projects valued at €1.76bn and accounting for about half the total investment between 2007-09. PPPs originated in the F-Model legislation in 1994, which permitted private sector DBFO tolled tunnels and bridges although few projects were built. The A-Model was introduced in 2005 as part of the new Federal government initiative to boost PPPs to privately finance widening of major roads from 4 to 6 lanes with heavy goods vehicle tolls. Several regional governments with responsibility for health and education have established PPP task forces. Public sector capital spending was divided between the federal government, regional and local authorities 21%, 20% and 59% respectively in 2004 (Deutsche Bank Research, 2007).

The range of PPP building projects has extended from schools and day-care centres to prisons, hospitals, municipal roads and the first defence sector PPP at the Furst-Wrede Barracks, Munich.

German construction companies have won about 80% of PPP projects and are also active in the UK, Australia, Ireland and North America. For example, Bilfinger Berger has 18 PPP projects with a further 9 in construction – 6% Germany, 38% UK, 17% Australia, Canada 32% and 17% rest of Europe. Its German projects include the District Administration Building, Unna; British Embassy, Berlin; and a €250m Cancer Therapy Centre, Kiel (with Siemens) and several transport projects including the €179m Herrentunnel, Luebeck.

Hochtief is building 65 schools in five PPPs in Cologne, Frankfurt, Leverkusen, Offenbach and Rodenkirchen with a capital value of €978m, plus the €44m Gladbeck City Hall and a €300m section of the A4 motorway. There is an estimated €60bn national infrastructure deficit in schools and a further €35bn in universities (PPP Bulletin, 2006 and 2008). Hochtief also has a share interest in the partially privatised Hamburg and Dusseldorf airports.

ACS, Spain's largest building company, acquired a 25% stake in Hochtief for €1.26bn in 2007 thus giving it access to construction and management contracts in Germany, Canada, Eastern Europe and Asia-Pacific. ACS also has share stakes in two of Spain's largest electricity generators, Union Fenosa (35%) and Iberdrola (10%).

Water supply and sewage is still highly fragmented, with about 6,600 municipally-owned companies and a further 8,000 sewage companies with joint venture and private companies having an 8% share (von Hirschhausen et al, 2002).

Private hospitals in Germany were significantly less efficient than public and non-profit hospitals over a five-year period in the 1990s (Helmig and Lapsley, 2001).

Arvato Services, part of the Bertelsmann group, operates strategic service-delivery partnership contracts, East Riding and Sefton in the UK and a services only contract with Wuerzburg in Germany. A Siemens and IBM consortium has a €7.1bn PPP contract to modernise the non-military ICT of Germany's armed forces.

United States

The long-term leasing of existing US public infrastructure assets is a new paradigm to extract value from existing assets through user fees and monetising future growth to provide a lump sum payment to revenue starved states. There have been a few examples where the private sector has financed and built private toll roads, for example the Dulles Greenway in Washington, and a handful of private prisons were built by prison companies who negotiated with county, state and federal corrections authorities to take prisoners.

Until the late 1980's federal policies discouraged states from building new toll roads or imposing tolls on existing roads on the grounds that they were '... *an impediment to interstate commerce*' (Congressional Budget Office, 1997). In 1916 Congress decreed that roads built with federal aid had to be toll-free and this was repeated in the Highway Act of 1956, which launched the Interstate Highway System (ibid). The US Department of Transportation introduced model legislation in 2007 to help states encourage private investment and PPPs for a range of transportation infrastructure. But to date only about half of the states have laws permitting PPPs.

A total of 235 toll-based highway projects were initiated in the US between 1992 and 2008, for 4,511 miles at a capital cost of US$161bn (Federal Highway Administration, 2009). Twenty-four toll roads had private sector involvement, representing 14% of length and capital investment, although the relevant database excludes long-term concessions. Private sector involvement is possible or yet to be determined in 79 projects whilst 57 projects have no private sector involvement and 74 projects do not currently contemplate such involvement. Only about 8.5% of the urban national highway system and 7% of the urban Interstate system is tolled. However, the fiscal crisis, increased use of pricing and new technology for congestion management and the use of toll revenues to support bond issues to finance new highway or public transport capacity, is likely to increase tolling and use of PPPs (ibid). The National Surface Transportation Police and Revenue Study Commission proposed that Congress increase the federal gas tax, currently 18.4 cents per gallon, between 5 cents and 8 cents annually for five years, followed by inflation-linked increases.

US local government has usually used the municipal (tax exempt) bond market to finance infrastructure projects, which has stymied the growth of PPP finance. There has been renewed interest in the US government's Transportation Infrastructure Finance and Innovation Act 1998 (TIFIA) which has provided over US$8bn of direct low-interest loans, loan guarantees and standby lines of credit for regional and national transport projects. Australian group Transurban used TIFIA funding to obtain US$589m debt at low fixed interest rates for Washington DC's US$1.4bn Capital Beltway HOT lanes project (Australia Productivity Commission, 2009).

PPP programme
335 PPP projects were funded between 1985 and 2008 with a total value of nearly fifty billion dollars (see Table 20). Roads accounted for half of the planned projects but for less than a third of funded projects, which were relatively evenly distributed between roads, rail and water followed by buildings.

Table 20: US PPP programme 1985 – 2008

Sector	No of projects		Cost $m	
	Total planned & funded since 1985	Funded by October 2008	Total planned & funded since 1985	Funded by October 2008
Roads	77	33	84,627	14,264
Rail	37	27	53,101	13,062
Water*	176	129	18,523	12,973
Buildings	152	146	12,588	9,123
Total	442	335	168,839	49,422

Source: International Public Works Financing, October 2008. * includes fees for long-term service contracts.

Asset monetisation – private leasing of public infrastructure
Asset monetisation creates large-scale investment opportunities, bigger than most social infrastructure projects. Asset monetisation is privatisation – a 50-99 year lease is virtually as good as ownership. Leases are likely to be resold to other investors during the lease period, each time ratcheting the pressure to increase tolls and make concessions on the terms of the lease. Ultimately, the government would 'own' less and less of the infrastructure, and conversely, more and more would be under private control. A continuing decline in the public asset base could lower the credit rating of public bodies and affect their ability to borrow for other infrastructure projects.

The new highwaymen
Goldman Sachs, JP Morgan and Citigroup promote asset monetisation in presentations to local government and public sector bodies across the US. This is often win-win work for which they either get to finance deals or receive large fees for advising government bodies. Unsolicited bids drive state and local government into commissioning consultants and advisers to assess them and to respond to campaigns initiated by corporate interests. Asset

monetisation reviews are becoming another lucrative activity for financial advisers and management consultants. An unsolicited bid for a US$500m upfront payment and 60-year lease for the Port of Virginia in March 2009 from CenterPoint Properties, a subsidiary of a company ultimately owned by the California Public Employees Retirement System (CalPERS), triggered the submission of other bids under Virginia's Public-Private Transportation Act. Not surprisingly, the Carlyle Group and Goldman Sachs sailed into port with rival bids for '... *what could become the first long-term lease of an entire US port*' (Infrastructure Investor, 2009).

Chicago City Council set the pace in asset monetisation, with a 99-year lease for the Chicago Skyway (US$1.83bn) and the downtown parking system (US$563m) and 35,000 parking meters (US$1.16bn), see Table 21.

The Mayor of Chicago claimed that the Skyway money would be invested in people and help '... *to protect Chicago taxpayers both today and in the future*' (TOLLROADSnews, 2005). Nearly half of the US$1.83bn obtained by Chicago City Council was used to pay off existing debt, which improved the city's credit rating and reduced the cost of borrowing. US$463m was used to refund Skyway debt and US$392m other debt. The City put US$500m into a long-term reserve fund, US$375m into a medium-term annuity to be used to support the budget in times of austerity and the remaining $100m was put into a fund to improve the quality of life in neighbourhoods, such as for jobs, housing programmes and facilities for children and the elderly.

Indiana and Chicago had not raised tolls since 1985 and 1993 respectively but the PPP ensures annual increases for 99 years! Tolls doubled from US$4 to US$8 on 1 April 2008.

The one-hour parking in the Millennium Park Garage has risen 31% to US$17 since 2006. Tolls on the Skyway are now 50% higher since the leasing deal (Chicago Tribune, 7 September 2008). The Chicago parking meter contract is based on graduated meter rate increases of over 50% over five years – high congestion downtown rates will more than double from US$3.00 to US$6.50 by 2013 after which rates are inflation linked plus scope for extending hours and more metering (Infrastructure Investor, 2 December 2008).

New Jersey Governor Jon Corzine, planned to asset monetize the New Jersey Turnpike, Parkway and Atlantic City Expressway to obtain between US$32bn – $38bn for a 75-year PPP which would be used to pay off half of the state's US$32bn debt and create a fund to repair

Table 21: Asset monetisation in the US

Asset	Authority	Consortia	Date	Upfront payment $m	Contract length (years)	Price – Revenue ratio
Chicago Skyway (7.8 miles)	City of Chicago	Cintra (Spain) and Macquarie (Australia)	2005	1,830	99	40
Dulles Greenway (14 miles)	Virginia	Original $350m PPP project opened 1995, acquired by Macquarie Infrastructure Group (Australia), operated by Autostrade (Italy)	2005	617	62.5	n/a
Indiana Toll Road (157 miles)	Indiana	Cintra (Spain) and Macquarie Infrastructure Group (Australia)	2006	3,850	75	40
Pocahontas Parkway, Richmond, 9 miles, unsolicited	Virginia	Original $324m PPP project opened 2002, acquired by Transurban Ltd (Australia)	2006	611	99	56
Northwest Parkway, Colorado, 11 miles	Colorado	Brisa (Portugal and CCR (Brazil)	2007	603	99	90
Capital Beltway, addition of HOT lanes	Virginia	Transurban Group (Australia), Fluor Corporation	2007	1,524	90	n/a
Chicago Downtown Public Parking System (9,178 spaces)	City of Chicago	Morgan Stanley Infrastructure and LAZ Parking (Vinci)	2006	563	99	n/a
On-street parking (36,000 meters)	Chicago City Council	Morgan Stanley Infrastructure and LAZ Parking (Vinci)	2008	1,160	75	n/a
Interstate 595	Florida	Actividades de Construccion & Servcios (ACS, Spain)	2009	1,800	35	n/a
LBJ 635 corridor rebuild	Texas	Cintra, Meridiam, Ferrovial, Macquarie (preferred bidder)	2009	n/a	52	n/a

Dexter Whitfield

Asset	Authority	Consortia	Date	Upfront payment $m	Contract length (years)	Price – Revenue ratio
Failed projects						
I-81, 325 miles, unsolicited	Virginia	STAR Solutions (KBR Inc) proposal then preferred bidder, 6 years of negotiations ended Jan 2008 with no contract.	2002	n/a	n/a	n/a
Stewart International Airport, New York	Port Authority of New York & New Jersey	National Express Group (UK), re-acquired – see Chapter 8	2000-2007	35	99	n/a
Pennsylvania Turnpike, 531 miles	Pennsylvania	Citigroup Inc and Albertis Infrastructure SA. Consortium withdrew September 2008	2008	12,800	75	21
Chicago Midway Airport	Chicago City Council	Citigroup (89%), Vancouver Airport (3%) and John Hancock Life Insurance (8%). Failed to raise equity for upfront fee	2009	2,500	99	28
Alligator Alley, I-75, 78 miles	Florida	No bids received. Four shortlisted included Alinda/Vinci.	2009	n/a	50	n/a

Source: US Federal Highway Administration, Chicago City Council, Wall Street Journal.

and maintain roads and bridges. In his 2008 State of the State speech, Corzine admitted that tolls would increase by 50% in 2010 and then 50% every four years until 2022. The project was abandoned after strong community opposition.

A US$12.8bn plan to lease the 537-mile Pennsylvania Turnpike failed in 2008. Two years earlier the state Transportation Funding and Reform Commission identified the need for US$1.7bn additional annual spending to maintain the current network. The following year, the Democratic Governor, Edward Rendell, proposed leasing the Turnpike, but met strong local opposition. The Turnpike Commission proposed a toll increase and sought Federal permission to toll Interstate 80. The state passed legislation (Act 44 of 2007), which guaranteed nearly US$1bn income annually for roads and public transport by issuing US$5bn special revenue bonds and US$4.1bn in bonds against tolls on the Pennsylvania Turnpike.

Shortly after the Act was passed, the Governor revived the leasing proposal and sought offers. Citigroup Inc and Albertis Infrastructure (Spain) joint US$12.8bn bid was accepted, ahead of a US$12.1bn bid from Goldman Sachs/Transurban Group (Australia) and a US$8.1bn from Macquarie Infrastructure Group/Cintra (Spain). The bids were below expectations (US$12bn – $18bn) which helped to galvanise opposition. The Governor's plan to save most of the proceeds and use the interest to pay for infrastructure projects also came unstuck, because it far exceeded the returns forecast by the State's pension funds and its own advisers (Pew Center, 2009).

State legislation authorising the use of PPPs became law in June 2008 but specifically prohibited leasing the turnpike. In autumn 2008 the US Federal Highway Administration rejected the I-80 toll proposal because it did not meet legal requirements for the correct use of toll revenue (Federal Highway Administration, 11 Sept 2008). A few weeks later Citi/Albertis allowed their bid to lapse because the state legislature had failed to approve the project.

Houston 'not for sale, not for lease'
Harris County Commissioners voted unanimously to continue to operate the Hardy, Sam Houston and Westpark toll roads after studying three options – publicly owned and operated, sale and concession agreement – prepared by Citigroup, Goldman Sachs and JP Morgan respectively in 2006 (Harris County, 2006).

The investment banks had forecasted that a sale or concession would have a gross value of between US$3bn and $20bn despite the toll road system generating US$373m revenue in 2006, which was spent in reducing the debt and improving the toll road system. The Harris County Toll Road Authority already uses toll-backed revenue bonds to fund publicly financed road projects – with a lower cost of capital than the private sector. Citigroup advised the County to value its own bonding capacity, which could be about US$8bn.

Goldman Sachs reported '... *a concession term of less than 50 years, linked with retention of strong oversight and decision-making by the county, and extraction of a percentage of ongoing operating revenues, would result in a low upfront yield for the county*' (ibid). A 99-year contract was valued at between US$10bn – $13bn with a low level of county control and no share of 'excess' toll revenue, compared to US$7.5bn – $10bn for a

50-year concession.

Texas also attempted to lease the 24 mile Dallas/Forth Worth Highway 121 and agreed a 49-year deal with a Cintra/JP Morgan consortia to provide a US$2.1bn lump sum plus $700m payments over the lease. However, opposition to the deal led to the North Texas Tollway Authority (NTTA), a state agency, submitting a higher US$3.3bn offer that was accepted. NTTA successfully borrowed US$3.5bn to use short-term notes to be replaced by long-term bonds in 2008. The right-wing Reason Foundation argued for the Cintra deal because if the company went bankrupt, private investors would bear all the financial losses, rather than Texas citizens. Simplicity itself!

The Dulles Greenway toll road, from Dulles International Airport, Washington DC, to Leesburg, Virginia, was a completely private venture, intended to exploit potential property development along the commuter route. The US$279m fourteen-mile highway opened in 1995 with a forecast of 34,000 daily traffic but actual demand was 10,500 causing a financial default (Bailey, 1996). Toll charges were reduced and the project was refinanced in 1999. Traffic slowly climbed to 70,000 vehicles per day by 2005, when Macquarie Infrastructure Group paid US$617.5m to acquire the project (Garvin and Bosso, 2008). The highway has a virtual monopoly because it is much faster than alternative routes and there is no mass transit system in the area. Tolls increased in January 2009, which led to an 8% drop in traffic, but toll income increased 11% to US$167,453 per day (Washington Post, 2009).

Some of the key implications of long-term leases for tolled highways were highlighted by a Government Accountability Office study:

'Though concession agreements can limit the extent to which a concessionaire can raise tolls, it is likely that tolls will increase on a privately operated highway to a greater extent than they would on a publicly operated toll road. To the extent that a private concessionaire gains market power by control of a road where there are not other viable travel alternatives that would not require substantially more travel time, the potential also exists that the public could pay tolls that are higher than tolls based on cost of the facilities, including a reasonable rate of return.

Furthermore, by leasing existing facilities, the public sector may give up more than it gains if the net present value of the future stream of revenues (less operating and capital costs) given up exceeds the concession payment received. Conversely, because the private sector takes on potentially substantial risks, the opposite could also be true – that is, the public sector might gain more than it gives up. Additionally, because large up-front concession payments have in part been used to fund immediate needs, it remains to be seen whether these agreements will provide long-term benefits to future generations who will potentially be paying progressively higher toll rates throughout the length of a concession agreement' (General Accountability Office, 2008).

States are forecast to have $230bn deficit from fiscal years 2008-2010 with at least a $45bn deficit in 2011 due to reduced sales, income and corporate tax receipts (National Association of State Budget Officers, 2009). The subprime and global credit squeeze has led to lower consumption of household items, furniture, construction materials and thus lower state tax income. States then cut elementary and higher education, public assistance, Medicaid, transportation and staffing levels to balance budgets.

A number of US states are planning to sell or lease lotteries. Utilities, water systems, parking and airports are likely to be next and any public asset, where there is a revenue stream from user charges or fees, is considered 'in scope'. Pittsburgh is also considering monetizing its 11 parking garages (Infrastructure Investor, 24 Feb, 2009). A New York State Commission study of asset monetisation and assets suitable for PPPs recommended transportation, schools, healthcare, the state university and energy projects overseen by a new State Asset Maximisation Board (New York State Commission on Asset Maximisation, 2009). A Citizens Budget Commission study had earlier recommended PPPs for New York City schools, parks and higher educational facilities (Citizens Budget Commission, 2008). A consultants study for the City of Los Angeles identified lessons learnt from previous PPPs, which included the public sector being allowed to compete with the private sector, PPPs being limited in size and phased over time and current pay and conditions maintained for staff (Public Financial Management, 2008).

Canada
The Federal Government launched a seven-year C$33bn Building Canada Infrastructure Plan in 2007 with five funding elements – C$25m annual base funding for Provinces and Territories, C$17.6bn over seven years to municipalities from the Gas Tax Fund and the Goods and Services Tax rebate, the Building Canada Fund for major infrastructure, a C$2.1bn Gateway and Border Crossings fund and a C$1.25bn fund to subsidise 'innovative' PPP projects. All projects

seeking over C$50m federal contribution must be assessed and considered for the P3 option (Infrastructure Canada, 2008). The government has financed PPP Canada Inc, a federal corporation, C$25m over five years to create a national PPP market. However, except for the Provincial/Territory base funding, all the Building Canada infrastructure funds are previous announcements that are being extended or repackaged, and will mean a declining level of federal infrastructure finance (Moist, 2008).

Responsibility for public infrastructure investment has shifted from national and provincial levels to the local level. In the period 1955 to 2007 the federal share of public infrastructure declined from 26.9% to 5.3% whilst local government responsibility increased from 26.7% to 54.9%. The provincial share declined from 46.4% to 39.8% in the same period (Brox, 2008). Local revenue sources, primarily property taxes, have not kept pace with infrastructure investment and maintenance needs, thus creating a 'municipal fiscal deficit' (ibid). This has been compounded by national and provincial legislation on 'balanced budgets'. The municipal infrastructure deficit reached C$123bn in 2007 (Mirza, 2007)

Canada has 58 signed PPP projects at a capital cost of over C$10bn plus 28 projects in procurement including a Federal police project not included in Table 22. Health accounts for 50% of projects with roads and bridges 25%. The Canadian PPP geography varies between provinces such as British Columbia, Alberta and Ontario with significant programmes compared with minimal programmes in other provinces to date. A series of failures and significant cost overruns in New Brunswick and Nova Scotia effectively stalled projects in these provinces.

A further 16 PPPs were abandoned, terminated or significantly reduced in scope in Canada between 1996-2009 (see chapter 8). Evidence of the use of Public Sector Comparators and the way that value-for-money was justified for several Canadian projects is examined in chapter 9.

PPP consortia in Canada include a number of international firms such as Babcock & Brown (Alberta schools), Bilfinger Berger (Edmonton ring road and Kelowna-Vernon Hospital, British Columbia), John Laing (Abbotsford Regional Hospital, Diamond Health Care Center and Kelowna-Vernon Hospital, British Columbia).

Although there has been a sale of equity in at least five Canadian PPP contracts (see chapter 7), the secondary market in refinancing and equity sales has been minimal to date.

Table 22: *Signed PPP contracts in Canada (in procurement)*

	British Columbia	Alberta	Ontario	Quebec	New Brunswick	Northwest Territories	Manitoba	Total Signed
Roads/ bridges	6 (1)	3 (1)	(1)	4	1	(1) 1	(2)	15
Rapid transit	1							1
Health	5 (2)		24 (5)	1 (4)				30
Water	1 (1)		1				(1)	2
Schools		1 (1)			(1)			1
Residential care	1							1
Courts		1 (2)		1 (1)				2
Other	1		4 (3)	1				6
Total	**15**	**4**	**30**	**6**	**2**	**1**		**58**

Source: PPP Project Tracker, CCPPP, July 2009 and Provincial PPP websites. Figures in brackets are projects in procurement.

Canadian public sector pension funds have been investing heavily in global infrastructure funds and acquiring previously privatised assets (see chapters 4 and 5). For example, the Ontario Municipal Employees Retirement System (OMERS) subsidiary, Borealis Infrastructure, increased its total investment in infrastructure to 15% and has acquired full or partial stakes in the Detroit-Windsor Tunnel, Associated British Ports, Scotia Gas Networks and projects in Canada. The Ontario Teachers' Pension Plan, with C$87.4bn assets in 2008, an 18% decline on the previous year, in the last two years spent C$926m acquiring 51% and 69% stakes in the second and third largest water companies in Chile and acquired SAESA Group, a Chilean electricity distribution, transmission and generation company, in a US$887m joint deal with Morgan Stanley Infrastructure. OMERS also acquired a 48% stake in Birmingham International Airport in the UK in a £420m joint deal with Australia's Victoria Funds Management Corporation, a state investment company.

In 1999, 'the largest toll road privatisation in the world' saw a Cintra/SNC-Lavalin and Capital D'Amerique consortium win a C$3.1bn 99-year lease for the Toronto 407 Express Toll Route. Macquarie Infrastructure Group acquired the Capital D'Amerique interest in 2002. Asset monetisation was also recently on the agenda of the Mayor of Toronto's Fiscal Review Panel, which recommended that Toronto Hydro (electricity distribution), Toronto Parking Authority and the Don Valley Parkway and Gardiner Expressway be considered for asset monetisation, which could net the city an estimated C$3.5 billion. Led by Blake Hutcheson, the president of commercial real estate giant CB Richard Ellis, the Panel recognised that the city has '... *chronic revenue and expense problems and huge unfunded capital requirements and other contingent liabilities*' but is not facing a financial crisis (Toronto City Council, 2008). It also recommended consolidating infrastructure assets into a new department, more outsourcing and centralized control of the city's 119 Agencies, Boards, Commissions and Corporations.

Alberta revised a 14-school PPP project by excluding four high schools, accounting for 37% of student capacity, which will now be design and build projects. The Alberta government claimed they had *'refined our model'* (Government of Alberta, 2009), but the first education PPP project for 18 schools in Calgary and Edmonton was signed in 2008 with Babcock & Brown, which has since been in financial crisis. An analysis of Alberta's first schools PPP concluded that '... *for every two schools financed using the P3 model, an additional school could be built if they were all financed using conventional public sector financing*' (MacKenzie, 2007).

Meanwhile on a totally different scale, the Alberta tar sands, with an estimated 175-200 billion barrels of recoverable oil, is the centre of an energy mega-corridor, linking the Arctic in the north (with estimated 90 billion barrels of recoverable oil) to the US in the south through vast network of pipelines (Clarke, 2008). '... *the infrastructure has been laid for the tar sands industry to extract, produce, deliver, and refine crude oil to fuel the US*' (ibid). Yet the '... *burning of natural gas to produce oil from the tar sands produces more than three times the amount of greenhouse gases conventional oil production does*' (ibid).

Russia

The mass privatisation of infrastructure and the economy, by voucher auctions, between 1992-94, was corrupt, disorganised and led to social disruption and a slump in production (Black *et al*, 2000). Renationalisation in the last five years, particularly of oil and gas interests, coupled with the consolidation of state owned banks, was part of Putin's strategy for the state to regain control over key profitable resources (Wisniewska, 2007).

According to a study of 3m working age men, mass privatisation was responsible for the early deaths of 1m people in Russia (Stuckler et al, 2009). Alcohol poisoning and poor diet were also major contributors to the surge in mortality figures. The architect of the mass privatisation programme, predictably, disagreed with these findings (Sachs, 2009).

The first PPPs were announced in 2005 following passage of a federal law permitting concessions. The St Petersburg Western High Speed Diameter, a 47km eight-lane motorway, 55% elevated across the city and the Gulf of Finland, became the flagship project. Initially there were four bidders, but a Basic Element-led bid (with Hochtief PPP Solutions, Strabag and Bouygues) was the only bidder in June 2008. The project has been delayed until 2011 after the transport infrastructure budget was cut by 90% (Infrastructure Investor, 2009) and St Petersburg's budget was cut by a third (Central and Eastern Europe Bankwatch Network, 2009). The project is 50% funded by the government with the concessionaire and city council funding 34% and 16% respectively. The government will provide guaranteed minimum revenue because of the limited track record of toll roads in Russia. The legal framework for PPPs remains untested.

Other large infrastructure projects in the pipeline include a US$15bn Moscow-St Petersburg highway; the Sochi 2014 Winter Olympics facilities; a joint Russian Aluminium and Unified Energy System, the power monopoly, hydropower plant and aluminium smelter in Siberia; and other St Petersburg projects such as the Orlovsky Tunnel, Pulkovo Airport reconstruction and the Nadex light rail link.

Unified Energy was divided into 24 generating companies with stakes sold to domestic and foreign investors including Eon (Germany), Enel (Italy) and Fortum (Finland) in return for a commitment to a US$59bn investment programme and a government agreement to liberalise the electricity market by 2011. However, this timetable appears to be in doubt (Financial Times, 2009).

The EBRD and the Russian Bank for Development (Vnesheconombank) signed a memorandum of understanding in 2008, to explore the possibility of co-financing projects in transport infrastructure, energy and municipal services and a special unit to promote PPPs. In June 2008 the government launched a US$570bn programme for roads, railways, airports and ports, of which US$215bn will be financed by national and regional expenditure with the remaining US$355bn from the Investment Fund and private investors. This programme has been significantly delayed by the global economic crisis.

Oligarch Oleg Deripaska owns Basic Element and Russian Aluminium and plans to invest US$20bn in St Petersburg projects by 2015. He also recently invested in German construction firms Hochtief and Strabag to gain PPP expertise.

Australia
Australia has had an important role in the global infrastructure market with over 80 PPP projects at various stages of planning, procurement and operation, plus its financial institutions, Macquarie Bank and Babcock & Brown in particular (see chapter 5), aggressively acquired infrastructure assets and/or financed PPPs in many countries.

Australia is also significant because it has a very high PPP failure rate. Seven projects have failed (see chapter 8) out of a total of 49 projects (five failed projects are no longer included in the national pipeline of PPP projects) giving a 14.3% failure rate (13.1% by value), which is more than twice the 6.1% failure rate (7.2% by value) of transport, energy, telecoms and water PPPs in developing countries between 1990-2007.

Two states, New South Wales and Victoria, dominate the PPP programme with other states and the Federal government each having only a handful of projects. As the Australian PPP programme has developed, the range of projects has diversified (roads, public transport, hospitals, schools, prisons and courts) which mirrors the scope of the much larger UK PPP programme (see Table 23).

12 projects were in procurement (schools, prisons, housing) with a further 20 projects at the planning stage in December 2008. The Brisconnections saga in Queensland, which involved major Australian PPP companies and Deutsche Bank, is a reminder of the price paid for deficient financial project design (chapter 5).

The Labour government established a A$20bn Building Australia Fund for critical economic infrastructure such as roads, rail, ports and broadband together with Infrastructure Australia (IA), which is responsible for developing a blueprint for long-term infrastructure needs. An existing Communications Fund was merged into the fund. Infrastructure Australia reports to the Council of Australian Governments (COAG) through the Federal Minister for Infrastructure, Transport, Regional Development and Local Government. Seven

Table 23: Signed and planned PPPs in Australia

State	No. of projects	Capital value A$	Signed Projects by sector	No. of projects	Capital value A$
Government of Australia	2	n/a	Public transport	3	4,446
New South Wales	17	11,953	Hospitals	7	5,120
Northern Territory	1	300	Schools	4	1,113
Queensland	3	1,760	Roads	5	7,096
South Australia	1	40	Housing	1	368
Tasmania	1	n/a	Police/Courts/Prisons	7	904
Victoria	18	6,038	Water/Wastewater	4	199
Western	1	69	Convention Centre	2	667
			other	7	578
Total	**44**	**20,160**		**44**	**20,491**

Source: National PPP Forum, Australia, December, 2008.

national infrastructure priorities were established in 2009 embracing the national broadband network, national energy market, international gateways, national rail freight network, increasing public transport in cities, improved indigenous infrastructure and improved water supplies (Infrastructure Australia, 2009a). Nine priority projects have been identified and a further 28 will be further assessed. The public/private balance is unclear, although IA is committed to PPPs and has produced best practice guidance (Infrastructure Australia, 2009b).

The government also established an A$11bn Education Investment Fund to finance capital investment in higher education and vocational training, absorbing the smaller Higher Education Endowment Fund. A A$10bn Health and Hospitals Fund was also established, bringing the initial investment to A$40bn. The three funds were initially funded from budget surpluses. The government also funded new water policy and renewable energy programmes.

South Australia's plan to locate new men's and women's prisons and a Forensic Mental Health centre at Murray Bridge, 80km east of Adelaide, has been delayed until 2013/14 because of the current economic crisis. Two Public Services Association commissioned studies revealed fundamental flaws in the PPP. Firstly, a review of primarily US evidence on the economic and social impact of relocating prisons in rural areas revealed a wide range of negative consequences for communities, staff, prisoners and their families (Whitfield, 2008). An

Australian Institute for Social Research survey of 252 existing prison staff (59.6% response rate) in autumn 2008, identified A$33m direct and indirect costs in the first year of operation arising from staff, family and friends commuting (AISR, 2008).

The government-led A$43bn high-speed National Broadband Network was launched in 2009 after the government cancelled a Singapore Telecommunications-led joint venture because it would serve only 72% rather than 90% of under-served premises. Telstra, Australia's largest telecommunication operator, privatised in three shares sales spread over a decade up to 2006, had earlier had their proposal for a high-speed network rejected. The government will establish a majority-owned company and utilise A$4.7bn allocated for the broadband project in the Building Australia fund and will raise additional finance by selling infrastructure bonds.

'It was always a private sector project' was how the then New South Wales Government Minister for Roads conveniently described Sydney's Cross City Tunnel (CCT), which went into receivership less than two years after opening in August 2005 (Australian Broadcasting Corporation, 28 December 2006). The CrossCity Motorway Consortium (CCM) of Cheung Kong Infrastructure Holdings (Hong Kong) and Bilfinger Berger (Germany), advised by Hyder Consulting, had forecast 91,000 trips per day by the end 2006, but only 30,000 vehicles used the tunnel daily. Even a toll-free period in October/November 2005 only increased traffic to just over 50,000 vehicles per day.

The New South Wales government adopted the PPP option to avoid increasing government debt and also sought a 'business consideration fee' from the bidders to cover the government's A$98m preparation and ancillary works costs (Asia Case Research Centre, 2007). CrossCity Motorway Consortium offered a fee of A$100.1m. CCM's proposals to increase the length of the tunnel by 300 metres and increase the eastern end depth by 30 metres were accepted – and increased daily capacity by 17,000 vehicles and increased potential toll income by A$10.98m per annum! CCM also proposed changes to the road network and traffic calming measures which had the effect of channelling traffic into the tunnel. CCM also required the government '... *to pay compensation if any changes to the Sydney public transport system had a material effect on the amount of traffic traversing the toll road tunnel ... and could amount to as much as A$100m annually*' (ibid).

The tunnel was acquired by investment bank ABN Amro and Leighton Holdings (Hochtief, Germany) for A$700m in June 2007.

CKI Holdings, Deutsche Bank and Westpac Bank were expected to receive less than a fifth of their equity in the project. Tolls rose 13% in February 2008 – described as a 'one-off adjustment' to take account of the toll free/freezes used earlier and return to the one per cent toll increase allowed every quarter under the contract. There is a dearth of traffic flow information.

Whether this project should ever have been constructed is a moot point. Selecting the PPP route and miscalculating the traffic forecasts (which meant revenue was significantly less than that required) and the likely community response to high tolls and the traffic management scheme, which curtailed access to some areas and funnelled traffic into the tunnel, were the fundamental failures.

An Australian secondary market is emerging, for example, through the sale of equity in the Lane Cove Tunnel. In July 2004 ABN Amro and Transfield Infrastructure sold their equity and AMP Life reduced its stake from 12.9% to 0.88% and Theiss and John Holland reduced their stakes from 10.13% each to 5.53% each. The 54.9% stake was sold to CKI Lane Cove Holdings (Malaysia) Ltd (40%) and Seamax Ltd, a subsidiary of Li Ka Shing (Overseas) Foundation (14.9%). In March 2007 these two shareholders sold a 19% stake to Macquarie Bank thus reducing their stakes to 30.5% and 5.4% respectively. AMP Life subsequently sold its remaining 0.88% stake.

China

Infrastructure investment has a key role in China's fiscal stimulus policies (chapter 2) continuing large-scale investment across all types of infrastructure. China now has 53,600km of toll expressways to rival the US interstate network and has a 70,000km target by 2020. The rail network is also being rapidly expanded after lagging behind road investment. China Railways now carry a quarter of the world's traffic on 6% of the global track length (World Bank, 2007). With US$42bn investment in 2008, compared to US$72bn in the previous five years, it has what is claimed to be the largest railway expansion of any country since the 19th century (The Economist, 2008). Projects include the 1,300km high-speed line between Beijing and Shanghai and the Beijing-Tianjin bullet train. China plans to have a 120,000km network by 2015, half of which will be electrified.

Annual investment in roads was US$24bn or 2.5% of GDP since 1998 and the capacity of water production and the length of the water network increased nearly 50% between 1990-98. The public sector financed 90% of infrastructure investment in the decade to 2002 (Bellier and Zhou, 2003).

China's 11th five-year programme development plan 2006-2010 includes US$175bn for five inter-city railways, plus upgrading of five existing routes, fourteen new expressways, improved facilities at 12 seaports and construction of the Yangtze golden waterway to increase shipping capacity. Water prices will be restructured, 70% of urban wastewater and 60% of residential garbage will be treated.

China has also invested heavily in PPPs and privatisation having 804 projects signed between 1990-2007 with a capital value of US$100bn. Transport, energy, telecoms accounting for 42.5%, 35.5% and 14.5% of the value of projects respectively with water and sewage accounting for 7.5%. Over half were greenfield projects.

Land reform has played a key role in providing finance for investment. The sale of State owned urban land has become very significant '... *amounting to almost 20 per cent of the total fiscal revenue nationally (Ministry of Finance, 2008) and over 50 per cent of total fiscal revenues locally in some cities. The majority of local governments have become more or less reliant on land sale receipts, taxes on development and transaction of property to finance massive infrastructure projects. As land sales revenues are extra-budgetary, those local governments that can sell more land at higher prices are more capable of investing in infrastructure and bringing about economic development*' (Cao, 2009).

An infrastructure market is emerging in China with the sale of toll roads. Road King Infrastructure Ltd has a HK$6bn investment in 19 toll road and bridge projects spanning 1,000km in eight provinces and has expanded into property development. The company has between 45%-70% interest in each project with 25-30 year concessions. Annual toll revenue almost doubled in the 2002 06 period. Road King has two major investors, Shenzhen Investment Ltd (which purchased its 23% stake from Stagecoach Group, the UK's bus and rail operator for US$93m) and Wai Kee Holdings, listed in Hong Kong. China Merchants Holdings Pacific, Singapore, acquired five toll roads for US$336.5m from China's Communications Ministry in 2004.

Not surprisingly, Macquarie is building investment stakes in China. Macquarie International Infrastructure Fund (MIIF) paid US$329.5m for an 81% stake in 2007 in the Guangzhou's Hua Nan Expressway, a 31km toll road connecting the city with the port of Nansha. It also has a 38% stake in the Chanshu Xinghua Port on the Yangtze River.

Continued economic growth, increasing population and urbanisation could mean that China will have 221 cities each with more than one million people by 2025, of which 23 cities will have more than five million inhabitants (McKinsey, 2009). The urban population is forecast to increase from 572m in 2005 to 926m in 2025, an increase larger than the present US population! The infrastructure implications are vast – between 700-900 Gigawatts of new coal-fired power, 170 cities needing mass transit systems, 28,000 kilometres of metropolitan rail lines, water and wastewater systems and a vast array of other infrastructure requirements. The level of infrastructure investment required will place severe strains on public finances plus foreign infrastructure investors and operators are likely to demand '... *greater protection and flexibility*', fiscal transparency of projects to evaluate risks and returns, and the fiscal stability of cities (Ibid).

Water companies such as Veolia and Suez have acquired water treatment plants and waste water operations in China, where foreign investors can acquire minority stakes (up to 49%) in water distribution networks in large cities and own or participate in joint ventures for wastewater plants. Foreign investment accounts for less than 10% of the total investment in this sector (KPMG, 2008). About half of public water investment in 2008 was concentrated in fortifying several thousand reservoirs and upgrading irrigation. Only 20% of the population has access to unpolluted drinking water and water shortages are a major problem in two third of Chinese cities.

China has significant investment in African infrastructure projects primarily to facilitate the extraction and transport of energy and mineral resources (chapter 2).

By May 2008, Chinese companies and financial institutions had 97 large dam projects in 39 countries, including 7 projects in Pakistan, 3 in Iran, 16 in Myanmar, 7 in Cambodia and 13 in Laos (International Rivers, 2008). Most are funded by the Chinese government's export credit agency, China Exim Bank. Its rules require at least 50% of materials must be sourced from China (ibid). This significantly reduces economic benefits for production and supply chains in the host country. China's interests are two-fold. It has built half of the worlds' largest dams and thus established a high capacity dam-building, equipment and financing industry and it wants to secure access to natural resources to secure economic development.

Following completion of the massive US$25bn Three Gorges Dam on the Yangtze River in China, which displaced 1.3m people, the government is building a cascade of 12 dams on the Jinsha River, a 13-dam cascade on the Nu River and an eight-dam project on the Lancang River.

The rapid rebound of the Chinese real estate market in 2009 – property prices in 70 cities were back to a 1% monthly increase on the previous month – led to China's property developers and their Wall Street backers '... *rushing to raise billions of dollars in initial public offering, rescuing real estate investments that just a few months ago were considered victims of the economic crisis*' (Wall Street Journal, 2009). However, the variable quality of infrastructure, the lack of democratic accountability in infrastructure planning, conflicting climate change/environmental sustainability and industrial policies and poor health and safety on building sites remain key issues.

India

Infrastructure investment in the Eleventh Five-year Plan (2007/08 to 2011/12) is expected to increase from 5% of GDP in 2006/07 to 9% at the end of the planning period. Planned total investment is Rs 2,027,169 crore (US$494bn in constant 2006/07 prices) with 70.3% financed by the public sector. The private sector is expected to increase its investment from the 18% achieved in the Tenth Plan to nearly 30% (Government of India, 2009).

Two hundred and thirty three PPP and privatisation infrastructure projects, valued at US$69bn reached financial close in India between 1990-2006. Telecoms accounted for just over half of the investment with energy (30%), transport (19%) and water a mere 0.2% (PPIAF, 2009). Privatisation accounted for only 13 projects but they accounted for 9% in value.

The National Highway Development Programme (NHDP) plans nearly 46,000km of new and upgraded major roads, of which, 86% will be via PPPs (Government of India, 2009). In addition, PPPs for nearly 5,000km of state highways were approved by March 2009. However, the NHDP did not receive a single bid for 38 out of 60 PPP projects by April 2009 (Wall Street Journal, 2009). Private sector investment of up to US$50bn over a five-year period is considered optimistic and '... *only a fraction of this amount is likely to be raised without substantive reforms*' (Asian Development Bank, 2007), by which they mean more privatisation, liberalisation and cost-based tariffs.

Two dedicated rail freight corridors, the 1,279km eastern and 1,483km western routes, are planned and private investment is being explored. The government has identified 26 stations in cities and major tourist centres to become '... *world-class stations through the PPP route*' by harnessing their real estate potential (Government of India, 2009). Two thirds of the planned investment in the twelve major ports will be via PPPs and global firms such as Maersk, P&O and Dubai Ports International are already established in some ports.

Four major airports, Delhi, Mumbai, Bangalore and Hyderabad, are privately operated and two-thirds of the 35 non-metro airports planned for modernisation, together with new mostly greenfield airports, will be PPP projects. City-airport rail links and extensions to metro rails systems in the four cities are also being developed as PPP projects.

Central and state governments provision account for 84.6% of electricity generation in India, although this is likely to fall as more private power projects are commissioned. Nine Ultra Mega Power Plants, each with an initial capacity of 4,000 megawatts, are planned and '... *the option of PPPs in nuclear power generation is being explored*' (ibid).

The government also plans 2,500 schools and 1,500 industrial training institutes via PPPs. Few health and water PPP projects are planned.

The government established a Committee on Infrastructure in 2004, chaired by the Prime Minister, to create a 'world class infrastructure' and maximise the role of public private partnerships. It also established a national PPP Appraisal Committee and introduced new legislation and regulations in 2005, together with 'viability gap' funding of grants to cover up to 40% of private sector project costs. It also set up the India Infrastructure Finance Company Ltd (IIFCL), which can provide loans up to 20% of project costs and refinance loans. In December 2007 the Asian Development Bank agreed to provide IIFCL with up to US$500m in loans to promote PPPs. It will also include capacity building and training for IIFCL staff. A US$40bn PPP road-building programme will extend the private sector toll road network.

Several private equity funds have launched new investment funds to finance projects in India. Citigroup and Blackstone Group teamed up with IIFCL and the Infrastructure Finance Development Corporation (IFDC) to launch the India Infrastructure Financing Initiative with US$5bn in 2007. Citigroup, Blackstone and IFDC will invest US$250m with the balance coming from international and domestic investors.

3i raised US$1.2bn from 16 investors in 10 countries for power, road, port and airport projects. *The Indian government are probably the smartest government in terms of policy in the infrastructure area of any country in the world. They have a very clear strategic agenda. Over the last four or five years they have put in place a series of policy measures to create a very good framework for enabling these projects to happen'* (Michael Queen, managing partner and head of 3i infrastructure, PPP Bulletin, May 2008).

Macquarie Capital Group, the State Bank of India (each with a 45% stake) and the International Finance Corporation (IFC), part of the World Bank group, raised an initial US$450m to launch the fund in April 2008. Within days Axis Private Equity (US$150m) and Quantum Equity Partners (US$500m) had also launched infrastructure funds for India (Emerging Markets Now, March and April, 2008).

Brazil

The World Bank PPP database reported 328 signed PPP and privatisation projects in Brazil between 1990-2007 with telecoms accounting for 50% of the capital value but only 11% of the total number of projects. Energy and transport accounted for 36% and 12% respectively of the capital value. Water and sewage accounted for 17% of projects but just 2% of total investment (Public Private Infrastructure Advisory Facility, 2009).

The Integration of Regional Infrastructure in South America (IIRSA) is a coalition of twelve national governments and multilateral financial institutions such as the Inter-American Development Bank and the Andean Development Corporation plus the national development banks such as Banco Nacional de Desenvolvimento Econômico Social (BNDES), the Brazilian Development Bank. Launched in 2000, IIRSA aims to improve the physical infrastructure in 12 South American countries to promote trade, competitiveness and economic development in the region. IIRSA has a portfolio of 514 projects of which 87% are transport, 11% energy and 2% telecommunications. In capital terms, transport accounts for sixty percent of investment with energy the remainder (Integration of Regional Infrastructure in South America, 2008).

By December 2008, finance had been arranged for two-thirds of the projects with US$17.6bn public funding of 190 projects, US$13.4bn funded with 29 public-private financed projects and US$7.2bn private funding for 28 projects (ibid). The Madeira hydroelectric complex is a major IIRSA project, which includes two dams to generate 6,450MW, a 2,500km transmission line and 4,200km waterway to transport barge trains upstream and downstream to the Amazon estuary and the Atlantic. New road links in the Peru-Brazil-Bolivia 'hub' would connect the Andes region and Peruvian Pacific ports, widening export routes for Brazilian grain, timber and other products (International Rivers, 2008).

The government has financed the paving/opening of new roads to expand cattle ranching and logging, which account for more than two-thirds of Amazonian deforestation (Vera-Diaz et al, 2009). The impact of paving roads is highlighted in a recent study of the 1,756km road (BR-163) connecting Santarem in the Amazon rainforest with Cuiaba, the capital of Mato Grosso state. Paving the remaining 56% of the road in the sparsely populated forest would increase the soybean growing area by 70%, reduce transport costs and a cost benefit analysis forecasts it would generate over US$180m for soybean farmers over a 20-year period. However, '... *if the destruction of ecological services and products provided by the existing forests is accounted for, then the Cuiaba-Santarem investment would generate a net loss of between US$762m and US$1.9bn*' (ibid).

Brazil's toll road concessions started with the tendering of six federal roads in 1995/96 followed by a further 20 concessions included in the 1997 Privatisation National Programme (Amorelli, 2009). Following a new federal PPP law, passed in December 2004, seven 25-year concessions for 2,600 km were signed in 2008 and a further four were in procurement.

The first toll road project launched under the new programme was to improve, maintain and operate a 633km section of the BR-116 and BR-324 roads in the State of Bahia, supported by International Finance Corporation and Brazilian Development Bank debt financing and with potential access to the government's PPP guarantee fund (International Finance Corporation, 2006). The 45 toll road concessions operating by mid 2009 account for 8% of the federal road network (Fitch, 2009).

Other PPPs include the 30-year concession to operate the Sao Paulo Metro Line 4, a new publicly-built line, which will add 21% capacity to the system. The concession to supply, operate and maintain trains was won by Companhia de Concessoes Rodoviarias (CCR), (Latin America's largest toll road operator), after the courts blocked trade union attempts to stop the contract on the basis that it was a disguised privatisation.

The second phase of the Plano de Aceleracao do Crescimento (PAC), the government's growth acceleration plan, will be launched in 2010 with BNDES launching an infrastructure fund coupled with a new portfolio of infrastructure projects to attract domestic and foreign investors (Bank Information Center, 2009). Brazil will host the 2014 World Cup and the 12 host cities are forecast to spend US$41.7bn on new stadiums, improved transportation and other facilities (Associated Press, 2009).

South Africa
Government departments, provincial and local government had signed 18 PPP contracts by January 2009 with a further 55 projects at different stages of development and procurement, under the 1999 Public Finance Management Act. This legislation led to Treasury regulations for PPPs and a national PPP unit was established a year later. This has since produced standardised contracts and guidance. The vaunted PPP guidance is comprehensive, however, the growth of PPPs is less evident to date.

Hospital and health projects accounted for 7 of the signed projects, which also included a toll road, rapid transit, office accommodation, fleet management, ICT and eco-tourism. Water and waste management, prisons, and defence facility projects were at the feasibility or procurement stage in 2009. The N3 and N4 toll roads, two maximum security prisons, two water projects and national park tourism concessions were early PPP projects in the 1997-2000 period.

The US$400m N4 Pretoria-Maputo (Mozambique) toll road was the first PPP to be refinanced in 2006 followed by an equity sale as Actis, a private equity group, sold its 26.9% stake in the Trans African Concession to existing shareholders.

The 77km Gautrain rapid rail system, Africa's largest PPP when the agreement was signed in 2006, will connect Johannesburg with the Oliver Tambo International Airport in time for the 2010 Soccer World Cup. It will later be extended to other areas. Unusually, the public sector is directly funding most of the capital costs of the Bombardier and Bouygues led consortium. '... *the public sector will provide a capital grant to the amount of R19,199million (US$2.6bn) over the five year development period in 2005 terms. This will be split in an equal share between the national and provincial governments. In addition to this amount, the public sector is responsible for the acquisition of land and the costs of managing and monitoring the Agreement by the newly established Gautrain Management*

Agency. The private sector will provide R3,094million (US$420m) in capital funding of which 85% is debt raised from the local banking sector' (National Treasury PPP Unit, 2006).

The provincial government signed the PPP agreement without the lender's financing documents being signed, to allow construction to begin several months before financial close. It signed a US$35m early works contract for the relocation of utilities prior to the contract being signed (ibid).

'*PPPs are good for Black Economic Empowerment*' claims the National PPP unit, which identifies the level of black enterprise involvement in project equity and subcontracting for each PPP project. Most signed projects have black enterprises contributing between 15%-50% of project equity, and obtaining up to 50% of subcontracting contracts. However, the claimed advantages and tangible economic benefits are virtually the same as those obtained from direct public investment. For example, '*where government is the buyer of a service, and insofar as the service is provided to the agreed standards, there is a steady revenue stream to the private party, reducing risk to new black enterprises*' (www.ppp.gov.za). Subcontracting and supplier opportunities and demand for black professionals would be equally significant.

CHAPTER 7

Trading portfolios of schools, hospitals and prisons

Buying and selling schools and hospitals like commodities in a global supermarket, is surely not what is meant by localism. This chapter shows how a trading system has developed from the refinancing and the sale of equity in PPP projects and growth of infrastructure funds. It highlights the consequences of this extension of marketisation of public services and also outlines new PPP models.

The refinancing of PPP projects and the sale of PPP equity appear to be financial mechanisms that are of little interest or consequence. This could not be further from the truth. The growth of a secondary market is already instigating changes in the ownership of projects, which could have a fundamental impact on the public sector, service users, staff and the future of public infrastructure. This market, not surprisingly, is most developed in the UK because of the scale and 'maturity' of the PPP programme. But other countries are also witnessing the growth of secondary markets.

'... by March 2006 40% of operational projects had changed ownership and in 50% of the cases of changed ownership the debt had been refinanced as well. The consolidation of ownership continued, despite levels of return on secondary holdings down to around 7% – 8 %' (DLA Piper, 2007).

Refinancing and the sale of equity in PPP projects are two separate transactions. Refinancing can occur after the construction phase is completed and the project is operating satisfactorily. Once the major construction risks are eliminated, the project can be refinanced by the original lenders or the original debt repaid and a new loan negotiated at lower interest rates. Banks and financial companies are prepared to refinance projects offering better terms to reflect the lower risks (National Audit Office, 2002). The prime objective of refinancing is to increase the rate of return. This is usually achieved by increasing the level of debt and extending the contract period. Projects can be refinanced by replacing the bank-funded debt or by issuing bonds, which will be sold, to insurance companies, pension funds and hedge funds. The large number of bondholders and bond conditions usually make any further refinancing prohibitively costly.

The sale of shares in the Special Purpose Vehicle or consortia company enables the original shareholders to gain the increased value of shareholding once the major risks are eliminated. They use the proceeds to fund further PPP projects or retain the money in their corporate accounts. A change in ownership is normally permitted following a lock-in period, typically one-year post construction.

Growth of a secondary market

Most of the risk in public infrastructure is in the design, site preparation, finance and construction of new building projects. Construction risks are eliminated or significantly reduced when construction is completed, leaving the operational risks. Many PPP companies want to sell their share equity to increase profits. The private sector argues that they are just managing their assets/investments and want to 'unlock value'. The demand for such assets increased rapidly in the last decade, as investment and pension funds sought to invest in long-term, low risk projects.

Some construction companies retain PPP equity but others recycle resources to finance new PPP projects. Some companies may be under financial pressure to sell their share stake. The sale of equity is often preferred to refinancing because the gains may be substantial and do not have to be shared with the public sector. A contractor can sell a shareholding in a PPP consortium but retain the Facilities Management (FM) contract, although they would no longer be represented on the PPP company board.

Secondary market funds are building portfolios of assets covering a variety of PPP projects. In turn, some of the secondary funds have been acquired by larger financial and property companies.

The term 'secondary market' is deceptive. It arises because the current focus is on the design, financing and construction of projects but these are short-term compared to the length of operational contracts. The 'secondary' market could become equally important and powerful, if not the prime market, as the stock of operational PPP projects increases and the portfolios of projects held by investment funds grow and consolidate. They will have a key role in influencing whether assets are transferred back to the public sector, refinanced and extended, or new projects are commenced.

Refinancing PPP projects

Demand for PPP investments
The other side of the coin is the demand for PPP investments from

infrastructure, pension and private equity funds. In addition to the long-term, low risk, inflation-linked attraction of infrastructure investment noted in Chapter 4, banks and investment funds believe there are opportunities to optimise the value of individual projects and to achieve further alleged efficiencies and economies of scale by combining projects in portfolios of assets. This means there is a demand for PPP asset investment in addition to those wanting to sell assets.

Refinancing which does not require consent or gain sharing
Public sector consent, and sharing of financial gains, are not required when contractors sell shares in PPP special purpose companies because HM Treasury in the UK regards PPP equity sales as standard company share disposals reflecting company performance. Nor is consent or benefit sharing required in a general refinancing of a contractor's company finance (excluding PPP project finance). If a project has a financial crisis, the contractor will not obtain refinancing gains above the financial returns agreed at the start of the contract (Office of Government Commerce, 2002).

In the UK, a voluntary code was introduced in 2002, in which the private sector agreed to provide the public sector with 30% of any refinancing gain. However, this was not made contractually binding. Refinancing of PPP projects is now on a 50/50 basis and an integral part of HM Treasury's 'Standardisation of Private Finance Initiative Contracts', requiring the contractor to obtain an authority's consent to refinance a project (HM Treasury, 2005).

Refinancing is complex and led the National Audit Office to establish principles in 2002 where the benefits should go to those bearing risks and if the private sector seeks to increase its profits by renegotiating a PPP contract, it is reasonable for the public sector to seek a share of refinancing benefits. The public sector should seek compensation for any increased exposure to termination liabilities arising from a refinancing. However, refinancing should not '... *jeopardise the stability and success of the long term contractual relationship*' between a consortium and the public sector client. Another so-called NAO principle stated that '... *substantial refinancing gains to the private sector may threaten the perceived value-for-money of the project*' (National Audit Office, 2006) hardly a principle but a rather feeble observation. There is nothing 'perceived' about value-for-money in what the NAO appears to regard as a cherished government policy. Refinancing increases private sector profits and drives a gaping hole in financial appraisal and value-for-money analysis at the procurement stage, which cannot anticipate the scale of potential future costs and benefits in refinancing.

Refinancing rules were changed again in the UK in November 2008 to ensure that '... *potential additional refinancing gains may be generated on projects signing in the current market, if credit margins or other terms were subsequently to move significantly towards pre-credit crunch levels*' (HM Treasury, 2008). A public body has thus been given the right to request a refinancing '... *where, in the absence of an equity-led refinancing request, the Authority believes that terms available in the market are more favourable than those within the existing agreement*' (ibid).

Refinancing experience
Refinancing twelve UK PPP projects between 1999-2005 resulted in a £142.6m gain for private finance initiative consortia, compared to £27.3m for the public sector (National Audit Office 2000, 2002, 2004, and 2005). Refinancing enables the private sector to increase the profitability of the PPP over and above the average 15% – 20% return that is built into projects before refinancing.

The UK Treasury model of a typical hospital project capital costs account for 54% of the total project costs, operating costs 29% and the cost to the public sector of the private sector taking the risks of constructing and operating the asset over the contract period accounts for 17% of total costs. Since debt finance accounts for about 90% of PPP/PFI project finance, with only about 10% equity investment, refinancing can substantially improve the terms of debt finance.

About half of the refinanced projects in the National Audit Office (NAO) survey increased borrowing by an average of 20%. This only serves to empower the private sector to accelerate the benefits to their shareholders by enabling them to pay out inflated dividends shortly after refinancing (National Audit Office, 2006).

The average internal rate of return in the refinancing of 22 PPP projects almost doubled from 14.91% to 27.23%. The survey included four hospitals, two school projects, five prisons, three road schemes and one of the London Underground contracts and was based on the NAO survey for its 2006 report plus additional information supplied for the House of Commons Committee of Public Accounts report in 2007. '*The IRR is the discount rate at which the present value of the investors' receipts from a project equals that of their payments, including their initial investment. The IRR percentage return aggregates a series of annual*

Table 24: Sharing of gains on refinancing PPP/PFI projects

Project	Total refinancing gains (NPV) £m	Amount shared with public sector (NPV) £m	% of gain shared with public sector
Norfolk & Norwich Hospital	115.5	33.9	29.3
Bromley Hospital	45.3	14.2	31.3
Darent Valley Hospital	33.4	11.7	35.0
14 other projects where gains were shared in accordance with Code	48.2	11.7	24.3
3 projects where no gains were shared	4.8	–	–
Total of 20 completed refinancings since Code came into operation	**247.2**	**71.5**	**28.9**

Source: National Audit Office, 2006.

percentages. It does not mean the investors will receive the IRR rate as a constant return each year' (National Audit Office, 2006).

Refinancing has led to the extension of contracts. Three were extended from between 5 and 7 years. The rationale for contract extensions was summarised as:

'Contract extensions are perceived to generate future savings (rather than the current gains derived from the sources discussed above). These future savings are assumed on supposition that the cost of the services secured now, by extending the contract, will be cheaper than those, which would be available in the future. Contract extensions are closely tied to the gains, which can be derived from increasing debt. By extending the contract the private sector is also able to extend the term of their debt and hence they are able to borrow more. For this reason the extension of a contract and the increase of debt often go hand in hand' (National Audit Office, 2006).

The increase in contract termination liabilities is often substantial. The refinancing of the Norfolk and Norwich Hospital in 2003 produced a windfall profit of £116m but the NHS Trust received just £34m (when it had a £15m deficit). The refinancing increased borrowing from £200m to £306m and imposed termination liabilities for the NHS Trust of £257m. The then Secretary of State for Health, Patricia Hewitt, described it as '… a great deal for the NHS' (Public Private Finance, 2006).

However, increased project debt means an inevitable increase in termination liabilities for the public sector. The public sector is forced to balance any immediate gains with the additional risks imposed by an increase in private sector debt.

Refinancing gain sharing does not apply to toll roads. PPP toll road projects usually require the concessionaire to accept all the revenue risks, so that when projects are refinanced, there is no sharing of the refinancing gains between PPP consortia and the public sector. For example, the £1bn M6 Toll motorway in the West Midlands (UK) was built by Macquarie Infrastructure Group (Australia) and Autostrade, the Italian motorway operator which later sold its 25% stake to Macquarie, giving them full ownership. In 2006, Macquarie agreed with the government to invest £112m in capital, operating and maintenance costs in the M54 Link Road and the M42 slip road, which Macquarie believes '... *will increase traffic on the M6 Toll motorway*' (Macquarie Press Release, 24 May 2006). Clearly an investment intended to secure higher toll income and larger profits. In the same year Macquarie took £392m in dividends after refinancing the original PPP project, increasing the debt of Midland Expressway from £620m to over £1bn.

The government failed to impose any controls on the level of tolls charged by Macquarie, which is expected to undertake further refinancing during the remaining 48 years of the concession and to pay itself further dividends. Government collaboration on a grand scale.

Macquarie and Cintra refinanced the Chicago Skyway toll road (see chapter 6) eight months after signing the US$1.83bn deal in January 2005. The project was originally financed by US$880m equity reflecting the Cintra/Macquarie 55%/45% ownership and US$1.19bn nine-year loans from European banks. The deal was refinanced when Cintra and Macquarie issued US$1.4bn in AAA-valued bonds plus US$150m subordinated debt, which reduced the equity holdings of the two companies giving them US$373m cash (Macquarie, 2005). '*This lower equity level could be recovered in full in 12 years based upon expected cash flows. After recovery the private operator is in the deal for the remaining 87 years with no equity at risk*' (NW Financial Group, 2006).

Secondary market investment funds
'*Secondary Funds are long term holders of PPP and PFI projects which have typically reached their operating stage. Returns to investors are principally by way of cash generated by the projects during the remainder of their concession lives*' (Innisfree, 2008).

Babcock & Brown and Abbey National set up the first, active, secondary market fund, Secondary Market Infrastructure Fund (SMIF), in 2001. Two years later, with 23 assets valued at £120m, it was acquired by Star Capital Partners. Halifax Bank of Scotland and AMP Capital Investors funded further growth. It formed a £115m partnership with Global Solutions (GSL) in 2005 acquiring £70m of GSL's PPP assets. There followed a series of acquisitions of PPP project share capital from construction companies such as Carillion, Jarvis, McAlpine and John Laing such that by its £927m acquisition by Land Securities Trillium in February 2007, the Fund had an interest in 80 PPP projects. Land Securities turned it into a joint venture company, Trillium PPP Investment Partners, raising £1.1bn debt and equity in 2008.

It was sold again in February 2009 to Semperian PPP Investment Partners when Land Securities sold Trillium to Telereal. Victorian Funds Management Corporation of Australia and Transport for London Pension Fund, acquired Trillium's 10% investment in Semperian, which by then owned and managed 108 assets with a value of £1.3 billion.

A number of other specialist secondary market investments funds have emerged. Infrastructure Investors (I2) is a joint venture between Barclays Private Equity, Societe Generale and 3i, formed in 2003 to acquire equity in operational PPP infrastructure projects in the UK and European euro currency countries. It has over 70 investments, valued at over £500m, in health, education, transport, utilities and defence. Projects include Wansbeck Hospital, Northumberland (£21m capital cost), Argyll and Bute schools (£100m – the first Non-Profit Distributing Organisation PPP project in the UK), Dockland Light Railway Lewisham extension (£270m), Highland Wastewater, Scotland (£45m), Ministry of Defence heavy equipment transport and accommodation.

Another specialist fund, Global Solutions (GSL), operates prisons and secure training centres, schools in Tower Hamlets and North Wiltshire and Building Schools for the Future in Leicester. It also operates hospitals in Oxford, UK and four LIFT projects, Governmental Communications Headquarters (GCHQ) in the UK and prisons in Australia and South Africa. It sold £70m PPP project equity to Secondary Market Infrastructure Fund (SMIF) in 2005 to focus on core outsourcing business support services in public and private sectors.

PPP investment fund Innisfree had been funding projects since 1996 when it formed a secondary fund £100m joint venture with M&G Investment Management Limited in 2004. Investments increased to £225m with two additional secondary funds opened in 2006 and 2008 with £350m and £600m funds respectively.

Another venture, Henderson PFI Secondary Funds, has two funds of £330m and £573.5m for operational PPP projects in the UK and Western Europe. Funders included the Merseyside, Greater Manchester and University pension funds.

HSBC Infrastructure Company Ltd (HICL): Launched in 2006 and listed on the London Stock Exchange with its headquarters in Guernsey, it began with 15 '... *long-term concessions based on public sector or government-backed revenues and "availability"-based rather than dependent on usage for revenue*' which had risen to 27 projects by early 2008 (HSBC, 2009).

The John Laing and Macquarie European Infrastructure Fund portfolios illustrate the range of assets held in two portfolios (see Tables 25 and 26).

Macquarie European Infrastructure Fund has over 100 infrastructure assets.

Table 25: *John Laing portfolio*

Sector	Number of PPP projects	Capital value £m
Defence	4	706
Health – Hospitals	12	2,577
Health NHS LIFT	6	169
Police and Criminal Justice	7	276
Roads and bridges	10	1,583
Education	10	1,069
Street lighting	3	75
Utilities	2	213
Housing and regeneration	3	125
Rail	5	357
Waste	1	350
Total	**63**	**7,520**

Source: John Laing, www.laing.com/portfolio/proj_portfolio.htm, accessed 20 August 2008.

Table 26: *Sample of Macquarie European Infrastructure Fund assets*

Asset	Stake %	Cost £m
Birmingham Airport	24.1	
Bristol Airport	100.0	198
Arlanda Express, rail service between airport and Stockholm	100.0	
Brussels Airport (other Macquarie companies own 70%)	10.0	
Wales & West Utilities (Gas distribution)	n/a	
Energy Power Resources, large renewable energy UK, France and Sweden	100.0	
Wightlink Shipping, ferry services to Isle of Wight	100.0	
East London Bus Group, from Stagecoach Holdings	100.0	264
Thames Water	100.0	8,000
National Car Parks (NCP)	100.0	790
Airwave – national digital network for polices and emergency services	100.0	1,900
CLP Envirogas, landfill gas fuelled power generation projects.	100.0	
Techem AG, meter reading & billing to energy & water companies	91.5	1,050
GWE, German energy supply (acquired from Star Capital Partners)	72.0	

Source: Macquarie Bank, 2009.

Sale of PPP project equity/assets

The sheer scale of investment is forcing some construction companies to sell some or all of their equity capital in private finance initiative projects, in order to bid for new projects. An NAO survey found that 40% of a sample of 80 PPP projects had a sale of equity, most more than three years after the contract had been signed, with half of those projects being subjected to refinancing (National Audit Office, 2006).

Mergers and acquisition often lead to a change in equity ownership, for example, in Carillion's takeover of construction companies Mowlem (2006) and McAlpine (2007), which owned equity in PPP projects they had developed prior to takeover.

Companies such as Amey and Jarvis, which had a financial crisis in 2003/04, were forced to sell their PPP assets. In the case of the East Lothian Grouped Schools PFI Project, administrators were appointed to Ballast UK companies nine months into construction. Balfour Beatty Construction took over the construction contract. John Laing sold its stake in Defence Management (Holdings) to Serco to enable it to be incorporated into a Defence Academy Campus with Serco appointed as Campus Integrator role but within a year Serco had sold this to the Infrastructure Investors Fund. John Laing engineered the fastest profiteering. It had a 50% stake in the M40 road project and acquired the remaining 50% interest from Carillion in June 2004 for £19.7m and in October that year sold the 50% stake to the Secondary Market Infrastructure Fund for £26.3m, making a profit of £6.3m after costs (John Laing, 2005).

Although it is clear that construction and investment companies gain from trading in PPP equity assets, there appear to be no benefits for the projects sold or to the public sector in general. The National Audit Office claimed that the expansion of a PPP equity market might bring benefits to the public sector '... *by attracting more investors into the PFI market. As the supply of equity in PFI projects increases this should, assuming efficient markets, drive down the relative cost of equity and bring benefits to the public sector in the pricing of PFI projects. The Treasury has said that it considers there is scope to reduce the returns of around 13–15 per cent which investors expect when PFI projects are bid for*' (National Audit Office, 2006). The almost doubling of the rate of return after refinancing demolishes this argument. It also claimed that the public sector '... *can learn from the management techniques employed by SMFs to reduce the operating costs of a portfolio of PFI projects*' (ibid).

The subsequent House of Commons Committee of Public Accounts inquiry compliantly concluded that the public interest was not affected if there is '... *an efficient equity market in which investor returns can be left to find their own level*' (Public Accounts Committee, 2007). They made no attempt to challenge the principle of PPP equity sales, private sector profiteering or the potential impact on the management and operation of contracts.

I have been able to identify the sale of equity in 628 PPP projects between 1998-2009 although the actual figure is much higher, because it does not take account of the acquisition of PPP assets by infrastructure funds such as Macquarie and Babcock & Brown where relatively small acquisitions are not disclosed (see Table 27). The annual rate of equity sales soared, as did the value of the assets sold. Information on profit levels was available for only a fraction of the equity sales so the £257.2m total is grossly under-stated.

Table 27:
Annual rate of PPP equity trading by UK PPP companies
(this Table combines Tables 28 and 31)

Year	Number of PPP projects in which equity sold	Value £m	Profit £m
1998	3	14	2.2
2001	7	105	n/a
2003	15	154	23.1
2004	72	176	25.7
2005	23	257	24.3
2006	35	167	91.8
2007	162	386	82.1
2008	*103	**285	8
2009***	198	1,300	n/a
Total	**618**	**2,840**	**257.2**

Sources: Company Announcements to the London Stock Exchange and Press Releases, PPP In-Depth, No. 6, 2006, PPP Bulletin, The Second Age of PFI, Collins Stewart, May 2004, Infrastructure and Secondary Market Fund websites, HM Treasury 2008, includes 39 identified in HM Treasury equity list. ** includes £217m representing 50% of the Bank of Scotland sale. *** to April, 2009.

The government belatedly began tracking changes in PFI equity in 2008. There were changes in equity in 39 out of 431 projects between February and November 2008 where data was available in the 637-project database (HM Treasury, 2008). They ranged across the sectors with Land Securities Trillium accounting for 17 transactions (44%).

Most of the large European contractors have PPP projects in various countries; for example, Hochtief, Berlinger, Balfour Beatty and secondary market funds such as SMIF and Macquarie Infrastructure are European-wide funds. Hence PPP equity sales are almost certain to become more common across Europe (assuming no legal restrictions). Vinci plc sold a 50% stake in a Cardiff road contract to its own pension fund, the Vinci Pension Scheme in 2003. The company still manages the contract.

SSP contracts are structured differently from standard PPP infrastructure projects and are not subject to refinancing or PPP equity sales. However, the authority's contractor is subject to merger and acquisition, for example, five SSPs had new 'partners' imposed on them when Mouchel acquired HBS Business Services Group in 2007.

Trading schools, hospitals, roads, prisons and courts
Hospitals, schools, roads, prisons and courts are now deemed tradable commodities with shareholdings in PPP companies sold to investors. But these are usually secret deals, which the PPP industry considers to be private transactions between private sector investors. There are no formal procedures to announce the sale of PPP equity, except where a company considers it prudent to make a formal stock exchange announcement. Most are undertaken covertly.

The list of equity sales in Table 28 was compiled from numerous company, media and PPP sources. 49 hospital, 39 school, 22 road and 21 criminal justice projects changed ownership via PPP equity sales between 2001-2009. This included the multiple sale of some projects. Most education PPP projects include several schools, although they have been treated as single projects in Table 28.

Equity in health, schools, transport and prison PPP assets, with an original project investment of £75.8m, were sold by UK construction companies for £253.1m, a 234% profit margin between 2003/06. They were acquired, all bar one, by infrastructure funds.

Sale of PPP teams and PPP contractors
In the sale of EDF Energy to Scottish and Southern Energy, a PFI adviser stated: *'Transactions of this type are be who advised on the deal becoming increasingly important in the PFI sector as the market matures. Street lighting has taken off over the last few years and has been fairly heavily commodified quite quickly. It's not the sexy end of PFI but with low risks and low margins it is the stable end,'* Stephen Wait, head of Stephenson Harwood's PFI/PPP practice (PPP Bulletin, May 2008).

Sale of secondary market funds

In addition to the sale of equity in individual PPP projects in the UK there have been four significant acquisitions of secondary market funds at a total cost of £1,160.4m between 2005-07. The combined sale of PPP assets between 2001-07 was over £3 billion.

The changing ownership of Global Solutions (GSL) is illuminating. GSL was originally established as the bidding vehicle for Group 4's prison and private security projects in the 1990s. When Group 4 merged with Securicor in 2004 the European Commission ruled that Group 4 must sell GSL. It was acquired by a private equity firm, Englefield Capital and Electra Partners, which added healthcare projects to their portfolio. The investment partnership between GSL

Dexter Whitfield

Table 28: *PPP equity sales 1998-2008*

Owner	Asset	Sold to	% share stake	Value £m	Profit £m (% in brackets)
1998					
Serco Ltd	DefenceHelicopter Flying School	FR Aviation Ltd Bristow Helicopter Group	n/a	3.4	2.2
n/a	Adelaide Airport and Northern Territories Airport	John Laing	14.5%	11.0	n/a
2001					
Hyder Investments	PFI assets – A55, A130 and M40 road projects, Nelostie toll road, Finland	John Laing	100	92.5	n/a
n/a	Macquarie European Infrastructure Ltd – Queen Elizabeth ll Hospital, Greenwich	John Laing	50	n/a	n/a
John Laing	A55 road scheme	Carillion plc	22.5 (retaining 50%)	3.2	n/a
John Laing	M40 road scheme	Carillion plc	22.5 (retaining 50%)	8.9	n/a
2003					
WS Atkins	3 assets – Connect Roads (A50 Derby-Stoke, A30/A35 Devon/Dorset and M77 Scotland	Balfour Beatty	32.2	13.3	Cost £4.4m (202%) Three times book value
Amey plc	8 assets – M6, A19 and another road project plus 5 accommodation projects including North Birmingham Mental Health Trust, MoD, British Transport Police, schools in Scotland.	John Laing	various	42.9	n/a
Mowlem	City Greenwich Lewisham Rail Link (Docklands Light Railway)	Infrastructure Investors	40.0	19.5	Cost £3.4m (471%)

Global Auction of Public Assets

Owner	Asset	Sold to	% share stake	Value £m	Profit £m (% in brackets)
Carillion plc	Darent Valley Hospital	Barclays Infrastructure Fund	50	5.2	Cost £4.1m also £11.2m refinancing profit (400%)
Vinci plc	City Link Cardiff	Vinci Pension Scheme	50	1.0	nil
Wackenhut Corrections Corporation Inc	Premier Custodial Group	Serco	50 – now has 100%	48.6	n/a
2004					
McAlpine and WS Atkins	Hereford Hospital	Secondary Market Infrastructure Fund	50 (two stakes of 25%)	11.2	£5.8m (107%)
Anglian Water Group	Tay Wastewater project, Scotland	Henderson Private Capital	33 Acquired stake when it acquired Morrison Construction in 2000	12.0	Sale £8m, £4.3m development gain
International Water (Bechtel: US & Edison: Italy joint venture	2 assets – Tay, Highland & Moray Wastewater projects, Scotland	Infrastructure Investors	n/a	n/a	n/a
Noble Primary Fund	19 PFI assets	Infrastructure Investors	n/a	n/a	n/a
Carillion plc	M40	John Laing plc	50	19.2	Profit £6m (46%)
Carillion plc	A249 road	John Laing	50	n/a	Profit £1m
John Laing	A249 road	Barclays European Infrastructure	50	n/a	n/a
PFI Infrastructure Company	Falkirk Schools Partnership	Secondary Market Infrastructure Fund	2.7	0.8	Cost was £0.56m with £0.24m (43%) profit
HBOS, Uberior and Quayle Munro	4 assets – Larkfield Hospital, Castle Hill Community Learning Centre, James Watt College of Further	PFI Infrastructure Company	various	8.2	n/a

Dexter Whitfield

Owner	Asset	Sold to	% share stake	Value £m	Profit £m (% in brackets)
	Education, Bannockburn MoD Housing				
Bank of Scotland	3 PPP assets – Aberdeenshire schools, Chester-le-Street Hospital & Stockton schools	PFI Infrastructure Company	8.8 increasing stake to 28.8%	0.63	n/a
Carillion	UK Highways which operates M40	John Laing	50	19.7	n/a
John Laing	UK Highways which operates M40	Secondary Market Infrastructure Fund	50	26.3	Cost £19.7m – £6.3m profit after costs in 3 months (32%)
Amec	Newcastle Estate Partnership	Secondary Market Infrastructure Fund	n/a	26.0	n/a
Jarvis plc	18 PPP assets includes 51% stake in Army Foundation College	Secondary Market Infrastructure Fund	n/a	18.0	n/a
Chiltern Securities Ltd	6 Community Health Projects – Chiltern Securities Group	Secondary Market Infrastructure Fund	n/a	10.0	n/a
Kajima Corporation	DEFRA building, Cambridge	Infrastructure Investors LP (Barclays, Societe Generale and 3i)	n/a	10.0	n/a
2005					
PFI plc	3 PPP assets – Aberdeenshire schools, Chester-le-Street Hospital & Stockton schools	Infrastructure Investors	28.6	3.2	£1.1m since acquisition in July 2004 (52%)
MJ Gleeson plc	Tiverton Community Hospital	PFI Infrastructure Company	40	1.1	n/a
Jarvis	Stake in Tube Lines (London Underground)	Amey plc	33	146.8	n/a

Global Auction of Public Assets

Owner	Asset	Sold to	% share stake	Value £m	Profit £m (% in brackets)
n/a	4 Health assets	Secondary Market Infrastructure Fund	n/a	40.0	n/a
United Medical Enterprises Ltd	Asset management business	Secondary Market Infrastructure Fund	n/a	5.0	n/a
UK bank	3 projects	Secondary Market Infrastructure Fund	n/a	25.0	n/a
Miller Group	3 schools projects	Secondary Market Infrastructure Fund	n/a	n/a	n/a
John Laing plc	Defence Management (Holdings) Ltd Joint Services Command & Staff College	Serco Group	50	5.9	7.8
John Laing plc	4 PPP assets – Gravesend and Cleveland Firearms Training Centres, South East London & Manchester Police Stations	Allianz PFI Holdings (Jersey) Ltd, subsidiary of Allianz AG	50	23.1	£12.19 plus £3.5m if projects are refinanced within 18 months)
Alfred McAlpine & WS Atkins	South Manchester University Hospital	Secondary Market Infrastructure Fund	n/a	7.6	Cost £3.3m (130%)
Barclays European Infrastructure and Noble PFI Fund	Ministry of Defence Heavy Equipment Transporters	Elbon PFI fund	50	n/a	n/a
2006					
Balfour Beatty	Connect Roads	Infrastructure Investors	15.0	13.5	Cost £3.0m (350%)
Innisfree, WS Atkins & Wates	Aberystwyth school	PFI Infrastructure Company	100	3.4	n/a
n/a	2 assets – Workington Community Hospital, West Cumbria Police Headquarters	PFI Infrastructure Company	100	6.0	n/a

Owner	Asset	Sold to	% share stake	Value £m	Profit £m (% in brackets)
n/a	3 assets – Mid-Argyll Community Hospital, Salisbury Hospital and Forfar Community Hospital	PFI Infrastructure Company	15, 60 and 60 respectively	7.4	n/a
Carillion	7 PPP assets – HM Prison Altcourse, HMP Rye Hill, Rainsbrook and Medway Secure Training Centres, East Anglia & Humberside Courts, Leeds Schools	Secondary Market Infrastructure Fund	n/a	32	£22m profit from 2 transactions (92%)
Carillion		Infrastructure Investors	n/a	14	
Serco	6 PPP assets – Ashfield, Dovegate & Lowdham Grange Prisons, Hassockfield Secure Training Centre, Joint Services & Command College, National Traffic Control Centre	Infrastructure Investors (forms investment partnership, SERCO retained FM cntracts)	100	76.5	Cost £19.9m (284%)
Bouygues	Barnet Hospital	HSBC Infrastructure	11.0 Increases stake to 41%	4.6	n/a
McAlpine	3 PPP assets – Conwy Schools, Exeter Courts & Stoke Mandeville Hospital	HSBC Infrastructure	10.0% Increases stake to 90%		n/a
McAlpine	3 Fife Council schools	HSBC Infrastructure	40%	5.5	n/a
Skanska	Bridgend Prison	Innisfree	9%	3.8	2.7 (245%)
2007					
Amec	8 PPP assets (transport, health & education – incl. Cumberland Infirmary and South Lanarkshire Schools) and 37 staff in Project Investments team	Land Securities Trillium	100%	152.4	n/a

Global Auction of Public Assets

Owner	Asset	Sold to	% share stake	Value £m	Profit £m (% in brackets)
United Medical Enterprises	9 assets – health	Land Securities Trillium	n/a	56.6	n/a
Hochtief PPP Schools Capital Ltd (51% retained by Hochtief)	6 PPP schools assets – Salford (2), Manchester Sports college, North Ayrshire (4), East Ayrshire (7), Bangor (2) and Cork School of Music	PFI Infrastructure Company	49	9.3	n/a
Kajima Partnerships	6 PPP assets – 14 Schools in North Tyneside, Ealing, Darlington, London, Northants & Health & Safety Executive HQ	HSBC Infrastructure (partnership formed with Kaijima)	50	30.2	18.00 profit
Carillion	3 PPP assets – Swindon, Harplands (North Staffs) and Glasgow Southern General hospitals	Land Securities Trillium	n/a	21.5	21.0 approx
Costain	2 PPP assets: Bridgend Prison and Sirhowy Enterprise Way, Wales	John Laing (already owned 50%)	50.0	9.4	Profit of £5.7m (61%)
Allianz PFI Holdings (Jersey) Ltd, subsidiary of Allianz AG4	PPP assets – Gravesend and Cleveland Firearms Training Centres, South East London & Manchester Police Stations	HSBC Infrastructure	50.0	36.5	Acquired by Allianz in 2005 for £23.1m
LFG Associates and Shepherd Construction	2 PPP assets – Barnet Hospital and Buxton Health & Safety Laboratory	HSBC Infrastructure	Increases Barnet stake to 51%. Increases Buxton stake to 80%	3.3	n/a
McAlpine	6 PPP assets – A1(M) Alconbury to Peterborough, A417/419 Swindon to Gloucester, East Leake Schools,	Infrastructure Investors	n/a	52.2	£24.9m (95.4%)

Owner	Asset	Sold to	% share stake	Value £m	Profit £m (% in brackets)
	Addenbrookes Elective Care Centre, A1 Darlington to Dishforth, Three Shires Mental Health				
Bank of Scotland	Home Office headquarters	HSBC Infrastructure	14.1	14.4	n/a
BAM PPP	Crawley Schools and 3 other projects	DIF Infrastructure Fund	25	n/a	11.25m profit
Barclays plc and G&J Seddon	Lancaster Care Units & Resource Centre and Residential Care Home in Surrey	Equitix Ltd	100	n/a	n/a
2008					
Kier Group	Hairmyres Hospital, East Kilbride	Innisfree M&G PPP Fund	50	13.8	16.0 includes refinancing profit in 2004
Carillion	4 assets – Lewisham hospital, James Cook University hospital, Barnsley schools and Redcar & Cleveland schools	Innisfree, Land Securities Trillium, Barclays European Infrastructure Fund and Robertson Capital Projects	n/a	35.9	n/a
Carillion	Oxford John Radcliffe Hospital	HSBC Infrastructure	50	18.0	n/a
Bank of Scotland	47 PFI projects and one infra- structure fund investment. Includes schools in Newcastle, Edinburgh, Aberdeenshire, Lancashire, Fife: housing in Leeds, Camden & Islington; Various hospitals, health centres and police stations	Pension funds of 4 'well known UK companies'	49.9	434.3	n/a

Global Auction of Public Assets

Owner	Asset	Sold to	% share stake	Value £m	Profit £m (% in brackets)
BAM PPP	Crawley schools plus 3 other projects	DIF Infrastructure Fund in JV with BAM	25 (now has 50%)	n/a	€10m profit
Accent Group	Leeds Mental Health – 7 facilities	Equitix Fund	100	34.0	n/a
Misc	45 equity sales in HM Treasury database	Misc	n/a	n/a	n/a
2009					
Barclays European Infrastructure Fund and Galliford Try Investments	148 Ministry of Defence houses	DIF Infrastructure Fund, Holland	100	n/a	n/a
Royal Bank of Scotland and Carillion Private Finance	1,600 student accommodation, University of Hertfordshire	DIF Infrastructure Fund, Holland	50	n/a	n/a
Siemens plc	Barnet Hospital	HSBC Infrastructure	30	2.7	n/a
Bouygues UK and Ecovert FM	Barnet Hospital	HSBC Infrastructure	19	1.7	n/a
Morrison Education	Highland Schools (10 primary & secondary)	HSBC Infrastructure	50	16.8	n/a
Carillion plc	Renfrewshire Schools (10 primary & secondary)	HSBC Infrastructure	30	6.8	n/a
Europe					
Skanska 2004	A1 Motorway, Poland	John Laing	30 (Skanska retains 30% Intertoll 15%)	11.4	n/a
Macquarie Infrastructure Group	Lusoponte, two toll bridges in Lisbon, Portugal	Mota and Vinci	30.6	€112m	n/a
Australia					
John Laing plc 2003	Adelaide Airport, Australia	Motor Trades of Australia Assoc Pension Fund	14.5	13.1	3.0 (42%)
John Laing plc	Northern Territory Airports	Perpetual Investment Management	14.6	6.5	2.0 (56%)

Owner	Asset	Sold to	% share stake	Value £m	Profit £m (% in brackets)
Macquarie Infrastructure Group	Westlink M7	Western Sydney Road Group	50	A$ 805m	n/a
Canada					
Capital D'Amerique 2002	Toronto 407 Express	Macquarie Group	18.4 (Macquarie also had 40% stake in Cintra)	C$ 568m	n/a
ABN AMRO Bank NV 2005	Abbotsford Regional Hospital, British Columbia	Macquarie Group	81.0 ABN AMRO retained 19%	n/a	n/a
Macquarie Group 2007	Abbotsford Regional Hospital, British Columbia	John Laing plc	81.0 ABN AMRO retained 19%	n/a	n/a
ABN AMRO Bank NV 2005	Diamond Health Care Centre, Vancouver General hospital	Macquarie Group	81.0 ABN AMRO retained 19%	n/a	n/a
Macquarie Group 2007	Diamond Health Care Centre, Vancouver General hospital	John Laing plc	81.0 ABN AMRO retained 19%	n/a	n/a
Others					
Brazil Skanska 2007	Ponte de Pedra hydroelectric power plant	Suez-Tractebel (also acquired remaining 50% from Impregilo)	50	85	45.0
Mozambique Skanska 2007	Maputo harbour	Grindrod, South Africa	12	10	6.0

Sources: Company Announcements to the London Stock Exchange and Press Releases, PPP In-Depth No. 6, 2006, PPP Bulletin, The Second Age of PFI, Collins Stewart, May 2004, Infrastructure and Secondary Market Fund websites, Contract Journal.

and Secondary Market Infrastructure Fund (SMIF) resulted in the £70m sale of GSL's PFI assets to SMIF and the establishment of a £45m investment partnership to finance new deals in the UK and Europe. GSL's PFI assets included two prisons, four LIFT projects, two hospitals, the Government's Communications Headquarters (GCHQ) and a schools project. Group 4 Securicor (re)acquired GSL in early 2008 (see Table 30).

SMIF's acquisition in 2005 of the asset management company United Medical Enterprises was the first time a secondary market

Global Auction of Public Assets

Table 29: *Analysis of profits from 10 PPP equity sales*

Date	Project	Seller	Buyer	Acquired for £m	Sold for £m	Multiple
Nov 03	Darent Valley Hospital	Carillion	Barclays/ Innisfree	4.1	16.0	3.9
Dec 03	Docklands Light Rail	Mowlem	Infrastructure Investors	3.4	19.4	5.7
Jan 04	Connect Roads	WS Atkins	Balfour Beatty	4.4	13.3	3.0
Jun 04	M40	Carillion	John Laing	13.1	19.7	1.5
Oct 04	M40	John Laing	SMIF	13.1	26.3	2.0
Nov 05	Manchester Healthcare	WS Atkins	SMIF Infrastructure	3.3 3.0	7.8 13.5	2.3 4.5
Jan 06	Connect Roads 15%	Balfour Beatty	Investors			
Mar 06	Glasgow- Edinburgh Schools	John Laing	SMIF	4.5	14.6	3.3
Sep 06	Various prisons, courts & schools	Carillion	SMIF	7.0	46.0	6.6
Dec 06	Various prisons & training centres	Serco	Infrastructure Investors	19.9	76.5	3.8
Total				75.8	253.1	3.7 Average

(SMIF: Secondary Market Infrastructure Fund)
Source: Bridgewell Securities, Daily Telegraph, 21 May 2007.

fund had acquired a non-PPP asset. The acquisition was intended to strengthen control over projects *'We're paying a premium for these assets, which means that we're generating a lower return. We need to protect that return by more active management'* (Public Private Finance, March 2005).

The consequences of refinancing and equity sales
The implications of equity sales and refinancing are profound. The long-term implications tend to be suppressed in the pursuit of short-term interests, which is a recurring theme of PPPs.

Refinancing ensures public infrastructure is first and foremost a financial asset and is a further significant stage in the financialisation, marketisation and privatisation of public assets. The motive for equity ownership and control is profit, not public service. Companies use

Dexter Whitfield

Table 30: *Sale of PPP teams and PPP contractors*

Owner	Asset	Sold to	% share stake	Value £m	Profit	Date
PPP Teams						
Jarvis plc	University Partnerships Programme – bidding & SPV management operations	Alma Mater Fund (joint venture Barclays and 3i)	100	0	'not material'	2004
Jarvis plc	PFI bidding operations. FM contracts for Belfast Courts and Irish schools sold for £100	Hochtief (Germany)	100	1.2	n/a	2004
Company acquisitions						
Group 4	Global Solutions Ltd (GSL) operates 3 PPP prisons and GCHQ in The UK, 2 prisons in Australia, 1 in South Africa	Englefield Capital and Electra Partners Europe	100	207	n/a	2004
Various shareholders	ITNET plc	Serco	100	235	n/a	2005
John Laing plc	Acquisition of Group	Henderson Infrastructure	100	1,004	n/a	2006
Mowlem	Construction company	Carillion	n/a	n/a	n/a	2006
McAlpine	Construction company	Carillion	n/a	n/a	n/a	2007
HBS	ICT and corporate services company, a Terra Firma private equity investment	Mouchel Parkman	100	46.2	Annual losses since 2001 and £100m investment	2007
EDF Energy	Street lighting contracts in Ealing, Islington and Dorset	Scottish & Southern Energy	100	7.8	n/a	2008
Englefield Capital and Electra Partners Europe	Global Solutions Ltd (GSL) – see above. Additional PPP projects – 4 NHS LIFT, North Wiltshire and Tower Hamlets schools, Leicester BSF, Met Office	G4S plc	100	355	n/a	2008

Sources: Company Announcements to the London Stock Exchange 2004-2008, Press Releases and various infrastructure journals in the same period.

financial engineering through refinance or sale of PPP equity solely for financial gain. It also puts the management and operation of facilities at the mercy of financial markets. The financial crisis and sale

Global Auction of Public Assets

Table 31: *Sale of Secondary Market Investment Funds*

Fund	Assets	Sold to	% Share stake	Value £m	Date
Grosvenor House Group plc	Noble PFI Equity Fund	n/a	12.5	4.0	2003
Global Solutions (GSL) acquired by Group 4 Securicor in 2008	See above – 10 projects	Secondary Market Infrastructure Fund	n/a	70	2005
Infrastructure Investors LP (Barclays, Societe Generale and 3i)	n/a	3i Group	33	n/a	2005
Investors in the Community Ltd (formed by Mill Group and Land Securities in 2005 to bid for BSF)	16 PPP projects, £650m portfolio of 17 schools & 22 local authority and community health facilities	Trillium (Land Securities)	50% (50% when joint venture formed in 2005)	7.4	2007
PFI Infrastructure Company	17 PPP projects	Infrastructure Investors LP (Barclays, Societe Generale and 3i)	100	156	2007
Secondary Market Infrastructure Fund (Star Capital Partners, Halifax Bank of Scotland, AMP Capital Investors)	79 PPP projects	Trillium (Land Securities)	100	927	2007
Trillium PPP Investment Partners	108 projects	Semperian PPP Investment Partners	100	1.3bn	2009
Infrastructure Investors LP (Societe Generale, 3i and Fleming stakes)	84 projects	Barclay Private Equity Integrated Infrastructure Fund	100	558.6	2009

Sources: Company Announcements to the London Stock Exchange and Press Releases, PPP In-Depth No. 6, 2006, PPP Bulletin, The Second Age of PFI, Collins Stewart, May 2004, Infrastructure and Secondary Market Fund websites.

of assets by Babcock & Brown and Macquarie are only two of many typical examples.

Private gain and public loss: The sale of equity allows companies to exit from PPP projects, which could lead them to take a short-term view of long-term financial risks. The emergence of secondary funds enables projects to be refinanced in groups or portfolios as a means of extracting higher profits. 'There must be some concern that, under such an arrangement, those ultimately owning the PFI debt may become so remote from the actual operation, and the debt instruments so bundled, that they are unable to form a true assessment of the actual risks involved: and be unable to play an effective role in scrutinising the management of the project. (At its worst, this could involve similar features to the bundling of debt instruments in the sub-prime market)' (Cuthbert, 2008). It also leads to an erosion of public interest – whose interests will dominate in the sale of portfolios between PPP consortia, investment trusts, private equity and sovereign wealth funds?

Balfour Beatty adopted a different strategy and retained equity stakes in PPP projects. A 2006 independent valuation concluded that the original investment of £180m was worth over £600m (Balfour Beatty, 2008). The financial value of PPP assets becomes another measure by which financial markets assess company performance. Contractors are adept at maximising additional income and minimising responsibility for delays and problems in publicly financed projects. In privately financed projects they charge the public sector a premium for taking responsibility for those same risks and thus have an incentive to deliver on time and to budget. Either way the public sector foots the bill. The solution is, surely, to improve public project management.

Invalidates value-for-money claims: Refinancing and/or sale of equity make a mockery of the value-for-money assessment in the procurement process. VfM is already fundamentally flawed (see chapter 9). It cannot be assumed that the public sector benefits from 'gain-sharing' when this is accompanied by changes to terms of the contract and there is clearly no direct benefit from the sale of PPP equity.

Accelerates marketisation: Equity sales increase the internationalisation and financialisation of infrastructure assets. They become commodified asset holdings traded in global markets. This is a long way from a local authority PPP schools contract in which Elected Members, teachers, parents and children believe that the Council or school effectively owns the buildings. They may deal with the Facilities Management (FM) contractor/help desk on a regular basis but do not identify the school as an infrastructure commodity valued and traded in the global marketplace. They are unaware of the longer-term implications such as the emergence of international FM companies employed by secondary market funds to manage and operate contracts. The 'internationalisation' of FM could lead to more complex consortia negotiations because there will be three private interests instead of simply the construction and financing interests.

Refinancing is creating new markets for companies undertaking due diligence in the refinancing process and in managing groups of special purpose vehicle companies established for each private finance initiative project (Hazell, 2005). Refinancing creates a new set of vested interests of financial institutions and corporate interests in the PPP lobby to widen secondary markets and promote the power, both financial and political, of private infrastructure ownership.

Erodes democratic control: The management and operational control of buildings by international companies, often headquartered in overseas tax havens, reduces accountability and transparency. It affects the flexibility, responsiveness and quality of service and further erodes public service principles and values. The interests of private investors influence the outcome at the end of the contract – either a transfer back to the authority, refinancing and extended contract or a new PPP contract and both at a cost.

Increases secrecy: Equity sales and refinancing extends 'commercial confidentiality' and significantly reduces disclosure and transparency. It is extremely difficult obtaining details of PPP equity sales and this is likely to get harder. Some companies issue a press release for a PPP equity sale but most are not required to issue a Stock Market Notice because the transaction is not a material financial interest. Privately owned companies have no comparable disclosure requirements.

Who benefits from operational efficiencies? The sale of assets creates pressure for additional operational efficiencies each time they are sold, in order that the new owner can extract profit and increase third party income from the use of buildings for other uses and by other organisations. This may include increased operational fees and charges for moving furniture and equipment, changing the use of rooms and redecoration over and above that specified. Even if some efficiencies can be obtained by batching FM operations on a regional/national basis to achieve economies of scale, the benefits for the public sector are likely to be small compared to the financial advantages gained by construction and finance capital.

The pressure to reduce management and operational costs will inevitably focus on jobs, terms and conditions of staff employed in FM service delivery. The consolidation of PPP projects by infrastructure funds is a classic private sector approach to 'shared services' or replacement of the traditional works department or Direct Service Organisation, which maintained a range of public buildings in a local authority. The new model cuts across public boundaries in managing and operating a variety of facilities for different client bodies and operates at a regional, national or international rather than at local level.

Privatising gains from public investment and development value: PPPs privatise the economic benefits and development gains but also commodify the organisational benefits. Once the project is completed the private sector can refinance and access the increased value of equity in the company that was responsible for finance and construction.

Longer-term implications: There are a number of key questions that must be addressed now, such as, will secondary funds grow into larger infrastructure funds or will they mutate into health and education funds, which might include core service delivery? Will the securitisation of PPPs lead to the next credit crunch? Who regulates the secondary market and what form of protection/security do these regulations provide?

The next generation of PPPs

Pressure to privatise, to recycle investment, to fund other infrastructure assets, will increase. For example, in 2007 the Czech Republic approved a plan to sell up to 7% of its 68% shareholding in the power company CEZ AS to raise US$1.74bn to fund highway construction. Privatisation is usually claimed to provide more resources for public investment but tying the receipts into specific funding of new infrastructure investment would signal a new development.

Neoliberalism is in crisis but 'new' forms of governance, 'strategic leadership', outsourcing and the transfer of assets and services to the partnerships with private sector or 'public interest companies' will continue. This will be couched as 'new and innovative' and 'accountable and empowering' but will be designed to make budget savings, corporatize the public sector and impose a contract culture, thus further eroding democracy and disempowering communities.

Increase in asset monetisation
The effect of the credit crunch and recession on public finance is likely to lead to an increase in asset monetisation. The lure of receipt of an immediate lump sum from the long-term leasing of public assets will be politically appealing. The relative security of long-term

infrastructure leasing may continue to be attractive to pension funds. These one-off lease payments are likely to be less favoured than those tendered in the last few years, due to the higher costs of finance, risk and investment market insecurity. Some infrastructure funds may consider it an opportune time to acquire cheap long-term leases in anticipation of 'better times' ahead!

Real estate
A wider role of Real Estate Investment Trusts (REITs) – see chapter 2 – is forecast. For example, REITs are being used to acquire healthcare facilities in the US (www.bio-medicine.org) and promoted to enable private equity investment in energy (Oil Gas Financial Journal, 2009). There is even discussion of enabling infrastructure investments to become REITs to exploit tax advantages (Reuters, 2009).

Real estate funds, such as the Whitehall funds operated by Goldman Sachs, are likely to acquire infrastructure assets. Whitehall raised US$31bn between 1991-2009 and owns office buildings, hotels, casinos and timeshares and acquired 95,000 public housing dwellings from the municipality of North Rhine-Westphalia, Germany, for US$3.5bn in 2008. Two years earlier, Dresden sold its stock of 48,000 dwellings to the private equity group Fortress Investments (Habitat International Coalition, 2008). Despite the collapse of property development, the conditions are being laid for further speculation and the next asset bubble.

New PPP/PFI models
The financial crisis, and slowdown in the flow of PPP deals, is being used as '... *an opportunity for radical new thinking*' which include changing the distribution of risk between the public and private sectors, reviewing the range of assets that are suitable for PPPs, examining new models '*that include permanent transfer of assets to the private sector*' and governments '... *taking long-term financial stakes in PPP projects*' (Freshfields Bruckhaus Deringer, 2009).

Joint or shared projects involving a number of public bodies to create larger contracts are also likely.

Project Delivery Organisation (PDO) or integrator model
This model attempts to reduce the length of the procurement process by requiring the private sector to provide procurement delivery and management skills (HM Treasury, 2008). However, it

would have far reaching consequences for the public sector.
'*Unlike an individual project, the project delivery organisation will manage the procurement of the underlying assets and then integrate those assets together with necessary component services to provide an overall service to the procuring authority. This may be beneficial in projects where there is a long construction period or where the service requires significant investment in new capital assets during the life of the contract or where there is a significant likelihood of material change in requirements throughout the life of the deal. This means that PFI investment can be managed alongside other forms of investment which are not suitable for PFI while still achieving improvements in service delivery*' (ibid).

A shift to delivering upgrades rather than new build and some PPP/PFI projects in technology and waste face '... *considerable future risks and uncertainties and the LIFT/BSF models are either untested or unsuitable in the circumstances*' (ibid). Hence 'competitive partnership', 'integrator' and 'incremental partnership' models, as further variants of the PPP, may emerge.

The Project Delivery Organisation (PDO), or integrator, approach is deemed be suitable where there is a need for '... *some uncertainty over the long-term requirement, with a resulting desire for flexibility and incremental acquisition, for example where new technology risk is present, end-user demands are subject to change, or policy changes are likely to affect how, where and what services are to be delivered in the future*' (HM Treasury, 2008). But this is applicable to virtually all-public and private services.

The Treasury claims this model is suitable when there is uncertainty about the timing or phasing of projects, a long construction phase and where efficiencies could be derived from dividing the project into distinct phases or parcels and where '... *limited supply-side competition to provide the entire project as one, but where the project can be sensibly divided into separate packages and competition introduced in the supply chain in a transparent manner*' (ibid).

'Alliancing' is another public/private delivery model advocated '... *where there is a high level of uncertainty about the nature of the infrastructure needed to meet the policy objectives, where there is significant technological risk, where there is a lack of a competitive supplier market, or where the project is large and not readily divisible into discrete parts that could be separately contracted*' (HM Treasury 2008). Leaving aside the usual requirement to specify outputs, create confidence and trust between the parties, sharing costs and benefits and open book accounting, this sounds like another recipe for public cost and private benefit.

Strategic Infrastructure Partnerships (SIP)
The Local Improvement Finance Trust (LIFT) and Building Schools for the Future (BSF) models are variations of a joint venture approach between the public and private sectors with a long-term strategic relationship. The UK government regards these models as still being in the '... *early stage of development*' (HM Treasury, 2006). It is claimed that this approach is suitable where there are successive phases of a similar type of work in national or regional programmes but uncertainty about its timing and phasing. Consolidating projects reduces procurement times and costs. This model also assumes to have advantages because it enables private sector commercial input into the planning of the project and to increase operational efficiency through continuous improvement and innovation.

Development of Strategic Service-delivery Partnership model
More multi-service SSPs with a larger infrastructure element may emerge: SSPs already provide new customer contact centres and promises of 'regeneration' through new business centres but this is likely to extend to the provision of new facilities. Furthermore, the extension of BSF to provide local authority capital projects for other services on school sites with the Local Education Partnership (LEP) taking on non-BSF work, could lead to a widening role of the LEP in service delivery. It creates a platform for the extension into core service delivery (DCSF, 2008).

Several trends are already evident. SSP projects now include planning and development functions (the Urban Vision Salford/Capita and Liverpool/Knowsley Mouchel projects) and highways/street scene (the Birmingham and Sheffield PPPs). The Oldham/Mouchel SSP combines professional and technical services such as highways engineering with corporate and ICT services. These projects could pave the way for directorate-based multi-function PPPs.

The extension of commissioning could lead to public bodies transferring a wide range of in-house services to commercial trading organisations, as recommended by PwC in a series of reports for the government (Department for Communities and Local Government (DCLG), 2008). Many are likely to be transferred to 'partnerships' with private contractors enroute to full privatisation, the same route taken by many Direct Service Organisations.

Shared services could be another driver for PPPs. Local, subregional and regional projects involving local government, health, employment training and other services could be developed as SSPs because of capability issues and failure to resolve democratic accountability matters. The 'strategic leadership' contract council model could also lead to large groups of services being transferred to 'partnerships', which would, in effect, be SSPs.

Whole service concept
'The days when public private financial structures were mainly about delivering chunks of capital – that's probably not going to be the focus in the future. The focus will be about delivering whole services, delivering outcomes that the taxpayer wishes to achieve. ... It isn't just about buildings and infrastructure, its about delivering whole solutions' stated Philip Hammond, the Shadow Chief Secretary to the Treasury (Public Private Finance, 2009).

Although the whole service concept has been implemented in SSPs in the UK, it has not been widely used for infrastructure and services, except in ICT. The division between core and non-core services remains. However, other PPP models, particularly in health, have included clinical services, for example in Latin America and Victoria, Australia. Four hospital PPPs in Portugal have a 30-year infrastructure contract and a 10-year renewable clinical services concession. However, the government has decided that future hospital PPPs will apply only to infrastructure, although procurement of the current projects will continue (Public Service Review, 2008). Entire hospitals have been transferred to private operators in Sweden (Capio) and Germany (Helios-Klinken) (Nikolic and Maikisch, 2006) and in the UK the first NHS hospital franchise, for the Hinchingbrooke Hospital, Huntingdonshire, including accident and emergency and maternity services, was agreed in July, 2009 (Health Service Journal, 2009). Other NHS Trusts and the private sector will be invited to bid.

The Sheffield City Council 'Streets Ahead' is an example of a long-term contract for a whole service via a £2bn 25-year PPP for highway maintenance (including street lighting, cleansing, design and build, grounds maintenance). The city is fast becoming a PPP City. It has a £1.3bn 35-year waste management, energy recovery, recycling and refuse collection PPP with Veolia; four school PPPs with a capital value of £300m; PPPs for building services, city centre offices and an £200m corporate services SSP with Capita. There are also PPPs for hospitals, courts and health centres in the city. The council previously transferred its residential care homes and sport and leisure facilities to trusts and council housing to an arms length company.

Hybrid approaches
The Ministry of Defence (MoD) Estate in London (MoDEL) project is an example of a hybrid approach and a variant on property outsourcing. VSM Estates (a joint venture between Vinci PLC and St. Mowlem Properties PLC) were appointed in August 2006 to fund and manage the development of a core site at RAF Northolt, the relocation of units and the sale of surplus sites, (about 100 hectares) within the M25. The MoD is investing £180m in new facilities at Northolt but the sale of surplus land is expected to exceed the cost of investment. The PPP provided a firm price for the first tranche of work and manages the procurement process for subsequent tranches but is barred from delivering development of these sites.

Claims that this is '... *an effective and economical way to deliver estate rationalisation within a constrained budgetary environment*' (Partnerships UK in Public Service Review 08) and provides a model for other public bodies, are grossly premature. Prime Plus Contracting (PPC) relies heavily on the location of sites, alternative uses and land values. MoDEL had the advantage of London sites, mainly housing use, and although the first site sold above expectations the fall in house prices and recession could reduce the value of the remaining sites. This PPP model is heavily dependent on incentivising the contractor to control costs and maximise receipts from land sales, a high-risk strategy at the best of times.

Integrating the delivery of new facilities, transfer of staff and the disposal of surplus sites is not rocket science. To date there is not a shred of evidence that this approach would be any more effective than a public sector rationalisation plan.

Strategic Estates Development Vehicle
Primary Care Trusts are being given the option of transferring their property assets to LIFT companies or to new Strategic Estates Development (SED) vehicles under the UK's transformation of community health services. In practice they are little different from the sale and lease back Property Partnerships described above.

Social private partnerships and community-owned assets
In the UK, the government has promoted community ownership of

public assets and service provision by voluntary and community organisations (Quirk, 2007). Whilst community and voluntary sector provision has a role to play, its capacity and ability to provide services is inflated in order to serve a political agenda to divert attention from outsourcing and privatising public assets to private companies.

In most cases, PPPs and operational providers are not interested in running community centres, which they regard as having a marginal economic function, fluctuating demand, limited scope for profit with too many political risks and liabilities. PPPs do not contribute to community empowerment, in fact quite the reverse, because they undermine and reduce community control of key assets.

PricewaterhouseCoopers have advocated Social Private Partnerships (SPPs), a '... *hybrid business model would seek to harness the best of the pure commercial sector to underpin a substantial expansion of social enterprise activity*' to secure a greater share of public sector contracts (PricewaterhouseCoopers, 2009). But they envisage more support and subsidies (tax and other incentives) will be needed to '... *scale up social enterprises.*'

Private towns and neighbourhoods
A more likely development is the growth of gated communities, regeneration areas and eco-towns where developers are responsible for building the infrastructure, operating basic services such as utilities, information and communications systems and community services. These services and 'community governance' would be provided through a management company, yet another PPP model but more clearly modelled and promoted as an alternative to local government!

CHAPTER 8

Abandoned and terminated projects

This chapter is a dossier of the performance of infrastructure PPPs and privatisation focusing on abandoned and terminated projects. The performance of outsourced services is excluded, except where they have been an integral part of PPPs.

Abandoned projects
A significant number of major projects have been abandoned before procurement began or was concluded. For example, in the UK they include the Leicester hospital (costs rose from £711m to £921 with £23.4m planning costs before the project was abandoned in 2007); Paddington Basin, London (£900m hospital incurred £15m costs before it was abandoned); Medway LIFT, Leeds Maternity, Southall Hospital, Plymouth Hospital, Wiltshire Primary Care Trust (abandons £85m LIFT project on value-for-money grounds after three bidders shortlisted); Whipps Cross MHS Trust (abandoned £350m PFI hospital contract after only one bidder remained); Colchester General Hospital (Amec preferred bidder on £170m project but abandoned on grounds of affordability, which cost Essex Rivers Healthcare £7.3m in aborted fees). The Higher Education Funding Council for England reported 23 abandoned projects compared to only 13 signed PPP projects in the 1997-2008 period. The Maiden Lane, London Borough of Camden housing project was also abandoned.

Seven Canadian PPP projects were abandoned including two hospital, one road, one water and three convention/arena/recreation projects up to 2005 (National Union of Public and General Employees). The Calgary Courthouse, Alberta, costs increased 66% to C$500m so the provincial government publicly financed the project. British Columbia ditched plans for the Port Mann bridge PPP in 2009, opting for a C$2.5bn design-build contract after failing to reach agreement with a Macquarie-led consortium which would have cost C$3.3bn using the same construction and engineering contractors.

Chapter 6 reported that five Dublin housing projects and the Thorton Hall prison complex were abandoned in 2008/09 and removed from Ireland's PPP programme.

Dexter Whitfield

Summary of privatisation and PPP failures
Nearly 1,000 PPP and privatisation projects have failed, were distressed or have been renegotiated with total value of an astonishing US$511bn (see Table 32). The total includes 262 cancelled and distressed projects in developing countries, 18 water contract failures globally (plus twenty in developing countries excluded to avoid

Table 32: *Summary of PPP and Privatisation failures*

Sector	No of projects	Total value of contracts US$billion	% Failure rates
PPP and Privatisation projects cancelled or distressed in developing countries: World Bank database	262	94.2	29% water, 8% transport, 8% energy and 4% telecoms (by value)
PPP failures – developed countries (see Table x)	58	43.7	n/a
Water privatisation failures in North America and Europe, excluding those in World Bank developing countries database	18	n/a	n/a
PPP and outsourcing ICT failures in The UK**	105	47.5	57% cost overruns, 33% major delays, 30% terminated
Additional ICT failures 2008/09 see text	5	14.3	n/a
Infrastructure privatisation failures* see text	12	10.0	n/a
Independent Sector Treatment Centres (Health) in The UK	n/a	1.5	Need to update situation
Renegotiated contracts (Latin America)	500	300.0	51% overall (water 81%, transport 65%, 22% electricity renegotiated on average 2.1 years after contract signed)
Total	**960**	**511.2**	

Sources: Public Private Infrastructure Advisory Facility database accessed 14 June 2009 – 194 cancelled and 68 distressed, 233 had been merged – all telecom and energy. Only water for 2007, 2009. Guasch, 2008, *ICT failures included in The UK: PPP and outsourcing ICT failures. ** Conversion rates to US$ were £1.61, €1.39, C$0.86, A$0.78 on 8 July 2009.

double counting), 50 PPP failures in the UK, Canada and Australia, plus 105 outsourced public sector ICT projects with major cost overruns, delays and terminations in the UK alone.

Terminated and troubled projects in developing countries
262 public infrastructure projects in energy, transport, telecoms and water were cancelled or distressed in developing countries between 1990-2007 (Public-Private Infrastructure Advisory Facility, 2009).

Cancelled projects were defined as those in which the private sector had withdrawn by selling or transferring its economic interest back to the government before fulfilling the contract terms, removing all management and personnel from the concern, ceasing operation, service provision, or construction for 15 percent or more of the license or concession period, following the revocation of the license or repudiation of the contract. Distressed projects were defined as those where the government or the operator had either requested contract termination or international arbitration.

The value of cancelled and distressed projects, by number of projects and value, was concentrated in Latin America/Caribbean and East Asia and Pacific which accounted for 89% of the total value and 74% of the number of projects (see Table 33). Cancelled and distressed projects accounted for one third of water investment in contrast to 11%, 10% and 4% of transport, energy and telecoms investment respectively (see Table 34).

The main reason for water project failures was opposition to large price increases and problems collecting charges from users. The main cause of transport project failures were levels of traffic use and toll income being well below the excessively optimistic forecasts, which were used in the financing of the project.

Some projects, such as the Mexican toll road programme, were large-scale failures. By the end of 1995, 34 projects had reached financial close with US$ 9.9bn private investment. However, construction cost overruns averaged 25% and average revenues were about 30% below forecasts (only 5 projects met or exceeded targets). The average toll road fee increased from US$ 0.02/km to US$ 0.17, a 750% increase (World Bank, 2008).

Renegotiated contracts
Over half of the one thousand PPP projects in Latin America between 1990-2001 were renegotiated an average 2.1 years after the award of

contract (Andries et al, 2008). The renegotiation rate in water was extremely high, 81%, followed by transport (65%) and electricity (22%), rendering competitive procurement almost meaningless. Nearly two thirds of renegotiations were initiated by the private sector. Concessions that were entirely privately financed were more likely to seek renegotiation. The main peaks in the rate of renegotiation of contracts coincided with economic fluctuations and political shocks, although not all shocks triggered waves of renegotiations. Four out of five contracts were awarded through competitive bidding but 46% of these were renegotiated compared to

Table 33:
Projects Cancelled or Distressed by region 1990-2007 (US$bn)

Region	No of projects	% of total projects	Value of cancelled or distressed investment US$bn	% of committed investment
East Asia and Pacific	79	6	34.4	12
Europe and Central Asia	21	3	3.8	2
Latin America & Caribbean	118	9	49.2	10
Middle East and North Africa	6	5	1.0	2
South Asia	7	2	3.9	3
Sub-Saharan Africa	31	9	1.9	3
Total	**262**		**94.2**	

Source: World Bank PPI database, accessed 14 June 2009. Water data includes 2008.

Table 34:
Projects Cancelled or Distressed by sector 1990-2007 (US$bn)

Sector	No of projects	% of total projects	Value of cancelled or distressed investment US$bn	% of committed investment
Energy	90	6	30.0	8
Telecoms	42	5	22.6	4
Transport	62	6	17.4	8
Water	68	10	24.2	41
Total	**262**		**94.2**	

Source: World Bank PPI database, accessed 14 June 2009. Water data includes 2008.

only 8% of bilateral negotiated contracts (World Bank, 2003). Renegotiation led to clear winners: 62% of renegotiated contracts included tariff increases compared with only 19% with tariff decreases, 69% agreed delays on investment obligation targets compared to 18% which accelerated investment, 62% reduced investment obligations, 59% increased the number of cost components with automatic pass-through to tariff increases, and 38% extended the concession period (Gausch, 2004). The most likely winner in renegotiation is not the most efficient operator but the one most skilled in renegotiation whilst many renegotiations '... are opportunistic and should be deterred' (Gausch, 2004).

Bearing in mind the evidence is limited to two sectors and five countries, nevertheless, it is an appalling record. PPP toll road projects awarded in the 1990s in Hungary, Indonesia and Thailand were taken over by the government. Renegotiation usually reflects political and community opposition, a 'social backlash' to price hikes, and exploitation.

Examples of failed privatisation
Rail: The UK's privatised railway system was carved up into three parts, a track operator, three companies own the trains which are leased to train operating companies which succeeded in winning operating franchises for routes and regions. Public subsidies and high rail fares were the other ingredients. Railtrack PLC, the rail infrastructure company, was placed into administration on 7 October 2001. Railtrack was sold for £1,904m in 1996 preceded by a £869m net debt write-off. The shares were priced at 390p, almost doubled in price within a year and by 1999 were over 1,600p, valuing the company at £8bn, four times its original sale price (Whitfield, 2001). Railtrack was replaced by Network Rail, a non-profit company.

The train leasing companies have been resold at inflated profits whilst the franchised services have fragmented the network (see Chapter 4). The southeast rail franchise operated by Connex was terminated by the Strategic Rail Authority in 2003 after seven years of poor performance, despite £779m in public subsides. The franchise was taken over by South Eastern Trains, a newly formed subsidiary of the Strategic Rail Authority (SRA). National Express walked away from the East Coast London-Scotland in 2009 after losing £20m in the first half of the year. It will have to pay a £72m penalty for terminating the contract. The company also has the East Anglia franchise, which it wants to retain because it is profitable. The company has naturally denied 'cherry picking'.

But its not the first time this company has walked away from a contract. In Australia, National Express abandoned three Victoria rail franchises in December 2002 after three years. It forfeited an A$130m performance bond plus an estimated A$300m in write-offs (Allsop, 2007). Bullish passenger forecasts, automated ticketing problems, fare increases and a failure to achieve significant cost savings contributed to the crisis. The government renegotiated the franchises with two other operators.

Estonia privatised its railways in 2001, having previously received €36m loans from the European Bank for Reconstruction and Development, European Investment Bank and EU-PHARE for reconstruction and upgrading. A 66% share stake was sold to Baltic Rail Services, but it was renationalised in January 2007 (Railroad Development Corporation, 2009).

Guatemala railway entered a 50-year partnership with Pittsburgh-based Railroad Development Corporation in 1998 but was in dispute from 2005 over removal of squatters on rail land and the finance of maintenance work and closed in 2007.

New Zealand was the first country in the world to fully privatise its railways as a single entity in 1993, selling the network for NZ$320m to a consortium headed by US-based Wisconsin Central and a local investment bank. The rail track was reacquired in 2004 for one dollar followed by rail and ferry operations in 2008 from Australia's Toll Holdings (which had bought a majority stake in 2003) for NZ$665m.

Air: Air New Zealand was re-acquired by the government in 2001, thirteen years after privatisation, with NZ$885m cash injection to prevent bankruptancy in return for an 83% stake.

The Argentina government renationalised the national airline, Aerolineas Argentinas, in 2008. It was originally sold to the Spanish airline Iberia in 1991 and sold to Marsans in 2001. The airline had debts of US$890m by May 2008, arrears of fuel payments and over half its fleet was grounded for lack of parts despite significant fare increases. *'The deterioration of a service that has stopped providing a service is how Argentina President Cristina Fernadez described the airline'* (Financial Times, 20 July 2008).

Energy: British Energy, the privatized nuclear power generator, supplying 20% of the UK's electricity, had to be bailed out by the government by £410m in 2002 to meet the company's debts. A restructuring deal was agreed, in which the company's creditors agreed a debt-for-equity swap in which they take control of 97.5% of the shares, leaving the existing shareholders with just 2.5%.

The cause of the California Electricity crisis in 2000/01, which led to blackouts and financial crisis, were rooted in the 1996 deregulation of California's electricity market, which was claimed would lower prices and spur economic growth. But by 2002 *'utilities were bankrupted, the state became the buyer of last resort, and the institutions established by the 1996 reform were dismantled'* (Public Policy Institute of California, 2003).

Telecoms: Bolivia renationalised ENTEL in 2008 from Euro Telecom Italia. Venezuela, renationalised CANTV (telecoms provider) and Electricidad de Caracas (EDC, electricity company) in 2006.

Ports: New Zealand, Auckland Regional Council reversed the part-privatisation of Ports of Auckland. Auckland Regional Holdings (ARH), the investment arm of the Auckland Regional Council, succeeded in acquiring 90% of the shares in Ports of Auckland Ltd (POAL) in 2005 enabling it to compulsorily acquire the remaining 10%. Much of the waterfront is industrial land, planned for urban and commercial development.

Examples of failed PPP projects
The PPP projects summarised in Table 35 suffered from financial collapse, large cost increases, the failure of partnership arrangements, over-ambitious user forecasts and/or community opposition to high user charges.

Service failures, delays and cost overruns
In the UK outsourced public sector ICT contracts in central government, the National Health Service (NHS), local authorities, public bodies and agencies had significant cost overruns, delays and terminations in the last decade (Whitfield, 2007). The contract models included outsourced contracts and PPPs in central and local government, the NHS and other public bodies. Whilst many outsourced ICT projects are delivered on time and within budget, some of the problems result from over-ambitious projects, a lack of design and development before procurement, and pressures for efficiency savings overtaking the ability to deliver. The technical complexity of projects is also often under-estimated. The research revealed that 105 PPP and outsourced public sector ICT projects in

Dexter Whitfield

Table 35:
Summary of key PPP Failures – Europe, North America and Australia

Project	Cost	Date	Consequences
The UK			
Metronet Rail SSL (WS Atkins, Balfour Beatty, Bombardier, EDF Energy, and Thames Water)	£15.7bn npv for 3 contracts	Started 2003, collapsed 2007 and no private sector buyer	Metronet had two 30 year PPP contracts for maintenance and renewal of the Bakerloo, Central, Victoria and Waterloo & City TUBE Lines and another for the 'sub-surface lines': the Circle, District, Hammersmith & City, Metropolitan and East London Lines. PPPs had £992m overspend by July 2007, projected to be £1.8bn by 2010. Transport for London took over work – maintenance in-house with individual contracts for upgrade and major new investment. The PPP 'ended in collapse and chaos. It was a spectacular failure' (House of Commons Transport Committee, 2008). Yet the Government claimed this was 'predominantly a corporate failure, and that the structural weaknesses of Metronet led to its own downfall' (Government response to Transport Committee, 2008). 'Metronet, which was originally contracted to upgrade two thirds of the network, was spectacularly inefficient' (London Assembly, 2009). Metronet was 'experiencing significant cost overruns and delays in delivering their obligations under the PPP contracts' and poor performance reflected 'the tied supply chain arrangements between Metronet and certain of its shareholders and weak governance, planning and risk management' (Cambridge Economic Policy Associates, 2008).
Skye Toll Bridge, Scotland (Miller Construction, Dyckerhoff & Widmann, Bank of America)	£42m	Opened 1995	Closed ferry service when bridge opened and vociferous community campaign against high toll fees. Tolls frozen at 1999 prices for remainder and abandoned in 2004 and concession terminated with £27m payment.

223

Global Auction of Public Assets

Project	Cost	Date	Consequences
Inverness Airport, Scotland	£9.6m cost of building	Opened 1998	Contract bought out for £25m by public agency in 2004.
Crymlyn Burrows waste treatment plant, Swansea, Wales	£40m	2002	HLC Environmental Projects, financed by Bank of Scotland. Terminated by Neath Port Talbot Council in 2005 because it was incapable of handling the daily tonnage of contracted waste. Long legal dispute over assets.
4 projects: Bedfordshire County Council (£265m, HBS) and West Berkshire Council (£104m, Amey) terminated: Redcar & Cleveland Council (£200m, Liberata) and Swansea City Council £100m, Capgemini) significantly reduced	£669m	2005-08	4 Strategic Service-delivery Partnership contracts terminated or significantly reduced because of poor performance (see ESSU, 2008 for details)
London Borough of Southwark: Education services	£100m	2002	Terminated after two of the five-year contract with WS Atkins – failed to meet targets. Termination cost Southwark Council £1.5m.
Royal Armouries	£43m	1996	Achieved only a third of 1.3m visitors forecast and plummeted to fewer than 200,000 within 2 years. Consortia refinanced deal twice but cumulative losses soared to £10m in 1999 and the Bank of Scotland refused further lending, forcing renegotiation of contract, ceased to be a PPP.
National Physical Laboratory (John Laing plc, Serco Group, Bank of America, Abbey National)	£96m capital value	1998 contract signed	Terminated in 2004 after long construction delays and failure to meet specification. 'Original private sector design of the new buildings was deficient' (NAO). John Laing plc lost £67m, subcontractors £12m, banks lost £18m and Laing's and Serco £4m in dividends. DTI invested £122m (including termination compensation, procurement costs, upfront payments and unitary payments) and left with £85m assets.
National Air Traffic Services	n/a	2001	Privatised but financial crisis forced refinancing in 2003 – government and BAA invested in company.

Dexter Whitfield

Project	Cost	Date	Consequences
East Lothian Council Schools	£43m	2003	Ballast UK went into administration in refurbishing 6 schools and community centre. Parent company withdrew funding. Unpaid subcontractors into liquidation. Replacement contractor but long delay.
Jarvis plc – range of PFI projects	n/a	2004	By 2004 company had 27 educational PFI contracts but did not have capacity to fulfil – forced to use subcontractors, higher costs, long delays and quality problems. Sold London Underground Tubelines PPP stake to help fund £120m shortfall.
Dudley Group of Hospitals	£150m	2001	Summit Healthcare (Sir Robert McAlpine, Interserve FM and Bank of Scotland) to redevelop and expand Acute Hospital. Additional refurbishment work required led to McAlpine suffering £100m losses. Firm sued NHS Trust for damages and received £23.2m in 2007.
Norfolk County Council	£300m	2009	Residual Waste Treatment project for 90,000-150,000 tonnes abandoned as preferred bidder costs increased 50% since March 2007 and no longer value-for-money.
Ireland			
West Link Toll Bridge, Dublin	€600m	2008	Originally opened in 1990 and new twin bridge operated from 2003, contract terminated to change to barrier free tolling but €600m compensation to original toll company.
5 housing PPPs	n/a	2008	Renewal of St Michaels, O'Devaney Gardens, Dominick Street estates in Dublin abandoned by developer McNamara/Castlethorn plus two McNamara projects housing land at Infirmary Road and Sean McDermott Street (Bisset, 2009)
Czech Republic			
D47 Motorway Ostrava	US$1.5bn	2003	Contract signed 2001 but cancelled
Na Homolce Hospital	€22m	2006	Contract cancelled
UJEP University campus	€89m	2006	Contract cancelled

Global Auction of Public Assets

Project	Cost	Date	Consequences
Poland			
A2 Motorway	n/a	2005	Completed Nowy Tomysl – Konin section but traffic well below forecast.
Hungary			
M1/M15 Motorway	n/a	1999	30-year concession in 1993, opened 1996, only 49% of toll revenue forecast achieved. Strabag and Transroute sought restructuring, renationalisation.
Bulgaria			
Sofia-Bourgas toll road	€715m	2008	Consortia including Sacyr Vallehermoso (Spain) awarded contract 2005 but Government cancelled contract after they failed to raise the funds.
Croatia			
Zagreb-Gorican toll road	US$460m	1998	Concession terminated after consortia unable to obtain financing.
USA			
Stewart International Airport, New York	US$35m	2000-2007	99-year lease won by National Express Group (UK), first US airport fully privatised in FAA pilot programme. National Express paid US$35m for lease and additional payment due after 10 years. Potential never developed and Group made strategic decision to get out of airports having sold its other airports. Re-acquired by Port Authority of New York and New Jersey for US$78.5m.
State Route 91, California	US$130m	2002	Toll road opened 1995 and first to use variable congestion pricing. Orange County Transportation purchased road for US$207.5m in 2002.
State Route 57 California	US$950m	2001	Contract for 4-lane 11.2 mile awarded to American Transportation Development, sought 6 year delay in start of construction but state terminated contract.
Mid State Tollway	US$600m	2001	40-mile toll road project suspended due to political opposition followed by termination.
Texas State Highway 121	US$3.3bn	2007	Unsolicited bid from Skanska then bidding process led to award to

226

Project	Cost	Date	Consequences
			Cintra, but eventually Regional Transportation Commission approved public-public partnership by North Texas Tollway Authority.
Camino Columbia Toll Road, Texas	US$90m	2004	Private project opened 2000 but high tolls and carried only 13% of traffic forecast. Bondholders foreclosed, John Hancock Financial Services bought back its investment for $12.1m at auction and then sold it to Texas Transportation Commission for $20m.
Westchester County Medical Center Car Park, New York	n/a	1999	Parking fees more than doubled in first three years. Acquired by state at a premium.
Canada			
Port Mann Highway	C$2.46bn	2009	Abandoned PPP, now design and build project
Prince Edward Wastewater Treatment Plant	C$25m	2009	Bids from Corix and Epcor rejected – high capital and 'operating costs far exceeding the known operating costs'. New design and build contract.
Cornwall Recreation Centre	n/a	2009	Council cancelled procurement and will proceed as conventional project.
Fundy Island Ferry Service	n/a	2008	Non-compliant bid received from only remaining bidder, New Brunswick the separated design and construction of 3 new ferries from operation and maintenance
Universite du Quebec, Montreal commercial and university project	C$333m	2005-08	Cost of redeveloped bus terminal, two university residence towers and parking garage soared to C$529m. Quebec Auditor General gave damning report of University Rector and senior advisers.
Ottawa Light Rail Transit	C$778m	2006	Council approved Siemen's led consortia but cancelled contract 5 months later
Hamilton-Wentworth Sewage Treatment Plant	n/a	2005	Two company failures – Philips Utilities then Azurix subsidiary of Enron, returned to city operation after decade of failures.
Whistler Wastewater Treatment Plant	n/a	2006	PPP procurement cancelled.
Swan Hills Waste Management Facility, Alberta, Canada	C$150m	2001	Bovar Inc. ran site for 12 years which cost taxpayers C$440m plus additional clean up costs.

Global Auction of Public Assets

Project	Cost	Date	Consequences
St Albert recreational facility, Alberta	n/a	2004	City council terminated contract.
Nova Scotia 33 schools PPP (Nova Learning)	C$350m	2001	PPP cancelled by Provincial Govt – 9 schools built but C$32m cost overruns. Nova Scotia announced non-PPP contracts for 17 new schools at lower cost.
City of Guelph Sports and Entertainment Centre	C$19.5m	1999	35 year contract but ticket sales lower than forecast, city council had to make loan repayments and taxes.
City of Cranbrook Arena	C$23m	2000	After five years project failed and reverted to council management
Victoria City Council Sports and Entertainment Centre	C$52m	1996	Agreement cancelled 1999, new contractor but increased costs and further delays.
Maple Ridge, British Columbia, town centre	C$80m	1999-2002	Agreement cancelled and city undertook project following court case ruled against legality of project.
Miramichi Youth Training Centre, New Brunswick	n/a	1995	Operation of centre excluded from contract with Wackenhut Corrections Corporation
Australia			
Australia: Sydney Airport Transit Link. 6.2 miles (Transfield/Bouygues PPP)	A$800m	2000	Receivership after 6 months as passengers only 25% of 48,000 forecast. A$704m government bailout.
Brisbane Airport Rail Link 5.3 miles (Transfield, Hyder, Macquarie, EGIS and ABN AMRO)	A$223m	2001	Ridership much lower than forecasts. Moody's sharply downgraded credit rating for operator Airtrain Citylink Ltd. State to acquire after 5 years of 35-year concession.
Cross City Tunnel, Sydney, Australia. 2.1km	A$1bn	2005	Opened mid 2005, receivership late 2006, sold 2007 after traffic and toll income only a third of forecast (see chapter 6).
Latrobe Regional Hospital, Victoria	A$440m	1998-2002	20 year BOO project with Australian Hospital Care Ltd, failed after two years, company sought additional recurrent funding for operational losses, operation and ownership transferred to state government in 2002.
St Vincent's Hospital, Queensland	A$48m	2002	Financial collapse of 200-bed hospital with A$10m losses, acquired by State.

228

Project	Cost	Date	Consequences
Deer Park Women's Prison, Victoria	A$21m	2000	Contract with Corrections Corporation of America terminated after 4 years due to poor performance. Acquired by state for A$20.2m, renamed Dame Phyllis Frost Centre.
Oasis Project, Liverpool	A$700m	2003	Sports arena and stadium with Macquarie Bank, failed at development stage, cost taxpayers A$20m, subject of Daly Public Inquiry.

Sources: Government and public sector audits, inquiries and studies 1996-2009.

the UK, contract value of £29.5bn, had significant cost overruns, delays and terminations in the last decade. 57% of contracts experienced cost overruns of £9bn, an average 30.5% increase. In addition, a third of contracts suffered major delays and 30% of contracts were terminated. The main ICT companies with contract cost overruns, delays and terminations are EDS (Electronic Data Service) – 13 contracts, Liberata (8), Fujitsu and IBM (6 each), Accenture, Atos Origin, Capita, ITNET (now Serco) and Siemens (5 each) and BT (British Telecom) (4).

There were further problems in 2008/09. The UK's largest defence PPP project, the £12bn Defence Training Review, centralised all non-military technical training for armed forces, is in crisis after property company Land Securities withdrew from the Metrix consortium with Qinetiq, and costs have risen by £1bn in two years. Another Ministry of Defence project, the Defence Information Infrastructure, saw costs soar from £2.3bn in 2006 to £7.09bn by July 2008. EDS costs on the National Offender Management Information System escalated from £234m in June 2004 to £793m by September 2008.

Transport for London sacked Oyster card operator after £1m fares were lost following two system failures in 2008. The NHS fired Fujitsu from an £896m electronic care record software contract. Nineteen key Department of Work and Pensions ICT contracts were either over-budget or late. IBM and the Department of Transport managed to turn planned savings of £57m on a shared services project into costs of £81m (NAO, 2008). Department for Children, Schools and Families terminated the Liberata contract to pay students Educational Maintenance Allowances after delays and 26,000 outstanding applications.

The UK's Audit Commission identified three strategic partnership failures in a sample of fourteen projects but claimed that the whole study was 'commercially confidential' (Audit Commission, 2008). This is a high failure rate. A critique of this report revealed that secrecy was only one of many fundamental flaws, which included inadequate methodology, no evidence base, employment issues ignored, questionable value-for-money and no audit of private investment (Whitfield, 2008).

There have been significant failures in privatised water services examples of privatised water services failing in both developed and developing countries. Table 36 summarises 46 project failures and twelve example where proposals for water PPPs and privatisation have been rejected.

Reasons for failures
The reasons for the high level of project failures vary between regions and sectors. There are five common factors.

Firstly, economic crises in East Asia and Latin America led to a decline in capital investment and contracts did not anticipate the effect of currency fluctuations with revenues on local currency and loan repayments (Connecting East Asia, 2005 and Leigland, 2008).

Secondly, flawed and inflated forecasts led to unrealistic expectations of traffic/user demand, which in turn reduced income from user charges and tolls, cash flow crises and threatened private sector profits.

Thirdly, increased tariffs and tolls, particularly after the renegotiation of contracts, strengthened community opposition already critical of job losses and the private takeover of public services.

Fourthly, the lack of comprehensive condition surveys of existing assets led to the level of disrepair being underestimated, plus poor quality of management and performance information was also a factor (Leigland, 2008).

Fifthly, the design of many projects was flawed – some projects were too ambitious and/or technically compromised, badly managed and failed to deliver the benefits claimed for PPPs and privatisation. Some projects were implemented as a result of '... *authoritarian decisions at the presidential level or through strict conditionalities imposed by international financial institutions and donors*' (Norwegian Forum for Environment and Development, 2006). Corruption, endemic in some countries, contributed to the financial instability of projects.

Finally, regulatory frameworks and monitoring systems were often

Table 36: Failed privatised and PPP water projects

Place	Country	Year started	Year ended	Reasons for rejection
Latin America				
Buenos Aires Province	Argentina	1999	2002	Frequent price increases, poor service quality, failure to honour contractual commitments.
Buenos Aires City	Argentina	1994	2005	Company sought huge tariff increase to compensate devaluation of currency but price hikes not allowed.
Tucuman	Argentina	1994	1998	Severe tariff hikes, intense public protests.
Santa Fe Province	Argentina	1995	2005	Non-compliance of contract and sought to re-negotiate contract.
Cochabamba	Bolivia	1999	2000	Drastic increase in water tariffs, intense public protests.
EL Alto and La Paz	Bolivia	1997	2005	Private operator refused to extend potable water supply to the poor areas of the city, peaceful but huge uprising and demonstrations by the people.
All	Uruguay	–	2004	Increased water tariffs, new law by plebiscite making water a fundamental right.
Bogota	Columbia	1994	–	City refused World Bank money due to privatisation conditionality.
Puerto Rico	Puerto Rico	1995	2003	Problems in service delivery and contractual obligations, violated environmental laws.
Honduras	Honduras	–	1995	Intense Public Protests.
All	Trinidad	1994	1999	Failure to fulfil contractual obligations.
North America				
Halifax	Canada	2002	2003	Private corporation refused to take responsibility for failing to meet environmental standards of the contract, also effective grassroots campaigning by citizens and environmentalist groups.
Hamilton	Canada	1994	2003	Municipal council voted to take back operation of city water and wastewater plants after the contract term ended.
Toronto	Canada	2002	2004	Huge public protests and campaigning against privatisation efforts.

Global Auction of Public Assets

Place	Country	Year started	Year ended	Reasons for rejection
Atlanta	USA	1999	2003	20-year deal, US$21.4m annual payment with United Water but level of repairs and investment grossly miscalculated. Contract terminated after United Water demanded extra US$80m.
Birmingham	USA	–	2000	n/a
New Orleans	USA	1999	2004	Bids received for US$1bn contract but rejected by Water Board. Campaign by a coalition of labour, environmental groups, churches and citizen activists.
Felton, California	USA	–	2008	Re-municipalised.
Montara, Cal.	USA	–	2003	Re-municipalised.
Houston	USA	2001	2008	$230m MWH Constructors water purification plant and operation terminated – now in-house.
Houston	USA	–	2007	American Water contract for southeast water plant and returned in-house
Fairfield-Suisun, California	USA	1976	2008	United Water contract terminated, return to in-house operation.
Petaluma, Calif.	USA	1979	2008	Veolia contract terminated, in-house operation of upgraded water plant
China				
Da Chang, Shanghai	China	1997	2004	Ended concession when government cancelled guaranteed rate of return.
Xian Water	China	–	2001	Ended concession when government cancelled guaranteed rate of return.
Shenyang	China	1996	1999	High price of bulk water, huge losses to state owned company due to high guaranteed returns, failure of concession contract.
Shantou	China	–	2002	Company exited in dispute over contract
Europe				
Paris	France	1985	2009	Re-municipalised
Cherbourg	France	–	2005	Re-municipalised
Castres	France	1990	2003	30 year contract terminated, high costs.
Durance-Luberon	France	1984	1997	Re-municipalised
Grenoble	France	1987	2001	Bribery scandal, public protests.
Potsdam	Germany	1998	2000	Unjustified price increases by private operator.
Lodz	Poland	1993	1995	Problems in terms of costs and failures, deadlines missed.

Place	Country	Year started	Year ended	Reasons for rejection
Poznan	Poland	–	2002	n/a
Asia				
Bangalore	India	2001	–	Very high cost of water, assured off-take from the company.
Delhi	India	-	2006	Intense public protests, exposé of contractual terms favouring private companies.
Kelantan Waters	Malaysia	1999	1999	Poor services provided by private company, huge debts, low number of connections, high amount of non-revenue water.
Indah Water	Malaysia	1996	1997	Private operator exited, eventually contract failed.
Manila West	Philippines	1997	2003	Failure to extend water connections to poor areas, no investments, increase in tariffs, non-fulfillment of other contractual obligations.
Thu Duc, Ho Chi Minh City	Vietnam	1997	2003	Company exited in dispute over contract terms.
Bangkok	Thailand	1993	1997	Private company found that it could not continue with the sewerage treatment plant construction contract, Government claimed that company not fulfilling contractual obligations.
Africa				
Dar es Salaam	Tanzania	2003	2006	Erratic water supplies, acute water shortages, failure to provide clean water to poor communities.
Nkonkobe	South Africa	1999	2002	Popular protests due to disconnection, price hikes.
Nairobi	Kenya	1999	2001	Severe price hikes, huge job cuts, guaranteed profits, no competitive bidding process.
Mali	Mali	2000	2005	Increased water charges led to high-level unpaid bills. PPP company compensated then withdrew.
Water privatisation proposals were rejected in 12 countries/cities				
Rio de Janeiro	Brazil	1999		
Montreal	Canada	1999		
Munich	Germany	1998		
All	Honduras	1995		
Debrecen	Hungary	1995		
All	Mauritius	2000		

Place	Country	Year started	Year ended	Reasons for rejection
All	Panama	1999		
All	Paraguay	2002		
Poznan	Poland	2002		
Lodz	Poland	1994		
Malmo	Sweden	1995		
Washington DC	USA	1996		

Source: Water: Private, Limited: Issues in Privatisation, Corporatisation and Commercialisation of Water Sector in India, 2007, by Gaurav Dwivedi, Rehmat and Shripad Dharmadhikary.and). Public Works Financing, March 2008; Hall, Lobina and de la Motte, 2005.

inadequate, understaffed and unable to cope with poorly designed and negotiated contracts.

A World Bank review of private investment from 1983 – 2004, concluded: *'PPI [private participation in infrastructure] has disappointed – playing a far less significant role in financing infrastructure in cities than was hoped for, and which might be expected given the attention it has received and continues to receive in strategies to mobilize financing for infrastructure ... PPI is inherently limited in scope for financing urban infrastructure for the wide array of non-commercial infrastructure services cities need. Even for commercial services like water supply, subsidies are prevalent all over the world ... Local governments need good sources of public finance to fund those services, and some form of government borrowing is needed for major investments in these areas to avoid inter-generational inequities'* (World Bank, 2006).

The level of abandoned, terminated and renegotiated contracts in developed and developing countries clearly indicates that there are fundamental flaws in the PPP model. Two decades of amending and adjusting the legal, financial and other aspects of the model have made little impact. Bigger, multi-service, longer-term contracts will only exacerbate this situation.

CHAPTER 9

Impact of infrastructure PPPs and privatisation

This chapter will evaluate the effect of PPPs and privatisation of public infrastructure. It examines the methods used to assess value-for-money and the Public Sector Comparator, a hypothetical assessment of the public and private investment options. The second part assesses the impact of projects on design, innovation and vision; affordability and cost; quality of service; accountability, governance and participation; economic and social impact; social justice; public sector capability and quality of employment.

Value-for-Money and the Public Sector Comparator

All governments claim that decisions made to proceed with PPPs and privatisation are made on grounds of Value-for-Money (VfM). No VfM-no PPP is their mantra. It is important to clarify some important points first.

Firstly, 'value' is primarily equated with cost. It is based on *estimates* of the costs and efficiency savings that *may* be achieved over the course of the contract. The project can draw on the experience of similar projects elsewhere but there is no certainty that the same conditions will apply. The PPP and privatisation lobby frequently imply that VfM is a rigorous, scientifically sound process, but in practice it is not.

Secondly, it is regularly *assumed* that the private sector will achieve larger efficiency savings both faster and at lower cost than the public sector. Differences in the estimates or forecasts, which is all they can be, for construction, maintenance, operational services, energy supply, the success of service transformation and so on can be significant over a long-term contract. Such assumptions can readily be tweaked to alter the overall figures.

Thirdly, risk assessment uses historic public sector performance to contrast with anticipated future private contractor performance, particularly with regard to the risk of construction delays and cost overruns. The flawed National Audit Office/Mott MacDonald evidence comparing public/private construction delays/cost overruns, has been widely promoted in development bank and PPP presentations. The analysis of retained, shared and transferred risks is usually internalised and rarely, if ever, subjected to public scrutiny.

This gives considerable scope for massaging impacts and the exclusion of ways in which some risks can be mitigated or eliminated by changes in public sector capacity and/or systems.

Fourthly, the reference or comparative projects are usually carefully *selected* to put the proposed project in the best possible light and to ignore alternative investment strategies. The quality and comparability of the evidence base for cost comparisons is crucial.

Finally, the full facts about Value-for-Money will only be known at the end of the contract when the facility is transferred to public ownership or due diligence takes place as part of a new procurement process. The Public Sector Comparator (PSC) is only a forecast or estimate. A contract agreement can never guarantee that the public sector will not be liable for significant additional costs during the lifetime or at the end of the contract.

On the other hand, the concept of 'public value' (Moore, 1995, Kelly et al, 2002, Benington 2007, Trades Union Congress, 2008) lacks the specificity required to evaluate public infrastructure options and projects and to assess their impact. It is little more than the articulation of public service principles (Whitfield, 2001). The public themselves would argue that the 'public value' of public and private activity includes its use or social value, the economic activity and employment it generates, the effect on social justice together with the political, public health, environmental and ecological values which have been known for decades, if not centuries. The sooner that all projects are evaluated on these terms, eliminating the PSC, value-for-money and other contrived terms, the better. They are contrived, because they are designed to narrow the criteria by which projects are evaluated.

A new Infrastructure Investment Evaluation Framework is set out at the end of Chapter 10 together with a PPP Infrastructure Stress Test.

The UK has a three-stage approach to value-for-money assessment – programme, project and procurement level quantitative and qualitative assessment. The project level assessment includes a specific soft services assessment to determine the inclusion or exclusion of soft services in addition to the viability, desirability and achievability criteria (HM Treasury, 2006). The assessment of capital expenditure, lifecycle costs, operating expenditure, residual cost (the level of investment required at the end of the contract to restore the facility to the required standard), transaction costs, revenue, indirect costs and benefits and tax income form the core of VfM, together with assessment and allocation of risk.

Partnerships British Columbia (Canada), Partnerships Victoria (Australia) and many other governments use the same basic approach. For example, the Ontario model compares a Public Sector Comparator comprising the base, financing, retained risks and ancillary costs with a Alternative Financing and Procurement (AFP) consisting of base costs including risk premium, financing costs, risks retained and ancillary costs. The difference between the PSC and the adjusted preferred bid is the claimed value-for-money in Net Present Value terms (Infrastructure Ontario, 2007).

PPP contracts specify that the facility must transfer back to the authority in good condition. There have been few PPP contract completions to date, however, contract clauses are likely to be open to different interpretation and disputes are inevitable. Unfortunately, major faults may not be readily evident or could be concealed at handover only to become evident a few years later. Whole life costs relate to the contract period, not to the life of the building or road.

Narrow evaluation criteria are justified on the grounds that the wider economic and social impacts will be the same under both options. This is usually not the case. Differences in operational policies, employment, training, supply chains and community benefits negotiated in procurement, will have economic and social impacts widening the difference between the public and private options. And where the PPP is contrived to be the 'only show in town', then the wider economic and social criteria have even more relevance.

The Public Sector Comparator
The Public Sector Comparator (PSC) is widely used to compare private finance options with a public sector alternative and to justify value-for-money. The PSC is said to promote full risk, inclusive cost pricing at an early stage, a reliable way of demonstrating the project's affordability; a consistent benchmark and evaluation tool that provides an initial indication of value-for-money; encourages bidding competition by creating confidence in the financial robustness and integrity of the feasibility process; helps to focus on the output specifications, costs and risk allocation and is sufficiently robust, that the service could be procured conventionally, if, at any stage, the PPP fails to show value-for-money (National Treasury Unit, South Africa, 2007).

Two points must be stated at the outset. Firstly, the PSC only has any status because of the absence of an in-house bid. An in-house bid makes the PSC irrelevant. Secondly, irrespective of the substantial shortcomings of the PSC, it is increasingly irrelevant, because public authorities are also asking for variant bids, giving the private sector much greater freedom to depart from the specification to change the scope, content and phasing of the project according to its ideas and interests. This makes alignment of the PSC even more difficult.

The PSC process in the UK has been described as being '... *less than real*' (Mayston, 1999) and creates '... *dubious behavioural incentives*' (Heald, 2003). '*The PSC is a hypothetical costing and not a real bid or operational concept*' (Partnerships Victoria, 2001). Most public sector officers and consultants have known that once an outline business case reaches a broad internal consensus, then a PFI/PPP would follow, unless there is significant external opposition. The PSC facilitates the impression that, if VfM was not evident, the project would be publicly financed, which is not the case. Even when there has been a relatively small difference in VfM, PFI projects have proceeded.

'*The decision to use PFI is taken on value-for-money grounds alone, and whether it is on or off balance sheet is not relevant*' (HM Treasury, 2003a) and '*... the Government only uses PFI where it offers value-for-money, considered over the long term*' (HM Treasury, 2003b).

'*The claimed efficiency gains of PFI over 'conventional' public investment appear to arise predominantly from the pricing of risk in the PSC and from the perceived overrun of costs under 'conventional' public investment.*' (Sawyer, 2005).

The Public Sector Comparator (PSC) is not an audited process. The focus on the cost of capital, construction, operational, transaction costs and the pricing of risk transfer, ignores the importance of the assessment of options, *before* the procurement process is started. Virtually all PPP schemes get embedded at option appraisal stage and more detailed appraisal against the PSC at bid evaluation is usually futile – the vagaries always permit, with a bit of tweaking, the PPP option to come out ahead in value-for-money assessments. The die has been cast much earlier. A narrow financial evaluation framework is deceptive, because, it implies that the decision hinges on those costs alone. Once the client and contractor are committed to a PPP, they will negotiate, unlike most standard outsourcing situations, to make any 'necessary' adjustments. To put it bluntly, the PSC is a charade and open to calculated manipulation and corruption.

The OECD recognises the potential misuse of a PSC: '*A good number of public-private partnerships are conceived due to the lack of public financial resources, in which case benchmarking efficiency against an infeasible policy* option is problematic. When affordability or the impact of a budgetary limit is the issue, the government might put less attention and effort into compiling the PSC than if public procurement was a viable possibility. The assessment might then be biased, particularly if such a PSC is compared to the PPP bid of a company that is willing to commit and that therefore puts significant effort into compiling its bid. In addition, if unaffordability and budgetary limits preclude traditional procurement, the government knows that – if the PSC shows that the bids submitted do not represent value-for-money – the project will not go ahead at all (i.e. no delivery will occur, neither through a public-private partnership nor through traditional procurement). This situation, together with a strong wish to deliver, may create an incentive to bias the public sector comparator so that it shows that a PPP will represent value-for-money' (OECD, 2008).

It is common for the PSC to be manipulated upwards and the PPP downwards to ensure the latter is lower. After all, '... a slight change in assumptions or in the assessment of risk may change the NPV calculations and cause the preference for a PPP to shift in its favour or against it' (OECD, 2008).

The PSC frequently under-estimates the ability of the public sector to improve and innovate. The proposals are not discussed with staff and trade unions and the figures and assumptions made, are not released for scrutiny. Furthermore, the ability of the public sector to improve project management and cost control is rarely, if ever, fully assessed.

Instead, historic evidence is used to project outcomes (construction completion) that ignore the fact that the private sector has systematically sought additional income through variation orders and other claims for additional work, unforeseen circumstances and delays caused by other contractors. One hundred and three contractors were fined £129.5m for rigging bids plus six recruitment firms supplying construction labour were fined £40m for price fixing (Office for Fair Trading, 2009).

The PSC cannot forecast negotiations and outcomes, economic conditions and financial deals, yet the project may be refinanced once it is operational, resulting in changes to the risk profile if the contract period is lengthened or other changes made. This could change the risk profile and transfer.

Critique of Public Sector Comparator
Demand forecasts and income from tolls and charges: Forecasting and predicting future demand over a 20-25 year period is extremely

difficult, particularly for transport projects, because demand is conditional on the state of the local/national/global economy, social needs and behaviour, improvements and changes elsewhere in road and rail networks. They are subject to optimism bias, and in some cases, political manipulation. Comparisons of forecast and actual flows at the end of the first year are spurious, given the lifespan of transportation projects.

Road traffic forecasts can, of course, be under- or over-stated. A study of 183 road projects in 14 countries found that 50% had a difference between actual and forecast traffic of more than plus or minus 20% (Flyvberg et al, 2005). Passenger forecasts for nine, out of ten, rail projects were overestimated with 72% being overestimated by more than two thirds. 'Deliberately slanted forecasts' were common in rail projects (ibid).

The issue is not new. Revenue exceeded the forecast in only two out of 14 US urban toll roads in the first four years of operation studied by JP Morgan. The revenue shortfall was between 20% – 70% in ten projects (JP Morgan, 1997). In 2009, Melbourne's ConnectEast toll road was forced into A$400m write-down of the value of the concession just a year after opening because traffic levels failed to meet expectations and forecasts have been downgraded (ConnectEast, 2009).

Demand forecasts are crucial because the level of use often determines whether facilities and services remain operational. The economic viability of transport, energy and water projects is dependent on the accuracy of demand forecasts, continuing public subsidies and the level of charges and tolls.

Employment policies: Irrespective of employment legislation on staff transfer, the PSC will include estimating future staffing levels and changes in efficiency, productivity and staffing/terms and conditions over the length of the contract. Labour costs form a significant part of whole-life operational costs.

The Public Sector Comparator is also open to manipulation in assessing strategic partnerships. An analysis of three PPP 10-12 year contracts awarded in the UK in 2007-08 valued at nearly £900m illustrates this point (based on Council reports obtained by European Services Strategy Unit under confidentiality agreements 2008). Procurement was the prime source of savings – accounting for 58% and 60.4% of total savings in two contracts. The PSC was lower than the bid price primarily by assuming lower and slower savings if delivered in-house, which had a higher cost of service delivery because of higher staffing levels and the additional cost of consultancy advice. Most SSP contracts forecast staffing reductions of between 25% – 40%, the prime source of savings (European Services Strategy Unit, 2008).

Construction costs – completion on time and to budget? Comparing the historic detailed performance evidence of private contractors in the 1990s, without making any adjustment for changes in systems, technology, types of projects or advances in project management, to compare with current and future public sector performance, would send business and the PPP industry into a justifiable rage. But that is precisely what occurs over construction costs and completion.

The UK Treasury 'evidence' that cost overruns occur in 73% of conventional construction projects compared to 22% for PPPs, and delays in project delivery are 70% in conventional procurement compared to 24% in PPPs has been repeated *ad nauseam* in presentations and reports by development banks, governments, consultants and the PPP lobby globally. Only one of the five studies cited by the Treasury is comparative and even this is fundamentally flawed (Pollock, Price and Player, 2007). The PPP track record of 24% projects late and 20% with cost overruns, is at odds with the rhetoric from the PPP lobby.

A rigorous evaluation of the evidence concluded that '... *the Treasury's claims about the superiority of the PFI is based on time and cost overrun arguments for which there is no evidence*' (Pollock, Price and Player, 2007). The Treasury claims are based on five studies: two NAO reports, *Modernising Construction* (2001) and *PFI Construction Performance* (2003); a Treasury internal research project in September 2002; and two private sector studies – *Agile Construction Initiative: Benchmarking Stage Two Study* (1999) and the Mott MacDonald *Review of Large Public Procurement in the UK* (2002). The Treasury report was predictably never published and disclosure was refused under the Freedom of Information Act on grounds that it might be detrimental to the commercial interests of PFI contractors. The remaining four studies demonstrate a failure to compare like with like, selection bias in the representation of standard and non-standard projects, samples which are too small and measurement bias in the use of different baselines (Pollock, Price and Player, 2007).

A study for Infrastructure Partnerships Australia of 21 PPP projects and 33 traditionally procured projects claimed PPPs had '... *superior cost efficiency*' because cost overruns (from original approval to completion) were 11.6% compared to 35.3% for traditional projects of which 23.5% suffered delays, whereas PPP projects were completed 3.4% ahead of time (Allen Consulting, 2007). However, it provided no analysis of the cost of risk transfer included in PPP contracts, no information on the size of contracts for each sector and avoided any analysis of the cause of differential performance. The additional cost of PPP projects reflects the payment required by private contractors to accept construction risk. In conventional procurement where risk is distributed between client and contractor, and additional costs are extracted through contingencies, 'negotiating' responsibility for unsatisfactory work, delays in design drawing delivery, supply chain problems and additional costs for groundworks. Another study for the National PPP Forum of 25 PPPs and 42 traditional public sector projects in Australia also claimed that PPPs performed better in terms of cost and completion and have the same limitations noted above (Duffield, 2008).

A study to promote the economic, social and environmental benefits of Sydney's eight PPP toll roads and tunnels revealed that the actual total capital costs were 33% higher than the planned capital costs when the projects were approved (Ernst & Young, 2008). Because the study was trying to prove the economic impact, the more that was spent, the bigger the contribution, so the cost increases were brushed aside as not surprising given the '... *nature of planning and the possibility for contingencies to arise during the final design and construction process*' (ibid). Operating and maintenance costs for the eight projects increased 30% over the projected cost at project approval stage.

It is important to take account of overall costs. But comparing traditional and PPP procurement models is like comparing oranges and lemons. It says nothing about the overall costs and the relative value/impact of delays and cost overruns to the different participants.

This point is reinforced by a European Investment Bank analysis of 227 new road projects, of which 65 were PPPs, in 16 European countries between 1990-2005. It estimated '... *the ex ante cost of a PPP road to be, on average, 24% more expensive than a traditionally procured road, all other things equal. This estimate corresponds by and large to reported ex post cost overruns in traditionally procured public roads. To the extent that the two measures are representative, this suggests that the largest part of the ex ante construction cost difference originates from the transfer of construction risk*' (Blanc-Brude, Goldsmith and Valila, 2006).

In the UK, the Outline Business Case for the Newcastle City Council PPP street lighting contract is a good example of how assumptions can be used to produce the 'right' result. The PPP model assumed 15% additional savings in capital costs ('... *economies of scale, supply chain management efficiencies, standardisation and optimisation of equipment and improved project coordination and management*'), 5% additional saving in ongoing asset renewal costs, 10% additional reduction in maintenance costs and 5% additional energy cost savings compared to the PSC costs (Newcastle City Council, 2001).

The business case claimed a reduction in night-time traffic accidents and crime but an analysis of city-wide traffic accident and crime statistics revealed that street lighting had a significantly smaller role, resulting in the community benefits being grossly exaggerated (Centre for Public Services, 2001). A neighbouring council, North Tyneside, later joined the project.

The London Borough of Haringey schools PPP appraisal began with a Public Sector Comparator (PSC) of £69.8m and PPP costs of £82.7m. Two years and various adjustments later and the difference had been reversed. Better school buildings were judged to improve school exam results and a 1% increase in school leavers gaining a job when they left school was estimated to benefit taxpayers by £4.8m. This was added to the PSC as a cost of not choosing the PPP option, ignoring the fact that it applied to all school improvement options (McFadyean & Rowland, 2002).

Several studies have surveyed PPP project managers about their perceptions of value-for-money and PPP performance (Cambridge Economic Policy Associates, 2005; National Audit Office, 2003). Such 'high level' surveys, restricted to people with a vested interest in implementing PPPs, may provide some insights, but are virtually worthless as evidence. But this did not deter the OECD from using these survey results in the same paragraph, which reported the flawed UK PPP/conventional procurement evidence (OECD, 2008).

Risk identification, allocation and pricing: PPP projects transfer some risks to the private sector. In practice the private sector insures against those risks, adds this cost to their bids and, in effect, transfers the risk back to the government. There is clearly a case for the public sector to directly insure against risks rather than pay the private sector's insurance premiums.

The degree of risk transfer is frequently exaggerated and/or mis-valued. There are numerous types of risk relating to the infrastructure, such as demand risk (school rolls, passenger numbers, traffic estimates, visitor numbers, changes in economic activity and demography), construction risk (design and site risks – planning permission, completion, cost, site difficulties); operational risk (availability of facilities, service performance); maintenance and lifecycle costs (damage to building, life-cycle replacement) and regulatory risk (changes in legislation and regulatory regimes). In conventional procurement, construction time and cost risks are divided between client and contractor, they are not automatically borne by the public sector. Contracts may have penalty clauses for delays and financial consequences of delays, and cost overruns are usually hotly contested and resolved by negotiation or dispute resolution.

The public sector pays a risk premium to the private sector for risk transfer. By April 2003 the National Audit Office (NAO) had undertaken only eight financial assessments (out of 450 operational projects) of central government PPPs and '... *the government's central justification for PFI in terms of risk transfer remains largely unaudited*' (Pollock and Price, 2004). The NAO had audited only 10 out of 622 PFI contracts signed up to 2007 and only 3 had examined the value of the risk transfer achieved (Pollock and Price, 2008). Data to allow auditing of the relationship between risk and risk premiums was not publicly available.

The principle is that risks should be borne by those with the skills and financial support to handle them. However, the private sector is risk averse and will usually manage risk by robust subcontracting and insurance. The public sector bears risks, which are not recognised or costed. For example, the financial and political costs of service failures, the difficulties of enforcing penalties, the cost of finding a new provider, not to mention the resulting disruption for users and staff (see Table 37).

The private sector is very reluctant to accept demand risk for hospitals, schools, prisons and similar facilities, because the Special Purpose Vehicle (SPV) has a very minor role in determining the level of demand. It will, however, accept demand risk in concession contracts, which are tied to road tolls, energy and water prices with built-in inflation increases.

There are also risks relating to the context, such as, regulatory and legal risk (changes in legislation or regulatory frameworks in the contract period), political risk (a change in political support/approval

Table 37: *Risk allocation*

Public sector		Private sector
Retained risks	*Shared risks*	*Transferred risks*
Demand risk	Inflation and interest rate risk	Design
Outline Planning permission	General regulatory risk	Detailed planning permission
Political risk	Force majeure (natural disasters, war, civil unrest)	Design
Land acquisition		Construction – cost overrun, delay, defects.
Land use	Obsolescence	
Specification		Maintenance
Residual value		Availability
Government guarantees and exchange rate risk		Operating performance and costs
		Project finance
Network/interface with other services risks		Environmental
Governance		Technology obsolescence
Legislation		

for the project), technological risk (changes in technology which may make systems redundant or speed up pace of renewal) and network risk (project is part of a larger network and decisions affect the network as a whole).

Some risks are specific to PPPs such as liquidity risk '... *ability to exit an infrastructure business quickly and at a good price*' (Deutsche Bank Group, 2005), partner risk (that a consortium partner or co-investor fails to carry out planned role), leverage/interest rate risk (increases in interest rates) and PPP management risk (effectiveness in delivering returns to investors!).

Risk transfer is a commercial decision. The Public Sector Comparator (PSC) process gives the impression that once a risk is transferred in a contract, that this is the end of the matter. If for any reason a costly event occurs that is not fully covered by insurance, a PPP consortia will inevitably review its commercial approach to all risks and will seek to recover any financial losses over the rest of the contract period. There is no commercial logic in merely accepting a financial loss.

The pricing of risk transfer is usually critical in determining value-for-money and ensuring the PFI option is cheaper than the PSC. The

Table 38: *The use of risk transfer*

Hospital PFI project	Cost advantage of the PSC over the PFI before risk transfer (£m)	Net present value of the risk transfer to the PFI (£m)	Percent difference between PSC and PFI	Risk as % of total construction cost
Swindon & Marlborough	16.6	17.3	0.05	16.5
Kings Healthcare Trust	22.9	23.8	0.03	37.2
St George's Healthcare Trust	11.9	12.5	0.11	31.3
South Durham	9.1	9.1	0.44	22.3
Hereford Hospitals Trust	14.4	21.9	1.08	35.3
South Tees Acute Hospital	28.8	67.8	14.47	70.6

Source: Shaoul, 2004.

PSC option had a cost advantage in six hospital projects in the UK before significant adjustments for risk transfer, ranging from £17.3m to £67.8m (NPV) led to the PFI option being the preferred option. However, in five projects, the cost difference was marginal, between 0.05% and 1.08%, which would otherwise have resulted in more detailed public policy analysis, and in four cases, risk represented an astounding 30% – 70% of the construction cost (see Table 38).

Further evidence is provided by the risk transfer NPV sums in another five PFI hospital deals closed in 1997-98 (Carlisle, North Durham, South Buckinghamshire, Norfolk and Norwich and Dartford and Gravesham). Risk transfer ranged from £7.6m to £83.7m, which meant that the PFI was cheaper by between 2.2% and 4.5%. Without the risk adjustment the PFI option would have been more expensive by 1.1% to 10.6% (Department of Health, 1998 quoted in Froud, 2003). The average difference between the PPP cost and the PSC for 56 NHS hospital projects in the 1998-2006 period was 2.9% (Serco Institute, 2007), although this figure is reduced by nearly a third if three projects with abnormally high differences (Barking 21.5%, South Tees 14.5% and Oxford Ratcliffe 12.9%) are excluded. The 2.9% average difference, even within PSC terms of reference, makes the 10% – 20% cost saving claims of the PPP lobby not credible (Asian Development Bank, 2008).

The Newcastle street lighting PPP, mentioned above, allocated a 137% additional risk cost to the Public Sector Comparator, whilst client and monitoring costs were claimed to be 47% higher for the PSC than for the PPP! The cost differentials totalled £16.1m, which produced a £2.1m (3.8%) Net Present Value (NPV) advantage for the PPP option.

Ability to achieve service delivery transformation: Operational efficiencies are distorted in several ways. Firstly, the in-house ability to improve service delivery so that it is more effective and efficient is understated, in contrast to private sector efficiency. Secondly, the exaggerated savings claims made for outsourcing, usually 20% despite empirical evidence that the savings are a fraction of those claimed, between 6% – 8% and turn into costs when other public costs are taken into account (UK Department of the Environment (DoE) 1993, Escott and Whitfield 1995, Centre for Public Services 1995, UK Cabinet Office 1996, DoE 1997 and other research studies summarised in European Services Strategy Unit, 2006). Thirdly, assumptions may also be made about reducing terms and conditions of operational staff over the contract period.

In Canada, the Auditor General of Ontario found that the Brampton Civic Hospital PPP had overstated the PSC by C$245m (2003 prices) by inflating certain design and construction costs and including costs for some non-clinical services, which were not included in the PPP (Office of the Auditor General of Ontario, 2008). In addition, some C$28m of the costs of employing 60 legal, financial, technical and other consultants on the PPP project were excluded. In addition, a C$67m risk transfer, equivalent to expecting a 13% cost overrun for conventional procurement, was added to the PSC. The cost of the 608-bed hospital had soared from C$357m in September 2000 to C$525m by November 2004, a C$168m increase, which far exceeded construction inflation in the same period. According to the funding agreement with the Ontario provincial government, the hospital was to bear 30% of the costs. However, the audit revealed that this might fall to 10%.

Cost of capital: Spain is Europe's largest user of private finance for roads with €14.5bn capital investment by the end of 2006. The cost of capital was 9%, double the cost of public finance, for 24 toll roads operating by 2003 (Acerete, Shaoul and Stafford, 2007). Road users paid almost twice the cost of public finance. The private toll road companies received €2,198m of public money in the 1995-2003 period in compensation payments, for not permitting a full increase in toll rates, capital grants and exchange rate insurance relating to the remaining debt of 8 concessions. The highly profitable state financial and regulatory regime, created a Spanish road operating industry, which enabled some companies to expand internationally (ibid).

The Special Purpose Vehicles (SPVs) of eight highways PPP contracts in the UK were paying an effective interest rate of 11% in 2001 and 9% in 2002, compared to the cost of Treasury stock, then 4.5% (Shaoul, Stafford & Stapleton, 2006). Operating profits increased from 13% to 68% in the 1997-2002 period and the companies paid an effective corporate tax rate of 8% on total operating profits of £384m. Analysis of Highways Agency and SPV accounts reveal that '... *in 6 years, the Highways Agency has paid the capital costs of the roads plus most of the operation and maintenance costs for the period (£859 million as opposed to £913 million). At the very least, this refutes one of the justifications for using private finance – that the government does not have the money to finance infrastructure investment*' (ibid).

The Ontario Auditor analysis of the Brampton Hospital PPP concluded: '*The province's 5.45% cost of borrowing at the time the agreement was executed was cheaper than the weighted average cost of capital charged by the private-sector consortium. Had the province financed the design and construction costs at its lower rate, the savings would be approximately $200 million over the term of the project's P3 arrangement ($107 million in 2004 dollars). However, WOHC had not considered the impact of these savings in its comparison of the traditional procurement approach with the P3 project*' (Office of the Auditor General of Ontario, 2008).

There are more Canadian examples of biased PSC methodology. The PSC for the Abbotsford Hospital, the Diamond Centre (health care) and the Sea-to-Sky highway projects showed a lower cost for the PPP by C$39.0m and C$17.0m for the two hospitals. The PPP cost of the highway project exceeded the PSC but it was approved on the grounds that it included additional highway improvements not included in the PSC, which indicates the PPP and PSC were not comparable. Forensic accountants compared the NPV and nominal cost (costs over the life of the contract at current prices), which revealed that the extra cost of the PPPs, were C$377.9m and C$114.0m respectively for the two health projects. The additional public cost of the highway projects was between C$319.5m and C$434.3m (Blair Mackay Mynett, 2009). Their analysis of discount rates on these projects and the Canada Line Rapid Transit PPP concluded that there was a degree of double counting of risk and were highly critical of the Partnerships BC methodology and lack of disclosure.

In the UK the average cost of private capital in the PFI schemes was 7%, compared to the cost of capital for buildings directly owned by the NHS, which was, in fact, only 3.5% (PricewaterhouseCoopers, 2002).

The cost of capital in SSP models is more complex because this often involves front-loading some investment in the early part of the contract, although payment may be spread over the entire contract period. This relies on related infrastructure and development. The cost of capital in regeneration PPPs is highly influenced by assumptions over land value and/or sale of assets and the acquisition of adjacent sites.

Transaction costs: PPP procurement transaction costs on European Investment Bank projects, average 12.5% of the capital value (Dudkin and Valila, 2005). This includes the public sector, winning bidder and failed bidder costs, but excludes contract monitoring costs, which have been estimated to between 3% – 7% of the capital value (Audit Commission, 2008). Thus total transaction costs range between 15.5% and 19.5%. In the UK procurement costs for the Somerset SSP projects were £3m, about 1% of the contract value, but this excluded private sector bidding costs (included in bid prices) and client contract management (European Services Strategy Unit, 2008).

Procurement costs for very large projects are likely to be a lower percentage of the total cost, for example, procurement costs for the London Tube Metronet PPP were 'only' 2.8% of the project value but totalled £455m (National Audit Office, 2004).

Cost of government guarantees: Some governments (Australia, Korea, Chile, Columbia, Argentina, Spain, India and South Africa) have provided revenue and/or exchange rate guarantees for PPP projects. The financial liabilities and risks need to be assessed at the evaluation of bids stage. Several guaranteed toll road revenues, for example in Korea, guaranteed 90% of a 20-year forecast for the Incheon airport toll road but traffic revenue was less than half that forecast, which cost the government millions (Irwin, 2005).

Tax concessions: Governments may benefit from tax payable by the private sector, but, in some cases, PPP projects can include potential tax deductions. For example, in the US, if the concessionaire has effective ownership of the facility (i.e. the length of the contract is greater than or equal to the economic life of the asset), they can claim tax deductions on the depreciation of assets. Hence the Chicago

Global Auction of Public Assets

Skyway and Indiana Toll Road PPPs can '... *claim full tax deductions for asset depreciation within the first 15 years of the lease agreement*' (General Accountability Office, 2008). Not only is the private sector benefiting financially from the depreciation of a publicly financed public asset but also significant tax concessions to the private sector, provide a vested interest to press for long-term contracts.

Treatment of state subsidies
There are basically four ways in which the state provides vital support for PPPs. Firstly, by providing direct and indirect subsidies for PPP projects. These take many forms including taxation benefits, guarantees and public finance of ancillary work. Secondly, by funding national PPP programmes and providing market-making support. Thirdly, by ensuring contractual arrangements and payment mechanisms satisfy the requirements of banks and financial institutions, major construction companies and facilities management operators. Finally, by endorsing flawed Public Sector Comparator and Value-for-money procedures. Some subsidies apply only in specific countries, for example, the loss of tax revenue when tax-exempt debt is used, and the cost of reviewing unsolicited proposals (USA).

Financial subsidies have taken many forms. For example, in the UK, the planned £2bn public funding of PPPs in 2009 discussed in chapter 3 was just the tip of the iceberg. The second Severn river crossing PPP project had to acquire the first Severn bridge for £120m for which HM Treasury agreed to make a £60m interest free loan until the end of the concession (Moles and Williams, 1995). They also conclude that state funding of approach roads, for example for Skye Bridge, Dartford Thurrock and Severn crossings, should be ' *considered as direct public investments*' (ibid).

Independent Sector Treatment Centres in the UK are an important example, because they combine the provision of clinical services, a core public service, with infrastructure provision. The first wave of ISTC contracts were on the basis of 'take or pay' in which health care companies received up to 90% of the monthly fee irrespective of the volume of patients treated. Nationally, up to £927m may have been paid to ISTCs for patients who did not receive treatment (Pollock and Kirkwood, 2009).

The first wave of eleven National Health Service (NHS) PFI hospitals received annual 'smoothing mechanism' payments totalling £7.3m to improve their affordability and '... *to manage the difference* between NHS capital charges – the 6% return on relevant assets – and PFI returns on capital' (Gaffney and Pollock, 1999). The London Borough of Lewisham financed nearly £6m of the costs of the extension of the Docklands Light Railway to the borough. The PPP project with Mowlem, as lead contractor, invested £3.4m, but soon after completion, sold its 40% stake to Infrastructure Investors for £19.5m, a 471% profit. The Council received nothing.

The Northumberland Strait Crossing (Confederation Bridge) PPP project between New Brunswick and Prince Edward Island in Canada receives C$41.9m per annum (1992 dollars indexed to inflation) for 35 years from 1997; in effect, the transfer of the ferry service subsidy. This was judged to be at the high end of the range of subsidies, and additional federal subsidies includes C$46m project management, C$41m for highway upgrading and C$15m regional development (Auditor General of Canada, 1995). The government also played a critical role by enhancing the credit rating of the C$661m bond finance. The audit also concluded that the financing costs could have been reduced by about C$45m, had the government financed the project.

European Investment Bank (EIB) funding of PPP projects contributes to keep funding costs lower than if they were entirely privately financed. Since EIB is publicly owned by the EU, and able to raise funds on capital markets more cheaply, this is a form of subsidy. Similarly, the US Transportation Infrastructure Finance and Innovation Act (TIFIA) 1998 provides credit assistance (secured (direct) loans, loan guarantees, and standby lines of credit) for public and private transportation projects. It provides up to one third of project costs at Treasury interest rates. The Pocahontas Parkway and the Washington Capital Beltway PPP projects recently benefited from $739m TIFIA finance.

National PPP programmes, such as the UK's Building Schools for the Future and LIFT in the health service, incur substantial annual central programme costs that are conveniently excluded from project cost analysis. These costs are incurred entirely in promoting PPPs and managing the private sector market. Four programmes in the UK (Partnerships for Schools, Community Health Partnerships, Waste Infrastructure Team and the Academies programme), spent £32m employing 265 staff (FTE) and consultants in 2007 (NAO, 2009). Central running costs represented an average 1.05% of annual spending programme – many PPP projects would have failed the PSC test, had these costs been taken into account. Many of these subsidies were not identified and quantified, let alone taken into account in the PSC and value-for-money assessments.

The Korean government amended the Promotion of Private Capital into Social Overhead Investment Act 1994 to introduce a Minimum Revenue Guarantee (MRG) mechanism in 1999 where operating revenue falls short of that forecast. Four road projects – the Incheon International Airport Expressway, Cheonan-Nonsan Expressway, Gwangju 2nd Beltway and the Woomyunsan Tunnel received a total of US$510m MRG subsidies in the 2000-05 period because traffic volume was 52.8%, 52.2%, 62.2% and 26.8% respectively of that forecast (Japan Bank for International Cooperation Institute, 2008). The government has since reduced the scale of MRG.

The evaluation of PPPs and privatisation proposals for public infrastructure is frequently not comprehensive or rigorous. Ideally, impact assessment should be carried out at four stages: at the needs assessment and planning stage, options appraisal, evaluation of bids and in monitoring contract performance. It should be publicly accountable, transparent in assumptions, forecasts and findings; comprehensive in scope and have a rigorous methodology, which assesses the economic, social, social justice, environmental, sustainable development and health impacts. It should take account of direct and indirect impacts, monetary and non-monetary effects, short, medium and long impacts, and different scenarios for development and finance (the latter should include the effects of refinancing and PPP equity sales).

Design, innovation and vision

Concern has been expressed over the quality of the design of PPP projects, that mundane public buildings were being produced with a relatively short life span, influenced by short-term contractual interests, rather than sustainable development and civic design strategies.

Only 3 out of 25 (12%) school designs were rated 'good' or 'excellent' in an assessment the first 25 BSF schools at the planning application stage or where a single design had been chosen (Commission for Architecture and the Built Environment, 2008). The remainder were judged by the schools design panel to be either 'not good enough' or 'mediocre'. A minimum design standard was introduced in May 2009 by the government and the Commission for Architecture and the Built Environment (CABE), after 82 of 187 school designs were classified as either mediocre or poor (The Guardian, 2009).

The degree to which a building can be physically adapted to accommodate future needs and requirements is a key aspect of design innovation. Design innovation, adaptability and 'future-proofing' of healthcare facilities was raised early in the PFI hospital programme. A study of six pre-PFI hospitals and six PFI hospitals assessed in 2005/06 concluded: *'Since the public sector still carries all the demand risk and because of the long-term contractual arrangements between the private and the public sector, it is essential that PFI delivers healthcare facilities that are able to accommodate future change and are optimally usable for the NHS during the entire lifecycle of the asset. A key question is therefore whether the PFI model is structurally capable of stimulating innovative design solutions to reduce the risk of potential future obsolescence arising from fast changing care delivery and technology lifecycles.'*

'the PFI model is unable to promote the level of innovation in the design of hospital built assets needed to optimise their lifetime clinical efficiency. This is partly due to the relationship between (1) the project delivery and (2) hospital operational systems. ... instead of promoting a higher degree of integration between the project delivery and hospital operational systems, the introduction of PFI has resulted in a separation between them. This has led to problems such as disrupted communications, complicated patterns of collaboration, misaligned goals and incentives and poor inter-project learning. The result is a project delivery model which may be producing facilities that are unable to adapt to future healthcare needs and health service innovations' (Barlow and Koberle-Gaiser, 2008).

There is a misguided assumption that the private sector is more innovative than the public sector and that a PPP project will benefit from this innovation at no additional cost. For example, the assumption is that the scale, timing and effectiveness of transformation and the implementation of change will be more extensive, faster and more effective when delivered by the private contractor compared to the public sector.

The PFI bidding process stifles innovation, future design adaptability, involved conventional solutions and *'PFI has not been supportive of innovation because SPVs were concerned with minimizing exposure to possible risks and clients needed to reduce project costs to meet value-for-money norms'* (Barlow and Koberle-Gaiser, 2009).

A study of integrated solutions in construction concluded that *'... the use of PFI and PPPs has just shifted the separation of design, construction and operation from government to the private sector, without creating higher levels of integration between the stages'* (Brady, Davies and Gann, 2005).

Loss of flexibility

The loss of flexibility in service redesign was highlighted by a National Health Service study of the fixed costs in four south east London acute hospital trusts, of which three were PFI funded hospital, two of which had separate 10-15 year PFI medical equipment contracts. The subregion currently has significant excess bed capacity, which is forecast to increase as hospitals improve day-case rates and shorten the length of stay (A Picture of Health, 2008). It also found a current surplus of facilities, which was expected to steadily increase as excess beds were closed. However, the availability and hard Facilities Management costs would remain, unless the excess estate can be sold or leased.

Occupation costs (comprising site availability costs, 'hard' facilities management such as building maintenance and utility costs and property taxes) were 12.3%, 13.1% and 14.7% total costs in the three PFI hospitals compared to 6.9%, 7.5% and 7.9% in the three non-PFI hospitals. The average availability cost in the three PFI hospitals was double the average cost of the non-PFI hospitals. Contract changes in the two whole hospital PFI schemes were not possible because one had been financed by bonds, which meant that refinancing, early repayment of the debt or re-profiling of the unitary charge was not practicable, and the other scheme had been refinanced in 2004/05 resulting in the availability payment being fixed for the remainder of the 35 year contract. But '... *without service redesign the excess estate will be stranded within acute sites and as a result the acute trusts will incur 'stranded' occupation costs. The stranded fixed costs will make it more difficult for acute trusts to restore and maintain financial balance*' (ibid).

The study concluded that, because there was least scope to reduced fixed costs in the PFI hospitals, service redesign should aim to maximise utilisation at these hospitals and release surplus estate at the non-PFI hospitals. It did not consider the effect of reconfiguration on service quality, access, choice and other costs and benefits. Proposed changes to the distribution of services were referred to the Secretary of State who authorised investigation by an Independent Reconfiguration Panel (IRP). Bexley's Overview and Scrutiny Committee referred to the '... *undue influence of financial factors and PFI schemes on reconfiguration*' (Independent Reconfiguration Panel, 2009).

The four acute trusts in the area had accumulated £121.5m debt at the end of 2007/08, projected to rise to £221.1m by the end of 2010/11. '*This level of debt is undermining the quality and sustainability of local services'* (ibid). Three of the trusts, Bexley, Queen Elizabeth and Queen Mary merged to form South London Healthcare in April 2009.

The government endorsed the proposals to close the accident and emergency department, maternity services and inpatient paediatrics at Queen Mary's, the non-PFI hospital, although a midwife-led maternity unit would be retained (Health Service Journal, 2009). The proposals required further £21.4m capital spend through '... *adjustments to PFI contracts*' plus development at the Queen Mary site and community health facilities, which would also be PFI-funded through LIFT projects (Independent Reconfiguration Panel, 2009). There were many other important factors in the reconfiguration of services but this example alone demonstrates the considerable influence of financial and contractual constraints of PPPs.

Another loss of flexibility is evident, when the demand for facilities forces their closure. Brighton & Hove Council had to pay the PFI contractor £4.5m when the Comart and Media Arts School, a revamped comprehensive, closed after six years in 2005. Similarly, the Northern Ireland Department of Education have to continue paying £370,000 per annum for the 18 years after the closure of Balmoral High school, Belfast (Children & Young People NOW, 12 March, 2009).

Architects have criticised PPPs as 'architecture through accountancy', in that it does not produce good buildings, and organisations such as Architects for Health have called for a new procurement process and more direct appointment of architects (Building Design, 6 March, 2009).

Affordability and cost

'Although PPPs, if well structured and implemented, offer the prospect of sizable efficiency gains in the construction of infrastructure assets and the provision of associated services, they can involve significant costs and risks for government over the longer term, and under certain circumstances can even threaten debt sustainability' (Ter-Minassian and Allen, 2004).

The difference between the Outline and Final Business Case costs is often substantial. Cost increases averaged 74% between Outline Business Case and contract in 43 Health PPPs in the UK (Hellowell and Pollock, 2007).

'On average NHS trusts with PFI schemes were having to pay 8.3% of their total income in charges and other payments linked to the PFI – more than the

5.8% of income allocated to each trust for capital costs. This funding gap of 2.5% has to be covered by drawing on income intended to pay for services' (Hellowell and Pollock, 2007).

All PPP projects are exposed to additional costs, despite the claim of 'whole life costing', which only covers the length of the contract, not the life of the building. They are hidden operational costs. Furthermore, once the project is operational, the PPP consortia impose charges for any changes required over and above the basic facilities management costs built into the monthly unitary payment. Additional capital costs and operational cost changes were £178m or 1.1% of the unitary charge in PFI projects in the UK in 2006 (National Audit Office, 2008). With outstanding unitary payments of £216.5bn between 2008/09 and 2033/34 (HM Treasury, 2008), PPPs could impose £2.4bn additional costs in this period and this excludes the additional costs incurred in the period prior to 2007/8. SPVs frequently impose additional management fees for processing change requests, which were estimated to cost the public sector £6m in 2006 alone (National Audit Office, 2008).

PPPs do not bring additional private sector investment because the cost of PPP/PFI is ultimately entirely funded by the public sector. Some SSPs have included private sector front-loading of investment, in effect bringing forward investment to the early years of the project. The public sector pays the additional finance and interest rate costs, which are included in the total contract price and payment mechanism.

'... *highway public-private partnerships are not a panacea for meeting all transportation system demands, nor are they without potentially substantial costs and risks to the public – both financial and non-financial – and trade-offs must be made. While private investors can make billions of dollars available for critical infrastructure, these funds are largely a new source of borrowed funds, repaid by road users over what potentially could be a period of several generations. There is no 'free' money in highway public-private partnerships*' (GAO, 2008).

Off balance sheet finance stores up potential future problems and intergenerational liabilities. '*The costs of off-balance-sheet financing have also come home to roost, as they always do. The spending of local authorities and National Health Service trusts will be squeezed by commitments they have incurred under the private finance initiative*' (Kay, 2009).

A high rate of return, or guaranteed profit, is built into PPP contracts – 15% is common in PFI contracts in the UK, 18% for the

US Dulles Greenway road, a limit imposed by Virginia State Corporation Commission rules. Examples of the dividends expected in PPP projects, are particularly high relative to the equity input, for example, an input of equity capital of £100 in Hairmyres Hospital, Scotland is projected to yield aggregate dividends of £89m (Cuthbert and Cuthbert, 2008a) – see Table 39.

Table 39: *Projected dividends in six UK PPP projects*

Project	Equity input (£m)	Projected dividends (£m)
New Royal Infirmary Edinburgh	0.5	167.90
Hairmyres Hospital	0.0001	89.14
James Watt College	0.08	7.14
Highland PP2 schools	0.000197	5.91
Perth and Kinross Office	0.136	24.36
Hereford Hospital	0.001	55.67

Source: Scottish Futures Trust: Consultation Paper, Jim and Margaret Cuthbert, March 2008.

Government has yet to address the increasing use of offshore locations of infrastructure funds and PPP companies, in effect legitimating their corporation, stamp duty and capital gains tax avoidance strategies.

The growth of the secondary market means that financial gains can be expected from refinancing, once the project is operational. There is at least one example, the Falkirk schools PPP in Scotland, where the anticipation of a £2m (Net Present Value) refinancing gain was key to making the project affordable (Cuthbert and Cuthbert, 2008b). This also indicates, that there is significant construction risk, which has not transferred to the private sector.

The requirement to publish International Financial Reporting Standard (IFRS) compliant accounts in 2010/11, will lead to the reclassification of PPP assets. Assets must be on a public sector balance sheet, when two control tests are met – where the public sector grants, controls or regulates what services the operator must provide with the asset, to whom and at what price; and where the public sector grants or controls, (through ownership, beneficial entitlement or otherwise), any significant residual interest in the infrastructure at the end of the contract. This has '... *potentially significant financial implications for individual authorities as assets coming on to the balance sheet will, for example, affect prudential ratios'* (Audit Commission, 2009), thus affecting borrowing levels for capital projects.

Brazil and Hungary have budget control mechanisms that limit revenue commitments to PPPs. The affordability test in Brazil, for example, requires a ten-year fiscal analysis and PPP expenditure is limited by law to 1% of the government's net current revenue (OECD, 2008).

The test for affordability should include future needs and demands on revenue expenditure, not just particular budgets, the likely scale of PPP operational cost increases, other investment plans and the potential loss of flexibility with large, long-term contractual obligations.

User charges and tolls
The 75-year privatisation of Chicago's 36,000 parking meters (see chapter 6) starts with a series of hourly price increases between 2008-11 ranging from US$3.00 to US$6.50 (117% increase) in the Loop, US$1.00 to US$4.00 (300% increase) in the non-Loop business district and 25 – 75 cents to US$2.00 (167%-700% increase) in neighbourhoods (Chicago Tribune, 2008). The operating hours of parking meters were increased so that most meters operate from 8.00hrs to 21.00hrs seven days a week – adding 35m operating hours to the parking system per annum! The installation of a Pay & Display system is expected to increase the number of parking spaces by 10%. The City Council made a US$19.3m parking meter profit in 2007 but this 'cash machine' is now in private hands.

The City's Inspector General Office audit of the US$1.15bn deal concluded that the city council received '… *conservatively, $974 million less for this 75-year lease than the City would have received from 75 years of parking-meter revenue had it retained the parking-meter system under the same terms that the City agreed to in the lease'* (City of Chicago Inspector General Office, 2009). But the city council locked itself into the contract. A month earlier, it had agreed the city council budget, assuming an immediate US$150m contribution from the parking PPP. The city council did not even assess the financial implications of retaining the system in-house and the IGO was highly critical of the lack of democratic debate on a *'momentous decision'* (ibid). Furthermore, the IGO estimated that 93% of the value of the upfront payment to the city council, comes from the first 37 years of the lease thus '… *it is highly questionable whether or not the City should have entered into a lease of this length'* (ibid).

Chicago Skyway concession agreement permits annual toll increases of nearly 97% in real terms between 2007-47 *'the potential exists that the public could pay higher tolls than those that would more appropriately reflect the true costs of operating and maintaining the facilities, including earning a reasonable rate of return'* (General Accountability Office, 2008).

If toll rates are set to maximize profit, where congestion is not a significant problem, they can *'... introduce substantial inefficiencies in the overall road transportation network and actually increase congestion and safety hazards in other parts of the system that they do not own and control'* (Swan and Belzer, 2008). Their study of the Ohio Turnpike and nearby free alternate routes showed, that, as the Turnpike toll increased, truck traffic increased on alternate routes as truckers balanced the monetary savings with the cost of longer journey times. But the alternative routes had much higher accident rates, dramatically increased maintenance costs and reduced the quality of life for people living along these routes. The costs of this are borne by the public and not by the private toll road operator.

Train fares on the UK's privatised network are on average 50% higher than in the rest of Europe. Despite continuing public subsidy, annual season tickets for short, middle and long distance commuters, are the most expensive in Europe. Return fares for immediate travel from the regions to the principal city are 1.9 times higher than those in the next most expensive country, Germany. Advance single tickets to the principal city purchased one week before date of travel were comparable with those in five other countries, while cheaper than in two. *'However, if you cannot get an advance ticket the GB price is significantly higher than in other countries'* (Passenger Focus, 2009).

Average water rates charged by privately or investor owned water companies were on average 33% higher than those of US municipal or local government utilities in 2009 (Food & Water Watch, 2009). Household sewer bills in eight states, including Texas, Florida, Ohio, and Indiana, were 63% higher in privately or investor owned utilities compared to municipal or local government utilities (ibid).

Quality of service

Terminated projects (chapter 8) have a significant impact on the quality of service, as do the issues evidenced in other sections in this chapter.

The level of financial deductions for poor performance is a useful indicator of quality. Nearly 70% of PPP operational projects surveyed by PartnershipsUK had imposed financial deductions for poor performance and/or lack of availability of a service, with 22% of projects imposing deductions more than 25 times (PartnershipsUK, 2006). Only half of the contract managers provided the total value of deductions, most of which were under £50,000. However, 18% were between £101,000 and £250,000, 12% between £250,000 and £1m and 2.5% more than £1m.

In the UK, delays and cost overruns contributed to a wide range of service quality failures in the 105 ICT contract failures discussed in chapter 8 (Whitfield, 2007).

Prisons
Some countries, for example the UK and USA, allow the private operation of prisons, but others have legislation that excludes the operational function from PPPs. Prisons are examples of 'whole service' provision ie infrastructure and service delivery and, therefore, an important benchmark. But this is much more than a debate about the relative efficiency of public private provision and well articulated by Dolovich (2005).

UK private prisons were performing worse than publicly operated prisons in 2008. Performance data for 132 prisons in England and Wales showed that 4 of the 10 private prisons, with 11% of the prison population, scored the second lowest rating 'requiring development' (The Independent, 2009). The four prisons were operated by Serco, G4S Justice Services and Kalyx. The private sector's average score in the second quarter was 2.6, some ten percent lower than the 2.85 score for publicly operated prisons. None of the private prisons achieved the maximum score of four, but 14 publicly run prisons were in the 'exceptional performance' category. Two former privately managed prisons, Blakenhurst and Buckley Hall, are now publicly operated.

In the US, Oklahoma's experience with private prisons is salutary. It was one of the first states to use private prisons. It began placing prisoners in private prisons in Texas in 1995 and commenced contracts with private prison companies in the state in 1997. A performance audit of the Department of Corrections showed that the use of private prisons declined 26% between 2002-07 primarily due to the state's purchase of the former Dominion private prison, the termination of an agreement with CCA for the Diamondback prison and the end of an agreement with Cornell Companies facilities (MGT of America, 2007). The audit revealed the three private prisons had an average of 0.42 serious incidents per 100 prisoners in 2006, twice the public prisons rate of 0.21 per 100 prisoners. Staff turnover rates were 40%, 61% and 95% in 2006 'dramatically higher' than state prisons. The Department's centralised custody classification system was plagued by a lack of accurate classification data from the private prisons.

A 4.8% cost efficiency of private prisons, based on comparative cost data '... *appears attributable to the fact that DOC institutions tend to be antiquated, poorly designed facilities that require higher staffing levels to compensate for severe security deficiencies inherent in their physical plant. The private prisons, by contrast, are relatively new institutions designed to facilitate the efficient use of staff resources and to enhance security*' (ibid).

A year later, little appeared to have changed – the Department withheld US$589,000 from Corrections Corporation of America and Geo Group in 2008 because of staffing shortages (Tulsa World, 2008).

In 2002, the State of Pennsylvania took control of the city of Philadelphia school district after years of low achievement and budget crises. It became the largest US experiment in the private management of public schools. The school board was replaced by a School Reform Commission, which adopted a 'diverse provider' model outsourcing the management of 45 poor performing elementary and middle schools to Edison Schools Inc and Victory Schools Inc (22 and 6 schools respectively), two non-profit organisations (9 schools) and eight schools to Temple University and University of Pennsylvania. In addition, it restructured another 21 poor performing schools providing additional staff support and funding and increased the funding for another 16 improving schools. After four years, a Rand Corporation study of 82 schools '... *found no evidence of differential academic benefits that would support the additional expenditures on private managers*' (RAND, 2007). '... *despite additional per-pupil resources, privately operated schools did not produce average increases in student achievement that were any larger than those seen in the rest of the district. Meanwhile, district managed restructured schools outpaced the gains of the rest of the district in math*' (ibid).

An investigation of Charter Schools in Washington DC revealed conflicts of interest in nearly US$200m business deals at over a third of the District's 60 charter schools. United Bank, whose senior vice president was also chair of the DC Charter School Board, had US$55m loans to schools and developers (Washington Post, 14

December 2008). More significantly, it exposed a system that '... *has benefited charter schools' landlords, developers, bankers and investors while taxpayers fund two separate school infrastructures*'(ibid). US charter schools are private, non-profit businesses, with control of educational programmes, staff, budget and premises.

'*Since 1996, the District has spent more than $2 billion in local and federal funds to build and operate charter schools. Much of that public money has gone to buy, lease and renovate school buildings that are now in private hands. Charter schools typically finance their property purchases or renovations with multimillion-dollar loans from banks and other lenders. They repay those loans using their guaranteed funding from the city*' (ibid). Chester Community Charter School, near Philadelphia, also illustrates the 'non-profit' claim to be a sham. In 2008 alone it paid US$14m in rent, management fees and salaries to a for-profit company. The school spent 44.6% of its income on administration and business in 2006/07 compared to the 17.3% average for charter schools (Philadelphia Inquirer, 28/29 December 2008). Several other charter schools in the state were under investigation for conflicts of interest and financial mismanagement.

Bus services were privatised in the UK in the mid 1980s and, as predicted, services are now dominated by a small group of multinational companies. Annual revenue, excluding London, is £2.4bn with £1.2bn public subsidy. A market investigation suspects that 'structural features' now '*prevent, restrict or distort competition*' and that '*local markets were more profitable once they were monopolised*' (Office of Fair Trading, 2009). Part of the problem is that '*bus users do not appear to "shop around" for local bus services*' and '*the concessionary fare regime distorts the market by creating an incentive for bus operators to raise fares*' (ibid). There is not one mention of the bus companies predatory employment practices in 176 pages of 'market analysis'.

There is clear UK evidence that PPP cleaning services in acute hospitals are of a lower standard than non-PPP cleaning services (UNISON, 2009). Healthcare Commission and NHS Estates studies revealed a higher level of cleanliness with in-house services, a high level of integration between domestic and clinical teams and staff with a better knowledge of hospital cleaning (ibid).

Strategic Service-delivery Partnerships:
IBM's shared services contract with the UK's Department for Transport's (DfT) forecast £57.0m savings by 2015, but these had

vanished by March 2008 and were replaced by a forecast of £81.1m additional costs (National Audit Office, 2008). A centralised Shared Services Centre in Swansea for the departments and its agencies such as the Driver and Vehicle Licensing Agency (DVLA) and the Driver Standards Agency (DSA), began in April 2005. The original estimate of the technical contract was £16.5m, yet the Department paid IBM over £54m by the end of March 2008 plus a further £18m to other contractors.

As costs escalated, IBM got approval to develop some of the software offshore. However, '... *the reduction was not as great as had been envisaged because of delays and additional costs associated with complying with the stringent government security accreditation requirements regarding software development abroad. Neither IBM nor the Department have been able to supply figures for the cost reduction, which resulted from this exercise, including the effect of increased security accreditation effort*' (National Audit Office, 2008). The Shared Service Centre had a poor performance record with delays in the availability of some services and delays in payments to suppliers. The cost per invoice processed was more than four times that of invoices processed by the National Health Service and Prison Service shared services centres.

In the US, Virginia signed a ten-year US$2bn ICT strategic partnership with Northrop Grumman in 2005, which was intended to avoid future costs, rather than achieve savings. However, an interim review of the Virginia Information Technologies Agency (VITA) identified delays in the transition to a managed services environment and state agencies believe that '... *the problems they have encountered are indicative of a longer-term inability of the partnership to provide adequate service*' (State of Virginia, 2008). The PPP was intended to avoid future cost increases but the savings are now only likely if the contract is extended and widened to include local government, colleges and universities.

Governance and accountability

'*Financing and ownership are secondary, what matters is how the public and private sectors share risk and reward, not whether infrastructure finance should be public or private*' (Asian Development Bank et al, 2005).

'*MIG recommends a series of changes to federal law to truly integrate private investment in the planning process. These include not only requiring consideration of private investment throughout the planning process, but requiring the inclusion of private operators of major modes of transportation*

Table 40: *Assessing governance and accountability template*

Governance and accountability framework	Project assessment
Functions and responsibilities Strategic planning Performance assessment and reporting Managing, monitoring and reviewing of retained and transferred risks Charges, tariffs, prices and tolls Transformation Implementation of social and economic commitments Contract management and monitoring (including employment) Retendering facilities management contracts Responding to criticism and complaints	
Organisational and accountability framework Organisational structure – JVC, strategic and operational levels Membership and representation rights (equitable representation) Accountability mechanisms Resources for governance Developing working relationships Alignment of objectives and values Resolution of disputes	
Participation Community organisations and service user participation Staff and trade union participation Technical support for community/trade union representatives	
Decision making Process for setting agendas Organisation of meetings and access Dispute resolution procedure	
Transparency Access to information Communications strategy and reporting Anti-corruption measures	
Scrutiny of governance Review and evaluation of governance framework	

Source: Whitfield, 2009.

on planning boards. Providing private operators with parity in planning organizations will help to change the mind set against private investment. It will also increase the chance that private investors will become aware of the investment potential of planned projects, thus increasing the flow of investment dollars to transportation projects' (James, Public Works Financing, 2003). So much for democratic accountability!

The scope and responsibilities of governance will vary according to the type of project with SSP projects and new PPP models having a wider range of functions and responsibilities than a traditional DBFO project. A six-part governance framework is proposed in Table 40 which sets out comprehensive governance and accountability issues to be taken into account.

PPP governance focuses on project management and procurement (Grimsey and Lewis, 2004) but there is little concern for governance and accountability once a contract is signed. There is a degree of conflict inherent in many partnerships, although the literature alleges to eliminate conflicts and disagreement in the name of 'partnership working' and 'alignment of objectives' (Zadek and Radovich, 2006, Audit Commission, 2005, Office of Government Commerce, 2005).

In the UK, PPPs in the Building Schools for the Future (BSF) and Local Improvement Finance Trust (LIFT) programmes establish local partnership boards with 10%-20% local public body representation.

Strategic Service-delivery Partnerships (SSPs) usually have a three-tier partnership board structure. A Strategic Partnership Board focuses on long-term strategic policies and partnership relations and comprises Council Leader and Chief Executive together with directors and contract managers from the contractor, and report directly to the Council's executive or cabinet. A second-tier Partnership Board will usually focus on medium term direction and operational overview. A third-tier Operational Board would focus on day-to-day operational delivery and implementation of the project objectives. A JVC will have a similar structure. Reports and minutes of Partnership Boards are either rarely published or are very difficult to obtain. Backbench elected members in SSP authorities frequently know little of what is reported or discussed at Board meetings.

The standard Design, Build, Finance and Operate (DBFO) model is sometimes described as not being a real partnership because co-production and risk-sharing is limited and relationships are purely contractual (Klijn and Teisman, 2005). The DBFO model does not encourage partnership – it is more of a commercial accountancy arrangement, which guarantees high fees and profits and only partial sharing of profits. The degree of joint working and sharing of costs is limited. High procurement costs leads to limited competition behind closed doors with a narrow group of construction companies, consultants, banks and FM contractor. Some would argue that this is a very expensive cocktail.

But with the private sector unwilling to accept demand risk (except for toll/energy projects with guaranteed hikes for inflation), contractors accept construction risk, which they have responsibility for anyway and for which they can insure, it is naïve to believe this can or will fundamentally change. It obscures the ways in which the state already subsidies and supports PPPs. I would argue that a PPP is little more than a glorified outsourcing model, financed entirely by the public sector and/or user charges.

Accountability of global investment funds
Where a Special Purpose Vehicle is owned by infrastructure funds, private equity and/or pension funds following the sale of PPP equity, there is no formal accountability other than the implementation of the contract. Infrastructure funds are usually a division or subsidiary of a bank or other financial institution. For example, Macquarie Infrastructure is part of Macquarie Bank (see Chapter 3). The opaqueness is further accentuated when large projects are owned by a consortia of banks and funds from different countries, headquartered in an offshore tax haven.

The veil of secrecy with less disclosure and transparency
'Commercial confidentiality' is widely used to prevent the disclosure of proposals, appraisals, business cases and reports to public bodies recommending decisions on contracts, land purchase and so on. A degree of confidentiality is essential to protect both public and private interests. However, this practice is systematically abused. There is a degree of collusion between public managers, contractors, consultants and lawyers to avoid accountability, scrutiny and challenge to their policies and proposals. These parties effectively use 'commercial confidentiality' to conceal the rationale and evidence base for what are, in effect, political decisions.

Options appraisals, business cases and large parts of bids contain public information about service delivery, how objectives will be achieved, services to be delivered, infrastructure designed, financed, built and operated, governance arrangements, employment policies and more.

This is not 'commercial' but public information, which falls into two categories.

Firstly, material must be shared with trade union and community representatives so that the procurement and development process can draw on their views and analysis and enable them to assess the impact of projects and submit evidence to elected bodies within the terms of confidential information. Protocols and Information Agreements provide a framework by which confidential information can be shared with a high degree of security and bidders concerns about retaining their intellectual property rights can be safeguarded. Genuine commercial information about the financial structure and costing of bids, detailed operating systems, technical data and a contractor's internal arrangements and management systems can remain confidential.

Secondly, information which should be in the public domain. The transfer of financial and operational risks to the private sector is frequently exaggerated for political and economic reasons.

A commissioning state will make secrecy even more widespread. It makes a mockery of a raft of government policies about community empowerment, workforce development, industrial relations, public scrutiny and so on. The UK government claims to have addressed some of the transparency issues and '... *has introduced a number of reforms that have significantly increased the transparency of PFI and improved accountability for service users and service providers*' (HM Treasury, 2006a). In practice they have systematically avoided any issue of substance. Full Business Cases have been made public in the NHS, hence the focus of health sector research, but not in the rest of the public sector.

In the UK, Southwest One joint venture is an example of secrecy and misuse of 'commercial confidentiality'. In summer 2007 Somerset County Council and Taunton Deane District Council, were negotiating with the preferred bidder, IBM, for a £400m SSP. The UNISON branches had demonstrated that the options appraisal was flawed and opposed the project (Centre for Public Services, 2005). The branches sought to legitimately examine the employment impact of the transformation strategy, IBM's 'social and economic transformation' proposals and undertake a comprehensive impact assessment of the project on the local/regional economy (European Services Strategy Unit (ESSU), 2008)

Although I, as the ESSU trade union adviser, had signed a confidentiality agreement, the local authorities and IBM steadfastly refused to provide any information to enable a critical public interest input to the process (European Services Strategy Unit, 2007 and 2008). Further, they delayed providing a copy of the staffing agreement until after the contract had been signed at 03.00 hours one Saturday morning in September 2007, after having emailed the staffing agreement to UNISON, which they received at 19.42 on the Friday evening! An employment tribunal ruled that there were '... *special circumstances which rendered it not reasonably practicable for them to consult*' (Employment Tribunal, 2008). This is being appealed.

Southwest One is 75% owned by IBM. Avon and Somerset Police Authority joined in early 2008, increasing the value of the contract to £585m employing 1,400 staff. Staff are seconded on existing terms and conditions with employment guaranteed for the 11 year life of the contract. The staffing agreement allows IBM to directly recruit up to 30% of the staff in the Joint Venture Company (JVC) but the company refuses to grant recognition for UNISON to represent new staff. The JVC voting powers give the clear impression of an IBM-controlled private company, rather than a genuine joint venture with the public sector.

The contract was procured with a framework agreement, which allows 33 other public bodies in the region to avoid a procurement process if they want services delivered by Southwest One. Although Southwest One has a clear commercial imperative to expand, two years into the contract and no other authority has joined. Somerset County Council's Chief Executive, who talked of 'organisational terrorists', resigned in July 2009 and was gone within days.

The two trade union branches used the Freedom of Information (FOI) Act to make over 40 formal requests for information disclosure. This approach was of very limited use in the procurement process because of the time factor and the scope for delay. The Council eventually disclosed the business plan but long after the contract had been signed. There are advantages and limitations of the FOI approach, which is reactive, subject to delay and dispute and reduces the value of the information in terms of influencing policy.

Even when the private sector wins contracts it refuses to divulge information even to the National Audit Office. For example 14 PPP contractors refused to supply financial information on their PPP projects in 2006 (National Audit Office, 2006).

Transparency is declining as more and more infrastructure and financial assets are owned by private equity and sovereign wealth funds (SWFs). Most sovereign wealth funds are opaque. For example, the Kuwait Investment Authority was established under Law No. 47 of 1982 in which Clause 8 prohibits the disclosure to the public of any information related to KIA's work and Clause 9 states the penalties for unauthorized disclosure of information to the public. Some SWFs reveal very general information, for example, GIC Singapore issues press releases on the acquisition/sale of real estate assets, but not for other investments.

The lack of information surrounding PPP is a common problem, much of which is treated as 'commercially confidential' and is exempt from Freedom of Information on the same grounds. Furthermore, confidentiality makes comparisons between public and private sector performance impossible and worthless because the precise quality and level of service, staffing levels, pay and conditions and other factors, which determine performance, is more difficult to obtain from privately operated contracts. This has implications for the benchmarking of facilities management contracts in PPP projects in terms of who is able to ensure rigorous and genuine analysis and comparison with similar contracts.

Rather than releasing information which further justifies a decision to use the PPP approach (see Chapter 7) the emphasis must be on accountability, transparency and disclosure of information in the planning and identification and appraisal of options before decisions can be made.

Reduced community and trade union involvement
User/community organisation and staff/trade union consultation and involvement in the planning, business case and procurement processes is usually limited to users consulted about building design of schools but few other facilities, and staff and trade unions consulted on bidders employment and transfer policies. Stakeholder Strategic Partnership Boards (SPB) are part of the organisational structure in BSF and LIFT projects and are intended to have local representation. However, SPBs are usually not established until the project is approved and underway and there are questions of accountability and representation, e.g. who selects participants, who is represented and how they are held accountable.

Studies of democratic accountability and community involvement in UK PPP projects in the London Borough of Haringey and Birmingham highlighted the restriction imposed by procurement and the limited attitude of public bodies and the private sector to accountability and disclosure (Macfadyen and Rowland, 2002).

UK Strategic Service-delivery Partnership projects often involve staff with twin-track consultation, the formation of consultative staff groups and formal, but limited, consultation with trade unions through the industrial relations machinery. PPP projects teams often establish separate staff forums. Consultation with trade unions is usually limited to employment matters. A series of reports for UNISON branches in various cities have exposed the deliberate and proactive undermining of participatory democracy (Centre for Public Services, 2002, 2004, 2005, European Services Strategy Unit, 2006, 2007, 2008).

Corporatisation of the public sector
PPP models such as the UK's Building Schools for the Future (BSF) and Local Improvement Finance Trust (LIFT) projects and SSPs place private sector corporate interests in the heart of local government and other public bodies. This is done in the name of 'partnership' but with virtually no debate about the effect on accountability, of '... *accountability being detached from the political process*' (Woodhouse, 2005) or the longer term consequences of a multiplicity of boards within local government or other public bodies. The public interest and the public service ethos appear to be expendable in the effort to 'modernise'.

Public sector share ownership in private or Joint Venture Companies could lead to public interest matters being compromised. For example, the financial benefits of shareholding would conflict with other economic, social and political priorities. The evaluation and negotiation of proposals may be biased by the possibility of long-term financial accumulation from shareholdings, taking priority over achieving medium-term corporate objectives.

PPPs and privatisation contribute to the growth of local special purpose companies, joint ventures and trusts, many of which are controlled by the private sector. Each company has its own, mostly unelected, directors, who are legally required to prioritise company interests, thus weakening accountability and the public interest. Companies frequently procure their own support services, use management consultants more extensively, have separate employment conditions and often duplicate participation consultation. Companies and trusts have their own accounting and financial systems, which encourages retention of excessive surpluses, for example, schools in England held £1.9bn unspent revenue at 31 March 2008, triple the level nine years ago (National Audit Office, 2009). Companies should operate within a corporate framework, although it is more difficult to subject this to public scrutiny. And as I have already illustrated, private Special Purpose Vehicles can be bought and sold.

Governance by contract is another aspect of corporatisation. The procurement process, together with soft market testing, options appraisal, business cases and framework agreements, increasingly dominate public management practice. Management, financial, legal and technical advisers are regularly involved in policymaking and project management. Shared services projects and joint economic development and regeneration projects often require multi-authority governance and management. This creates a web of common interests for contractors, consultants, clients, financial institutions, business organisations and politicians. They have a shared ideology, contract culture, value system and vested interests and seek to consolidate policy and legal frameworks, minimise regulations and maximise private finance and business opportunities (Whitfield, 2001).

Maximising public subsidy, whilst being risk averse, are two other core parts of the shared ideology and business practice. Banks and financial companies have frequently obtained state and local economic development subsidies to relocate or finance 'regeneration' schemes. In the US, Citigroup received US$289.9m subsidies in New York, New Jersey, Texas and Kentucky between 1989-2007 (Good Jobs New York, 2007). These subsidies take the form of economic development grants, property tax holidays, subsidies for new roads, parking and sewers or sales tax breaks on the purchase of furniture and equipment for new buildings. Many subsidies did not create new jobs and the threat to relocate was often false. Citigroup announced 17,000 worldwide job losses in April 2007 and a further 25,000 in April 2008.

The PPP industry forms a corporate welfare sub-system, in which the same private sector consultants, lawyers, banks and financial companies, infrastructure funds, construction companies and advisers, are used in the options appraisal, soft market testing, design, procurement, build, finance and operation of projects. They constitute different projects, sectors and countries, but feed off each other. Framework agreements for corporate and technical services effectively lock-in the big four consultancies and consolidate continuity! Democratic accountability is weakened and fragmented by the transfer of functions and services to a plethora of local, regional and national arms length companies, trusts, quangos and public-private partnerships.

Change of power relations within a city
The continuance of PPPs and privatisation and these parallel developments is almost certain to lead to increased private sector control of the public infrastructure, land and development rights. An increasing share of a city's infrastructure could be on long leases under concession contracts operated by the private sector. State withdrawal from direct ownership of departmental and governmental buildings, replaced by PPP property partnerships, could reinforce this concentration of private control. Such changes are certain to increase the power and influence of developers, construction companies, consultants and managed services companies in the public policy making process at all levels.

Corporate power and machinery to resolve disputes
The International Centre for the Settlement of Investment Disputes (ICSID), part of the World Bank Group, operates investor dispute tribunals. It '... *provides multinational corporations with powers to sue governments when they impose domestic laws or regulations that have a significant detrimental effect on corporate profit-making*' (Institute for Policy Studies and Food & Water Watch, 2007). Far from being independent, the ICSID is embedded in the World Bank network. Investors can have loans from the International Finance Corporation, have purchased risk guarantees from the Bank's Multilateral Investment Guarantee Agency (MIGA) or the World Bank can have had a key role in the design and implementation of privatisation and deregulation programmes.

Many of the 167 concluded and 127 pending ICSID cases (August 2009) concerned infrastructure projects such as energy projects, railroads, water services, telecoms and road contracts. It is a catalogue of multi-million or billion dollar claims by transnational corporations against smaller countries in Eastern Europe, Africa and Latin America (ICSID case database, http://icsid.worldbank.org/ICSID/Index.jsp). Just over a quarter of unresolved cases were claims against the

Argentinian government for action it took to protect citizens in the 2002 economic crisis. Hochtief registered a claim against the government of Argentina, in December 2007, over a highway construction contract. Other countries have also cancelled contracts, changed prices and regulations, taken assets into public ownership, to protect citizens in economic crises, or stopped development, which threatened indigenous communities or the environment.

Economic and social impact

Two hundred and forty five new prisons were built in 212 rural US counties in the 1990s. Many small towns actively lobbied for the benefits of construction jobs, prison guard jobs and the commercial benefits from the supply of goods and services and visitors. However, a literature review of studies in Wisconsin, Minnesota, California and Colorado revealed high levels of prison staff commuting whilst economic impact studies of communities in Missouri, New York, Texas and Oregon revealed recruitment and environmental problems and limited economic benefits (Whitfield, 2008).

The loss of regional production and supply chains as PPP consortia resort to their global sourcing of goods and services, could slow growth or sustainability in the region (Centre for Public Services, 2003). The rationalisation of PPP contracts on a subregional/regional basis, either by PPP consortia or a change of Facilities Management (FM) supplier after refinancing, could also result in similar changes in the supply chain.

Another concern is the export of profit from a city/region to national and foreign investors and from developing countries to infrastructure, pension and private equity funds in New York and London. This includes the transfer of profits from the provision of finance, construction, FM and management consultancy advice, plus profits from the sale of equity and/or assets in successful PPP and privatisation projects are economically significant.

In the UK, large PPPs have particular economic consequences, for example, the Joint Waste PPP projects, which cover a subregion and are designed to include waste and recycling collection, street scene, grounds maintenance and strategy/service development. They also established new Joint Committees as a single client organisation, headed by a managing director, on which the partner authorities are represented. Seven authorities in Hampshire plan a £500m fourteen-year contract. Veolia Environmental Services currently operates a waste disposal and recycling plant in the largest authority, Portsmouth. The company is expected, because of its strategic position, to win the contract.

PPPs and privatisation can affect the ability of local and regional bodies to plan and implement growth strategies and development. Planning and integrating transportation policies are more difficult to implement when an increasing part of networks are owned and operated by different transnational private sector companies. Coordinating strategies to encourage economic development and implement growth strategies is more difficult with a fragmented control of infrastructure. What happens to education and health policy making when the private sector own portfolios of assets – portfolios of schools from different authorities in different countries – when their interest is simply to maximise returns to shareholders and to create opportunities for subsidiaries to provide an ever-widening range of services to those schools?

These are implications due to the reduction in the public sector asset base as a result of long-term leasing of public land, control and access to development potential and sharing of development gains, and the consequences of co-location policies, for example Independent Sector Treatment Centres (ISTCs) and private hospitals collocated with public hospitals in Ireland. There is an assumption that the private sector do not 'own' the land and buildings and, therefore, the private sector only has a lease and the assets will eventually return to the public sector, or that PPPs are just a short-term means of getting investment, which we would, not otherwise have, so there is no fundamental problem! Well, many PPPs are unlikely to be terminated at the conclusion of the contract because further investment will be required for improvement, restructuring, expansion and so the public sector will face the same financial issues. However, it is likely to have less capability of undertaking the work itself, because of the marketisation and privatisation of other public services and assets during the period of the PPP contract. Furthermore, the PPP/infrastructure market will have developed and be making demands on government/EU to continue expansion.

The development of regional business centres to win additional work from other public bodies and create 'additional' employment are a core feature of most SSPs. The basic premise is that a new ICT infrastructure and service transformation will provide the basis for winning contracts from other local authorities and thus 'create' new jobs in the host authority. This ignores the fact that there will be a net loss of jobs at a subregional or regional level. The earlier market leaders in SSPs had ambitious claims to create networks of regional business centres. However, for example, HBS (Mouchel) did not create any additional jobs in Bedfordshire and claims to have created only 137 after over 6 years in Middlesbrough despite a target of between 487 and 750 new jobs (European Services Strategy Unit, 2008).

The strategy has been almost a total failure in the UK. Only one of 35 authorities met the job creation target and this was not achieved by organic growth but by the contractor, Capita, winning a large TV licence contract and relocating a large chunk of the work from Bristol to Blackburn in 2002. Most local authorities face political pressure to maximise public and private economic benefits within their locality and have different ICT and related systems and organisational cultures.

'One innovative approach to identifying areas for increased use of the PSI [Public Services Industry] is to hand the question over to the private and third sector providers themselves by creating a framework for unsolicited bids to run parts of the public services' (Julius, 2008). This is merely copying US asset monetisation (see chapter 6). This is not 'innovation' in any normal use of the word but rather an example of crude neoliberal public policy making. The costs and consequences are not even mentioned in the report. So having created a market free-for-all, will the public sector have the right to make unsolicited bids for private and third sector operated services? The Australian state of New South Wales allows unsolicited bids which 'demonstrate community benefit' and alignment with government plans and priorities and will normally seek other bids (New South Wales Treasury, 2009). However, unsolicited bids inevitably focus on the size of the upfront payment (the ransom!) and private equity/infrastructure fund views of long-term interests rather than public needs and priorities.

Economic effect of mergers and contract renewals
What will happen when a PPP contract is close to completion and it is part of a portfolio of infrastructure fund assets? The asset would, in theory, transfer to the client public sector body on completion and the fund would have one less asset. However, other scenarios are more likely. The fund is more likely to try to persuade the public sector body to draw up a new PPP contract based on another whole-life renewal and improvement. It would be naive to believe that the fund will remain idle and simply wait to transfer the asset to the public sector on completion

of the contract. Of course, the public sector may want full ownership and would not contemplate another contract. However, lump sum upfront payments could change that situation. Much will depend on the returns achieved by the fund and the longer-term prospects for the asset, for example, the condition of the building, expected lifespan, service demand and potential for conversion to other uses.

Infrastructure funds and FM contractors will constantly seek to achieve economies of scale, efficiency savings, productivity increases and risk reduction, by increasing the scope and size of the portfolio, consolidation of service providers (for example, merging groups/federation of schools) and acquisition of other FM companies, diversification into core service provision i.e. if you manage and operate the building then why not provide the services too. Some funds or property companies could face pressure to sell their equity in PPP projects. For example, some investors in Land Securities/Trillium (now Semperian) believed the assets were 'undervalued' and sought a sale to get higher returns.

Four large hospital projects in the UK, signed before the introduction of a standard contract, which ensures that leases and contracts expire at the same time and have leases, which extend well beyond the PPP contract. Cumberland, Greenwich, Hereford and Darent PPP hospital projects have leases from 75 – 125 years in contrast to 30 – 60 year project contracts. The Colchester Garrison, a Ministry of Defence PPP, has a 150 years lease! (Building Magazine, 2007).

Social justice

Governments in developed countries have usually taken a very limited approach to an economic, social, health and environmental impact assessment of PPP projects. The process is ruled by the imperative for PPPs to demonstrate value-for-money in a narrow financial sense, otherwise the project would not proceed. This concentrates minds on the pricing of risk transfer. The process creates an attitude that just getting the project agreed and approved is a major contribution to the local economy and community and means that social justice and class issues (see chapter 1) are treated as secondary matters, if at all.

Public infrastructure is a class issue (chapter 1) with respect to what gets built where, when, how, who pays and how facilities and services are managed, staffed and are held democratically accountable.

Ownership is being redefined. As risk is traded on, through

derivatives and securitisation, it is becoming evident that traditional ownership is changing into a complex array of share dealings resulting in multi-layered ownership. PPPs, co-location and strategic partnerships may be temporary, because they will not be necessary in a fully privatised service (which might still be state funded) but the buildings and services will be owned and operated by the private sector.

The OECD recommends that a poverty reduction strategy for infrastructure will need to:

i) *Target infrastructure interventions to areas that enable the largest possible number of poor people to engage in productive activities and access social services, using a cross-sector approach linked to MDG outcomes.*
ii) *Encourage the involvement of poor communities through, for example, decentralised planning systems that incorporate explicit poverty reduction goals (such as universal coverage for basic services).*
iii) *Propose technological and commercial options tailored to investment areas' long-term service needs.*
iv) *Support tariff policies that poor users can afford – including smart subsidies and flexible payment structures – and ensure that users are consulted on needed tariff increases.*
v) *Provide technical and financial incentives (certification, risk insurance) for local private sector involvement.*
vi) *Promote employment creation in infrastructure construction, operation and maintenance.*
vii) *Systematically address gender-specific needs when designing infrastructure projects.*
viii) *Prevent or mitigate negative impacts on vulnerable groups and promote inclusion of the disabled, the elderly and minority groups'* (OECD, 2006).

Quality of employment

The impact on jobs depends heavily on the prevailing legislation. The European Acquired Rights Directive gives workers a degree of protection when services are transferred from one employer to another. This excludes pensions, but the UK has a Code of Practice, which strengthens both pensions provision and the terms and conditions of new staff to try to avoid a two-tier workforce.

Average employment fell 24% in electricity and 22% in water in PPP and privatisation projects over and above employment levels in state operated services in a study of utilities in 71 developing and transition economies (Gassener et al, 2009). Although staff reductions were small relative to the national labour force, *'that does not take away from the seriousness with which governments need to address the employment question'* (ibid).

Employment in electricity distribution in eight Latin American countries declined 26.4% in the pre-privatisation period and 17.6% in the post-privatisation period. Job losses were concentrated in Argentina, Brazil and Columbia. Telecoms employment reduced by 9.2% and 23.2% in the same periods, again concentrated in certain countries – Argentina, Brazil and Peru. Water and sewage employment also declined by 16.5% and 17.6% respectively. Not surprisingly, labour productivity in terms of the number of connections per employee, increased substantially.

In the UK, a Best Value Code of Practice on Workforce Matters applies across the public sector. It requires contractors (and sub-contractors) to employ new staff working alongside transferred staff on *'fair and reasonable terms and conditions, which are overall no less favourable than those of transferred employees'* (Department for Communities and Local Government, 2005). Contractors must consult with trade unions to agree the terms and conditions for new starters. However, the legislation and code are rarely monitored by public sector bodies or trade unions. Secondment, rather than the transfer of staff in some UK PPPs, has helped to maintain public sector terms and conditions and pensions.

New PFI prisons in the UK are 'full service' contracts (buildings and prison services) and thus avoid the European staff transfer regulations. Consequently, prison contractors employ staff on private rather than public sector terms and conditions. Since labour costs account for the bulk of prison operating costs, significant pay differentials are the prime source of PFI 'efficiencies' (Justice Forum, 2002). Prison officer/custody officer and supervisor average basic pay is between 8% – 44% lower in the private sector than in the Prison Service (MCG Consulting Group, 2006). The difference is, in fact, larger because Prison Service staff receive additional payments for extra hours, which averaged £620 and £689 per annum for Prison Officers and Senior Officers respectively in the year to 31 March 2006. Prison Service staff were also entitled to a range of allowances, which averaged £715 and £655 per annum respectively in the same period. These are usually not payable in private prisons. Prison Service staff receive locality payments in London and the South East, again not payable in private prisons. Only governors and senior managers are better paid in private prisons (ibid).

The salary value of a Prison Service pension, based on employer contribution rates in 2006, was between 11.3% and 15.6% more valuable than pensions in privately managed prisons. There are also substantial differences in holidays, with the Prison Service offering between 5.75 and 8 more days per annum (ibid). Longer working hours (39 – 44 hours in private prisons compared to 39 hours in the public sector) with private prisons having significantly less generous sickness benefits than the Prison Service (Justice Forum, 2003).

New private prisons are able to make use of modern security arrangements, which is part of the reason for lower staffing levels in private prisons (Scottish Executive, 2002), also applicable to new public prisons. The significant pay differentials account for the bulk of cost savings, not the 'innovative management practices' claimed by the PPP industry. A study of Scottish prisons concluded that the private sector saving in labour costs is achieved '... *not just by a reduction in the absolute numbers of staff, but also by a radical change in the skills/experience mix of staff*' and thus lower pay rates (Taylor and Cooper, 2003).

In the UK, the average hourly pay rate for middle management, supervisors, clerical and manual staff was lower in all the surveyed PFI contracts between the time of transfer and October 2004. Only senior management increased their average hourly pay rate (National Audit Office, 2008).

The treatment of staff in privatised residential care homes in Essex and Barnet operated by Excelcare Holdings and Fremantle Trust respectively, was scandalous (European Services Strategy Unit, 2007). Pay cuts and radical changes in terms and conditions made a mockery of the European staff transfer regulations. Private contractors often operate local/regional pay rates when employing new staff, thus creating different tiers of staff.

Privatisation and PPPs effectively force staff to transfer to the private sector when many are committed to working in the public sector. Whilst privatisation may provide some staff with new career opportunities, it denies many others the opportunity of a career in public service.

More fragmented trade union organisation
In the UK, PPP contractors frequently only recognise trade union representatives from the company or Joint Venture Company (JVC) workforce, instead of continuing with the existing local authority branch representation. They have often reduced trade union facility

time. They refuse to recognise trade unions to represent new staff (IBM refuses to recognise UNISON for new staff in Southwest One – the JVC with Somerset CC, Taunton DC and Avon and Somerset Policy Authority); refuse to directly debit trade union membership fees and/or require staff to re-sign (Capita in Southampton), which leads to the fragmentation and weakening of trade union organisation and representation.

Public sector capability and planning

Large projects and PPP programmes must take account of the impact on public sector capability and planning. Because PPPs are assessed on an individual basis, the accumulated impact on public sector service delivery, technical knowhow and intellectual knowledge, planning and the future of public service provision is rarely assessed.

The transfer of public sector design, finance and facilities management, and in some cases construction, to the private sector leads to the loss of skills, experience and knowledge. When staff may transfer to a new employer, in-house sections are often run-down or closed. As PPP contracts get larger and more complex, public bodies rely more heavily on external consultants and advisers. Reduced capability is evident in project management skills, appraisal and evaluation, technical knowledge, managing procurement, legal and financial management, sector and market analysis (see chapter 3).

Commissioning further reduces public sector capability. A client-contractor split leads to the transfer of in-house services to arms length trading organisations or companies and their eventual privatisation through trade sales or 'partnerships'. If the state is reduced to merely selecting providers through the procurement process, this will radically and dramatically change public management. Commissioning would not then remain a public function. Some Primary Care Trusts (PCTs) in the UK have already considered outsourcing commissioning, which would involve management consultants and contractors assessing needs and services, writing specifications, selecting outputs and outcomes, carrying out options appraisals, managing the procurement process, evaluating bids from other private contractors and monitoring their performance. The role of the Project Delivery Organisation or integrator model was described in Chapter 7.

Public sector capability is reduced by the diversion of resources to 'making markets' by shaping contracts to suit business interests and designing business-friendly regulatory frameworks. The notion of creating a 'mixed economy' and a 'level playing field' are simplistic and ignore the economic realities of private sector cherry picking, cross subsidising contracts, loss leader strategies, labour exploitation and gaming tactics, to take advantage of market forces and weak regulatory regimes. Business practice and commercial values will increasingly dominate public management and thus erode public service principles to be replaced by profit-driven motives. Monitoring and contract management is frequently under-resourced.

It is almost inevitable that having created a 'market' in PPPs (between construction companies, banks, financial institutions and facilities management companies) and a secondary market in refinancing and PPP equity, the market will expand and develop new forms of marketisation and privatisation of public services.

The private sector strategy could be described as one of attrition, to systematically reduce the responsibility, capability and power of the state in the provision and delivery of services. The objective is to weaken democratic institutions by fragmenting collective, area-wide public authority provision into separate stand-alone companies and trusts running individual schools and hospitals, organised and operated with business structures and values, which, in turn, will be unable to resist further phases of privatisation. This provides future opportunities for the private sector to achieve economies of scale and increase profitability by merging and consolidating these separate companies and trusts to create area/regional organisations, again but firmly in the private sector.

Asset monetisation has significant implications for planning cities and regions – concessionaire companies, PPP consortia and secondary market portfolio funds could have a major influence on the level of integration, and have the power to influence change. Initial highly fragmented network of concessions and PPP contracts is almost certain to consolidate into control by transnational companies. This would be a corporate complex on grand scale!

Conclusion
These are not isolated examples of flawed development and failed projects. The evidence shows that the flaws in PPPs are systemic. It is not ameliorated by the projects that are built on time, to budget and are operating satisfactorily (recognising that most of that evidence comes from surveys of project managers and the PPP sector itself).

There is overwhelming evidence to demonstrate the inadequacy of the value-for-money and PSC evaluation models. They are deliberately designed to ensure PPPs are never fully and comprehensively assessed. This has grave implications for public services as the scope of PPPs is widened.

Table 41 summarises the long list of public costs and impacts of PPPs and compares them with the limited public benefits of PPPs.

Table 41: *The case against PPPs and privatisation*

Public costs and impacts	Public benefits
Widens global infrastructure market in public infrastructure assets.	Construction companies reduce delays and cost overruns because they take responsibility for risks.
Does not significantly increase investment in infrastructure because PPPs are publicly financed. Even if the debt is off-balance sheet, it still has to be financed from public sector revenue budgets for the contract period, and remains a public liability.	Whole life costing to take account of maintenance and renewal.
Erodes democratic accountability and governance.	Higher degree of price certainty.
Value-for-money unproven and in many cases contrived.	Construction companies proactive in introducing green building systems and controls.
Risk transfer is frequently exaggerated, misallocated and mispriced.	Corporate-wide approach to application of ICT to improve access and efficiency.
Increase in user charges – tolls, fees and third party income. Locked into a market-based financial strategy to widen infrastructure tolls may increase revenue depending on level and changes in usage. But has profound implications for urban spatial planning, equalities and social justice.	National building programmes for schools, colleges and health centres.
Affordability and potential financial impact on other services when budget cuts imposed because PPP payments protected.	
Creates opportunities to extend private provision of core services.	

Public costs and impacts	Public benefits
Renegotiation of contracts shortly after commencement.	
Loss of flexibility with long-term contract and constraints of contract culture in public services.	
Reduces public sector capability through transfer of intellectual knowledge to private sector.	
Quality of service variable with high additional costs for variations or changes.	
Quality of design and buildings highly variable.	
Widens commercial confidentiality and lack of transparency.	
High programme and transaction costs.	
Outsourcing of support services and facilities management except if retained in-house or staff seconded.	
Weakens in-house delivery organisations.	
Creates two-tier workforce and complete-service PPPs reduce pay, pensions and conditions of service.	
Fragments and weakens trade union representation and organisation.	
Business interests influence in determining social needs and public policy.	
Refinancing and sale of equity in PPP company.	
PPP industry created of construction companies, banks and financial companies, consultants and lawyers.	
Loss or erosion of public sector principles and values.	
Impact of loss of local/regional production and supply chains.	
Full cost of public subsidies, guarantees and PPP programme costs rarely quantified.	

Source: Whitfield, 2009.

CHAPTER 10

Strategies for public investment

The preceding analysis indicates that a radically different approach is necessary for public infrastructure investment. We need a strategy which tackles today's crises with new priorities on addressing climate change, urban policies and alternative public service reform. This must go hand in hand with radical reform of global and nation state financial markets and regulatory frameworks and a new public sector transformation strategy.

The response to the fiscal crisis has failed to address reform of the global infrastructure market whilst the PPP industry has sought to expand the role of private finance. The Global Unions/ITUC Washington Declaration made no reference to privately financed infrastructure (November 2008). The ATTAC (international network in the global justice movement) statement *'The time has come: Let's shut the financial casino'* made brief reference to infrastructure privatisation but made no recommendations to challenge the global infrastructure market and PPPs (October 2008). Meanwhile, infrastructure funds have continued to receive substantial investments and banks have continued to create PPP platforms.

The chapter begins with a vision for an infrastructure strategy with new priorities followed by proposals on how public infrastructure should be financed, new global policies and regulations, the critical importance of revitalizing the role for government and concluding with meeting the needs of the 21st century through public management and governance.

A vision for an infrastructure strategy with new priorities

Tackling today's critical issues
We need to reinvigorate and inform people's imagination by showing the potential of new concepts of public provision, combining infrastructure and services in new configurations. There is enormous scope for more imaginative integrated cross-sector provision in general and more multi-service projects for particular population groups, such as children and the elderly. For example, community health complexes (combining doctors surgeries, medical centres, domiciliary care and a variety of independent living options); multi-

modal transport hubs (integrating public and other transport systems); learning centres (combining schools, adult learning and training, leisure and community facilities); multi-service centres (integrating access to a range of local services).

Vision and long term planning are essential in so far as they can be based on 'affordable reality'. Major projects often have a 15-20 year planning period before they are approved and construction begins. In the US a '... *broad and compelling vision is needed*' to focus on a future of '... *economic competitiveness, energy independence, environmental sustainability, and quality of life, not a legacy of concrete, steel, and cables*' (National Research Council, 2009). The Council recommended focus on providing the essential services involving water and wastewater, power, mobility, and connectivity – in contrast to upgrading individual physical facilities. Any vision should focus on collaborative, systems-based approaches, cost-effective solutions across institutional and jurisdictional boundaries and '... *greater transparency in decision making by quantifying the links among infrastructure investments, the availability of essential services, and other national imperatives*' (ibid).

Four strategies are required to make an infrastructure vision.

1. Climate change and the low carbon economy
This strategy requires a drive for renewable energy such as wind power, solar photovaltaics, solar power and solar thermal energy to accelerate the shift to a low carbon economy; to transform energy efficiency of buildings, household appliances and combined heat and power; and broader environmental activities, such as conservation, to preserve biodiversity, and bringing back contaminated or abandoned land into use.

There is considerable scope to develop local/regional manufacturing of clean energy equipment and components given the scale on national and global investment over the next 20-30 years. Although labour and living wage standards can be required, imposing production and supply conditions invariably fall foul of procurement regulations. Although there is often scope for applying preferences at the selection stage of procurement, these regulations and the single market concept from which they are based, will have to be challenged if sustainability and local/regional economic development is to have any effective meaning.

Thirteen studies of the economic and employment impact of clean energy industry in the US and Europe have concluded that '... *the renewable energy sector generates more jobs than the fossil-fuel energy sector per unit of energy delivered*' (Kammen et al, 2004). The switch to clean energy will result in job losses in fuel processing and operations and maintenance, whereas the majority of jobs created in renewable energy will be in manufacturing and construction, after taking into account that fossil-fuel plants have a 40-year life in contrast to 25 years for renewables. In addition, '... *supporting renewables within a comprehensive and coordinated energy policy that also supports energy efficiency and sustainable transportation will yield far greater employment benefits than supporting one or two of these sectors separately*' (ibid). A US$300bn US federal investment over ten years in diversifying US energy sources, clean technology manufacturing, high performance energy efficient buildings and smarter infrastructure, would add 3.3m jobs to the economy, repay the investment, produce US$284bn net energy cost savings and stimulate the economy (Apollo Alliance, 2004). Communities dependent on fossil fuel industries must be supported economically and financially to transform the local economy and improve community well-being.

2. *Sustainable economic development and employment strategies*
The focus should be on socially useful jobs, not just 'green jobs', within an overall strategy of reducing poverty and inequalities, developing local production and supply chains, minimising waste and negative environmental impacts and maximising renewables and recycling. Developing the research, innovation, manufacturing and service linkages evident from infrastructure and service investment in the health economy can spur economic development and employment, providing important local/regional benefits. For example the health and social care economy studies in the North West and East of England, illustrate the wider economic and social benefits of investment (Centre for Public Services 2003 and 2005). Similar economic and employment linkages are evident in other sectors such as education.

The linkages should be developed through public sector support for research and development; investment, premises and technical advice for enterprise expansion and start-ups; financial assistance to encourage the location of manufacturing plants linked to infrastructure investment strategies; training and skills programmes; the integration of infrastructure investment with economic development strategy to plan provision; and constant monitoring of regulations and controls to minimise the negative effects of markets.

3. Urban development and regeneration

The strategy must seek to reduce speculation in public assets and housing to prevent the conditions arising for further asset bubbles. It should plan investment in land and property and change the focus of infrastructure funds.

The formation of publicly owned National and/or Regional Infrastructure Development Banks could have a significant role. They would issue bonds, which would provide a solid investment for pension funds and other investors. Their remit would include reclaiming areas blighted by foreclosures and putting vacant and under-used land and buildings back into effective occupation and use; undertaking urban regeneration; climate change infrastructure adaption programmes retrofitting building, irrigation and other projects; supporting local/regional economic development by creating new opportunities for local production and employment; assisting the development process to maximise public sector, social enterprise and small and medium enterprise involvement; and contributing to creating a different set of public values, priorities and wrest a degree of control away from existing banks and financial markets.

The lessons from successful European eco-towns demonstrate the need for a high level of infrastructure investment, often funded by land value uplift, location in growing and prosperous areas close to existing settlements with easy access to jobs and services and a demand for new homes. *'They are built on land owned by a public agency, which also commissions the master plan and installs the basic infrastructure to enable plots to be sold to small builders and cooperative groups. They include a significant proportion of social housing (25 – 30%)'* and a major commitment from local authorities to eco-town principles (European Regional Business and Economic Development Unit, 2009). Another study of European regeneration emphasised the need for public investment in high quality infrastructure and a high quality public realm, to devolve real power and resources to cities and to drive democratically accountable development agencies (Cadell et al, 2008).

Equally important, alliances of community, trade union, civil society and political parties must ensure that the articulation of priorities does not get hijacked by powerful business lobbies and political hierarchies. They also have the ability to be first in line to scoop the pool of available resources. High profile capital-intensive infrastructure projects must not proceed at the expense of the revenue-based needs of deprived communities.

4. Economic realism

The financial crisis and global recession has forced a reassessment of how investment in public infrastructure should be prioritised and how it should be financed and controlled. Infrastructure planning has always required the reconciliation of addressing urgent social needs within financial constraints, competing public policy priorities, accommodating demands from different areas and interest groups and meeting long-term needs to expand, renew and reconfigure networks.

There are clearly differences between the needs and priorities of developing and developed countries. In developing countries the emphasis is usually on the provision of new public infrastructure. Developed countries have the option of readjusting values and expectations to focus on the better use of existing facilities through rehabilitation and retrofitting.

Ideally, all sections of public infrastructure will be 'fit for purpose' but, as discussed in chapter 2, there will always be provision and/or maintenance deficits of one type or another. They have existed in periods of high growth because resources are expropriated or channelled into other uses. Now, it is even more essential for reasons of financial prudence and sustainability that the demands for public infrastructure be reconfigured.

The claims that new schools and hospitals are 'essential' to 'transform' education and healthcare have to be challenged. There is evidence that new schools have a potentially positive impact on pupil aspiration and behaviour and teacher morale, but the impact of capital expenditure on pupil attainment is *'... quite small'* (PricewaterhouseCoopers, 2008). In addition, *'... there is the potential for substantial diminishing returns to investment ... and some weak evidence that returns differ across the different types of investment'* (ibid). Another study made the obvious point that the school environment *'... is just one of many interacting pedagogical, socio-cultural, curricular, motivational and socio-economic factors'* (Centre for Learning and Teaching, 2005). This study concluded that whilst there was evidence that inadequate school building had negative detrimental effects on health, concentration, well being and attendance *'... once provision reaches a reasonable standard, the complexity of environmental interaction comes into play'* and *'... much of the evidence is inconclusive'* (ibid).

The benefits of new buildings are similar to those obtained from rehabilitated buildings. Furthermore, the location of rehabilitated buildings may have advantages over the greenfield location of new facilities. The size and scope of benefits must be clearly identified, their value assessed relative to other priorities with all rehabilitation alternatives fully investigated in options appraisal.

Infrastructure deficits have traditionally been used by government departments, professions and the construction industry to make the case for investment in resource 'bidding wars'. However, the basis on which deficits are calculated should be more comprehensive and take account of adaption to climate change, sustainability and new infrastructure priorities.

Banks, financial markets and governments assume that those governments that have recapitalised and nationalised banks will, at some point in the future, sell those assets to reduce public debt. But there are so many unknowns and it is impossible to forecast if, or when, this may occur.

It is crucial to reiterate that private debt is not an alternative to public debt. If government's cannot 'afford' public sector capital expenditure, then they cannot afford the same level of debt in the form of contractual commitments to PPP consortia. Irrespective of whether a PPP is on or off balance sheet and irrespective of the type of partnership or its organisational structure, the partnership concept does not extend to the private sector sharing the cost of public infrastructure. Banks and financial institutions provide all or part of the initial finance but projects are generally entirely paid for by the public sector and/or charges and tolls imposed on service users. There are no free or cheap solutions. And the more complicated the partnerships arrangements, particularly when public assets are used to 'leverage' private sector involvement, the more those assets are put at risk and the more that private interests will take precedence over the public interest.

Asset monetisation merely shifts the financial burden from government to service users who have to pay higher tolls and charges. It is another form of taxation. Quick-win lump sums from asset monetisation and privatisation are not a sustainable option for governments and public bodies. They should strenuously oppose unsolicited bids. This will asset strip the public sector, tie ownership and control into long-term inter-generational contracts and impose tolls and charges for an increasing range of services. The same interests that oppose modest pay and pension increases for working people, also promote 99-year contracts that guarantee sweeping increases in tolls and charges. Yet governments don't guarantee inflation-proof pensions for a decade, let alone 99 years.

Extending the marketisation and privatisation of the public infrastructure is not a solution. The UK's rail 'market' has led to the quasi-renationalisation of Railtrack, gross profiteering in the sale and resale of the three train leasing companies, increasing failure of franchises and increasing public subsidy. Imposing market prices for energy, water, transport and public housing require large state subsidies to protect the poor, but also ensure profits for private investors and operators.

Setting new priorities
Infrastructure programmes must be rooted in economic performance and a government's fiscal policy to determine what is affordable. Social and economic needs and full cost/benefit impact assessments should identify priorities between expenditure on different types of infrastructure and options for particular projects. Crude comparisons with previous levels of investment or with investment levels in other countries should be avoided. Most existing frameworks are inadequate, for example, centralising infrastructure policy, new special purpose long-term bonds, common assessment of costs and benefits and wide application of new infrastructure management technologies (Center for Strategic and International Studies, 2006) or the OECD's Principles for Private Sector participation in Infrastructure which fail to address the criticisms of PPPs and merely consolidate their role (OECD, 2007).

The re-prioritisation of infrastructure must be four-dimensional.

Firstly, economic and spatial plans, together with planning controls, should determine what gets built where, how and for whom. Infrastructure plans should identify immediate, medium and longer-term needs, identify options, estimated costs and implementation programmes. They should prioritise projects that meet local needs and maximise economic and social benefits within national and regional priorities. Public bodies should undertake capability reviews to ensure they have the capacity and skills for effective project management.

Public expenditure programmes should ensure resources are distributed between new, replacement, improvement, upgrades and maintenance. There must be a balance between brownfield and greenfield projects based on needs and priorities. The private sector promotes greenfield rather than brownfield projects because the rate of return of greenfield projects is usually in the 10% – 15% range compared to 8% – 11% for brownfield projects (Infrastructure Management Group, 2008).

The balance between infrastructure and public service expenditure (capital and revenue) is crucial because both contribute to economic development and community well being. New public infrastructure may attract political kudos but increased revenue spending, for example, on more teachers and better health services, may be a higher community priority and achieve similar economic benefits.

Condition and adaption audits should identify how better maintenance and management, and the level of adaption required for climate change, could improve and extend the useful life of existing infrastructure assets. Joint or shared infrastructure projects between public bodies should be encouraged to make more effective and efficient use of existing infrastructure with a subregional approach to management and maintenance of assets. Design must incorporate flexibility for alternative future uses and sustainability in construction and operation and employment within those areas.

Secondly, the connection between taxation (corporate, personal, consumer taxes and user charges) and the quality of public infrastructure needs to be reaffirmed. In other words, it is economically impossible to have high quality public transport, roads, schools, hospitals and other facilities with low taxes and user charges. Transparency must replace the opaqueness of privately financed PPPs and the illusion that private debt ratcheted up in PPPs is not public debt embodied in long term contracts. I highlighted earlier how off-balance sheet financing was one of the causes of the financial crisis.

Thirdly, democratisation and a high level of transparency of public infrastructure planning, procurement and operational stages, is essential in enabling community and trade union participation at each stage of the process.

Finally, demand forecasts for passengers, traffic, visitors and users and the relative potential performance of public and private sectors in managing the construction process on time and to budget, must be subject to rigorous, independent review and assessment.

Mis-trust the 'impossibility' and 'inferiority' arguments

There is a commonly held belief that a publicly operated system cannot increase tolls or user charges to the same extent as a privately operated system sector, because of a lack of political commitment. In other words a privately operated system is able to extract higher tolls and charges than the same publicly operated system. The audit of the Chicago parking PPP refers to this as the *'impossibility argument'* and was used to justify why the city council did not calculate the financial benefits, if it retained control of parking under the same terms as those in the proposed lease. This ran parallel with the *'government inferiority argument'* that the city council could not operate the parking system as efficiently as the private sector (City of Chicago Office of the Inspector General, 2009). However, the Inspector General demolishes these arguments. The city council approved significant increased charges (see chapter 9) when it signed the lease and other cities have retained parking systems and increased parking charges. The efficiency argument was shown to have no merit when city council intervention was required to fix 'teething problems' in the first few months of the contract. Increased efficiencies in the contract *'... are expected to come from capital improvements that are well within the City's capability and expertise'* (ibid).

Financing public investment

Public investment must come from a combination of different sources, which will vary between countries, and include capital and revenue public expenditure programmes, new green taxes and charges, infrastructure and revenue bonds, government infrastructure funds, development banks, planning gain/land value uplift, special funds, joint investment and public-public partnerships.

In one sense, money itself is not the problem. There are vast global resources. How it is spent, and how it is classified under the financial/accounting rules and values attributed to levels of debt and the way these are used to further economic and political interests, are the key issues.

Future levels of public spending are couched in 'armageddon scenarios' in which the level of cuts is the dominant theme. There is not the space to discuss this here. However, capital and revenue expenditure on public infrastructure will continue and should be subject to the priorities and strategies set out in this chapter.

The debt problem
The current level of public debt in developed and developing countries was highlighted in chapters 1 and 2. This will be affected by the length and depth of the recession and the speed and scale of a return to economic growth. Much will also depend on whether fiscal stimulus measures are required and the scale and type of measures taken. It is clear that the levels of public debt in most countries will

remain high at least in the medium term, possibly for more than a decade.

Public debt may increase in some countries, for example Ireland's planned National Asset Management Agency could have up to €90bn liabilities in taking over developers' land and property assets. Some banks and financial institutions may have to be fully nationalised. The sale of assets acquired in the recapitalisation and nationalisation of banks and other companies may eventually reduce public debt, although there is almost certainly a political economy case for retaining public ownership.

The global debt of developing countries must be subjected to a 'debt work-out process'. *'38 of the 43 countries that the World Bank calculates are most vulnerable to the economic crisis already required substantial debt cancellation before the current crisis, in order to meet the needs of their people'* (Jubilee Debt Campaign, 2009). Legislation must outlaw the so-called 'vulture funds' who buy up debts at a steep discount and pursue the debtor country for the full amount.

Public spending
Countries where the fiscal stimulus included bringing forward infrastructure expenditure may face declining capital programmes after 2010/11. A low tax, low public expenditure model is fundamentally incompatible with providing good schools and hospitals, quality public transport, adapting building to meet the challenge of climate change, providing water and sanitation, energy networks, social housing and infrastructure.

The OECD recommended that governments diversify and expand traditional revenue-raising sources on the grounds that *'... there remains some scope in OECD countries for exploring new ways of raising tax-based revenues'* (OECD, 2006). This could include new ways of raising tax-based revenue nationally through vehicle licence fees and fuel taxes and locally, through more innovative bonds, general and selective sales taxes, parking and local fuel taxes. The OECD referred to the use of leasing arrangements for water treatment facilities, solid waste disposal and power plants. The recommendations did not refer to funding more infrastructure by increasing corporate and personal taxation. Consistent with the OECD's neoliberal ideology, it recommended more PPPs, using diversified business models, more infrastructure investment by pension funds and other large institutional investors, wider use of user charges, more outsourcing of the operation and maintenance of infrastructure and developing competition and markets by '... *exploring the possibilities for expanding the scope for privatization of assets*' (ibid).

New taxes and/or charges
A 2009 UN Interagency statement called for fiscal reforms to '... *shift the burden of taxation from jobs, income and savings to the overuse of resources, resource depletion and environmental degradation, thereby encouraging green investments*' (United Nations, 2009).

Targeted taxes should be more widely introduced such as the tax on air travel tickets introduced by several countries. This would reduce ultra-low cost travel where the ticket price bears no relation to the cost of travel, use of airports or the environmental damage. A Workplace Parking Levy could be used to finance public transport investment – a study by Nottingham City Council in the UK showed that it could generate £10.8m annually by 2014 (Core Cities Group, 2008).

Reformed tax structures could include increased taxes on the wealthiest citizens and a tax on trading financial assets – trading has little to do with raising funds for investment and would help to discourage speculation (Pollin, 2008).

Congestion pricing can be effective when it is linked to investment in public transport, for example in Singapore, London and Stockholm. There are 70,000 fewer vehicles entering central London daily whilst bus passengers increased 45% between 1999/2000 and 2006/07. In some countries, local, general or selective sales taxes, parking and fuel taxes can make a contribution to infrastructure projects.

Changes in tax regulations
A number of proposals have been made to eliminate cross-border tax evasion and limit the scope for tax avoidance, so that large corporations and wealthy individuals pay tax in line with their ability to do so; increase citizens' influence in the democratic control of taxation, and restrict the power of capital to dictate tax policy solely in its own interest; restore similar tax treatment of different forms of income, and reverse the shifting of the tax burden onto ordinary citizens; remove the tax and secrecy incentives that encourage the outward flow of investment capital from countries most in need of economic development; and prevent the further privatisation and degradation of public services (Tax Justice Network, 2009).

Offshoring in tax havens must be stopped. Tax rates and tax bases for highly mobile capital, such as that controlled by large corporations and wealthy individuals, should by under-pinned by a degree of harmonisation. (Eighty-three of the 100 largest publicly traded U.S. corporations had subsidiaries in jurisdictions listed as tax havens or financial privacy jurisdictions – Citigroup had 427, Morgan Stanley 273 and News Corporation 152 in 2007). Tax breaks and loopholes, for example 'carried interest', for private equity funds and other financial companies, must be terminated (Trades Union Congress, 2008).

Other changes needed include a new 'general anti-avoidance principle' that treats all tax avoidance as unacceptable and, therefore, open to challenge. Abolish unnecessary tax reliefs enjoyed primarily by the wealthiest individuals. Apply income tax to all capital gains on assets held for less than a year, make it much harder to abuse Capital Gains Tax by shifting the ownership of assets prior to their sale. Introduce a minimum rate of tax to be paid on the income of those earning more than £100,000 a year, to ensure that they do not unduly benefit from tax reliefs and allowances.

In addition, public disclosure in all states and territories of tax laws and treaties should be mandatory; comprehensive and automatic information exchange must operate between all tax authorities to facilitate assessment and collection of taxes, including imposing obligations on states to obtain information from financial institutions, lawyers, accountants, auditors, and other relevant intermediaries.

Transnational corporations should be taxed on the unitary basis to permit tax authorities to effectively reverse the false shifting of profits to low-tax jurisdictions. The residency principle should be universally applied for corporate taxation. A country-by-country reporting system of accounting should be required for multinational corporations (Murphy, 2009).

Infrastructure funds and banks
Infrastructure Canada and Infrastructure Australia are examples of national agencies responsible for national infrastructure plans or priorities supported by infrastructure funds. Canada has several funds, the Building Canada Fund (C$8.8bn over seven years), a Gas Tax fund with C$11.8bn to invest in municipal infrastructure to 2014 supplemented by C$5.8bn from the Goods and Services Tax Rebate Provincial-Territorial Base Funding, that allocates C$25m per annum base funding to each province, a Gateways and Border Crossing Fund

(C$2.1bn). It also has a Public-Private Partnership Fund with C$1.25bn to '... *support innovative projects that provide an alternative to traditional government infrastructure procurement*' (Infrastructure Canada, 2009).

The A$20bn Building Australia Fund was established in the new Labour government in 2008, with funds sourced from expected budget surpluses in 2007/08 and 2008/09. However, by early 2009 the government conceded that planned surpluses had been eroded by the global financial crisis leaving only A$12.5bn, of which A$4.5bn is allocated to the national broadband plan.

Switzerland set up a €20bn railway infrastructure fund in 1998, partially funded by heavy goods vehicles fees, VAT and excise duties. A €13.5bn road transport infrastructure fund was launched in 2006 to expand trunk roads and motorways and public transport. This fund is financed by vehicle fuel taxes and motorway tolls.

These funds promote national priorities and channel additional funding to reduce the level of debt otherwise incurred by local/regional authorities. However, there are key issues such as the extent to which these funds represent 'new' money as opposed to rolling-in existing programmes, democratic governance, capture by PPP interests and the extent to which they enhance or reduce local/regional powers and accountability.

Pension fund investment in infrastructure

Pension funds should immediately revise their strategy for infrastructure investment and realign priorities from maximising returns to a combination of reasonable return with social and public benefit. Firstly, all planned investments in private infrastructure funds and the privatisation of public assets should be stopped. Secondly, plan the withdrawal of existing infrastructure fund investments with priority given to those located in offshore tax havens. Thirdly, consider investment in local/regional/national public infrastructure funds and/or bonds. Fourthly, work with public agencies to develop new innovative funding mechanisms to increase investment to achieve a low carbon economy and strengthen economic growth through local/regional production and supply chains. Finally, all pension funds should have stringent quality of employment/trade union recognition, environmental and sustainable development policies. They should also actively support the adoption of a strengthened EU-style employment protection globally.

Regional and development bank funding
The European Union and several development banks have special funds or programmes that provide grants or loans to assist capital investment, for example, the European Commission's €105bn cohesion fund for 2007-2013 to create green jobs and growth. However, the European Investment Bank and the European Bank for Reconstruction and Development should focus on public investment and cease to promote PPPs and private investment in public infrastructure.

Special funds
The US Highway Trust Fund, established in 1956, using income from Federal fuel taxes and truck-related taxes to fund highways and transit projects, is an example of hypothecated funding – specific taxes or charges being earmarked for a specific use. The fund has been described as a revenue sharing mechanism rather than an infrastructure policy because Federal funds are handed over to states that decide projects (Ehrlich and Landy, 2005).

Federal gas taxes have not increased for over a decade and drivers currently pay about 3 cents in tax revenue per vehicle mile while the actual cost of using a highway in congested conditions are on average 10 – 29 cents per vehicle mile travelled. By 2012 the highway element of the fund is forecast to have a negative balance of US$25bn with the transit balance at zero. A US$8bn transfer of funds from the government's general funds was required in 2008 to keep the fund afloat (Wall Street Journal, 2009). The National Transportation Infrastructure Financing Commission (NTIFC) recommended the *'Federal fuel tax be increased from 5 to 8 cents per gallon per year over the next 5 years, after which it should be indexed to inflation'* (National Transportation Infrastructure Financing Commission, 2009).

The UK's proposed Independent Next Generation Fund, financed by a 50 pence per month on all fixed copper lines to provide a part subsidy for the deployment of next generation broadband to the 'final third' of homes and businesses, is another example of a specific tax funding a specific infrastructure. The disadvantages of hypothecated funds include a loss of flexibility in allocating public resources and rigidity in terms of how the money is spent.

Planning gain/urban renewal
Local authorities have various potential sources of infrastructure funds. For example, cities and larger authorities in the UK can levy

an additional two pence supplement on the national business rate in their area, the Business Rate Supplement, to help finance infrastructure investment. A Community Infrastructure Levy, used alongside planning obligations to obtain affordable new housing, is a charge related to the size and character of development levied on developers, to ensure new development contributes to infrastructure provision. The Core Cities Network consider these funding streams to be helpful, whilst being inadequate for larger projects and are seeking Accelerated Development Zones (ADZs), based on the US model of Tax Increment Financing, and Regional Infrastructure Funds.

But ADZs are another zone model '... *designed to allow cities to 'participate in the growth dividend' – or, in other words, allow local authorities to capture incremental value in the form of tax revenue generated from new development. In order to do this, cities require the power to retain long-term local tax revenues generated from development, such as business rates, allowing funds to be raised for investments through securitisation of those revenues*' (Core Cities Network, 2008). The US Economic Stimulus Act allows state and municipal authorities to divert business, sales and property taxes to developers, extending existing Tax Increment Financing. But Greg LeRoy, executive director of Good Jobs First, described TIF as '... *a gamble with taxpayers' money far into the future, at the expense of public education and other public services*' (New Jersey Policy Perspective, 2009).

In the US, many local and state governments have developed Housing Trust Funds. Those funds are pledged toward the development of housing for lower income families, and they draw on a variety of sources of public funding. These sources include repayment of the principal on government urban renewal bonds, exactions from developers of new commercial, industrial and residential developments, and special taxes on hotel rooms and other sources (Centre for Community Change, 2009).

Local Asset Backed Vehicles (LABV) in the UK are another mechanism to pool public and private finance and land assets in PPPs or Joint Venture Companies (JVCs) to develop areas and to share increased property values. But again, these models promote speculation, securitisation and expose public assets to unnecessary risk.

Infrastructure and revenue bonds
There are significant differences between countries in the way that infrastructure is funded. Infrastructure bonds are commonly used in the US where local authorities and public bodies issue bonds to raise

funds for capital investment and in some cases, revenue spending. Some European Members of Parliament have called for 'Eurobonds' to be issued to raise finance for large infrastructure schemes (EurActiv, 25 September 2008).

A private sector alternative to the standard DBFO project would require a complex organisational structure. Local infrastructure investment funds would raise capital from domestic, institutional and foreign private equity investors with second tier investment trusts established to buy equity stakes from investors in the first local infrastructure investment funds who wanted to exit their investment (Noel and Brzeski, 2005). A second component would consist of breach-of-contract insurance or guarantee facilities to '... *alleviate sub-sovereign policy risks faced by first and second round funds*' (ibid). An 'output-based subsidy scheme' (required because steep tariff increases will cause hardship for low income households) and a 'contract transparency monitoring system' (operated by a 'neutral' third party to assist contract negotiations between the public and private sectors) make up the four-part structure. This is not an acceptable alternative model. It encapsulates all the criticisms of PPPs made to date.

Joint investment and public-public partnerships
Public-public partnerships describe joint investment between two or more public bodies, for example, shared services projects, in which authorities pool their resources, such as capital investment and technical know-how, to develop infrastructure assets.

For example, in the UK, local and sub-regional Public-Public Partnerships were promoted by several UNISON branches and European Services Strategy Unit (ESSU), in developing alternative strategies to Strategic Service-delivery Partnerships (Centre for Public Services, 2002 and European Services Strategy Unit, 2008).

Infrastructure increases economic activity, which is normally taxable, thus potentially benefiting local and national income, although financial benefits may not accrue where assets are privatised and controlled by transnational companies, with transfer pricing strategies and offshore locations for tax purposes.

In the US the Texas State Highway 121 demonstrates the importance of offering a public bid when PPPs are planned. Highway 121, a 26-mile road in northeast Dallas, had a complicated history between 1999-2007 before it became a Public-Public Partnership between the North Texas Tollway Authority (NTTA) and Collin

County (Battaglio and Khankarli, 2008). Skanska submitted an unsolicited bid in 2005 and, later that year, four firms were shortlisted – Cintra, Macquarie, Skanska and Dallas Mobility Link. A US$2.88bn Cintra proposal was accepted in early 2007 only to be rescinded following state legislation with new highway finance and tolling regulations. A few months later NTTA was allowed to submit a US$3.3bn bid, which was evaluated with the Cintra bid. The Regional Transportation Commission accepted the NTTA bid as providing best value, with higher income.

Mega projects, which are currently dependent primarily on private finance, must be rigorously challenged in terms of whose needs are being met, financial viability and risk. If a strategic economic and/or political decision is made to have a degree of private sector investment in large complex public infrastructure projects, this should be based on specific terms, which include public sector control of joint venture companies, democratic accountability, good quality employment with trade union recognition, full transparency and disclosure, participation and consultation with community organisations and trade unions, and comprehensive impact assessments capable of extracting authentic information.

User charges and tolls
Congestion pricing, particularly where it is accompanied by investment in alternative services such as public transport, is more likely to attract support. The introduction of new or higher charges, fees or tolls can increase revenue depending on the level of increase, the cost of alternatives and the impact on demand. It is important that user charges and tolling regimes are also adjusted for inflation.

The US Harris County Toll Authority decided to retain ownership of a toll road system after a study concluded that '... *the implementation of more aggressive tolling would generate financial gains close to those under the long-term concession scenario and still allow the county to retain full control of its toll roads*' (Transportation Research Board, 2009). This is not to suggest that public sector charges should simply mirror those advanced by the private sector in PPPs but, where the principle of charging has been established, should be effective, fair, index linked to inflation, and justifiable.

Do people have a more positive attitude to charges and tolls than income, property and sales taxes? A full debate on tolls and charges is not within the scope of this book but they must be considered within the framework of public service and welfare state principles and values. There are real dangers that the extension of charges and tolls will accelerate the marketisation and privatisation of public services.

A 'Non-profit' approach
The Non-Profit Distributing Organisation (NPDO) model for PPP projects allows reinvestment of profit in the local community and greater involvement of local stakeholders in the governance of the project company. Whilst this model has two key advantages over the standard PPP model, it is, nevertheless, very similar to a standard PPP model. The same criticisms therefore applies.

Argyll and Bute Council in Scotland became the first local authority in the UK to establish an NPDO for a PPP schools project in 2005 (Ernst & Young, 2005). Profits generated by the project company are given to a specially created charity to avoid the profits being distributed to shareholders. The Charity appoints a stakeholder director to the NPDO board. There are six other directors, five appointed by the debt providers (Royal Bank of Scotland and Quayle Munro) and an independent director appointed by Partnerships UK. The NPDO is classified as a private sector company for corporate income tax and accounting purposes. *'Therefore, in the vast majority of respects, it is much the same as any other PPP project company'* (ibid). The infrastructure fund Infrastructure Investors own the equity in the Argyll and Bute project.

Potential resources – UK example
The potential resources that could be redirected to public infrastructure investment vary between countries. But the scale of potential resources is significant. The following example is based on UK policy changes by stopping or reducing current expenditure, (for example, operating the Trident defence system, the marketisation of public services and the operation of quangos), changing tax regulations and rates to reduce tax avoidance and by the rationalisation and making more effective use of public assets (see Table 42).

The cost of the marketisation of public services in the UK was estimated to be £8bn in one-off capital and revenue costs by 2006 plus over £3bn annual costs (Whitfield, 2006). These costs cover subsidies, debt write-offs, capital spending and the revenue costs of 'making markets'. A large part of these resources could be available for

Table 42: *Potential resources in the UK*

Potential resources	Cost saving over 10 year period (£bn)
Cancellation of Trident – construction costs of £25bn with total lifetime costs (maintenance etc) of £76bn*	76
The annual cost of government measures to establish public service markets (excludes one-off costs)**	30
Reducing corporate (£11.8bn) and individual (£12.9bn) tax avoidance plus £8.4bn tax planning by wealthy individuals: Assume 50% reduction (Trades Union Congress, 2008)	165
Consolidation and elimination of quangos – arms length agencies, companies and trusts (estimate)	2
Improved public sector asset management***	140
Total	**313**

Source: * Campaign For Nuclear Disarmament, March 2009. ** Whitfield, 2006. *** Operational Efficiency Programme, HM Treasury, 2009.

additional capital investment and associated revenue expenditure, if the marketisation strategy were to be terminated.

The potential resources are £313bn over a ten-year period, which would significantly reduce public debt *and* divert substantial resources into public infrastructure investment. These resources could finance high speed digital infrastructure to every home and business in the UK broadband, a smart power grid and intelligent transport systems, £15bn in year one and £5bn thereafter, (£60bn), 1,000 new schools with community and leisure facilities (£20bn), 1,000 new health centres and 50 new hospitals (£25bn), a rapid transit system in 30 cities (£23bn) and still leave £25bn for other public infrastructure. The digital investment would create or retain 700,000 jobs in the first year alone (London School of Economics, 2009).

New global policies and regulations

This section summarises the key changes required to help increase public revenue and investment and impose effective constraints on the operation of the global private infrastructure market machine.

New operating principles for international/national economies are required to set the context for welfare state and public infrastructure policies. The first four principles, '... *the subordination of finance in the* economy, democratic governance, accountability and transparency, the provision of health and financial security, and social stability having priority over market efficiency and shareholder value' are vitally important (Elliot and Atkinson, 2008). They also propose a principle of 'the undesirability of a semi-detached super-rich class', '... the principle of social justice' (ibid). Other principles include only seeking '... economic growth which is sustainable and tackles climate change; the trade and exchange of agriculture, natural resources, goods and services should not be dependent on creation of global/regional markets; state intervention, regulation and direct provision has a key role in economic, social and political relations; and a collective responsibility to ensure each state implements the development/poverty reduction agenda' (ibid).

Stop the financialisation of pensions and other services: There is a connection between the growth of private finance for public infrastructure and how hedge fund activity is tied to the withdrawal of the state from pensions provision (CornerHouse, 2006). Financial programmes related to public service provision, such as student financial support, should be provided directly by the state as it is cheaper and more efficient and avoids extending the investment market. This has recently been demonstrated by the US student loan program in which the private sector component underperformed the public programme (Morris, 2008).

Stop public service marketisation: World Trade Organisation (WTO), General Agreement for Trade in Services (GATS) and EU Services Directives proposals to liberalise and marketise public services should be immediately abandoned as well as nation state transformation of public services by marketising local services (see chapter 3). Financial services liberalisation should be excluded from the Doha Development Agenda, until such time as new international and nation regulations and supervision are in place and excluded from Free Trade Agreements, as currently negotiated, or being submitted for ratification. Developing countries, which have already opened up their financial services markets according to GATS rules, should be allowed to reverse their current GATS commitments on financial services, without the need for compensation after withdrawal (Vander Stychele, 2008).

Prohibit off-balance sheet financing: Off-balance sheet financing in public and private sectors should be prohibited through legislation. All structured investment vehicles and other companies, trusts and arms length organisations, designed to transfer and retain assets off-balance sheet, should be required to be included in public and private accounts.

New controls on private equity and hedge funds: New controls need to be put firmly in place to include short-selling (which can drive the stock price of financial institutions to exaggeratedly low levels and thereby undermine their viability and led to short-term curbs on the practice in 2008). Alongside this, new regulations covering risk management processes and valuation techniques should replace self-regulatory codes of practice, impose liquidity and transparency and disclosure regulations, applicable to all financial companies. Private equity and hedge funds should be legally required to meet the same information disclosure requirements as publicly listed companies.

Financial conglomerates should be demerged into separate banking, insurance, investment banking and securities trading activities (Elliot and Atkinson, 2008 and Vander Stichele, 2008).

Regulate securitisation: Prohibit the sale of financial securities too complex to be sold on exchanges (80% of Collaterised Debt Obligations (CDOs), Credit Default Swaps (CDSs) and other exotic financial instruments are currently traded off-market). Required trading on exchanges would reduce risks and increase transparency (Political Economy Research Institute (Crotty and Epstein, 2008). All new financial products and processes must be subjected to a regulatory precautionary principle on the same principle used for the licencing of drugs in US, Europe and other countries (ibid).

Increase capital or asset reserve requirements of banks and financial companies (including private equity funds, hedge funds, investment banks) so that they have similar solvency and liquidity requirements, applicable to all lending entities, including intermediaries like mortgage bankers, who warehouse deals for securitisation (Morris, 2008). Regulators should impose counter-cyclical capital-asset ratios and/or provisions. As the value of assets increases, capital requirements would increase, this would restrict the degree to which they could increase lending and drive up asset prices still further (Crotty and Epstein, 2008).

More stringent and comprehensive audit standards are essential, in consort with tightening of company law, restrictions on the use of off-balance sheet financing/companies, new due diligence and disclosure requirements. Evidence of a lack of standards have been a series of failures, for example PricewaterhouseCoopers failing to detect a US$1bn fraud at Satyam Computer (Wall Street Journal, 2009) and Ernst & Young's claim they were '... *unaware of the refinancing* *transactions undertaken by the former Chairman of the bank'* in the eight-year concealment of €84m loans to the chairman of Anglo Irish Bank (Ernst & Young, 2009). The existing system is designed for 'complexity and obfuscation' to undermine regulators and avoid public disclosure. Stringent controls are needed on auditors to constrain the provision of management consultancy and financial advice to the same client, including the promotion of tax avoidance products (KPMG recently paid US$456m to US government to settle tax shelters assessments in 2005).

New global investment standards are required so that social, environmental, sustainable development, climate change, governance and transparency, poverty reduction and employment performance can be regularly monitored, scrutinised and subject to public disclosure.

New labour legislation is paramount to strengthen job security, terms and conditions in mergers, acquisitions and outsourcing; rights to organise, represent and take industrial action; and rights/procedures for participation and access to information.

Development aid: Governments should follow Norway's example that '... *aid should not go to programmes that contain requirements for liberalisation and privatisation*' (Soria Moria Declaration on International Policy, Norway, 2007). The Government made an exemplary commitment to '... *strengthen poor countries' opportunities for and ability to engage in trade, building of democratic institutions and development of public welfare services such as health and education*' (ibid).

Reform of investor protection regulations in multilateral and bilateral treaties: There is compelling evidence that foreign investors should be subjected to the same laws as domestic investors. Bilateral investment treaties have '... *not deepened the commitment of host states to the rule of law reform enterprise. It has systematically diverted the interests of potentially influential foreign investors from demanding the creation of good generalized laws and legal institutions, and has further encouraged them to enter into long term arrangements that impair the state's capacity to regulate effectively in the public interest and which further increase the risk of corruption and abuse*' (Daniels, 2004).

Daniels concludes that '... *committing to a regime of strict national treatment, the interest of foreign investors in advocating for good rule of law reforms will be enhanced, and, in this respect, will become more closely aligned with dispersed and often voiceless citizen interests in the host country. One way of achieving this goal would be the revival of the much maligned Calvo Doctrine, which was committed to equal treatment of foreign and host state investors under the municipal laws and courts of the host country*' (ibid).

The Australian Government set an important precedent in the 2004 US-Australia Free Trade Agreement when it refused to include an investor state dispute resolution. Several countries including Brazil, have not signed the Convention on the Settlement of Investment Disputes Between States and Nationals of Other States, which continues to attract high levels of foreign direct investment. Furthermore, World Bank research concluded that: '*... analyzing twenty years of bilateral FDI flows from the OECD to developing countries finds little evidence that BITs have stimulated additional investment. Those countries with weak domestic institutions, including protection of property, have not gotten significant additional benefits; a BIT has not acted as a substitute for broader domestic reform*' (World Bank, 2003). Other studies have similar findings (Gallagher and Birch, 2006). '*These cases show that the rights given to foreign investors may not only exceed those enjoyed by domestic investors, but expose policymakers to potentially large-scale liabilities and curtail the feasibility of different reform options*' (ibid).

Policy reform of multinational and global bodies
The World Bank, International Monetary Fund, World Trade Organisation, United Nations and Development Banks must adopt macroeconomic and financial policies with effective regulatory frameworks, strengthen domestic capability, improve public sector provision and employment, and cease the prescription/conditionality of neoliberal policies. Multilateral development banks should stop pressurising borrowing countries to pass legislation to facilitate wider use of '*alternative financial instruments*' (Fried, 2008) and should eliminate privatisation and PPP requirements from Bilateral/Multilateral Agreements.

An effective monitoring system should be established for state and international implementation of the United Nations Convention Against Corruption together with more decisive rules and binding procedures put in place to minimise fraud, corruption and bribery (Transparency International, 2008).

Revitalising the role for government

It is plainly evident by now that it *does* matter who plans, designs, finances, builds and operates public infrastructure. Governments have a key responsibility for planning and investment in the public infrastructure and economic development; regulation of markets and services; democratic governance and accountability; progressive taxation, rents and service charges and a public management model centred on public provision.

Three immediate priorities for government action are:

Firstly, recognition that government has a key role in the provision of public infrastructure and that this should *not* be transferred or outsourced to the private sector. Government must abandon the creation of markets in public sector and welfare state services. Notwithstanding this, the private sector has an important role in construction because most, if not all, building and civil engineering work is untaken by the private contractors. There are also many large architectural and engineering consultancies.

Four organisational models should be used for the provision of public infrastructure:

1. Public sector – a single public body or a consortia of local public bodies.

2. Public sector – national/regional organisation such as a government department or agency (cross border projects could have a joint government body).

3. Joint Venture Company between the public sector and a community/social enterprise.

4. Joint Venture Company with a private company with the public sector having majority control.

These models will not automatically ensure that public infrastructure planning and investment will address the economic, employment and social justice issues in deprived communities. Radical changes will be required in economic strategies and resource priorities, which are often based on flawed models of the local economy and spurious trickle-down economics. The abolition and transfer of functions from the raft of unaccountable arms length companies, trusts and quangos will take time. The private sector currently retains disproportionate and unaccountable influence on many economic and regeneration bodies in the UK and other countries.

Secondly, to integrate the infrastructure planning and implementation process and to increase public sector capacity to manage this process. This requires reversing the separation of strategic planning, commissioning and provision into distinct activities, often carried out by different organisations. This should be part of a paradigm shift to a progressive public sector reform outlined below.

Thirdly, a new public infrastructure contract is required for design and finance responsibilities with the public sector client. The answer is not to revert to design and build contracts, although this model may be suitable for projects that require a combination of design, manufacturing and installation skills. Construction Management At-Risk (CMR) has been successfully used for US building, transportation and highway projects. The American Institute of Architects support this model. The client selects the construction manager, based on qualifications, before the design stage is completed. The architect and construction manager work together in the final stage of the design process and the latter gives the client a guaranteed maximum price and coordinates all the subcontracted work. This approach strengthens coordination, enhances transparency, delivers efficiencies and minimises delays (Triangle Business Journal, 2009).

There also is scope for the packaging of similar infrastructure projects and/or the use of framework agreements where one or more construction companies are awarded contracts over a rolling programme of work. Public bodies have important multi-functional design responsibilities (Centre for Public Services, 2004).

Reform of existing PPPs

A ten-point reform plan is proposed, with the objective of imposing new criteria in the appraisal and evaluation of PPP projects currently at the planning and procurement stage; to improve the governance, accountability and transparency of operational PPP projects; and to transfer support services to public provision at the earliest opportunity.

1. Public investment options, including shared/joint and public/public models, should be reassessed for all projects in the planning stage. For projects already in procurement, the process should be terminated, where this can be justified on the grounds of changed circumstances, so that procurement cost compensation claims from bidders can be avoided.

2. A new comprehensive evaluation and impact assessment methodology must be adopted for all options appraisals and bids – see Table 44, in conjunction with an Infrastructure Stress Test – see Table 45.

3. Governance arrangements should be reviewed to include the membership and effectiveness of PPP Partnership Boards, the quality of accountability and the need to increase the frequency and scope of

scrutiny. In addition, all PPP projects should have rigorous and regular monitoring procedures and performance assessment to improve the quality to ensure availability of facilities and fulfilment of employment responsibilities. Public bodies should review their policies and procedures in dealing with requests to refinance projects and to be informed of a planned sale of shares. Public bodies should ensure that in-house bids are always considered in the retendering of facilities management contracts. Independent scrutiny, oversight and reporting of performance must include a wide network of community, trade union and civil society organisations in addition to statutory bodies to enhance accountability and transparency.

4. UK Local Education Partnerships in BSF projects and LIFT projects should be restricted to the provision of new buildings and the provision of hard facilities management services.

5. Support services should be excluded from PPP projects and should be returned to public provision when retendering is triggered by the contract or if performance is not satisfactory.

6. Radical changes are needed in the procurement process and operational stage to increase public disclosure of PPP documentation including options appraisals, business cases, procurement documents, contracts, minutes of Partnership Board meetings, monitoring and performance reports. New protocols with trade unions and community organisations should set out the scope, process, methodology, participation, information disclosure and evaluation criteria for future planning and implementation of infrastructure projects. Contracts must have adequate termination agreements that are non-punitive to the public sector. For example in the US, Chicago's Inspector General's Office recommended a 60-day review period between reaching agreement on PPP terms but before bids are submitted. The review period would include an independent cost/benefit analysis, public hearings and a full council debate and decision.

New disclosure requirements must apply to individual projects and to PPP programmes to ensure disclosure for public access and to facilitate trade union/community involvement in the procurement process. Every PPP project or group of similar projects, government budget documents and year-end financial statements, should provide information on future service payments and receipts specified in PPP contracts for a 20-30 year period; details of contract provisions for guarantees, shadow tolls, profit-sharing arrangements, events triggering contract renegotiation; the amount and terms of financing and other support for PPPs provided through government on-lending or via public financial institutions and other entities owned or controlled by government; the effect on fiscal balance and public debt, and whether PPP assets are recognized as assets on the government balance sheet (International Monetary Fund, 2006).

Every government guarantee should include a description of its nature, intended purpose, beneficiaries, and expected duration; the government's gross financial exposure and, where feasible, an estimate of the likely fiscal cost of called guarantees; payments made, reimbursements, recoveries, financial claims established against beneficiaries, and any waivers of such claims; and guarantee fees or other revenue received. In addition, budget documents should provide an indication of the allowance made in the budget for expected calls on guarantees, and its form (e.g., an appropriation, a contingency), plus a forecast and breakdown of new guarantees to be issued in the budget year (ibid).

7. New policies/codes of practice should be drawn up which limit the transfer of public assets to arms length companies, Joint Venture Companies or the private sector. They would also apply in the reorganisation of public services and development of a shared services infrastructure.

8. Government PPP agencies and departmental units should be closed and staff transferred and retrained to public infrastructure investment and management units.

9. When PPP contracts reach completion, the assets should be returned to the public sector. There should be no contract renewals or new PPPs, at least not without comprehensive scrutiny. Punitive termination clauses should be excluded from PPP contracts, which should also include a minimum 50% public sector share from all elements of future refinancing of the project.

10. Public sector bodies, PPP consortia and trade unions should draw up comprehensive agreements to protect the terms and conditions of transferred and new staff, pension provision, fulfilment of labour rights and engagement in workforce planning.

PPP projects usually have punitive termination clauses, which make a public sector option of buying out the project untenable. The Skye Bridge and Inverness Airport PPP projects in Scotland were bought out by the public sector, but at considerable cost. Even if the private sector agreed to accept less than full payment for the remaining contract period, there would be little advantage because legal fees, termination costs and new management costs would swallow up the initial benefit to the public purse.

Meeting the needs of the 21st century
through public management and governance
A new approach is required for public sector management in the 21st century. We need public bodies whose functions, responsibilities, organisation and management that will deliver progressive public service renewal to replace the marketising, commissioning, contracting and asset stripping neoliberal policies of recent decades. Progressive public service renewal should be underpinned by a commitment to public service principles and social justice in taxation, rents and charges and allocation of resources – see Table 43. The devolution of powers to city and regional government should include effective implementation of economic development and community well-being policies.

The governance of local public bodies in many countries is partial and fragmented with varying degrees of accountability and transparency. Few have any meaningful participation. Therefore, the development of new holistic, democratically governed public bodies, coupled with new alliances or networks of community, trade union and civil society organisations must run parallel with progressive public service renewal.

Holistic public sector perspective: A whole-public sector approach – geographic, functional and jurisdictional – is required for the provision, governance, resources and asset management across all public services. Full implementation of the principles of democratic accountability, participation, transparency, social justice, public interest, sustainability, universal provision, quality of service, integrated and well-coordinated services and quality employment are vital in the planning and delivery of public services. This includes a parallel commitment to social justice in taxation, rents and charges and allocation of resources.

Public investment: Maximum use of public resources, including joint/pooled budgets between public bodies and development of new funding mechanisms.

In-house delivery: Each stage of the infrastructure process – design, planning, procurement and operation – must be subject to democratic accountability, transparency, participation and scrutiny. Each project must incorporate high quality design, maximise flexible use of space and green technology, contribute to sustainable development and to the local/regional economy and employment.

Table 43: *Progressive Public Service Renewal*

Progressive Public Service Renewal	
Objectives	**Policies**
Improve collective provision to meet economic, environmental and social needs. Increase capability and capacity of public organisations. Improve governance, accountability, participation, transparency and scrutiny. Regulate sectors, markets and private & voluntary sector contractors. Public investment to improve quality and sustainability of public infrastructure. Progressive taxation and charging. Value skills and improve ability of staff to manage and deliver.	Holistic public sector perspective with strategic planning integrating economic, social, environmental and sustainable development policies. Public investment. In-house delivery, build networks & work collaboratively with other public/community bodies. Strategic planning integrating economic, social, environmental and sustainable development policies Capability and capacity building programme: – project management with systematic monitoring, review and scrutiny. – evidence based evaluation of policies, projects and options. – research sectors and markets. – retain and enhance technical knowledge and public sector information. – organisational development to promote innovation and learning. – financial management and investment. – service innovation and improvement. – commitment to public service principles and values. Regulation of markets to protect public health, labour standards and legal rights. Democratisation and consolidation of public bodies and agencies. Involvement of service users, community and civil society organisations and staff/trade unions Commitment to social justice in taxation, rents and charges and allocation of resources.
Neoliberal Public Sector Reform	
Objectives	**Policies**
Marketisation of services to widen markets. Services shaped by market forces. Direct payments, individual budgets and vouchers. Commercialisation of public sector. Private control of public infrastructure Privatisation of public assets. Reduce the cost of labour and weaken trade union organisation. Minimum government. Low direct taxation.	Financialisation and individualised/personal budgets. Commodification of services. Commissioning (and client/contractor separation). Outsourcing and offshoring. Public Private Partnerships. Performance management through indicators and targets. Creation of arms length companies, trusts and joint venture companies. Transfer of staff between employers. Deregulation and removing red tape.

Source: Whitfield, 2009.

This will require in-house capability of project management, design and technical services and facilities management and support services. Joint or shared public infrastructure investment and service provision should be commonplace.

Strategic planning integrating sectors: Re-invigoration of local and regional government with powers to regulate, provide and deliver, which consolidates public resources and intervenes in markets in the public interest; ensures effective and efficient cooperation between public bodies with sharing/joint provision of support services where relevant and viable; strong and effective government organised to meet needs and deliver services and meet responsibilities, and not financial wheezes designed to meet private interests or create new organisations to serve narrow and/or vested interests; an integrated infrastructure planning and implementation process should avoid or minimise gaps in provision, common in much new development and regeneration projects; long-term whole-life costing integrating investment costs with maintenance and operational costs not limited to contract periods.

Capability and capacity building programme: Infrastructure planning and project management, including access to technical resources to design and manage projects from inception to completion should minimise delays, cost overruns and improve quality. Public sector capability and intellectual knowledge must be reflected in the organisational culture, the working practice of middle management and front-line staff and its approach to innovation. The options appraisal and procurement process must include comprehensive assessment, financial and resource planning, construction and contract management, monitoring and review and in-house technical support with minimum use of external consultants. When external consultants and advisers are required, their contracts must include knowledge transfer, capacity building and commitment to public service principles. All public bodies should operate an integrated impact assessment methodology to assess the full economic, social, health, social justice, environmental and climatic impacts of projects so that the costs and benefits, advantages and disadvantages are transparent (see below).

Regulation of markets to protect public health, labour standards and legal rights: New regulatory frameworks are required to enable the state to regulate, monitor, review, and where necessary, intervene in markets to ensure people's needs and local economy interests are achieved.

Democratisation and consolidation of public bodies and agencies: The consolidation of arms length companies, trusts, off-balance sheet companies and quangos is essential to improve governance, accountability and participation. Radical changes are needed in transparency and disclosure to avoid the narrow approach adopted by the UK's Audit Commission which claims that even the names of terminated PPP contracts are 'commercially confidential'. This is a flagrant misuse of 'confidentiality' to protect private capital and a reluctance to protect the public interest. Confidential information is a product of the procurement process, but there must be a degree of disclosure and transparency if staff, service user and community participation are to be meaningful and projects subjected to effective scrutiny and rigorous impact assessment. Relying on obtaining information through Freedom of Information requests is inadequate in procurement because it is frequently dealing with post-decision making information and can be a drawn-out process if the authority/bidders decide to delay or dispute the release of information.

The OECD's global infrastructure study concluded '... *citizens have had relatively little direct involvement in infrastructure planning*' and processes need to be '... *inclusive and representative; provide for genuine deliberation; allow access to accurate information; and offer the prospect of effectively influencing outcomes and achieving clear results*' (OECD, 2007)

Involvement of service users, community and civil society organisations and staff/trade unions: Public bodies must involve community, civil society and trade union organisations are involved in the public policy making process. This should include financial resources to obtain their own organising and technical advice.

Quality employment and workforce development: Local authorities and public bodies are, directly or indirectly, major employers in any local economy. The standard or quality of employment, training, workforce development, pensions and industrial relations has a major influence in the local labour market and the local economy. There is a direct connection between the quality of service and the quality of employment (skills, experience, training, workforce development and terms and conditions). Therefore, it matters greatly who provides and who delivers services. For example, the health and social care economy has direct economic linkages to local and regional firms in the production and supply chains and hence employment.

A new evaluation framework

A new evaluation methodology is needed to improve the prioritisation and effectiveness of projects; to make decisions about public

Table 44: *Public Infrastructure Investment Evaluation Framework*

	Assessment Criteria
1	*Design and scope* – to meet strategic objectives, current and future needs, address national and network priorities; changes in demand, innovation and vision, design standards, regulatory framework.
2	*Construction and operational proposals* – construction method, phasing, site management, facilities management, maintenance and renewal.
3	*Forecasts of demand* – projected use/fare/traffic/toll revenue; impact of changes in user tariffs/charges/prices; third party income; stability and reliability of revenue.
4	*Financial assessment* – cost of capital, whole life and transaction costs; security of finance; potential effects of refinancing and sale of equity; government guarantees, subsidies and share of risks; affordability and effect on public sector budgets; taxation/evasion issues in private finance/provision; validity of savings and job creation forecasts; impact on land and property values.
5	*Risk analysis* – identification, assessment of impact, likelihood of risk arising, pricing and allocation, political and social risks, risk avoidance, reduction and mitigation.
6	*Quality of service and performance* – accessibility, responsiveness, reliability, security, service user/customer service proposals.
7	*Service transformation and integration* – networks, connectivity, operational flexibility; plan for continuous improvement; effect on other public policies, sectors and markets.
8	*Delivery plans* – method statements, mobilisation, phasing of implementation and development, use and deployment of resources, project management, assessment and review.
9	*Management* – approach to public service reform, use of consultants and sub-contractors. Commitment to public service principles.
10	*Organisational structure* – options, scope for collaboration, consortia and joint arrangements with other public bodies, control and responsibilities in joint ventures, legal powers to act, flexibility to respond to changing circumstances, effective partnering arrangements.
11	*Economic costs and benefits* (direct, indirect and induced) – for local/regional/national economy and community well being through economic activity and development; agglomeration impact; affect on productivity; impact on competitive advantage of communities; economic costs of congestion, accidents and journey times; availability of alternative routes/services; access to public transport; community capacity building; relocation and transitional severance effects.
12	*Economic development opportunities* – potential local/regional production of equipment and supplies; research and development opportunities; job creation; links to health, education and other sector economies.

Global Auction of Public Assets

	Assessment Criteria
13	*Social justice, equity and poverty reduction* – reduce existing social, income, geographic inequalities; promote generational equity (charge current/future users for current/future benefits); impact of charges/tolls on geographic/social class distribution of users; equity of access to employment, healthcare, education, retail and leisure.
14	*Quality of employment* – staffing levels, terms and conditions, labour standards, pensions, training and workforce development, industrial relations framework, financial resources to meet transfer/secondment obligations; trade union recognition rights, impact of outsourcing/transfer on rest of public body.
15	*Climate change* – achievement of low carbon economy targets/zero emissions; energy efficiency, smart metering, adaption of buildings.
16	*Environmental Impact Assessment* – direct and indirect impacts at local/regional/national levels; internal – noise, air quality; external – landscape & cityscape, heritage, water supply and drainage, biodiversity.
17	*Governance, accountability, participation and transparency* – governance arrangements and reporting, monitoring and scrutiny; ease/cost of monitoring and compliance;
18	*Public health* – health and safety, contribution to physical fitness and reduction in health inequalities.
19	*Impact on service users and civil society* – distribution of user benefits, collective and personal safety, programme and compensation if relocation or resettlement required.
20	*Support for regeneration* and development, housing provision, urban/rural impact.
21	*Public sector capability* – potential gain/loss of intellectual knowledge, application of public service principles, impact on corporate skills, scope for collaboration and shared services.
22	*Sustainable development* – local supply chains; recycling, reuse and minimising waste; construction methods/code for sustainable building standards.
23	*Added value and community benefits* – local training and employment opportunities, provision of local facilities or services over and above specification; community/trade union organisational impact.
24	*Corporate impact* – impact on costs in other services, continued viability of in-house organisations.
25	*Bidders proposals* – acceptability for managing implementation, governance and participation and monitoring and contractual terms, such as no-compete conditions on related services, termination costs.

Source: Whitfield, 2009.

investment, the merits of sustaining existing infrastructure or investment in new facilities and take account of all the potential costs, impacts and benefits (see Table 44). It is also necessary to provide an alternative to assessing asset monestisation PPPs and urban renewal projects by the size of the cash offer. It is not within the scope of this book to detail the criteria nor their relative weighting, which will vary according to the type and scope of projects.

Forecasts and assumptions must be clearly explained; they should be comprehensive and rigorous and communicated to the public; it is not a tick-box methodology and any lack of evidence must be explained and not concealed or distorted by academic complication or political rhetoric; 'commercial confidentiality' must be redefined to increase transparency recognising where non-disclosure of information may be in the public and/or private interest.

PPP Infrastructure Stress Test

This Stress Test (Table 45) is designed to provide a forward-looking assessment of the ability to achieve the project's stated objectives in the public interest. The Stress Test supplements the evaluation framework and is designed to reveal the overall viability of the project with regard to public need, affordability, economic and community well being and political support.

Partnerships Victoria and New South Wales, Australia use a Public Interest Template to assess whether the project delivery of the project is in the public interest, by assessing effectiveness, value-for-money, accountability and transparency, affected individuals and communities, equity, public access, consumer rights, security and privacy – with an emphasis on individual rights (Partnerships Victoria, 2009). This, at least, establishes a public interest agenda, but does not go far enough.

The Stress Test extends the principles of the public interest test in the Freedom of Information legislation, now common in many countries. The Stress Test is designed to further the understanding of and participation in public debate; promote accountability and transparency by public authorities for decisions taken by them and the spending of public money; allow the public, organisations and companies to understand decisions made by public authorities and, in some cases, assist individuals in challenging those decisions; and, to bring to light information affecting public health and public safety.

Table 45: *PPP Infrastructure Stress Test*

Stress Test criteria
Financial security • How realistic are the planned sources of revenue? • What are the main user/traffic and other demand forecasts and what assumptions are they based on? • What is ratio of debt/equity investment of the project company? • Are the parent companies with equity in the special purpose company and the financial institutions proving loans have adequate financial resources and commitment to this project? • Has the potential for refinancing the project been taken into account in the financial structure with adequate public sharing of benefits included in the contract clauses? • Do the SPV equity holders plan to retain or sell their equity stakes? • Does the project have the ability to absorb losses in an economic downturn? • Which risks are retained by the public sector and which risks are transferred to the private sector? • What is the scope and nature of the revenue/profit sharing clauses in the contract?
Affordability • What impact will funding of the project have on other services and investment during the contract period? • Have adequate resources been secured for client management and monitoring of the project? • What are the annual minimum/maximum price increases allowed over the contract period? • How will the sale of surplus land and buildings, be managed in the public interest?
Users • Are the planned charges, tariffs and tolls sustainable and equitable and under what conditions can they be amended? • If the project is relying on continuing public sector subsidies are they guaranteed, if not, what conditions apply? • How will user rights be protected and enhanced? • How will community health and safety be secured? • Has the design been fully vetted and tested?
Equity • How will the project achieve poverty reduction targets and reduce inequalities? • How will equality of access be achieved and sustained?
Governance, accountability, participation and transparency • How will the planned governance structure operate, who is represented on project boards, who is accountable to whom, and what is the status and reporting system for reports and minutes?

Stress Test criteria
• How will community participation proposals be implemented? • What mechanisms are in place to ensure that changes in the design, scope and scale of the project (the change control mechanism) are subject to full governance accountability, participation and transparency? • If a Joint Venture Company is planned, what are the power sharing arrangements? • What are the proposals for the disclosure of information in procurement and operational stages?
Services • How will services be integrated with other public services? • What impact will the project have on the delivery of core services – have all the potential risks been identified? • If facilities are not available when required, what is the fall-back plan? • Does the project have the capability and resources to comply with regulatory frameworks and statutory responsibilities?
Implementation • What systems will be used to ensure completion targets are achieved and is there Plan B if there are delays? • Do the construction companies have other conflicting commitments which may also effect the quality of community benefits such as local employment and training obtained during construction? • If the private sector is responsible for additional investment during the contract period, what assurances and systems are in place to make this happen? • Are the job creation targets realistic, what assumptions are they based on and how will they be achieved? • Has the ICT implementation plan been approved?
Employment • What staffing levels, terms and conditions have been built into the project, how will they change over the contract period, and are adequate financial resources allocated to meet transfer of undertakings regulations, labour standards and codes of practice? • Has a workforce development plan been agreed with the trade unions? • What arrangements have been made for staff and trade union participation in the planning and implementation of change? • Have the trade unions agreed the industrial relations framework? • How will worksite and community health and safety be maintained during construction and operation of the project?
Economic and community benefits • How will the job creation targets be achieved and are they a condition of contract? • What is the timetable and methodology for implementation of social and economic projects? Who will carry out this work? • How will social and economic projects be financed and are any conditions imposed on how they operate?

Source: Whitfield, 2009.

CHAPTER 11

Strengthening strategic alliances for the future

This chapter sets out the broad strategies needed to achieve and sustain the progressive changes advocated in the previous chapter.

Experience has shown the most successful campaigns against marketisation and privatisation are those that follow a strategy which:

1. Critically assesses the direct and indirect impacts (economic, social, equity, employment, environment and ecological), costs and benefits of policies and projects and expose the underlying values, assumptions and vested interests.

2. Develops community/trade union alternative plans, progressive change in public sector provision and management and makes the case for public investment.

3. Organises and mobilises in the workplace, community and civil society to build strong, effective and independent organisations.

4. Forges local, regional, national and international alliances and coalitions to organise support.

5. Intervenes in the planning, public sector reform, service review, options appraisal and procurement processes.

6. Builds political support through research, education and communications strategies including evidence of PPP and privatisation impacts and failures.

7. Adopts action strategies that include selective joint civil and industrial action.

8. Challenges the pro-PPP and privatisation business alliances, services directives, multi-lateral agreements and World Bank/OECD neoliberal policies.

This strategy must be applied at the local, national and international levels. Firstly, it must focus on public investment strategies and public sector transformation policies including in-house improvement and innovation strategies, a locality-wide public sector approach that embraces reorganisation, restructuring and asset rationalisation. It must be an integral part of the infrastructure planning and development process. Secondly, it must challenge the policies and rules of internal markets (EU, North American Free Trade Agreement (NAFTA) etc) that promote competitive markets for public services. Thirdly, it should focus on strengthening the provision and monitoring of employment legislation, codes, standards and living wage agreements at local, national and international levels. Finally, trade unions and community organisations should target the investment strategies of pension funds as part of the strategy to retain and improve pension provision.

Opposition to PPPs is often difficult to sustain because they are developed on a one-by-one project basis, in a context of need, and claimed to be 'the only show in town' with no other option. Furthermore, as stated before, community organisations and trade unions are confronted by a state-corporate alliance of government, banks, financial companies and major construction firms supported by consultants and lawyers, using 'commercial confidentiality' to conceal project details. Despite these constraints, campaigns in many countries have succeeded in stopping PPP projects, reversing outsourcing and privatisation and changing public policy to increase public investment.

National and international alliances

The UK currently has the world's largest PPP programme, an extensive marketisation-dominated public sector transformation programme and three decades of privatisation. It holds important lessons for other countries. The main public sector trade unions adopted a twin-track strategy to oppose the Private Finance Initiative. The principle of a twin track strategy, opposing PPPs nationally while negotiating locally on individual projects, crucially relies on the scope and power of a national campaign, supported by EU and global union federations. But this strategy is fundamentally flawed if no attempt is made to build and mobilise a national alliance of trade unions, community and civil society organisations opposed to PPPs and privatisation.

PPPs cannot be stopped by research or arguments about economics and value-for-money alone – rather they are propelled by ideology and business interests. Similarly, lobbying government ministers may sometimes appear to be effective, but in practice this action alone rarely leads to change.

Public sector trade unions in the UK published research and analysis of the impact of PPPs, gave evidence to Parliamentary select committees and lobbied Members of Parliament with breakfast meetings and other events. A decade of criticism of PFI succeeded in getting the 'brand' a widely known bad name. Opposition to PPPs did reduce the scope of some facilities management contracts and to the secondment employment model in some health and local government projects. It also contributed to a successful campaign for a relaxation of local authority borrowing controls. This led to a wider use of public finance in the Building Schools for the Future programme. The anti-PPP campaign also led to more rigorous Outline Business Cases (OBCs) and impact assessment, than would otherwise have been the case.

These gains have been marginal in the circumstances. The New Labour government expanded the PPP programme in any case, introduced new models and freely exported PPPs and privatisation to the rest of Europe and developing countries. Whilst some PPP projects have been stopped or stalled, in reality, trade union opposition often has had only a minor influence in these decisions.

Trade unions in the UK failed to organise and mobilise nationally against PPPs/privatisation and for public investment, primarily because they did not want to organise against a Labour government following eighteen years of Thatcherism. They also possibly feared that they would lose control of an alliance, although that is insufficient grounds not to build an alliance. National campaigns were organised by individual unions against privatisation and spending cuts but they did not have the strategy or resources to mobilise nationally with community and civil society organisations. It is also questionable whether they had the resources to sustain such a mission.

It might be argued that a twin track strategy was designed to fail because there was never any intention of organising a national alliance. Local pragmatism ruled, as most trade union branches were confronted with a fait accompli and had to intervene or respond at the formal procurement stage, after PPP projects had been approved at the options appraisal stage. In many cases, trade union involvement in the procurement process was limited to employment matters and branches inevitably attempted to negotiate the best deal for their members.

The twin track approach also reflected the wider failure to fully challenge government policies for public sector transformation. The overriding desire was to limit criticism and minimise opposition to the Labour Government. The fear was that too much opposition could pave the way for a Conservative government. This was 'unthinkable', yet it was 'acceptable' to keep a government in power that had marketised, and in some cases privatised, faster and further than the Thatcher era, precisely because New Labour had trade union support.

Local alliances of trade union, community and civil society organisations are essential to winning these struggles to promote public investment and democratic values. Broadly based alliances should include public bodies, political parties and campaigns. Intervention strategies can succeed when they combine organising and political action with technical know-how but success is always going to be limited if the response is on a project-by-project basis. The Canadian Union of Public Employees' work with the Council of Canadians on water, energy and trade campaigns is a good example of alliance building.

Blueprints and worker/community plans

The global economic crisis has spurred many blueprints, plans and frameworks for green new deals, fiscal stimulus strategies, reform of financial markets and strategies for economic recovery.

Community plans, workers and users plans, blueprints, improvement plans or policies for projects, services, sectors and areas at neighbourhood, city, regional, national or international level must play a key part in any public infrastructure strategy. They must be politically feasible, operationally and financially viable and rooted in peoples' needs and experiences. Idealistic wish lists are irrelevant. The plans should establish a vision of public service provision and infrastructure for the future, address economic and social needs, social justice and equity, climate change and sustainable futures and the contribution of public investment in the local/regional and wider economy. Opportunities abound to prepare blueprints to show how all public services in an area or city can be integrated and democratised under a 'one public sector' approach. Community, trade union and civil society organisations should pre-empt or respond to 'whole service' PPPs with counter proposals.

There are also opportunities to initiate and/or be involved in preparing service improvement plans for infrastructure and the operational needs of individual services where participative and employment protection frameworks have been agreed. Alternative proposals should be drawn up before the options appraisal stage, prior to the start of the formal procurement process. They also have an important role in in-house bids and service transformation (Wainwright and Little, 2009) and shared/joint services provision (Whitfield 2007). There are also important opportunities for regional, sub-regional and citywide socio-economic analysis of the role of the public sector, for example highlighting the contribution of the health and social care economy (Centre for Public Services, 2003 and 2005).

We have to change the political culture from responding with '*Keep the ...*' campaigns to a practice of articulating demands and ideas about the future provision, finance, governance and delivery of services in alternative plans. Thus, progressive blueprints are an important tool for creating alliances and building public support when they are collective statements for the future of communities, economies, services and/or equality groups. Defending the status quo is rarely a viable option, particularly when the scope for a project-by-project response gets narrower as the marketisation and privatisation of infrastructure expands.

Staff and service users, trade unions, community and civil society organisations must own and control how these plans and proposals are used to leverage or negotiate changes in public policy for infrastructure and service delivery (Whitfield, 1992). Harnessing their intellectual knowledge and experience, regular communications and meetings of members to discuss negotiating positions and action strategies and collective decision making is the only way to ensure that alternative proposals strengthen organisations, mobilise broader support and increase political leverage and control.

Organising and action

Little of any significance can be achieved without organising and mobilising. This is a political and economic fact of life. Strong representative organisation is the bedrock of all workplace and community campaigns, particularly in directorates and departments that have large capital programmes and in communities requiring new schools and hospitals or with regeneration projects.

Community and other civil society organisations should insist that they be involved throughout the planning, options appraisal, and design and implementation stages of infrastructure projects. Organising around key issues, researching examples of public investment, identifying companies involved in failed projects, and visits of delegations to other campaigns and projects to share experience, lessons and exchange information, can be effective and rewarding.

New alliances or networks of community, trade union and civil society organisations must not only campaign for progressive public service renewal but also the formation of holistic, democratically accountable, participative and transparent public bodies.

Selective and targeted industrial and community action should take account of the dynamics applicable at the particular stage of the infrastructure investment process. Boycotts of private sector services/facilities and support for users opting for public sector options may also be effective.

Good communications are essential to keep the membership fully informed at each stage of the process. Regular meetings are essential to make people aware, build support and solidarity. Links should be established with other trade unions, trades/labour councils and community organisations.

Developing and deepening community and workplace understanding of the strategies needed to improve public infrastructure and the forces promoting PPPs and investment funds is a key organising tool. As this book demonstrates, there is no shortage of evidence to facilitate better understanding of the local/regional economy, power structures and global development. Education and publicity should focus on building up the evidence base to support alternative plans and blueprints, exposing vested interests and identifying issues around which people can organise. Organiser training in community organisations and trade unions must increase understanding of each other and develop joint strategies.

Trade unions, living wage and community organisations should support international alliances. Examples include the European alliance between trade unions (European Trade Union Confederation/European Public Service Unions ETUC/EPSU) and civil society organisations including European Public Services Network/European Social Forum (EPSN/ESF) and ATTAC, to exchange experience and information, undertake joint research and develop alternative policies. They should also draw on the support of national and international Non-governmental Organisations (NGOs) who are opposing the World Trade Organisations General Agreement for Trade in Services and European Union Services Directives – NGOs need to link their opposition to services liberalisation by opposing PPPs and privatisation in their host country.

Procurement is a political, technical and legal process. Elected members, the media and the public must be made aware of the key issues at each stage of the process. Evidence of PPP failures, delays, overspends, increased charges and tolls, job losses, cuts in terms and conditions and conflicts of interest provide vital information to elected members, managers and the public. Unfortunately, they rarely stop procurement by themselves.

The process, by which public infrastructure projects are approved or rejected, is usually a long technical and legal process. Intervention in this process must run parallel with other strategies. Relying solely on intervention in the options appraisal and procurement process is a very high-risk strategy irrespective of the strength of a case, organisation or support. The objective should be either to avoid the need for procurement, or where it is required in such areas as construction, to subject it to protocols, good practice and stress testing frameworks. A procurement process is rarely stopped midstream and, although a public body can decide not to conclude a contract at the end of the procurement process, this is all too infrequent.

Early intervention in planning and procurement

Opposition to PPPs in the UK highlights the importance of building a campaign at the earliest possible stage and before the procurement process begins. It requires intervention in the options appraisal stage to make the case for public investment, improved public sector capability and the economic, social, environmental and health criteria and decision-making framework. The strategy must strengthen organisation and representation in the affected workforce and build alliances with community and civil society organisations. It must include challenging the track record and policies of private companies and the strategic use of industrial action.

The primary objectives of intervention should be to shape the planning, appraisal and procurement processes in terms of how options are identified, including in-house/public sector options/bids, and how they are evaluated. Protocols should set out the scope, processes, participation and information access for the planning, commissioning, options appraisal, procurement and monitoring/scrutiny stages. They should facilitate trade union and community involvement in the scoping, short-listing, specification and evaluation stages, access to information and employment options to protect terms and conditions and pensions.

Options appraisal and outline business cases need to be rigorously assessed to determine whether they have established need, considered public sector options, assessed the impact on the local economy, addressed equalities and sustainable development (production and supply chains), examined private sector performance, assessed secondment employment models and made the case for the exclusion of support services from PPP projects.

Demand that Scrutiny Committees investigate the performance of contracts and partnerships, procurement policies and projects using integrated impact assessment to identify the full effects on services, jobs, economies and communities. Scrutiny Committees must have adequate resources so that they can operate independently and have the power to set agendas and require the attendance of those being scrutinised.

Providing evidence of the performance of similar projects and the same architect, construction company, bank or financial company and facilities management company, can be very effective at the appraisal, selection and evaluation stages.

Public bodies, community, trade union and civil society organisations need access to independent strategic advice, research and policy analysis, who can assist with the preparation of alternative plans, evaluate projects and advise in the planning and procurement process. The Centre for Public Services (and subsequently the ESSU) provided such a model in the UK that was independent of employer's organisations and academic institutions. It enabled local, national and international public sector organisations, trade union and community organisations to commission projects and published its own research and good practice. Such organisations need part public funding or foundation support/endowment to ensure their long-term sustainability.

Public infrastructure projects are likely to get more technically, financially and organisationally complex. This could stretch the capacity of public organisations (leading to further outsourcing to consultants), making political understanding and control more difficult, thus reinforcing the trend towards managerialism.

Public sector capability in infrastructure planning and project management must be strengthened in three ways. Firstly, by minimising the use of external consultants; and when they are required, negotiating capacity building training of public sector staff. Secondly, by ensuring that infrastructure planning has procedures for community and trade union engagement; that asset management policies and systems are regularly reviewed, and updated; and implementing sustainability strategies. Finally, by ensuring that a comprehensive appraisal and evaluation framework is designed for key stages of the planning and procurement process.

Conclusion

The demand for public infrastructure will always exceed the economic and political ability to supply new buildings, transportation, housing, schools, hospitals and communications networks. Deficits, gaps and backlogs must be minimised even when they are an inevitable consequence of innovation, development and obsolescence. The solution is not to turn public infrastructure into commodities to be traded on global markets. Marketisation and privatisation only create new types of shortages, crises and price increases.

PPPs and privatisation are ultimately publicly financed, either directly by government or indirectly through user charges, fares and tolls. Pay-as-you-go provision of public infrastructure and services will be costly, inequitable and undermine the public interest. There is no quick fix or a cheap, low tax solution.

Reform of the PPP model will achieve little. Powerful vested interests, business, political and academic, will ensure any re-assessment will be focused on the minutia of PPP finance, risk transfer and governance arrangements. Corporate business interests including finance capital, construction companies, lawyers and consultants, political ideologues and governments will continue to advocate the neoliberal PPP and privatisation agenda to expand the global infrastructure market. They have no intention of challenging the model, merely massaging contractual matters to ensure deal flow continues.

The PPP 'partnership' concept is fraudulent. No amount of rhetoric can disguise the fact that divisions of labour exist at different stages of the planning, design, construction, finance and operation of infrastructure. Contracts, payment mechanisms and tolling regimes do not constitute a partnership.

The provision of public infrastructure through PPPs changes power relations between government and the private sector, between road users and toll road operators, between staff and their employer, and between community organisations and facilities management operators. These changes have economic, social and political consequences but are rarely recognised, let alone identified in the evaluation of projects. Yet another reason why a comprehensive evaluation framework is needed to assess every project in a rigorous and transparent manner.

So who will own public infrastructure in 2025 and beyond? It is often claimed that PPPs and privatisation will account for no more than 15% – 20% of public infrastructure investment and that the state will continue to directly provide the rest. On the contrary, continued commodification, marketisation and privatisation will expose these assumptions to be baseless and redundant.

The division between public infrastructure and the services provided within buildings (teaching, medical practice, justice) is not sustainable in the long term, because there are no formal barriers or technical frontiers between the provision of building, networks and services. It is ultimately down to the struggle between the strength of political opposition and the corporate interests and capability of transnational companies.

The development process is equally important for developed/developing countries, urban/rural areas and for different population and equality groups. All public infrastructure projects create economic activity and employment, and they increasingly create wealth for distant investors. The focus must be on economic, social and environmental benefits, not financial returns. If the necessity is to make PPPs work *before* they can work for the poor, then this indicates that the model is fundamentally flawed. Further private ownership and control of land, private design and private management of the remaining public assets will be the final stage in the privatisation of the public infrastructure. Only then will PPPs be redundant!

Fiscal stimulus infrastructure programmes, green new deals and job creation programmes must combine renewable energy and infrastructure strategies to generate sustainable economic growth and employment through local/regional production and supply chains.

There is no alternative to public investment, to implementation of the new infrastructure priorities, to radical reform of the infrastructure planning process, to new methods of public finance of public infrastructure investment and to the transformation of public sector management. It is more urgent than ever before to have comprehensive strategies with resources to organise and undertake action research and investigation; organise and take action in the workplace, community and political institutions; prepare blueprints, worker/user and alternative plans and to advocate public service reform; intervene in the planning and procurement process and to build alliances and coalitions at local, regional, national and international levels.

References

A Picture for Health (2007) *A 'Picture for Health' Project Team Perspective on the Implications of Fixed Costs and PFI Schemes for Service Redesign in SE London*, April, www.apictureofhealth.nhs.uk

Accounts Commission (2002) *Taking the Initiative – Using PFI to Renew Council Schools*, June, Edinburgh.

Acerete, B., Shaoul, J. and Stafford, A. (2007) *Taking its Toll: The Private Financing of Roads in Spain*, Working Paper No 44, Centre for Research on Socio-Cultural Change, University of Manchester, www.cresc.ac.uk

Adams, J., Young, A. and Zhihong, W. (2006) 'Public Private Partnerships in China: System, Constraints and Future Prospects', *International Journal of Public Sector Management*, Vol. 19, No. 4, p384-396.

Aecom Consult (2005) *Synthesis of Public Private Partnership Projects for Roads, Bridges and Tunnels from Around the World, 1985 – 2004*, for US Department of Transportation, Washington DC, www.fhwa.dot.gov

Aecom Consult (2007) *Case Studies of Transportation Public Private Partnerships in the United States*, for US Department of Transportation, Washington DC, www.fhwa.dot.gov

Aecom Consult (2007) *Case Studies of Transportation Public Private Partnerships Around the World*, for US Department of Transportation, Washington DC, www.fhwa.dot.gov

Age, The (2009) 'Why BrisConnections has courted battle with unit holders', 31 March, Melbourne, www.theage.com.au

Age, The (2009) 'MacBank bank buys into BrisConn', 30 March, Melbourne, www.theage.com.au

Agenor, P-R. (2006) *A Theory of Infrastructure-Led Development*, Centre for Growth and Business Cycle Research Discussion Paper Series, University of Manchester, http://EconPapers.repec.org/RePEc:man:cgbcrp:83

Agenor, P-R. and Moreno-Dodson, B. (2006) *Public Infrastructure and Growth: New Channels and Policy Implications*, Policy Research Working Paper 4064, World Bank, Washington DC.

Alberta, Government of (2009) *Plan to build 14 new schools moves to next stage - Approach will combine P3 and design-build*, Press Release 1 May, Edmonton.

Allen Consulting (2007) *Performance of PPPs and Traditional Procurement in Australia*, for Infrastructure Partnerships, Australia, www.allenconsult.com.au

Allsop, R. (2007) 'Victoria's Public Transport: Assessing the Results of Privatisation', *IPA Backgrounder*, April, Vol. 19/1, Institute of Public Affairs, Melbourne, www.ipa.org.au

Alpha Magazine (2008) 'Best-Paid Hedge Fund Managers', 15 April, www.alphamagazine.com

Altenberg, T. (2005) *The private sector and development agencies: How to form successful alliances - Critical issues and lessons learned from leading donor programmes*, Discussion Paper to the DIE-GDI working group, 10th International Business Forum 2005, New York, German Development Institute, Bonn.

Altshuler, A. and Luberoff, D. (2003) *Mega-Projects: The Changing Politics of Urban Public Investment*, Brookings Institution Press, Washington DC.

American Society of Civil Engineers (2009) *2009 Report Card for America's Infrastructure*, January, Washington DC, www.asce.org

Amorelli, L.C. (2009) *Brazillian Federal Road Concessions: New Challenges to the Regulatory Framework*, George Washington University, Washington DC.

Andres, L., Guasch, J.L., Haven, T. and Foster, V. (2008) *The Impact of Private Sector Participation in Infrastructure: Lights, Shadows and the Road Ahead*, World Bank, Washington DC.

Annez, P. (2006) *Urban Infrastructure Finance from private Operators: What Have We Learned from Recent Experience*, Policy Research Working Paper 4045, November, World Bank, Washington DC.

Apollo Alliance (2004) *New energy for America: The Apollo Jobs Report: For Good Jobs and Energy Independence*, www.apolloalliance.org

Aschauer, D. A. (1989) 'Is public expenditure productive?' *Journal of Monetary Economics* 23(2): 177-200.

Asia Case Research Centre (2007) *Infrastructure Finance: The Sydney Cross City Tunnel*, University of Hong Kong.

Asian Development Bank (2005) *Connecting East Asia: A New Framework for Infrastructure*, with Japan Bank for International Cooperation and the World Bank, www.adb.org/

Asian Development Bank Institute (2007) *Infrastructure Challenges in South Asia: The Role of Public-Private Partnerships*, Geethanjali Nataraj, September, Tokyo, www.adb.org

Asian Development Bank (2007) *India: Case Studies on Private Sector Development and Operations*, June, Operations Evaluation Department, Manila, www.adb.org

Associated Press (2009) *Brazil needs $40bn for World Cup Infrastructure*, 22 July.

Attac (2008) *The time has come: Let's shut down the financial casino*, a statement from Attac's European Network on the financial crisis and democratic alternatives, 15 October.

Audit Commission (2003) *PFI in Schools*, January, London, www.audit-commission.gov.uk

Audit Commission (2005) *Governing Partnerships: Bridging the Accountability Gap*, London, www.audit-commission.gov.uk

Audit Commissions (2008) *For better, for worse: Value for money in strategic service-delivery partnerships*, January, London. www.audit-commission.gov.uk

Audit Commission (2009) *Managing the Transition to IFRS*, Briefing Papers, London, www.audit-commission.gov.uk/

Auditor General of Canada (1995) *Public Works and Government Services*

Canada—Northumberland Strait Crossing Project, Chapter 15, October, Ottawa.

Auriol, E. and Picard, P. (2006). *Infrastructure and public utilities privatisation in developing countries*, World Bank Policy Research Working Paper, No. 3950. World Bank, Washington, DC

Australian Broadcasting Corporation (2006) *Cross City Tunnel placed into receivership*, 28 December, www.abc.net.au

Australian Institute for Social Research (2008) *A preliminary analysis of direct and indirect costs associated with the relocation of prison facilities to the Murray Bridge district*, University of Adelaide, October, www.cpsu.asn.au

Australian Productivity Commission (2009) *Public Infrastructure Financing: An International Perspective*, Staff Working Paper, March, Sydney, www.pc.gov.au

Babcock & Brown (2008) *Investor Information*, www.babcockbrown.com/ accessed 9 January.

Bailey, E. (1996) *Driving up the learning curve*, Infrastructure Finance, July-August 9-10.

Bailie, A., Bernow, S., Dougherty, W., Lazarus, M., Kartha, S., Goldberg, M. (2001) *Clean Energy: Jobs for America's Future*, World Wildlife Fund, Tellus Institute and MRG & Associates, Boston.

Balfour Beatty (2008) *Is Public-Private Partnership right for your next Education Project?* Presentation, Florida.

Balfour Beatty (2008) *Annual Report 2007*, London, www.balfourbeatty.com

Bank of International Settlements (2007) *77th Annual report*, 1 April 2006 – 31 March 2007, June, Basel, www.bis.org

Bank Information Center (2009) *Lula to announce PAC ll in 2010*, 29 July, www.bicusa.org

Banker, The (2009) 'Redrawing the Landscape', 1 April, London.

Barclays Capital (2009) *Hedge Funds To See At Least $50 Billion Of New Allocations Before End Of 2009*, Press Release, 2 June, London, www.barcap.com/

Barlow, J. and Koberle-Galser, M. (2008) 'The Private Finance Initiative, Project Form and Design Innovation: The UK Hospitals Programme', *Research Policy*, Vol. 37, Issue 8, pp 1392-1402.

Barlow, M. (2007) *Blue Covenant: The Global Water Crisis and the Coming Battle for the Right to Water*, New Press.

Barretta, A. and Ruggiero, P. (2008) 'Ex-ante Evaluation of PFIs within the Italian Health-Care Sector: What is the basis for this PPP?', *Health Policy*, 88, pp 15-24.

Battaglio, R.P. and Khankari, G.A. (2008) 'Toll Roads, Politics, and Public—Public Partnerships: The Case of Texas State Highway 121', *Public Works Management & Policy*, Vol. 13, No. 2, 138-148.

Baxandall, P. (2007) *Road Privatisation: Explaining the Trend, Assessing the Facts and Protecting the Public*, September, US PIRG Education Fund, Boston.

Bayliss, K. amd Kessler, T. (2006) *Can Privatisation and Commercialisation of Public Services Help Achieve the MDGs? An Assessment*, International Poverty Centre, Working Paper 22, UNDP, Brasilia, Brazil, www.undp-povertycentre.org

Beeferman, L. (2008) *Pension Fund Investment in Infrastructure: A Resource Paper*, December Harvard Law School.

Bell, M.G. (2006) 'Policy Issues for the Future Intelligent Road Transport Infrastructure, Intelligent Transport Systems', *IEE Proceedings*, Vol. 153, Issue 2, p147-155, June.

Bellier, M. and Zhou, Y.M. (2003) *Private Participation in Infrastructure in China*, Working Paper No 2, Washington DC.

Benington, J. (2007) *From Private Choice to Public Value*, London, www.centreforexcellence.org.uk

Benito, B., Montesinos, V. and Bastida, F. (2008) 'An Example of Creative Accounting in Public Sector: The Private Financing of Infrastructures in Spain', *Critical Perspectives in Accounting*, Vol. 19, Issue 7, pp 963-986.

Bensman, D. (2009) *Port Trucking Down the Low Road: A Sad Story of Deregulation*, Demos, New York, www.demos.org

Bestani, R. (2008) *Rebuilding America's Infrastructure: Lessons from Abroad*, Working Paper 42, Collaboratory for Research on Global Projects, Stanford, www.crgp.stanford.edu

Bisset, J. (2008) *Regeneration: Public Good or Private Profit*, New Island, Dublin.

Black, B., Kraakman, R. and Tarassova, A. (2000) 'Russian Privatisation and Corporate Governance: What Went Wrong', *Stanford Law Review*, 52, p1731-1808.

Blackburn, R. (2008) 'The Subprime Crisis', *New Left Review* No 50, Mar-April.

Blanc-Brude, F, Goldsmith, H. and Valila, T. (2007) *Public-Private Partnerships in Europe: An Update*, European Investment Bank Economic and Financial Report 2007/03.

Blair, Mackay and Mynett Valuations (2009) *Evaluation of Public Private Partnerships: Costing and Evaluation Methodology*, for Canadian Union of Public Employees, www.cupe.bc.ca

Brady, T., Davies, A., & Gann, D. (2005) 'Can Integrated Solutions Business Models Work in Construction?' *Building Research & Information*, 33 (6): 571-579.

Brenner, N. (2004) 'Urban Governance and the Production of New State Spaces in Western Europe', *Review of International Political Economy*, 11:3, August p447-488.

Broadbent, J. and Laughlin, R. (2003) 'Public Private Partnerships: An Introduction', *Accounting, Auditing & Accountability Journal*, Vol. 16, No. 3, p332-341.

Brox, J.A. (2008) 'Infrastructure Investment: The Foundation of Canadian Competitiveness', *Institute for Research on Public Policy, Policy Matters*, Vol. 9, No. 2.

BNET (2009) *Hedge Funds to Prosper By Hedging Out the Toxic Waste*, 31 March, http://industry.bnet.com

Building (2007) '125-year PFI hospital lease comes to light', Issue 19, www.building.co.uk

Building Design (2009) 'Government should scrap PFI, says Rogers, and we can't kill PFI, let's cure it', 6 March, www.bdonline.co.uk/

Bull, B., Jerve, A. and Sigvaldsen, E. (2006) *The World Bank's and the IMF's Use of Conditionality to Encourage Privatization and Liberalization: Current Issues and Practices*, Report prepared as background for the Oslo Conditionality Conference, University of Oslo.

Business Week (2007) 'Roads to Riches: Why investors are clamoring to take over America's highways, bridges, and airports—and why the public should be nervous', 7 May, www.businessweek.com

Business Spectator (2008) 'Charging Up B & B Power', 3 September, Commentary T. Boyd, and 'Babcok's Rapacious Appetite', 4 September, Commentary, A. Kohler, www.businessspectator.com.au

Cadell, C, Falk, N. and King, F. (2008) *Regeneration in European Cities: Making Connections*, Joseph Rowntree Foundation, York, www.jfr.org.uk

Calderón, César, and Luis Servén (2004) *The Effects of Infrastructure Development on Growth and Income Distribution*, Policy Research Working Paper, No. 3400, World Bank, Washington, DC

Cambridge Economic Policy Associates (2005) *Public Private Partnerships in Scotland: Evaluation of Performance*, www.cepa.co.uk

Cambridge Economic Policy Associates (2007) *Analysis of the Causes of the Queen Elizabeth Hospital Trust Deficit*, January, www.cepa.co.uk/

Cambridge Systematics (2009) *Connecticut Electronic Tolling and Congestion Pricing Study*, for Connecticut Transportation Strategy Board and Connecticut Office of Policy and Management, April, www.camsys.com

Campaign Against Climate Change Trade Union Group and Neale, J. (2009) *One Million Climate Change Jobs Now*, London, www.campaignncc.org

Canadian Centre for Policy Alternatives (2003) *The True Cost of P3s*, April, Ottawa, http://policyalternatives.ca

Canadian Centre for Policy Alternatives (2008) 'A Pipeline through a Troubled Land: Afghanistan, Canada, and the New Great Energy Game', *Foreign Policy Series*, Vol. 3, No. 1, June, Ottawa, http://policyalternatives.ca/

Canadian Union of Public Employees (2009) *Privatisation Watch*, monthly, http://cupe.ca/privatizationwatch

Canning, D and Bennathan, E. (2000) *The Social Rate of Return on Infrastructure Investments*, Policy Research Working Paper No. 2390, World Bank, Washington DC.

Cao, J.A. (2009) 'Developmental State, Property-Led Growth and Property Investment Risks in China', *Journal of Property Investment & Finance*, Vol. 27, No. 2, p162-179.

Carbon Trade Watch (2008) *Carbon Trade-Off*, August, http://carbontradewatch.gn.apc.org

CEE Bankwatch (2008) *Never Mind the Balance Sheet: The dangers posed by public private partnerships in Central and Eastern Europe*, www.bankwatch.org

Center for Community Change (2006) *Dismantling a Community*, Washington DC, www.communitychange.org

Center for Community Change (2009) *Housing Trust Fund Project*, Washington DC, www.communitychange.org/our-projects/htf

Centre for Learning and Teaching (2005) *The Impact of School Environments: A literature review*, University of Newcastle, Newcastle, www.ncl.ac.uk

Centre for Public Services (2001) *Private Finance Initiative and Public Private Partnerships: What Future for Public Services?* www.european-services-strategy.org.uk

Centre for Public Services (2001) *Shedding the Light on the Newcastle/North Tyneside Street Lighting PFI Project*, Newcastle UNISON. www.european-services-strategy.org.uk

Centre for Public Services (2002) *No Corporate Takeover of Council Services: Newcastle City Council Information Technology and Related Services*, Newcastle City Council Trade Unions. www.european-services-strategy.org.uk

Centre for Public Services (2002) *An Alternative to Privatisation by Partnership: A New Vision for Local Government in Milton Keynes and Northamptonshire*, Milton Keynes and Northamptonshire UNISON Branches, www.european-services-strategy.org.uk

Centre for Public Services (2003) *The Health and Social Care Economy in the North West*, for North West Regional Assembly, www.european-services-strategy.org.uk

Centre for Public Services (2004) *City Design: the new agenda, a report for Newcastle City UNISON*, www.european-services-strategy.org.uk

Centre for Public Services (2004) *How to Exclude Support Services from BSF and PPP/PFI Projects, A Best Practice Report for UNISON, GMB, NUT and NASUWT in Tyne and Wear using HM Treasury VfM Methodology*, December, Sheffield. www.european-services-strategy.org.uk

Centre for Public Services (2005) *Health and Social Care and Sustainable Development in the East of England*, for Department of Health, East of England Regional Assembly, East of England Development Agency, Health Development Agency, COVER and the Environment Agency, www.european-services-strategy.org.uk

Centre for Public Services (2005) *Strategic Partnership in Crisis, Bedfordshire UNISON*, March, Sheffield. www.european-services-strategy.org.uk

Centre for Public Services (2005) *The Flawed Options Appraisal and Outline Business Case for a Strategic Service-delivery Partnership, Somerset County UNISON*, www.european-services-strategy.org.uk

Chamberlain, G. (2009) 'India prays for rain as water wars break out', *The Observer*, 12 July.

Chicago Tribune (2008) 'You pay a lot more: What happens when the city leases public assets to private investors?' 7 September, www.chicagotribune.com

Chicago Tribune (2008) 'Meter Mania: 1 Hour Parking = 26 Quarters by 2013', 2 December, www.chicagotribune.com

Children and Young People NOW (2009) *Failed PFI Schools Cost Millions*, 12 March, www.cypnow.co.uk

Citizens Budget Commission (2008) *How Public-Private Partnerships Can Help New York Address Its Infrastructure Needs*, December, web www.cbcny.org

City & Financial Publishing (2006) *PPP In-Depth*, Bulletin Issue No 6, April/May, London, www.cityandfinancial.com

City of Toronto (2008) *Blueprint for Fiscal Stability and Economic Prosperity – a Call to Action, Mayor's Fiscal Review Panel*, February, Toronto. www.toronto.ca

City of Chicago Office of the Inspector General (2009) *An Analysis of the Lease of the City's Parking Meters*, June, Chicago, www.chicagoinspectorgeneral.org

Clarke, T. (2008) *Tar Sands Showdown*, Lorimer, Toronto.

Collins Stewart (2004) *The Second Age of PFI*, May, London, www.collins-stewart.com

Colonial First State Global Asset Management (2008) *The Credit Crisis and Implications for Investment Markets*, Investment Market review, October, www.firststate.co.uk/

Colonial First State Global Asset Management (2009) *Changing Gears: Navigating the Road Ahead in Infrastructure*, Infrastructure Research Paper, June, www.firststate.co.uk/

Colonial First State Global Asset Management (2009) *Changing Gears: Navigating the Road Ahead in Infrastructure*, June.

Commission for the Built Environment (2005) *Design Quality and the Private Finance Initiative*, London. www.cabe.org.uk

Commission for the Built Environment (2008) *Threshold needed to improve school design*, Press Release, 24 July, www.cabe.org.uk

Committee of Public Accounts (2005) *Value for Money Report No 48: Grouped Schools Pilot Partnership Project*, 21 April, Dail Eireann, Dublin.

Commonwealth Development Corporation (2008) *Portfolio*, www.cdagroup.com

Commonwealth Scientific and Industrial Research Organisation (2006) *Infrastructure and climate change risk assessment for Victoria: Report to the Victorian Government*, Aspendale, www.csiro.au

Comptroller and Auditor General (2004) *The Grouped Schools Pilot Partnership Project*, Department of Education and Science, Dublin, www.audgen.gov.ie

Confederation of British Industry (2003) *Delivering for Local Government: The impact of public-private partnerships*, London.

Congressional Budget Office (1997) *Toll Roads: A Review of Recent Experience*, Washington DC www.cbo.gov

ConnectEast (2009) *ASX Release and IMIS Traffic Projections*, 21 August, www.connecteast.com.au

Construction (2006) *US Roads are Being Built and Run by Other People's Money*, 28 August. www.construction.com

Core Cities Network and PricewaterhouseCoopers (2009) *Unlocking City Growth: Interim Findings on New Funding Mechanisms*, Manchester, http://www.corecities.com

Cornerhouse (2006) *Too Many Grannies: Private Pensions, Corporate Welfare and Growing Insecurity*, Briefing No 35, www.thecornerhouse.org.uk

Council for Foreign Relations (2006) *Foreign Investment and National Security: Getting the Balance Right*, Alan P. Larson and David M. Marchick, CSR No 18, July, New York www.cfr.org

Crafts, N. and Leunig, T. (2005) *The Historical Significance of Transport for Economic Growth and Productivity*, London School of Economics, Prepared for the Eddington Report, www.dft.gov.uk/

Crane, D. (2008) 'California's Infrastructure Deficit', *Public Works Management & Policy*, Vol. 12, No 3, January, p476-478.

Crotty, J. (2007) *If Financial Market Competition is so Intense, Why are Financial Firm Profits so High? Reflections on the Current 'Golden Age' of Finance*, Working Paper 134, Political Economy Research Institute, University of Massachusetts, Amherst, www.peri.umass.edu

Crotty, J. and Epstein, G. (2008) *Proposals for Effectively Regulating the U.S. Financial System to Avoid Yet Another Meltdown*, October, Political Economy Research Institute, University of Massachusetts, Amherst, www.peri.umass.edu

Cummings. C. and Dyson, A. (2007) 'The Role of Schools in Area Regeneration', *Research Papers in Education*, Vol. 22, No. 1, March, p1-22.

Cuthbert, M. and Cuthbert, J. (2008) *PFI Refinancing*, May, www.scottish.parliament.uk

Cuthbert, J. and Cuthbert, M. (2008) *Response to Scottish Futures Trust: Consultation Paper*, March.

Cuthbert, J. and Cuthbert, M. (2008) *Inquiry into the Methods of Funding Capital Investment Projects: The Royal Edinburgh Infirmary: A case study on the workings of the Private Finance Initiative*.

Dail Eireann (2006) *Eighth Interim Report of the 2003 Report of the Comptroller and Auditor General*, Committee of Public Accounts, October, Dublin.

Dail Eireann (2007) *First Interim Report of the 2007, Access to the Private Element of the Public Private Partnerships: An International Comparison*, March, Dublin.

Daniels, R. and Trebilcock, M. (1996) 'Private Provision of Public Infrastructure: An Organizational Analysis of the Next Privatization Frontier', *The University of Toronto Law Journal*, Vol. 46, No. 3, pp. 375-426.

Daniels, R. (2004) *Defecting on Development: Bilateral Investment Treaties and the Subversion of the Rule of Law in the Developing World*, draft, University of Pennsylvania.

Davis, K. (2008) *Listed Infrastructure Funds: Funding and Financial Management, Department of Finance*, University of Melbourne, http://ssrn.com

Deloitte & Touche Corporate Finance (2003) *London Underground Public Private Partnership: Emerging Findings, Transport for London*, www.tfl.gov.uk/

Deloitte (2006) *Building Flexibility: New delivery models for public infrastructure projects*, London. www.deloitte.com

Demetriades, P. and Mamuneas, T. (2000) 'Intertemporal Output and Employment Effects of Public Infrastructure Capital: Evidence from 12 OECD Economies', *The Economic Journal*, 110, July, p687-712.

Department for Children, Schools and Families (2008) *The Management of Building Schools for the Future waves 7 to 15*, Consultation, April, London.

Department for Environment, Food and Rural Affairs (2005) *Securing the Future: The UK Government Sustainable Development Strategy*, March, London.

Department for Education and Skills (2004) *Building Schools for the Future: The Local Education Partnership Model*, London.

Department for Homeland Security (2007) *Key Framework for Infrastructure Protection*, www.dhs.gov/index.shtm

Department for International Development (2007) *Literature Review on Private Sector Infrastructure Investment*, Working Paper No 24, London.

Department for International Development (2009) *Eliminating World Poverty: Building Our Common Future, Background Paper to the DFID Conference on the Future of International Development*, March, London, www.dfid.gov.uk/

Department of Communities and Local Government (2005) *Best Value Code of Practice on Workforce Matters in Local Government*, London, www.communities.gov.uk

Department of Communities and Local Government (2008) *Local Government Services Market - series of reports*, London, www.communities.gov.uk

Department of Health (2008) *Prioritised Capital Schemes*, November 2008, accessed 10 August 2009, www.dh.gov.uk

Department of Health (2009) *Transforming Community Services: Enabling new patterns of provision*, January, www.dh.gov.uk

Department of Transport (2008) *Kelly announces £6bn motorway improvements*, Press Release, 16 July, London, www.dft.gov.uk

Department of Transport (2009) *Britain's Transport Infrastructure: High Speed Two*, January, London, www.dft.gov.uk

Deutsche Bank Group (2005) *Understanding Infrastructure: A burgeoning global asset class*, RREEF, London.

Deutsche Bank Group (2007) *Performance Characteristics of Infrastructure Investments*, RREEF, San Francisco.

Deutsche Bank Group (2008) *Infrastructure Goes Global*, RREEF, San Francisco.

Deutsche Bank Group (2008) *Megacities: Boundless Growth*, http://www.dbresearch.com

Deitz, R. and Garcia, R. (2007) 'The Demand for Local Services and

Infrastructure Created by an Ageing Population', *Upstate New York Regional Review*, Federal Reserve Bank of New York, Vol. 2, No. 1, Buffalo.

DLA Piper Rudnick Gary Cary (2007) *European PPP Report 2007*, London.

Dolovich, S. (2005) 'State Punishment and Private Prisons', *Duke Law Journal*, Vol. 55, No. 3.

Dudkin, G. and Valila, T. (2005) *Transaction Costs in Public-Private Partnerships: A First Look at the Evidence, Economic and Financial Report2005/03*, European Investment Bank, www.eib.org

Duffield, C. (2008) *Report on the performance of PPP projects in Australia when compared with a representative sample of traditionally procured infrastructure projects*, for National PPP Forum, University of Melbourne.

Dwivedi, G., Rehmat and Dharmadhikary, S. (2007) *Water: Private, Limited: Issues in Privatisation, Corporatisation and Commercialisation of Water Sector in India*, Manthan Adhyayan Kendra, Badwani.

Economist, The (2008) 'Rushing on by road, rail and air: China's infrastructure splurge', 14 February.

Economic Policy Institute (2008) *Strategy for economic rebound: Smart stimulus to counteract the economic slowdown*, EPI Briefing Paper 210, Washington DC, www.epi.org

Economic Policy Institute (2009) *Tools for Assessing the Labour Market Impacts of Infrastructure Investment*, EPI Working Paper, April, Washington DC, www.epi.org

Economic Policy Institute (2009) *Transportation Investments and the Labour Market: How many jobs could be generated and what type?* Issue Brief, April, Washington DC, www.epi.org

Economic Policy Institute (2009) *Green Investments and the Labour Market: How many jobs could be generated and what type?* Issue Brief, April, Washington DC, www.epi.org

Edwards, P., Shaoul, J., Stafford, A. and Arblaster, L. (2004) *Evaluating the Operation of PFI in Roads and Hospitals*, Association of Chartered and Certified Accountants, London.

Ehrlich, E. and Landy, B. (2005) *Public Works, Public Wealth: New Directions for America's Infrastructure, Center for Strategic and International Studies*, Commission on Public Infrastructure, Washington DC, http://csis.org

Elliott, L. and Atkinson, D. (2008) *The Gods that Failed: How Blind Faith in Markets has Cost us Our Future*, Bodley Head, London.

Emerging Markets Now (2008) 'SBI, Macquarie, IFC to Launch Infrastructure Fund, 17 April, and Axis Private Equity Raises $150m for Infrastructure Fund', 25 April, http://emergingmarketsnow.evalueserve.com

Employment Tribunals (2008) *UNISON v Somerset County Council*, Taunton Deane Borough Council and South West One Ltd, Reserved Judgment, 19 November.

English, L. and Baxter, J. (2008) *Using Contracts to Govern Hybrid Public-Private*

Partnerships: A Case Study of Australian Prisons, Draft, Discipline of Accounting, University of Sydney.

Environment Agency (2009) *Investing for the Future: Flood and coastal risk management in England - A long-term investment strategy*, London, http://publications.environment-agency.gov.uk

Enwright, D.J. (2007) *The Public verses Private Toll Road Choice in the United States*, NW Financial Group, LLC, New York.

Ernst and Young (2005) *Australian PPP Survey: Issues Facing the Australian PPP Market*, November, Sydney.

Ernst and Young (2005) *Transaction Advisory Services: That's the way the money goes – a non-profit distributing schools PPP in Argyll & Bute*, Edinburgh.

Ernst and Young (2007) *Investing in Global Infrastructure 2007: An Emerging Asset Class*.www.ey.com

Ernst and Young (2008) *Bridging the Gap: Investing in European Infrastructure 2008*, April, New York www.ey.com

Ernst and Young (2008) *The Economic Contribution of Sydney's Toll Roads to NSW and Australia, for Transurban Limited*, July, www.ey.com.au

Ernst and Young (2009) *Ernst and Young Statement on Anglo Irish Bank*, Press Release, 16 January, Dublin, www.ey.com/

Escott, K. and Whitfield, D. (1995) *The Gender Impact of CCT in Local Government, Equal Opportunities Commission*, Manchester.

Estache, A. (2005) *PPI partnerships versus PPI divorces in LDCs (or are we switching from PPPI to PPDI?)*, Working Paper, No. 3470. World Bank, Washington, DC.

Estache, A. and Goicoechea, A. (2005). *How widespread were infrastructure reforms during the 1990s?* World Bank Research Working Paper, No. 3595. World Bank, Washington, DC.

Estache, A. (2006) *Infrastructure: A Survey of Recent and Upcoming Issues*, April, Mimeo, World Bank, Washington DC.

Estache, A. and Fay, M. (2007). *Current debates on infrastructure policy*, Policy Research Working Paper, No. 4410, World Bank, Washington, DC.

EURODAD (2008) *Critical Conditions: The IMF maintains its grip on low-income governments*, April, www.eurodad.org

Euromoney (2008) 'Monoline Insurance: Fitch triggers meltdown', 1 February, www.euromoney.com

European Bank for Reconstruction and Development (2007) *Infrastructure: Public Private Partnerships Factsheet*, www.ebrd.org

European Communities (2004) *Facing the Challenge: The Lisbon Strategy for Growth and Employment*, Report of the High Level Group chaired by Wim Kok, Brussels.

European Commission (2004) *Working Together for Growth and Jobs: A New Start for the Lisbon Strategy*, COM (2005) 24, Brussels.

European Commission (2006) *European Programme for Critical Infrastructure Protection*, COM(2006) 786 final, Brussels.

European Commission (2007) *Handbook on the Implementation of the Services Directive*, http://ec.europa.eu/

European Commission (2009) *White Paper: Adapting to Climate Change – Towards a European Framework for Action*, COM(2009) 147 final, http://eur-lex.europa.eu

European Investment Bank (2004) *The EIBs Role in Public Private Partnerships* www.eib.org

European Investment Bank (2005) 'Innovative Financing of Infrastructure – the role of public private partnerships', *EIB Papers*, Vol. 10, No 2., 2005 www.eib.org

European Investment Bank (2005) *Evaluation of PPP Projects Financed by the EIB*, March. www.eib.org

European Investment Bank (2008) *The European Investment Bank: building bridges for PPPs*, September, www.eib.org

European Parliament (2006) *Resolution on public-private partnerships and Community law on public procurement and concessions (2006/2043 (INI))*, Strasbourg.

European Regional Business and Economic Development Unit (2009) *Eco-Town Report: Learning from Europe on eco-towns*, Leeds, www.lmu.ac.uk/lbs/erbedu

European Union (2003) *Guidelines for Successful Public-Private Partnerships*, http://ec.europa.eu

European Union (2004) *Resources Book on PPP Case Studies*, http://ec.europa.eu

Eurostat (2004) *Long-term contracts between government units and non-government partners (Public Private Partnerships)*. http://epp.eurostat.ec.europa.eu

European Services Strategy Unit (2006) *North Tyneside – A Commissioning Council? Evidence Base for the Alternative Plan, for UNISON Northern*. www.european-services-strategy.org.uk

European Services Strategy Unit (2006) *Employment Risk Matrix*, www.european-services-strategy.org.uk

European Services Strategy Unit (2007) *Does Excelcare Really? An investigation into the transfer of 10 residential care homes by Essex County Council to Excelcare Holdings PLC*, Essex UNISON, www.european-services-strategy.org.uk

European Services Strategy Unit (2007) *Somerset ISiS or Crisis? An Assessment of the proposed Strategic Service-delivery Partnership with IBM*, Somerset County and Taunton Deane UNISON Branches, www.european-services-strategy.org.uk

European Services Strategy Unit (2008) *PPP Briefing: Strategic Service-delivery Partnerships and Outsourced Shared Services Projects*, www.european-services-strategy.org.uk

European Services Strategy Unit (2008) *Southwest One: Lessons and New Agenda for Public Services in the South West*, Somerset County and Taunton Deane UNISON Branches, www.european-services-strategy.org.uk

European Services Strategy Unit (2009) *PPP Database: Strategic Service-Delivery Partnerships for local authority ICT, corporate and technical services in Britain*, www.european-services-strategy.org.uk

Fankhauser, S., Sehlleier, F. and Stern, N. (2008) 'Climate Change, Innovation and Jobs', *Climate Policy*, No 8, p421-429.

Farber, N. (2008) 'Avoiding the Pitfalls of Public Private Partnerships: Issues to be Aware of When Transferring Transportation Assets', *Transportation Law Journal*, 35, p24–44.

Fay, M, and Morrison, M. (2005) *Infrastructure in Latin America and the Caribbean: Recent Developments and Key Challenges*, World Bank, Washington DC, www.worldbank.org

Federal Highway Administration (2003) *Highway Operations Spending as a Catalyst for Jobs Growth*, July, Washington DC, http://ops.fhwa.dot.gov

Federal Highway Administration (2008) *Employment Impacts of Highway infrastructure Investment*, www.fhwa.dot.gov

Federal Highway Administration (2008) *Dulles Greenway Case Study*, www.fhwa.dot.gov

Federal Highway Administration (2008) *Indiana Toll Road Case Study*, www.fhwa.dot.gov

Federal Highway Administration (2009) *Current Toll Road Activity in the US: A Survey and Analysis*, January, www.fhwa.dot.gov

Federal Reserve System (2009) *Flow of Funds Accounts of the United States: Flows and Outstandings, First Quarter 2009*, Washington DC, http://www.federalreserve.gov

Federation of Canadian Municipalities (2008) *Infrastructure as Economic Stimulus*, November, Ottawa, www.fcm.ca

Financial Times (2006) 'Infrastructure and private equity set to compete', 29 October, www.ft.com

Financial Times (2008) 'Argentina to buy back floundering state airline', 20 July, www.ft.com

Financial Times (2008) 'Infrastructure', 3 December, www.ft.com

Financial Times (2008) 'B & B Defends A$106m Bill', 4 September, www.ft.com

Financial Times (2009) 'Goldman amasses $164bn war chest', 14 April, www.ft.com

Financial Times (2009) 'Russian Energy Liberalisation', 5 May, www.ft.com

Fitch Ratings (2004) *Public-Private Partnerships: the Next Generation of Infrastructure Finance*, August, New York, www.fitchratings.com

Fitch Ratings (2007) *Infrastructure Project Ratings: Resilient in Inclement Markets*, Special Report, 14 November, New York, www.fitchratings.com

Fitch Ratings (2008) *Global Infrastructure & Project Finance Outlook 2008: Balancing Government and Capital Market Needs*, Special Report, 3 March, New York, www.fitchratings.com

Fitch Ratings (2008) *Brazil's Toll Roads Concessions: A new Cycle of Opportunities in a more Stable Environment*, May, New York, www.fitchratings.com

Fitch Ratings (2009) *Latin America Toll Roads: Global Credit Crisis Causes Bumpy*

Road Ahead, June, www.fitchratings.com
Florio, M. (2004) *The Great Divestiture*, MIT Press, Cambridge, Mass.
Flyvbjerg, B., Bruzelius, N. and Rothengater, W. (2003) *Megaprojects and Risk*, Cambridge University Press, Cambridge.
Flyvbjerg, B., Skamris, M. and Buhl, S. (2005) 'How (In)accurate Are Demand Forecasts in Public Works Projects? The Case of Transportation', *Journal of the American Planning Association*, Vol. 71, No. 2, Spring.
Food and Water Watch (2009) *A Cost Comparison of Public and Private Water Utility Operation*, June, www.foodandwaterwatch.org
Freshfields Bruckhaus Deringer, (2009) *Outlook for Infrastructure 2009 and Beyond*, June, London, www.freshfields.com
Froud, J. (2003) 'The Private Finance Initiative: risk, uncertainty and the state', *Accounting, Organisations and Society*, Vol. 28, Issue 6, August, p567-589.
Gaffney, D. and Pollock, A. (1999) 'Pump-Priming the PFI: Why are privately financed hospital schemes being subsidised?' *Public Money & Management*, March, p55-62.
Gann, D. and Salter, A. (200) 'Innovation in project-based, service-enhanced firms: The construction of complex products and systems', *Research Policy*, Vol. 29, p955 – 972.
Garvin, M. and Bosso, D. (2008) 'Assessing the Effectiveness of Infrastructure Public Private Partnership Programs and Projects', *Public Works Management & Policy*, Vol. 13, No 2, p162-178.
Gassener, K., Popov, A. and Pushak, N. (2009) *Does Private Sector Participation Improve Performance in Electricity and Water Distribution?* World Bank and Public-Private Infrastructure Advisory Facility, www.worldbank.org
Gibson, M. (2007) *Credit Derivatives and Risk Management*, Finance and Economics Discussion Series Divisions of Research & Statistics and Monetary Affairs, Federal Reserve Board, Washington DC.
Gibbons, S. and Machin, S. (2006) *Transport and Labour Market Linkages: Empirical Evidence, Implications for Policy and Scope for Further UK Research*, Paper for the Eddington Transport Study, Department for Transport, www.dft.gov.uk
Global Pensions (2006) *Building returns on infrastructure investment*, March.
Global Unions/ITUC/TUAC (2008) *The Global Unions 'Washington Declaration, Trade Unions Statement on the 'G20 Crisis Summit'*, November, www.global-unions.org
Glyn, A. (2006) *Capitalism Unleashed: Finance, Globalisation and Welfare*, Oxford University Press, Oxford.
Gomez-Ibanez, J.A, Lorrain, D. and Osius, M (2004) *The Future of Private Infrastructure, Working Paper, Taubman Center for State and Local Government*, Kennedy School of Government, Harvard University, Cambridge www.hks.harvard.edu

Gonzalez, J., Guasch, J.L. and Serebrisky, T. (2007) *Latin America: Addressing High Logistics Costs and Poor Infrastructure for Merchandise Transportation and Trade Facilitation*, World Bank, Washington DC.

Good Jobs First (2009) *High Road or Low Road: Job Quality in the New Green Economy*, Washington DC, http://www.goodjobsfirst.org

Good Jobs New York (2007) *Pay, Or We (Might) Go: How Citigroup Games the States and Cities*, New York, www.goodjobsny.org

Government Accountability Office (2008) *Highway Public-Private Partnerships: More Rigorous Up-front Analysis Could Better Secure Potential Benefits and Protect the Public Interest*, February, Washington DC, www.gao.gov

Government Accountability Office (2008) *Physical Infrastructure: Challenges and Investment Options for the Nation's Infrastructure*, GAO-08-763T, Washington DC.

Government Accountability Office (2009) *International Taxation: Large U.S. Corporations and Federal Contractors with Subsidiaries in Jurisdictions Listed as Tax Havens or Financial Privacy Jurisdictions*, GAO-09-157, Washington DC.

Government of India (2009) *Private Participation in Infrastructure, Secretariat for the Committee on Infrastructure*, New Delhi, wwww.infrastructure.gov.in

Government of Ireland (2007) *National Development Plan 2007-2013: Transforming Ireland – A Better Quality of Life for All*, Stationery Office, Dublin.

Gowan, P. (2009) 'Crisis in the Heartland: Consequences of the New Wall Street System', *New Left Review* 55, Jan-Feb, pp 5-29.

Gray, G.J., Cusatis, P.J. and Foote, J.H. (2008) *For Whom the Road Tolls - Corporate Asset of Public Good? An analysis of Financial and Strategic Alternatives for Pennsylvania Turnpike*, prepared for Democratic Caucus of the Pennsylvania House of Representatives, February.

Grimsey, D. and Lewis, M.K. (2005) 'Are public private partnerships value for money? Evaluating alternative approaches and comparing academic and practitioner views', *Accounting Forum*, vol. 29, no. 4, pp. 345–78.

Guardian, The (2009) 'Architects to vet new school designs', 12 May, London, www.guardian.co.uk/

Guasch, J Luis (2004) *Success Factors in Awarding Highway Concessions*, Presentation, Transport Forum, World Bank, Washington DC.

Guasch, J. Luis (2004). *Granting and Renegotiating Infrastructure Concessions: Doing it Right*, WBI Development Studies, World Bank, Washington, DC.

Guasch, J. Luis, Jean-Jacques Laffont and Stephane Straub (2003). *Renegotiations of concession contracts in Latin America*, World Bank Policy Research Working Paper, No. 3011, World Bank, Washington, DC.

Habitat International Coalition (2008) *Cash-strapped German councils are selling their homes to private investors*, www.hicnet.org

Hansard (2005) Written Answer, 1 February, Column 825W, Departmental Costs/Expenditure, Fiona Mactaggart, for Secretary of State for the Home Department, London.

Harris County (2006) *Commissioners Court: Capital Improvements*, 20 June, Texas.

Harriss-White, B. and Harriss, E. (2006) 'Unsustainable Capitalism: The Politics of Renewable energy in the UK, incoming to Terms with nature', *Socialist Register 2007*, Merlin Press.

Hart, O. (2003) 'Incomplete Contracts and Public Ownership: Remarks and an Application to Public-Private Partnerships', *Economic Journal*, Vol. 113, March, p69-76.

Harvey, D. (2005) *A Brief History of Neoliberalism*, Oxford University Press, Oxford.

Hayes, C. (2007) 'The NAFTA Superhighway', *The Nation*, August 27, www.thenation.com

Heald, D. (2003) 'Value for Money Tests and Accounting Treatment of PFI Schemes', *Accounting, Auditing, and Accountability Journal*, Vol. 16, No. 3, pp. 342–71.

Hearne, R. (2009) 'What Future for the Regeneration of Social housing Estates', *Village*, April/May, p44-46, www.villagemagazine.ie

Health Service Journal (2009) 'Alan Johnson Approves South East London NHS Reconfiguration', 8 May, www.hsj.co.uk

Hebson, G., Grimshaw, D., Marchington, M. and Cooke, F. (2002) *PPPs and the Changing Public Sector Ethos: Case Study Evidence from the Health and Local Authority Sectors*, Working Paper No 21, Manchester School of Management, UMIST, Manchester.

Heintz, J., Pollin, R. and Garrett-Peltier, H. (2009) *How Infrastructure Investments Support the US Economy: Employment, Productivity and Growth*, Political Economy Research Institute, University of Massachusetts, http://www.peri.umass.edu/

Hellowell, M. and Pollock, A. (2007) *Private Finance, Public Deficits: A report on the cost of PFI and its impact on health services in England*, Centre for International Public Health Policy, Edinburgh, www.health.ed.ac.uk/CIPHP/

Hellowell, M. and Pollock, A. (2007) 'New Development: The PFI: Scotland's Plan for Expansion and its Implications', *Public Money & Management*, November, p351-354.

HM Treasury (1999) *The Government Client Improvement Study*, Agile Construction Initiative, London.

HM Treasury (2003) *Meeting the Investment Challenge*, London. www.hm-treasury.gov.uk

HM Treasury (2003) *The Green Book, HM Treasury*, London, www.hm-treasury.gov.uk

HM Treasury (2005) *Application Note - Value for Money in Refinancing*, London, www.hm-treasury.gov.uk

HM Treasury (2006) *PFI: Strengthening Long-Term Relationships*, March, London. www.hm-treasury.gov.uk

HM Treasury (2006) *Releasing the resources to meet the challenges ahead: value for money in the 2007 CSR*, July, London, www.hm-treasury.gov.uk

HM Treasury (2006) *PFI: Meeting the Investment Challenge: Further Background*

Information, March, London, www.hm-treasury.gov.uk
HM Treasury (2008) *Budget 2008*, March, London. www.hm-treasury.gov.uk
HM Treasury (2008) *Infrastructure Procurement: Delivering Long-Term Value*, London www.hm-treasury.gov.uk
HM Treasury (2008) *Amended Refinancing Provisions: Standardisation of PFI Contracts*, Version 4, Addendum, October, London, www.hm-treasury.gov.uk
HM Treasury (2008) *PFI Equity Holders – November*, London, www.hm-treasury.gov.uk
HM Treasury (2009) *UK International Financial Services - The Future*, May, London, www.hm-treasury.gov.uk
HM Treasury (2009) *Safeguarding Government Infrastructure Investment, Written Ministerial Statement*, 3 March, London, www.hm-treasury.gov.uk
Hochtief (2007) *Public-Private Partnerships (PPP): Concessions Business at Hochtief Position Paper*, www.hochtief-pppsolutions.com
House of Commons Public Accounts Committee (1998) *The Skye Bridge*, June, London.
House of Commons Public Accounts Committee (2005) *PFI: The STEPS Deal*, HC 553, Session 2003-04, June, London.
House of Commons Public Accounts Committee (2006) *NHS Local Improvement Finance Trusts*, HC 562, Session 2005-06, July, London.
HSBC Global Research (2009) *A Climate for Recovery*, February, London.
Hurst, C. and Reeves, E. (2004) 'An Economic Analysis of Ireland's First Public Private Partnership', *International Journal of Public Sector Management*, Vol.17, No.5, p379-388.
Hypo Real Estate Holding (2007) *Recommended Offer Document for DEPFRA Bank plc*, www.depfra.com
Independent, The (2009) 'Private Prisons 'Performing Worse than State-Run Jails'', 29 June.
Independent Reconfiguration Panel (2009) *Advice on proposals for changes to the distribution of services between Bromley Hospitals, Queen Elizabeth Hospital Greenwich, Queen Mary's Hospital Sidcup and University Hospital Lewisham and the associated development of community services*, Submitted to Secretary of State for Health, March, London.
Infrastructure Australia (2008) *Discussion Paper No 1: Australia's Future Infrastructure Requirements*, www.infrastructureaustralia.gov.au
Infrastructure Australia (2009a) *National Infrastructure Priorities*, May, Sydney, www.infrastructureaustralia.gov.au
Infrastructure Australia (2009b) *National PPP Policy and Guidelines*, www.infrastructureaustralia.gov.au
Infrastructure Canada (2006) *Adapting Infrastructure to Climate Change in Canada's Cities and Communities*, A Literature Review, Ottawa.
Infrastructure Canada (2007) *Infrastructure and Productivity: A Literature Review*, PricewaterhouseCoopers, Ottawa.

Infrastructure Canada (2008) *Building Canada*, www.buildingcanada-chantierscanada.gc.ca

Infrastructure Canada (2009) *Targeted Funding Programmes* – accessed 10 August 2009, http://www.infc.gc.ca

Infrastructure Investor (2008) 'Macquarie Group writes down A$684m in managed assets, co-investments', 18 November, www.infrastructureinvestor.com

Infrastructure Investor (2008) 'Morgan Stanley wins $1.2bn Chicago parking deal', 2 December, www.infrastructureinvestor.com

Infrastructure Investor (2009) 'RE softens OMERS' C$8bn loss in 2008', 25 February, www.infrastructureinvestor.com

Infrastructure Investor (2009) 'Pittsburgh takes next step in parking system monetisation', 24 February, www.infrastructureinvestor.com

Infrastructure Investor (2009) 'Private investors flee Russian infrastructure', 18 March, www.infrastructureinvestor.com

Infrastructure Investor (2009) 'Ireland Budgets for 4.8bn of private infrastructure investment', 9 April, www.infrastructureinvestor.com

Infrastructure Investor (2009) 'The end of Project Finance?' Issue 1, April, www.infrastructureinvestor.com

Infrastructure Investor (2009) 'Carlyle, Goldman steam into Port of Virginia', 27 July, www.infrastructureinvestor.com

Infrastructure Investor (2009) 'ABP Investments', April, p43, www.infrastructureinvestor.com

Infrastructure Management Group (2008) *Valuing Concessions: Making Equity Work in P3s*, Presentation, 13 January, Bethseda, www.imggroup.com

Infrastructure Ontario (2007) *Assessing Value for Money*, Toronto, www.infrastructureontario.ca

Infrastructure Partnerships Australia (2009) *Financing Infrastructure in the Global Financial Crisis*, March, Sydney, www.infrastructure.org.au

Innisfree (2008) *Primary Funds*, accessed 23 December, www.innisfree.co.uk

Integration of Regional Infrastructure in South America (2008) *IIRSA Portfolio 2008*, December, www.iirsa.org

Intergovernmental Panel on Climate Change (2007) *Climate Change 2007: Climate Change Impacts, Adaptation and Vulnerability*, Fourth Assessment Report, www.ipcc.ch

International Finance Corporation (2008) *Annual Report*, Washington DC, www.ifc.org

International Finance Corporation (2009) *Road Map 2009/11*, Washington DC, www.ifc.org

International Finance Corporation (2009) *Issue Brief: IFC Infrastructure Crisis Facility*, December, Washington DC, www.ifc.org

International Financial Services London (2008) *PFI in the UK & PPP in Europe 2008*, London www.ifsl.org.uk

International Financial Services London (2008) *Fund Management 2007*, www.ifsl.org.uk
International Financial Services London (2008) *Economic Contribution of UK Financial Services 2008*, www.ifsl.org.uk
International Financial Services London (2009) *PFI in the UK & PPP in Europe 2008*, London, www.ifsl.org.uk
International Financial Services London (2009) *International Financial Markets in the UK*, May, London, www.ifsl.org.uk
International Monetary Fund (2004) *Public Private Partnerships*, Washington DC, www.imf.org
International Monetary Fund (2006) *Public-Private Partnerships, Government Guarantees and Fiscal Risk*, Fiscal Affairs Department, Washington DC, www.imf.org
International Monetary Fund (2008) *Fiscal Policy for the Crisis, Staff Position Note*, December, Fiscal Affairs and Research Departments, Washington DC, www.imf.org
International Monetary Fund (2009) *The State of Public Finances: Outlook and Medium-Term Policies After the 2008 Crisis*, March, Fiscal Affairs Department, Washington DC, www.imf.org
International Monetary Fund (2009) *Companion Paper—The State of Public Finances: Outlook and Medium-Term Policies After the 2008 Crisis*, March, Fiscal Affairs Department, Washington DC, www.imf.org
International Monetary Fund (2009) *Fiscal Implications of the Global Economic and Financial Crisis*, June, Washington DC, www.imf.org
International Rivers (2008) *The New Great Walls: A Guide to China's Overseas Dam Industry*, Berkeley, http://www.internationalrivers.org
International Rivers (2008) *Muddy Waters: Consequences of Damming the Amazon's Principal Tributary*, http://internationalrivers.org
Institute for Fiscal Studies (2006) *The IFS Green Budget: The Fiscal Policy Framework*, January, London, www.ifs.org.uk
Institute for Fiscal Studies (2008) *Green Budget 2008*, January, London. www.ifs.org.uk
Institute for Fiscal Studies (2009) *Green Budget 2009*, January, London, http://www.ifs.org.uk
Institute for Public Policy Research (2001) *Building Better Partnerships: Commission on Public Private Partnerships*, London.
Institute for Public Policy Research (2004) *3 Steps Forward, 2 Steps Back: Reforming PPP Policy*, London.
Institute for Policy Studies and Food and Water Watch (2007) *Challenging Corporate Investor Rule: How the World Bank's Investment Court, Free Trade Agreements, and Bilateral Investment Treaties have Unleashed a New Era of Corporate Power and What to Do About It*, Sarah Anderson and Sara Grusky, Washington DC, www.ips-dc.org

Institute for Policy Studies (2008) *How the Bailouts Dwarf Other Global Crisis Spending*, November, Washington DC, http://www.ips-dc.org

Irish Examiner (2009) 'Superprison Plans Hit by Economic Climate', 7 January, http://archives.tcm.ie

Irons, J.S. (2008) *Testimony, Economic Policy Institute on Infrastructure Investment and Economic Recovery*, US House of Representatives Committee on Transportation and Infrastructure, 29 October, Washington DC.

Irwin, T. (2007) *Government Guarantees: Allocating and Valuing Risk in Private Financed Infrastructure Projects*, World Bank, Washington DC.

James, N. (2003) *Private equity and debt poised to help build US transportation*, Public Works Financing, December.

Jefferis, C. and Stilwell, F. (2006) 'Private Finance for Public Infrastructure: the case of Macquarie Bank', *Journal of Australian Political Economy*, Vol. 58, p44-61.

Jen, S. (2007) *How big could Sovereign Wealth Funds be by 2015?* Morgan Stanley Perspectives, May 4, New York.

John Laing (2005) *Creating Value: Annual Report and Accounts 2004*, London.

Jones, A. (2008) *Public Money, Private Gain*, West Eye View, ITV, Broadcast 24 July.

JP Morgan (1997) 'Examining Tollroad Feasibility Studies', *Municipal Finance Journal*, Vol. 18, No. 1. Spring.

Jubilee Debt Campaign (2009) *A New Debt Crisis? Assessing the impact of the financial crisis on developing countries*, London, www.jubileedebtcampaign.org.uk

Julius, D. (2008) *Public Service Industry Review: Understanding the public service industry, how big, how good, where next?* Department for Business Innovation and Skills, www.berr.gov.uk

Justice Forum (2002) *Privatising Justice: The Impact of the Private Finance Initiative in the Criminal Justice System*, Centre for Public Services, London. www.european-services-strategy.org.uk

Kagarlitsky, Boris (2008) 'Communism's new crisis', *The Moscow Times*, 8 May 2008, www.tni.org

Kammen, D.M., Kapadia, K., Fripp, M. (2006) *Putting Renewables to Work: How Many Jobs Can the Clean Energy Industry Generate?* Report of the Renewable and Appropriate Energy Laboratory, University of California, Berkeley, April.

Kamps, C. (2004) *New Estimates of Government Net Capital Stocks for 22 OECD Countries 1960–2001*, Working Paper 04/67, International Monetary Fund, Washington DC.

Kaul, I., Grunberg, I. and Stern, M. (1999) *Global Public Goods: International Cooperation in the 21st Century*, Oxford University Press, Oxford.

Kaul, I., Conceicao, P., Le Goulven, K. and Mendoza, R. (2003) *Providing Global Public Goods*, Oxford University Press, Oxford.

Kay, J. (2009) 'Britain has sunk itself into a fiscal black hole', *Financial Times*, 7 July, www.ft.com

Keane, A. G (2006) 'Line Up for Tolling', *Traffic World*, 27 November.

Kelly G, Mulgan G, Muers S, (2002) *Creating public value: an analytical framework for public service reform*, Strategy Unit, Cabinet Office, London, www.cabinetoffice.gov.uk

Kelsey, J. (2008) *Serving Whose Interests? The Political Economy of Trade in Services Agreements*, Routledge-Cavendish, Abingdon.

Klare, M. (2008) *Rising Powers, Shrinking Planet: How Scarce Energy is Creating a New World Order*, Oneworld Publications, Oxford.

Klein, N. (2007) *The Shock Doctrine: The Rise of Disaster Capitalism*, Penguin Books, London.

Klijn, E. and Teisman, G. (2005) 'Public private partnerships as the managing of coproduction: strategic and institutional obstacles in a difficult marriage'. In Hodge, G. and Greve C. (Eds), *The Challenge of Public-Private Partnerships: Learning from International Experience* (Edward Elgar, Cheltenham).

Kohlberg Kravis Roberts (2008) *KKR Announces Plans for Investments in Global Infrastructure Assets*, 16 May, New York, www.kkr.com

Kok, W. (2004) *Facing the Challenge: The Lisbon Strategy for Growth and Employment*, Report of the High Level Group, Brussels.

KPMG (2008) *The Water Business in China: Looking Below the Surface*, Beijing, www.kpmg.com.cn

KPMG (2009) *Financing Australian PPP Projects in the Global Financial Crisis*, May, www.kpmg.com.au

KPMG (2009) *PFI in school building – does it influence educational outcomes?* London, www.kpmg.co.uk

Krause, F., DeCanio, S., Hoerner, A., Baer, P. (2003) 'Cutting carbon emission at a profit. Part II: Impacts on U.S. competitiveness and jobs', *Contemporary Economic Policy* 21(1), 90–105.

Lapavitsas, C. (2008) *Financialised Capitalism: Direct Exploitation and Periodic Bubbles*, May, Department of Economics, SOAS, University of London.

Lattman, M. (2008) 'China's African Infrastructure Investment', *Global Infrastructure*, Vol. 2, Fall.

Leigland, J. (2008) *The Rise and Fall of Brownfield Concessions*, Working Paper No 6, Public-Private Infrastructure Advisory Facility, Washington DC. www.ppiaf.org

Levina E. and Adams, H. (2006) *Domestic policy frameworks for adaptation to climate change in the water sector*, OECD, Paris, www.oecd.org

Leyshon, A. and Thrift, N. (2007) 'The Capitalization of Almost Everything: The Future of Finance and Capitalism', *Theory, Culture and Society*, 24; 97.

Linklaters (2006) *PPP in France – 2006*, Paris, www.linklaters.com.

Lobina, E. and Hall, D. (2006) *Public-Public Partnerships as a catalyst for capacity building and institutional development: Lessons from Stockholm Vatten's experience in the Baltic region*, PSIRU, University of Greenwich, London.

Local Partnerships (2005) *Sheffield City Council – Corporate and Transactional Services*, London.
Local Partnerships (2006) *Workforce Matters in Local Authority PFI and PPP Agreements: Guidance and Standard Drafting*, March, London.
Local Partnerships (2008) *Frequently Asked Questions (FAQ) on the Credit Crunch*, London.
Lohmann, L. (2006) *Carbon Trading A Critical Conversation on Climate Change, Privatisation and Power*, www.thecornerhouse.org.uk.
Lohmann, L. (2009 *Climate Crisis: Social Science Crisis*, Cornerhouse, www.thecornerhouse.org.uk.
LSE Enterprise Ltd (2009) *The UK's Digital Road to Recovery*, April, London, www.itif.org/
Ma, J. and Pineiro, C. (2006) *Infrastructure as an Emerging Alternative Asset Class*, Goldman Sachs, 12 December, presentation.
Mabizela, M. (2005) *The Business of Higher Education: A study of public-private partnerships in the provision of Higher Education in South Africa*, Human Sciences Research Council, Cape Town, www.hsrcpress.ac.za
Mackenzie, H. (2007) *Doing the Math: Why P3 for Alberta Schools Don't Add Up*, Canadian Union of Public Employees, www.cupe.ca
McCartney, S. and Stittle, J. (2008) 'Taken for a Ride: The Privatization of the UK Railway Rolling Stock Industry', *Public Money & Management*, Vol. 28, Issue 2, April, p93-100.
McFadyean, M. and Rowland, D. (2002) *The PFI Verses Democracy? The Case of Birmingham's Hospitals*, Menard Press, London.
McKinley, T. (2006) T*he Monopoly of Global Capital Flows, International Poverty Centre*, Working Paper 12, UNDP, Brasilia, Brazil www.undp-povertycentre.org
McKinsey Global Institute (2007) *The New Power Brokers: How Oil, Asia, Hedge Funds and Private Equity are Shaping Global Capital Markets*, October, www.mckinsey.com/mgi
McKinsey Global Institute (2008) *Mapping Global Capital Markets: Fourth Annual Report*, San Francisco. www.mckinsey.com/mgi
McKinsey Global Institute (2009) *Preparing for China's Urban Billion*, www.mckinsey.com/mgi
Macquarie (2005) *MIG – Refinancing of Skyway Concession Company*, 17 August, www.macquarie.com.au
Macquarie Group (2009) *The Infrastructure Asset Class*, www.macquarie.com
Macquarie Group (2009) *Macquarie Group 2009 Annual Report*, July, Sydney, www.macquarie.com.au
Manley, J. and Guadagnuolo, L. (2006) 'Breaking New Boundaries: Essential Public Infrastructure Capital ll (EPIC ll)', *The Journal of Structured Finance*, Fall.
Massachusetts Infrastructure Investment Coalition (2007) *Infrastructure Status Report: Massachusetts Drinking Water*, May, Boston, www.engineers.org

Matsukawa, T. Habeck, O. (2007) *Review of Risk Mitigation Instruments for Infrastructure Financing and Recent Trends and Developments*, PPIAF, Washington DC, www.ppiaf.org

Mayston, D. (1999) 'The Private Finance Initiative in the National Health Service: An Unhealthy Development in New Public Management', *Financial Accountability and Management*, August-November.

Mehra, N. (2005) *Flawed, Failed, Abandoned: 100 P3s, Canadian Union of Public Employees*, http://cupe.ca

MGT of America (2007) *Performance Audit of the Department of Corrections for the Legislative Service Bureau of the Oklahoma Legislature*, Austin. www.mgtofamerica.com

Ministry of Defence (2005) *Review of MoD PFI Projects in Construction and Operation*, MoD Private Finance Unit, December, London.

Miraftab, F. (2004) 'Public-Private Partnerships: The Trojan Horse of Neoliberal Development?' *Journal of Planning Education and Research*, 24, 89.

Miraz, S. (2007) *Danger Ahead: The Coming Collapse of Canada's Municipal Infrastructure*, Federation of Canadian Municipalities, Ottawa, www.fcm.ca

Moist, P. (2008) 'Building Canada: A P3 Push?' *Municipal World*, July, p27-28.

Moles, P. and Williams, G. (1995) 'Privately funded infrastructure in the UK: Participants' risk in the Skye Bridge project', *Transport Policy*, Vol. 2, Issue 2, April, p129-134.

Monmouth University Polling Institute (2007) *New Jersey Says Hands Off Our Assets*, July, New Jersey www.monmouth.edu

Moody's Global Infrastructure (2009) *Canadian Public Private Partnership Sector – 2009 Outlook*, www.moodys.com

Moore, M. (1995) *Creating Public Value: Strategic Management in Government*, Harvard University Press.

Morales (2008) *Statement on the draft European Union Return Directive*, Evo Morales Ayma, President of the Republic of Bolivia.

Morgan Stanley (2008) *Morgan Stanley Closes $4.0 Billion Global Infrastructure Fund*, Press Release, 12 May, New York, www.morganstanley.com

Morris, C. (2008) *The Trillion Dollar Meltdown: Easy money, high rollers and the great credit crash*, Public Affairs, New York.

Mother Jones (2007) 'The Highwaymen', January-February www.motherjones.com

Mott MacDonald (2002) *Review of Large Public Procurement in the UK*, London.

Munnell, A. H. (1990) 'Why has productivity growth declined? Productivity and public investment', *New England Economic Review*, Jan/Feb. 3-22.

Murphy, D. and Devlin, M. (2009) *Banksters: How a Powerful Elite Squandered Ireland's Resources*, Hachette, Dublin.

Murphy, R. (2009) *Country-by-Country Reporting: Holding Multinational Corporations to Account Wherever They Are*, Task Force on Financial Integrity & Economic Development, June, Washington DC, www.financialtaskforce.org

Nataraj, G. (2007) *Infrastructure Challenge in South Asia: The Role of Public Private Partnerships*, Asian Development Bank Institute, Discussion Paper No 80, www.adbi.org

National Audit Office (2001) *Modernising Construction*, HC 87, Session 2000-2001, January, London.

National Audit Office (2001) *The Re-negotiation of the PFI-type deal for the Royal Armouries Museum in Leeds*, HC 103, Session 2000-01, January, London.

National Audit Office (2002) *The Public Private Partnership for the National Air Traffic Services Ltd*, HC 1096, Session 2001-02, July 2002, London.

National Audit Office (2003) *PFI: Construction Performance*, HC 371, Session 2002/03, February, London.

National Audit Office (2004) *London Underground: Are the Public Private Partnerships likely to work successfully?* HC 644, Session 2003-2004, June, London.

National Audit Office (2004) *Refinancing of the Public Private Partnership for National Air Traffic Services*, HC 157, Session 2003-04, January, London.

National Audit Office (2004) *PFI: The STEPS Deal*, HC 530, Session 2003-04, May, London.

National Audit Office (2005) *Darent Valley Hospital: The PFI Contract in Action*, HC 209, Session 2004/05, February, London.

National Audit Office (2005) *Improving Public Services through Better Construction*, HC 364-ll, Session 2004-2005, London.

National Audit Office (2005) *Innovation in the NHS: Local Improvement Finance Trusts*, HC 38, Session 2005/06, May, London.

National Audit Office (2005) *The* Refinancing of the Norfolk and Norwich PFI Hospital: How the deal can be viewed in the light of refinancing, HC 78, Session 2005/06, June, London.

National Audit Office (2006) *PFI and PPP Focus*, No. 1, April, London.

National Audit Office (2006) *Update on PFI Debt financing and the PFI Equity Market*, HC 1040, Session 2005/06, April, London. www.nao.org.uk

National Audit Office (2006) *The Termination of the PFI Contract for the National Physical Laboratory*, HC 1044, Session 2005/06, May, London.

National Audit Office (2006) *The Paddington Health Campus Scheme*, HC 1045, Session 2005/06, May, London.

National Audit Office (2006) *A Framework for Evaluating the Implementation of Private Finance Initiative Projects*, Volumes 1 and 2, May, London.

National Audit Office (2007) *Improving the PFI Tendering Process*, Report for the House of Commons, HC 149 Session 2006-07.

National Audit Office (2008) *Shared Services in the Department of Transport and its Agencies*, HC 481, Session 2007-2008, May, London, www.nao.gov.uk

National Audit Office (2008) *Making Changes in Operational PFI Projects*, HC205, Session 2007-2008, January, London, www.nao.gov.uk

National Audit Office (2008) *Protecting Staff in PPP/PFI Deals*, March,

London, www.nao.gov.uk

National Audit Office (2009) *The Building Schools for the Future Programme: Renewing the secondary school estate*, HC 135, Session 2008-2009, February, London, www.nao.gov.uk

National Audit Office (2009) *Financial Management in the Department for Children, Schools and Families*, HC 267, Session 2008-2009, April, London, www.nao.gov.uk

National Capital Region Transportation Planning Board (2008) *Evaluating Alternative Scenarios for a Network of Variably Priced Highway Lanes in the Metropolitan Washington Region*, February, Washington DC, www.mwcog.org

National Intelligence Council (2008) *Global Trends 2025: A Transformed World*, November, Washington DC, www.dni.gov

National Research Council (2009) *Sustainable Critical Infrastructure Systems: A Framework for Meeting 21st Century Imperatives*, National Academic Press, Washington DC, www.nap.edu

National Statistics (2006) *Including Finance Lease Liabilities in Public Sector Net Debt: PFI and Other Economic Trends 636*, November, London..

National Surface Transportation and Revenue Study Commission (2009) *Transportation for Tomorrow: Report of the National Surface Transportation Policy and Revenue Study Commission*, http://transportationfortomorrow.org/

National Treasury PPP Unity (2006) *PPP Quarterly*, October, www.ppp.gov.za

NERA Economic Consulting (2005) *Understanding Changes in NHS Inputs and Outputs: A Report for BUPA*, London.

Newcastle City Council (2001) *Street Lighting Improvements: Outline Business Case*, May, Newcastle.

New Jersey Policy Perspectives (2009) *Proposed Tax Increment Financing Law: Developer Windfall Could Result in Significant Revenue Losses for the State and Localities*, Press Release, 22 June, www.njpp.org

New South Wales Treasury (2009) *NSW Treasury Submission to Infrastructure Australia*, March, www.treasury.nsw.gov.au

New York Attorney General (2009) *Merrill Lynch 2008 Bonuses, Letter from Andrew Cuomo to House Committee on Financial Services*, US House of Representatives, 10 February, New York, www.oag.state.ny.us

New York State Commission on State Asset Maximization (2009) *Final Report*, June, www.nysamcommission.org

Nikolic, I. and Maikisch, H. (2006) *Public-Private Partnerships and Collaboration in the Health Sector - An Overview with Case Studies from Recent European Experience, Health, Nutrition and Population (HNP) Discussion Paper*, World Bank, Washington DC, www.worldbank.org

Noel, M. and Brzeski, W. (2005) *Mobilising Private Finance for Local Infrastructure in Europe and Central Asia: An Alternative Public Private Partnership Framework*, Working Paper No. 46, World Bank, Washington DC, www.worldbank.org

Norfolk and Norwich University Hospital NHS Trust (2005) *Private Finance Initiative - Norfolk and Norwich University Hospital*, Norwich.

NW Financial Group (2006) *The Chicago Skyway Sale: An Analytical Review*, May, Jersey City. www.csgeast.org

North Atlantic Treaty Organisation (2008) *Bucharest Summit Declaration* Issued by the Heads of State and Government participating in the meeting of the North Atlantic Council in Bucharest on 3 April.

Northern Way and Deloitte (2008) *The Northern Way Private Investment Commission, Financing the long-term future of the regions*. Issues Paper, December, Manchester, www.thenorthernway.co.uk

Northern Way and Deloitte (2009) *The Northern Way Private Investment Commission: Preparing the ground - Private investment in the regions, in the recovery phase and beyond*, July, Manchester, www.thenorthernway.co.uk

Norton Rose (2005) *The Development of Global PPP*, June, London.

Norwegian Forum for Environment and Development (2006) *Privatisation of Water: Public-Private Partnerships – Do they deliver to the poor*, Oslo.

Norwegian Union of Municipal and General Employees (2008) *The EU Services Directive and the Public Services*, Oslo, www.fagforbundet.no

O'Fallon C. (2003) *Linkages Between Infrastructure and Economic Growth*, December, Ministry of Economic Development, Wellington, New Zealand.

Office of Fair Trading (2009) *Constructions firms fined for illegal bid-rigging*, London, www.oft.gov.uk

Office of Fair Trading (2009) *Local Bus Services*, August, London. www.oft.gov.uk

Office of Government Commerce (2005), *Guidance Note: Calculation of the Authority's Share of a Refinancing Gain*, London, www.ogc.gov.uk

Office of Government Commerce (2005) *Managing Risks with Delivery Partners*, London, www.ogc.gov.uk

Office of the PPP Arbiter (2006) *Annual Metronet Report, 2006*, November, London.

Oil & Gas Financial Journal (2009) 'Using REITs Structure to Enable Private Equity Investment in Energy', 1 March, www.ogfj.com

Ontario Auditor General (2008) *Annual Report*, Section 3.03: Brampton Civic Hospital Public-Private Partnership Project, Toronto, www.auditor.on.ca

OECD (2003) *The Policy Agenda for Growth – an overview of the sources of economic growth in OECD countries*, Paris, www.oecd.org

OECD (2006) *Infrastructure to 2030: Telecom, Land Transport, Water and Electricity*, Paris, www.oecd.org

OECD (2006) *Promoting Pro-Poor Growth: Infrastructure*, Paris, www.oecd.org

OECD (2006) *Promoting Pro-Poor Growth: Private Sector Development*, Paris, www.oecd.org

OECD (2007) *Infrastructure to 2030: Mapping Policy for Electricity, Water and Transport*, Paris, www.oecd.org

OECD (2007) *OECD Principles for Private Sector Participation in Infrastructure*, Paris, www.oecd.org

OECD (2008) *Public-Private Partnerships: In Pursuit of Risk Sharing and Value for Money*, May, Paris, www.oecd.org

OECD (2009) 'Pension Fund Investment in Infrastructure', *Working Papers on Insurance and Private Pensions* No 32, Georg Inderst, Paris, www.oecd.org

Orr, R. and Kennedy, J.R. (2008) 'Highlights of Recent Trends in Global Infrastructure: New Players and Revised Game Rules', *Transnational Corporations*, Vol. 17, No. 1, April.

Palley, T. (2007) *Financialisation: What it is and Why it Matters*, Working Paper No 525, The Levy Economic Institute, Annandale-on-Hudson, www.levy.org

Panggabean, A. (2006) *Expanding Access to Basic Services in Asia and the Pacific Region: Public Private Partnerships for Poverty Reduction, Economics and Research Department*, Working Paper No. 87, November, Manila. www.adb.org

Partnerships for Schools (2008) *PfS Announces Review of Operational Local Strategic Partnerships*, Press Release, 21 May, London.

Partnerships UK (2006) *Operational PFI Projects*, March, London.

Partnerships UK (2007) *PFI: The State of the Market*, October, London, www.partnershipsuk.org.uk

Partnerships UK (2007) *PUK 5-Year Review*, London, www.partnershipsuk.org.uk

Partnerships UK (2008) *The Impact of the Credit Crisis on the PPP Market*, November, London, www.partnershipsuk.org.uk

Partnerships Victoria (2001) *PPP Guidelines*, Melbourne, www.partnerships.vic.gov.au

Passenger Focus (2009) *Fares and Ticketing Study, Final report*, February, London, www.passengerfocus.org.uk

Peck, J. (2006) 'Neoliberal Hurricane: Who Framed New Orleans? in Coming to Terms with Nature', *Socialist Register 2007*, Merlin Press, London.

Pennsylvania (2008) *2008-09 Budget Briefing*, February, Philadelphia, www.budget.state.pa

Pessoa, A. (2008) 'Public Private Partnerships in Developing Countries: Are Infrastructures Responding to the New ODA Strategy?' *Journal of International Development*, 20, p311-325.

Peterson Institute for International Economic (2009) *Assessing Global Fiscal Stimulus: Is the World Being Short-Changed?* 24 February, Washington DC, www.piie.com

Pew Center (2009) *Driven by Dollars: What States Should Know When Considering Public-Private Partnerships To Fund Transportation*, March, Washington DC, www.pewcenteronthestates.org

Philadelphia Inquirer (2008) 'Charter School Corruption 2009 Style', 29 December, Philadelphia.

Player, S. and Leys, C. (2008) *Confuse and Conceal: The NHS and Independent Sector Treatment Centres*, Merlin Press, Monmouth.

Plender, J. (2008) 'The return of the state: How government is back at the heart of economic life', *Financial Times*, 21 August, www.ft.com

Pollin, R. (2008) 'Ending Casino Capitalism', *The Nation*, 13 October, www.peri.umass.edu/

Pollin, R., Wicks-Lim, J. and Garrett-Peltier, H. (2009) *Green Prosperity: How Clean-Energy Policies Can Fight Poverty and Raise Living Standards in the United States*, Political Economy Research Institute, University of Massachusetts.

Pollock, A. M, Shaoul, J. and Vickers, N. (2002) 'Private finance and 'value for money' in NHS hospitals: a policy in search of a rationale?' *British Medical Journal*, vol. 324, pp. 1205–9.

Pollock, A. (2004) *NHS plc: The Privatisation of our Health Care*, Verso, London.

Pollock, A. and Price, D. (2004) *Public Risk for Private Gain? The public audit implications of risk transfer and private finance*, for UNISON, www.unison.org.uk

Pollock, A., Price, D. and Player, S. (2007) *An Examination of the UK Treasury's Evidence Base for Cost and Time Overrun Data in UK Value-for Money Policy and Appraisal, Public Money & Management*, April, 127-133.

Pollock, A. and Price, D. (2008) 'Has the NAO Audited Risk Transfer in Operational Private Finance Initiative Schemes?' *Public Policy & Management*, June, p173-178.

Pollock, A. and Kirkwood, G. (2009) 'Independent Sector Treatment Centres: Learning from a Scottish case Study', *British Medical Journal*, 30 April, 338:b1421.

Pomeranze, K. (2009) 'The Great Himalayan Watershed: Agrarian crisis, mega-dams and the environment', *New Left Review*, No 58, July-August.

Postigo, A. (2008) 'Financing Road Infrastructure in China and India: Current Trends and Future Options', *Journal of Asian Public Policy*, Vol. 1, No. 1, p71-89.

PricewaterhouseCoopers (2002) *Study into Rates of Return Bid on PFI Projects*, London.

PricewaterhouseCoopers (2004) *Partnering in Practice: New Approaches to PPP Delivery*, London. www.pwc.com

PricewaterhouseCoopers (2005) *Delivering the PPP promise: A Review of PPP issues and activity*, London.

PricewaterhouseCoopers (2007) *Infrastructure Funds*, London. www.pwc.co.uk

PricewaterhouseCoopers (2008) *Population Ageing and Public Infrastructure: A Literature Review of Impacts in Developed Countries*, Infrastructure Canada.

PricewaterhouseCoopers (2008) *Building New Europe's Infrastructure: Public Private Partnerships in Central and Eastern Europe*.

PricewaterhouseCoopers (2009) *Social Private Partnerships – innovation in public service delivery*, Public Sector Research Centre, www.pwc.co.uk

Private Equity Intelligence (2008) *Prequin Infrastructure Review*, www.prequin.com

Privatisation Barometer (2008) *PB report 2007: Reporting on Privatisation in the Enlarged Europe*, Milan, www.privatisationbarometer.net

Probitas Partners (2007) *Investing in Infrastructure Funds*, September, San Francisco, www.probitaspartners.com

Prodkul, C. (2009) 'Blown Away', *Infrastructure Investor*, Issue No 1, p33-35, www.infrastructureinvestor.com

Project on Emerging Nanotechnologies (2009) http://www.nanotechproject.org

Prowle, M. (2008) 'New Development: Developing Contestability in the Delivery of Public Services', *Public Money & Management*, August, p255-260.

Prud'homme, R. (2004) *Infrastructure and Development, Annual Bank Conference on Development Economics*, May, Washington DC.

Public Financial Management Inc (2008) *Special Study to Assess Opportunities to Develop Public Private Partnerships*, for Office of Controller, December, City of Los Angeles.

Public Policy Institute of California (2003) 'What can be Learned from California's Electricity Crisis', *Research Brief*, Issue 66, San Francisco, www.ppic.org

Public Private Finance (2005) 'Secondary Market takes new turn', March, p5.

Public Private Finance (2006) 'Hewitt: Norfolk and Norwich deal was 'great'', July, p7.

Public Private Finance (2007) Most PFI projects off balance sheet, December, p9.

Public Private Finance (2009) 'Interview with Philip Hammond, Shadow Chief Secretary to the Treasury'.

Public-Private Infrastructure Advisory Facility (2006) 'Financing Infrastructure in Africa', *Gridlines* No 13, September, Washington DC, www.ppiaf.org

Public-Private Infrastructure Advisory Facility (2008) *New private infrastructure projects in developing countries have started being affected by the financial crisis*, ppiaf.org

Public-Private Infrastructure Advisory Facility (2009) *Building Bridges: China's Growing Role as Infrastructure Financier for Sub-Saharan Africa*, Washington DC, www.ppiaf.org

Public-Private Infrastructure Advisory Facility (2009) *Assessment of the impact of the crisis on new PPI projects – Update 3*, June, Washington DC, www.ppiaf.org

Public-Private Infrastructure Advisory Facility (2009) Database, www.ppiaf.org, accessed 8 August.

Put People First (2009) Beyond the London Summit: Assessing the UK Government's Response to the Financial Crisis and Charting a Way Forward, June, London, www.putpeoplefirst.org.uk

Public Services International Research Unit (2005) *Water privatisation and restructuring in Asia-Pacific*, January, www.psiru.org

Public Services International Research Unit (2008) *PPPs in the EU: A Critical Appraisal*, D. Hall, October, London, www.psiru.org

Public Service Review (2008) 'Better Build for Better Health', October, www.publicservice.co.uk

Quarmby, K. and Fazackerly, A. (2009) *Building Blocks? An investigation into Building Schools for the Future*, Policy Exchange, London, www.policyexchange.org.uk

Quiggin, J. (2004) 'Risk, PPPs and the Public Sector Comparator', *Australian Accounting Review*, July, 14:2.

Quiggin, J. (2004) 'Financing our roads, rail, tunnels and bridges: The case for infrastructure bonds', *Kings Counsel*, Issue 22, Autumn, King & Co Property Consultants, Brisbane.

Quiggin, J. (2006) *There's nothing intrinsically wrong with public debt*, June, www.uq.edu.au

Quirk Review (2007) 'Making Assets Work: The Quirk Review of community management and ownership of public assets', Department of Communities and Local Government, London, www.communities.gov.uk

Railroad Development Corporation (2009) *Estonian Railways*, www.rrdc.com/op_estonia_evr_past.html (accessed 8 August 2009).

Rand Education (2007) *State Takeover, School Restructuring, Private Management, and Student Achievement in Philadelphia*, www.rand.org

Ravillion, M. (2008) *Bailing Out the World's Poorest*, October, Policy Research Working Paper No 4763, Development Research Group, World Bank, Washington DC.

Regan, E. (1999) 'A New Approach to Tax-Exempt Bonds: Infrastructure Financing with the AGIS Bond', *Public Policy Brief* No 58, Jerome Levy Economics Institute, New York.

REUTERS (2009) 'Infrastructure Investments May Become REITs', 7 May, www.reuters.com

Reyes, O. (2009) 'Climate Crunch', *Red Pepper*, April/May, p24-25.

Rohatyn, F. (2009) *Bold Endeavours: How Our Government Built America and How Why it must Rebuild Now*, Simon & Schuster, New York.

Riskmetrics Group (2008) *Infrastructure Funds: Managing, Financing and Accounting: In Whose Interests?* April, New York, www.riskmetrics.com

Riskmetrics Group (2008) *Breaking Up is Hard To Do: Lessons from Privatising, Internalising and Winding Up Externally Managed Entities*, Melbourne.

Robinson, P., Hawksworth, J., Broadbent, J., Laughlin, R. and Haslam, C. (2001) *The Private Finance Initiative: Saviour, Villain or Irrelevance?* IPPR, London.

Roland-Holst, D. (2006) *Infrastructure as a Catalyst for Regional Integration, Growth and Economic Convergence: Scenario Analysis for Asia*, ERD Working Paper No 91, Asian Development Bank, Manila, www.adb.org/economics

Romer, C. and Bernstein, J. (2009) *The Job Impact of the American Recovery and Reinvestment Plan*, Washington DC, http://krugman.blogs.nytimes.com

Romp, W. and de Haan, J. (2007) 'Public Capital and Economic Growth: A Critical Survey', *Perspektiven der Wirtschaftspolitik 8* (Special Issue) p6-52.

Royal Bank of Scotland (2007) *RBS Adds Dana Levenson, Former CFO of City of*

Chicago, to North American Infrastructure Team, Press Release, 16 March, New York. www.rbsgc.com

Roy, R., Heuty, A. and Letouze, E. (2006) *Fiscal Space for Public Investment: Towards a Human Development Approach*, UNDP, prepared for G-24 Technical meeting, Singapore, September.

RREEF (Deutsche Bank) (2009) Global Ports: Trends and Opportunities, April, www.rreef.com

Ruane, S. (2008) "One Modet Brick'? Independent Sector Treatment Centres, Accountability and the Re-Commercialisation of the NHS', *Radical Statistics*, No 96, www.radstats.org.uk

Rude, C. (2008) *The Global Financial Crisis: What Needs To Be Done*, Briefing Paper, Friedrich Ebert Stiftung, New York.

Sachs, J. (2005) *Investing in Development: A Practical Plan to Achieve the Millennium Development Goals*, Report to the UN Secretary-General, New York. www.unmillenniumproject.org

Sachs, J. (2009) "Shock Therapy' had no adverse effect on life expectancy in Eastern Europe', Letter, *Financial Times*, 19 January.

Sawyer, M. (2005) *The Private Finance Initiative: the UK Experience*, University of Leeds.

Scottish Executive (2002) *Consultation on the Future of the Scottish Prison Estate*, June, www.scotland.gov.uk

Serco Institute (2007) *Competitive Edge. Does Contestability Work?* London, www.serco.com

Service Employees International Union (2008) *Sovereign Wealth Funds and Private Equity: Increased Access, Decreased Transparency*, April, Washington DC, www.seiu.org

Shaoul, J. (2005) 'A Critical Financial Analysis of the Private Finance Initiative: Selecting a Financing Method or Allocating Economic Wealth', *Critical Perspectives on Accounting*, 16, p441-471.

Shaoul, J., Stafford, A. and Stapleton, P. (2006) 'Highway Robbery?: A Financial Analysis of Design, Build, Finance and Operate (DBFO) in UK Roads', *Transport Reviews*, Vol. 26, No. 3, p257-274.

Shaoul, J., Stafford, A. and Stapleton, P. (2008) 'The Cost of Using Private Finance to Build, Finance and Operate Hospitals', *Public Money & Management*, April, p101-108.

Sheppard, R. (2003) *Capital Markets Financing for Developing-Country Infrastructure Projects, Department of Economic and Social Affairs*, United Nations, Discussion paper No. 28, January.

Siemens Financial Services (2007) *Financial Solutions and Public Services: A study of trends in investment & financing in the public services sectors across six European countries*, Munich.

Siemens Financial Services (2007) *Public infrastructures and private funding. Financial solutions for the energy, industry and healthcare sectors*, http://www.siemens.de/finance

Soria Moria Declaration on International Policy (2007) 'Chapter 2: International Policy, Office of the Prime Minister', 2 February, Norway, www.regjeringen.no

South Africa National Treasury PPP Unit (2005) *Municipal Service Delivery and PPP Guidelines*, Pretoria, www.ppp.gov.za/

South Africa National Treasury PPP Unit (2009) *PPP Quarterly*, Pretoria, www.ppp.gov.za/

Sovereign Wealth Fund Institute (2008) *What is a Sovereign Wealth Fund?* www.swfinstitute.org

Spackman, M. (2002) 'Public-Private Partnerships: Lessons from the British Approach', *Economic Systems*, Vol. 26, Issue 3, September, pages 283-301.

Speigel, E, McArthur, N. and Norton, R. (2009) *Energy Shift: Game-Changing Options for Fuelling the Future*, McGraw-Hill, New York.

Spoehr, J., Whitfield, D., Sheil, C. Quiggin, J. and Davidson, K. (2002) *Partnerships, Privatisation and the Public Interest*, Centre for Labour Research, University of Adelaide for Public Service Association of South Australia, Adelaide, www.european-services-strategy.org.uk

Standard and Poor's (2003) *Octagon Healthcare Funding PLC Refinancing*, London.

Standard and Poor's (2006) *The Amazing Growth of Global Infrastructure Funds: Too Good to be True?*, November, London, www2.standardandpoors.com

Standard and Poor's (2007) *The Changing Face of Infrastructure Finance: Beware the Acquisition Hybrid*, September, London, www2.standardandpoors.com

Standard and Poor's (2007) *How Infrastructure Assets have Weathered a decade of Storms*, October, London, www2.standardandpoors.com

State of Virginia (2008) *Interim Review of the Virginia Information Technologies Agency*, Joint Legislative Audit and Review Committee, http://jlarc.virginia.gov

Statistics Canada (2008) 'Infrastructure Capital: What Is It? Where Is It? How Much of It Is There?' *Canadian Productivity Review*, Ottawa, http://www.statcan.gc.ca/

Stichele, M.V. (2008) *How Trade, the WTO and the Financial Crisis Reinforce Each Other*, Centre for Research on Multinational Corporations, www.tni.org

Stiglitz, J.E. (2009) 'Capitalist Fools', *Vanity Fair*, January.

Straub, S. (2008) *Infrastructure and Development: A Critical Appraisal of the Macro Level Literature*, Policy Research Working Paper, No 4590, World Bank, Washington DC.

Stuckler, D. and King, L. (2009) 'Mass Privatisation and the Post-Communist Mortality Crisis: A Cross-National Analysis', *The Lancet*, Vol. 373, Issue 9661, January, p360-362.

Sussex, J. (2001) *Economics of the Private Finance Initiative in the NHS*, Office of Health Economics, London.

Sustainable Development Commission (2004) *St Bartholomew and the London Hospitals Private Finance Initiative Development*, Progress in Practice, May,

London.
Swan, P. and Belzer, M. (2007) *Empirical Evidence of Toll Road Traffic Diversion and Implications for Highway Infrastructure Privatisation*, School of Business Administration, Pennsylvania State University, Harrisburg.
Sydney Morning Herald (2007) 'Macquarie Media buys US newspaper business', 24 January, Sydney, www.smh.com.au
Sydney Morning Herald (2009) 'Brisconn hunts investors', 24 August, Sydney, www.smh.com.au
Tax Justice Network (2009) *Economic Crisis and Offshore*, accessed 12 August 2009, www.taxjustice.net
Taylor, P. and Cooper, C. (2003) *Privatised Prisons and Detention Centres in Scotland: An Independent Report*, http://visar.csustan.edu/aaba/Cooper&Taylor.pdf
Ter-Minassian, T. and Allen, M. (2004) *Public Investment and Fiscal Policy*, Fiscal Affairs Department, International Monetary Fund, Washington DC.
Texas Department of Transportation (2009) *Innovative Connectivity in Texas: Vision 2009*, Austin, www.txdot.gov
Todorvich, P. (2009) 'America's Emerging Megaregions and Implications for National Growth Strategy', *International Journal of Public Sector Management*, Vol. 22, No. 3, p221-234.
TOLLROADSnews (2005) 'Chicago Skyway handed over to Cintra/Macquarie after wiring $1,830m', 24 January, http://www.tollroadsnews.com
Toronto City Council (2008) *Blueprint for Fiscal Stability and Economic Prosperity – a Call to Action*, Mayor's Fiscal Review Panel, www.toronto.ca
Trade Union Congress (2008) *The Missing Billions: The UK Tax Gap*, London. www.tuc.org.uk
Trade Union Congress (2008) *Rethinking Public Service Reform: The 'Public Value' Alternative*, London, www.tuc.org.uk
Transportation Research Board (2008) *Potential Impacts of Climate Change on US Transportation*, Special Report No 290, Washington DC, www.TRB.org
Transportation Research Board (2009) *Public Sector Decision Making for Public Private Partnerships: A Synthesis of Highway Practice*, NCHRP Synthesis 391, Washington DC, www.TRB.org
Transnational Institute (2005) *Reclaiming Public Water Achievements, Struggles and Visions from Around the World*, Amsterdam, http://www.tni.org
Transnational Institute (2006) *Public Water for All: The Role of Public-Public Partnerships*, Amsterdam, www.tni.org
Transport for London and Mayor of London (2006) *London Underground and the PPP: The third year 2005/06*, July, London.
Transportation for Illinois Coalition (2008) '*Lease the Illinois Tollway*' *Public Ownership is Better*, January www.tficillinois.org
Triangle Business Journal (2009) 'Construction Management At Risk draws mixed reviews', 13 March, http://triangle.bizjournals.com
Tuck, L., Schwartz, J. and Andries, L. (2009) *Crisis in LAC: Infrastructure*

*Investment and the Potential for Employment Generatio*n, World Bank, Washington DC.

Tulsa World (2008) 'In get-tough stance, DOC withholds prison payments', 16 December, www.tulsaworld.com

Turner, G. (2008) *The Credit Crunch: Housing Bubbles, Globalisation and the Worldwide Economic Crisis*, Pluto Press, London.

Tyne and Wear Pension Fund (2005) *Report and Accounts 2004-05*, South Tyneside.

UK Trade & Investment (2009) *Transportation: India's Sunrise Sector*, London, www.uktradeinvest.gov.uk

UNISON (2003) *Positively Public Briefing*, August, London, www.unison.org.uk

UNISON (2004) *Public Risk for Private Gain: The public audit implications of risk transfer and private finance*, July, London, www.unison.org.uk

UNISON (2006) *In the Interests of Profit at the Expense of Patients*, Rachel Aldred, London, www.unison.org.uk

UNISON (2008) *The Rise of the 'Public Services Industry'*, a report by Paul Gosling, September, London, www.unison.org.uk

UNISON (2009) *Making the Connections: Contract Cleaning and Infection Control*, Steve Davies, London, www.unison.org.uk

United Nations (2009) *The Millennium Development Goals 2009*, New York, www.un.org

United Nations (2009) *Green Economy: A Transformation to Address Multiple Crises: An Interagency Statement of the United Nations System*, www.unep.org

United Nations Development Programme (2005) *Making Infrastructure Work for the Poor: Synthesis Report of Four Country Studies: Bangladesh, Senegal, Thailand and Zambia*, New York, www.undp.org

United Nations Conference on Trade and Development (2007) *World Investment Report 2007*, Geneva, www.unctad.org

United Nations Conference on Trade and Development (2008) *World Investment Report 2008: Transnational Corporations and the Infrastructure Challenge*, Geneva, www.unctad.org

United Nations Development Programme (2006) *Fighting Climate Change: Human Solidarity in a Divided World*, Human Development Report, 2007/2008, Geneva.

United Nations Economic and Social Commission for Asia and the Pacific (2004) *Understanding Pro-Poor Public Private Partnerships*, October, Colombo, Sri Lanka, www.unescap.org

United Nations Economic and Social Commission for Asia and the Pacific (2008) *Public Private Partnerships: A Financier's Perspective*, Bangkok, www.unescap.org

United Nations Educational, Scientific and Cultural organisation (2009) *A New Dynamic: Private Higher Education*, Paris, www.unesco.org

U.S. Commission on Ocean Policy (2004) *An Ocean Blueprint for the 21st Century*,

Final Report of the U.S. Commission on Ocean Policy, Washington DC, http://oceancommission.gov

US Public Interest Research Group (2009) *Private Roads, Public Costs: The Facts About Toll Road Privatization and How To Protect The Public*, Spring, Boston, www.uspirg.org/

University and College Union (2008) *Challenging the Market in Education: Marketisation and the growth of the private sector in tertiary education: a preliminary report*, London, www.ucu.org.uk

University and College Union (2009) *Fighting Privatisation: A branch activists' guide*, May, London, www.ucu.org.uk

Vera-Diaz, M., Kaufmann, R, and Nepstad, D. (2009) *The Environmental Impacts of Soybean Expansion and Infrastructure Development in Brazil's Amazon Basin*, Working Paper No. 09-05, Global Development and Environment Institute, Tufts University, www.fufts.edu/gdae

von Klaudy, S, Sangi, A. and Dellacha, G. (2008) *Emerging Market Investors and Operators*, Working Paper No 7, Public-Private Infrastructure Advisory Facility, World Bank, Washington DC.

von Hirschhausen, C., Beckers, T. and Tegner, H. (2002) 'Private Participation in Infrastructure (PPI) in Germany – The Gradual Awakening', *Infrastructure Journal*, June.

Wade, R. (2008) 'Financial Regime Change', *New Left Review*, No 53, Sept-Oct.

Wade, R. (2008) *A Crisis of the System*, Presentation at Tufts University, http://ase.tufts.edu/gdae

Wainwright, H. and Little, M (2009) *Public Service Reform – But not as you know it: How Democracy can transform public services*, Picnic Publishing, Hove.

Wall Street Journal (2009) 'Pricewaterhouse Defends its Audit Procedures', 8 January, www.wsj.com

Wall Street Journal (2009) 'American's See 18% of Wealth Vanish', 13 March, www.wsj.com

Wall Street Journal (2009) 'Toxic-Asset Plan Sends Stocks Soaring', 24 March, www.wsj.com

Wall Street Journal (2009) 'U.S. Highway Fund Low on Cash Again', 3 June, www.wsj.com

Wall Street Journal (2009) 'Are Sovereign Funds Ready to Spread the Wealth Again?' 6 June, www.wsj.com

Wall Street Journal (2009) 'India's Road Builder Plans 'Huge' Upgrade', 8 July, www.wsj.com

Wall Street Journal (2009) 'Macquarie Model Is Hit at Airport Fund', 27 July, www.wsj.com

Wall Street Journal (2009) 'Chinese Developers Race to Launch IPOs', 2 September, www.wsj.com

Walker, C. and Smith, A.J. (1995) *Privatised Infrastructure: The BOT Approach*,

Thomas Telford, London.

Warner, M. (2009) *Child Care Multipliers: Stimulus for the States*, Department of City and Regional Planning, Cornell University, http://economicdevelopment.cce.cornell.edu

Washington Post (2008) 'Letting the Market Drive Transportation', 17 March, Washington DC. www.washingtonpost.com

Washington Post (2008) 'Regional Panel wary of Toll Plan', 20 March, Washington DC. www.washingtonpost.com

Washington Post (2008) 'Public Role, Private Gain', 14 December, Washington DC, www.washingtonpost.com

Washington Post (2009) 'Greenway Revenue, Traffic At Odds', 5 July, Washington DC, www.washingtonpost.com

Wharton Risk Management and Decision Processes Center (2008) *Managing Large-Scale Risks in a New Era of Catastrophes*, University of Pennsylvania.

Whitfield, D. (1983) *Making it Public: Evidence and Action Against Privatisation*, Pluto Press, London.

Whitfield, D. (1984) *Privatisation and International Restructuring, World View 1985*, Pluto Press, London.

Whitfield, D. (1992) *The Welfare State: Privatisation, Deregulation, Commercialisation of Public Services*, Pluto Press, London.

Whitfield, D. (2001) *Public Services or Corporate Welfare: Rethinking the Nation State in the Global Economy*, Pluto Press, London.

Whitfield, D. (2002) 'Impact of Privatisation and Commercialisation on Municipal Services in the UK', *Transfer – Journal of the European Federation of Public Service Unions*, Brussels.

Whitfield, D. (2006) *New Labour's Attack on Public Services: Modernisation by Marketisation*, Spokesman Books, Nottingham.

Whitfield, D. (2006) 'The Marketisation of Teaching', *PFI Journal* No 52, April, London. www.european-services-strategy.org.uk

Whitfield, D. (2006) *A Typology of Privatisation and Marketisation*, Research Report No 1, European Services Strategy Unit www.european-services-strategy.org.uk

Whitfield, D. (2007) *Financing Infrastructure in the 21st Century: The Long-Term Impact of Public Private Partnerships in Britain and Australia*, Paper 2/2007, Don Dunstan Foundation, University of Adelaide www.european-services-strategy.org.uk

Whitfield, D. (2007) *Cost Overruns, Delays and Terminations: 105 outsourced public sector ICT projects*, European Services Strategy Unit, Research Report No 2. www.european-services-strategy.org.uk

Whitfield, D. (2008) *Public Private Partnerships: Confidential 'Research'*, A Critique of the Audit Commission's study of Strategic Service-delivery Partnerships, www.european-services-strategy.org.uk

Whitfield, D. (2008) *Economic Impact of Prisons in Rural Areas: A Review of the Issues*, European Services Strategy Unit for Australian Institute for Social

Research, September, www.european-services-strategy.org.uk

Wisniewska, I. (2007) *The Invisible Hand ... of the Kremlin, Capitalism 'a la russe'*, Centre for Eastern Studies, February, Warsaw.

Wolf, G. (2004) *The Risks and Benefits of Globalisation and Privatisation of Fresh Water*, in Cabrera, E. and Cobacho, R. *Challenges of the New Water Policies for the 21st Century*, Taylor & Francis, London.

Woodhouse, D. (2005) *Changing Patterns of Accountability in Westminster Systems: A UK perspective*, Political Science Program, Australian National University.

World Bank (2003) *Renegotiation of Concession Contracts in Latin America*, Policy Research Working Paper 3011, Washington DC www.worldbank.org

World Bank (2003) *Infrastructure Projects: A Review of Cancelled Private Projects*, Public Policy for the Private Sector, Note No 252, January, Washington DC.

World Bank (2005) *Infrastructure Development: The Roles of the Public and Private Sectors*, November, Washington DC.

World Bank (2006) *Infrastructure at the Crossroads: Lessons from 20 years of World Bank Experience*, Washington DC.

World Bank (2007) *An Overview of China's Transport Sector – 2007*, Washington DC.

World Bank Group (2008) *Sustainable Infrastructure Action Plan FY 2009-2011*, July, Washington DC,

World Bank (2008) *Successes and Failures of PPP Projects*, Presentation, V. Cuttaree, Europe and Central Asia Region, Warsaw, 17 June.

World Economic Forum (2005) *Building on the Monterrey Consensus: The Growing Role of Public-Private Partnerships in Mobilising Resources for Development*, September, Geneva, www.weforum.org

Yescombe, E.R. (2007) *Public Private Partnerships: Principles of Policy and Finance*, Butterworth-Heinemann, Oxford.

Zadek, S. and Radovich, S. (2006) *Governing Collaborative Governance: Enhancing Development Outcomes by Improving Partnership Governance and Accountability*, Working Paper No 23, Corporate Social Responsibility Initiative, Harvard University.

Zandi, M. (2008) Written Testimony, *House Committee on Small Business Hearing on 'Economic Stimulus For Small Business: A Look Back and Assessing Need For Additional Relief*, Washington DC.

Index

Abandoned projects 216-234
Abbotsford Hospital 167, 248
ABN Amro 173, 174
Accelerated Development Zones 204, 298
Accountability 259-269,
Acquired Rights Directive 277
Added value 312
Additionality 75
Affordability 255-259, 314
Afghanistan 28
Africa 82, 91, 114, 133, 149, 233, 272
Ageing 25
Airports 175
Alberta 167, 169
Albertis 154, 164
Alinda Capital Partners 115
Alligator Alley 37
Alternative investment 91
Amazon 180
American International Group 115
American Society of Civil Engineers 41, 58
Amey plc 191
Andean Community 86,
Angel Trains Contracts Ltd 115
Anglian Water 99
Angola 149
Apax Partners 128
Apollo 130
Arequipa 148
Argentina 57, 148, 146, 221, 273, 278
Argyll and Bute 301
Arms length companies 64
Arvato Services 69, 158
Ashley House PLC 129, 138
Asia 82, 98, 114, 116, 118, 121, 233
Asian Development Bank 33, 140, 177, 263

Asset class 91
Asset management 48
Asset monetisation 36, 47, 101, 160, 209, 275, 289
Asset backed securitisation 106
Associated British Ports 96, 110, 118
ATTAC 284, 325
Audit Commission 153, 229
Australia 24, 49, 57, 91, 95, 98, 110, 112, 115, 117, 121, 122, 123, 125, 126, 127, 130, 171-174, 198, 209, 217, 228-229, 302
Australian Institute for Social Research 171
Australian Securities and Investments Commission 131
Austria 143
Autoroutes du Sud de la France 153
Autoroutes Paris-Rhin-Rhone 153
Autostrade 116
Avon and Somerset Police Authority 268, 280
Babcock & Brown 59, 86, 92, 98, 108, 110, 115, 124, 127, 129, 167, 171, 185, 189
Balfour Beatty 60-61, 138, 192, 190, 207, 209, 219
Banco Santander 116
Bangladesh 23
Banglalore 178
Bank of England 108
Bank of International Settlements 108
Bank of Scotland 86
Barclays Bank 123, 127, 129
Barclay Private Equity 189
Bedfordshire County Council 275
Beijing 174
Belgium 143
Berlin 42

Bermuda 110, 125
Bertelsmann 69
Bilateral agreements 88, 305
Bilfinger Berger 167, 173
Biodiversity 29
Birmingham 270
Birmingham International Airport 168
Black Economic Empowerment 182
Blackstone Group 178
Blueprints 323
Bolivia 88, 122, 148, 180, 222
Bonds 100, 105, 298
Borealis 27, 120, 123, 168
Brampton Civic Hospital 247, 248
Brazil 59, 58, 137, 148, 149, 179-181, 258, 278
Brazilian National Development Bank 87, 179
Brisbane 130
Brisbane Toll Road Link 133
BrisConnections 132-134, 171
British Columbia 167
British Energy 222
British Virgin Islands 111
Bromley Hospital 193
Brussels 125
Building Australia Fund 171, 291
Building Canada Fund 295
Building Canada Infrastructure Plan 166
Building Schools for the Future 38, 63, 71, 152, 208, 251, 270, 322
Bulgaria 143, 226
Caisse des Depots 38
California 59, 103, 222, 273
California Public Employees Retirement System 123, 161
Cambodia 176
Canada 24, 25, 26, 57, 62, 95, 113, 123, 124, 129, 132, 164-167, 199, 216, 227-228, 247, 295
Canada Line Rapid Transit 248

Canada Pension Plan Investment Board 99, 124
Canadian Council for Public-Private Partnerships 141
Canadian Union of Public Employees 323
Capio 130, 213
Capita Group PLC 138, 275
Carbon trading 24
Carlyle Group 122, 130, 131, 161
Carrillion 189, 191
Care homes 110
Cayman Islands 111
Center for Community Change 90, 298
Centre for Public Services 267, 270, 273, 299, 304, 319, 327
Channel Tunnel Rail Link 150
Charter schools 261
Chicago 101, 136, 258, 292
Chicago City Council 161, 162, 254
Chicago City Inspector General Office 258, 292, 309
Chicago Midway Airport 37, 160
Chicago Skyway 104, 161, 188, 250, 259
Chile 97, 99, 124, 148, 166
Children's Investment Fund 131
China 21, 23, 28, 29, 56, 59, 82, 116, 120, 121, 122, 123, 137, 145, 149, 174-176, 232
China Export-Import Bank 149
China State Investment Corporation 122
Cintra 124, 154, 184, 300
Citigroup 101, 123, 129, 139, 160, 164, 178, 271, 295
Citizens Budget Commission 166
Climate change 22-24, 70, 285, 312
Code of Practice on Workforce Matters 278
Colonial First State 94, 99
Colorado 160, 273

Columbia 88, 97, 148, 278
Competition 72-73
Commercial confidentiality 266-269
Commercialisation 67, 68
Commission for Architecture and the Built Environment 252
Commissioning 64, 66-68, 78, 267, 280
Commodification 14, 67-68, 70, 325
Commonwealth Bank of Australia 99
Commonwealth Development Corporation 122
Community asset ownership 214
Community benefits 312
Community Health Partnerships 151, 251
Community involvement 269, 310
Community Realisation European Aid Masterplan 144
Community well being 50
Concession agreement 47, 101, 135, 151, 219
Confederation Bridge 251
Confederation of British Industry 141, 153
Congestion pricing 300
Connectivity 41
ConnectEast toll road 240
Consolidation of public bodies 313
Construction companies 137
Construction costs 241-243
Construction Management At-Risk 308
Contestable markets 79
Copenhagen 125
CornerHouse 299
Corporate impact 312
Corporate power 268
Corporate welfare 271
Corporatisation 271
Corrections Corporation of America 261
Cost overruns 241

Council of Europe Development Bank 143
Council on Foreign Relations 122
Credit Suisse 109, 130
Critical infrastructure 30
Critical Infrastructure Protection Programmes 42
Croatia 226
Cross City Tunnel 173
Crowding out 56
CSX 131-132
CVC Capital Partners 130, 131
Cyberspace 30
Cypress 143
Czech Republic 144, 209, 225
Czech Republic Public Private Partnerships Association 141
Dallas 295
Darent Valley Hospital 183
Debt write-off 74
Defend Council Housing 153
Deficits 54, 289
Delhi 178
Deloitte 139
Demand forecasts 239, 291, 311
Democratic accountability 204, 272, 291, 313
Department for International Development 18
Department for Transport 258
DEPFA Bank 37, 86, 94, 108
Deregulation 53, 67
Derivatives 107
Design 248-251
Design, Build, Finance and Operate 46, 265
Deutsche Bank 27, 93, 95, 116, 127, 132-133, 157, 169, 174
Developing countries 101, 135, 140, 293
Development aid 301
Dexia 86
Digital economy 30

Dominican Republic 148
Dubai Ports World 27, 122
Dublin 121
Dublin City Council 76, 154
Dulles Greenway 159, 165, 257
Durham 52
Eastern and Central Europe 117, 272
East Asia 144, 214, 215, 230
Econometric modelling 50
Economic costs and benefits 50, 311, 315
Economic development 54, 311
Economic growth 51-65
Economic infrastructure 39
Economic models 50
Economic Policy Institute 61
Economic realism 283
Eco-towns 287
Ecuador 88, 148
Education 288
Efficiency 73, 207
Embedding business interests 66
Employment 53, 59, 77, 240, 277-280, 285, 286, 314, 316
Energy 79, 134, 145, 222
Environmental Impact Assessment 312
Ernst & Young 139, 238
Estonia 221
Ethiopia 149
Europe 31, 91, 98, 114, 121, 125, 144, 145, 147, 215, 232
European Bank for Reconstruction and Development 87, 144
European Commission 80
European Court of Justice 80
European International Contractors 140
European Investment Bank 38, 56, 87, 140, 143, 144, 156, 242, 249, 251
European Network for Debt and Development 89

European Public Services Network 325
European PPP Expertise Centre 87, 140
European Regional Business and Economic Development Unit 287
European Services Strategy Unit 73, 240, 268, 270, 275, 279, 299, 327
European Spatial Development Perspective 144
European Trade Union Confederation 325
European Union draft Migrant Return Directive 88
European Union Services Directive 78, 325
Eversholt Leasing Ltd 116
Excelcare Holdings 110, 279
Express LIFT 151
Externalities 39
Facilities management 100, 98
Federal Highways Administration 62
Federal Reserve Bank, 21, 110
Federation of Canadian Municipalities 62
Financial crisis 64, 283
Financial engineering 106
Financialisation 14, 22, 66, 70, 102, 109, 303
Finland 143
Fiscal crisis 35
Fiscal stimulus 59, 61, 83, 329
Florida 160-161
Fondi Italiani per le infrastructure 115
Foreign Direct Investment 134
Foreign exchange reserves 119
Foreign policy 87
Framework agreement 271
France 57, 134, 143, 153-154
Freedom of Information 317
Fremantle Trust 279
G20 group of countries 57

Gatwick Airport 37
Gender 34
General Agreement for Trade in Services 32, 80, 79, 303, 325
General Healthcare Group 130
Geneva 136
Geo Group 257
German Financial Markets Stabilisation Fund 37
Germany 21, 26, 37, 57, 88, 97, 120, 124, 142, 144, 157-158, 210, 213
Global credit crisis 109
Global Infrastructure Partners 115
Global Solutions 189, 194
Global trade 26-27
Global Unions 284
Globalisation 78
Goldman Sachs 27, 36, 38, 99, 116, 120, 124, 130, 139, 161, 164, 210
Good Jobs New York 271
Governance 259-269, 314
Governance and accountability framework 260
Government Accountability Office 165
Greater Manchester Waste 87
Greece 143
Gross Domestic Product 13
Growth wedge 104
Guangzhou 175
Guarantees 95, 249, 310
Guatemala 221
Guernsey 110
Harris County Commissioners 164
Harris County Toll Road Authority 164, 300
HBOS 35, 55, 128
Health 77, 152, 242, 288
Hedge funds 109, 116, 119, 129, 304
Henderson PFI Secondary Funds 54, 124, 190
HSBC Infrastructure Company 110, 116, 124, 127, 190
Highways 62

Highway Trust Fund 297
Hochtieff 130, 138, 156, 158, 190, 273
Hospitals 63, 154, 158, 213, 246, 249, 253, 276
Hospital Corporation of America 131
House of Commons Public Accounts Committee 189
Housing 76, 152, 156-157, 210
Housing Trust Funds 298
Hungary 144, 226, 258
Hyderabad 178
Hypo Real Estate 37, 96
IBM 138, 229, 262-263, 267, 280
Independent Next Generation Fund 297
Independent Sector Treatment Centre 48, 63-64, 76, 250, 274
India 28, 30, 56, 57, 116, 137, 145, 177-179
India Infrastructure Finance Company 178
Indiana Toll Road 104, 161, 250
Individualisation 67
Indonesia 57, 145
Information and Communications Technology 46, 77, 222, 229, 263, 270
Infracapital Partners 54, 128
Infrastructure 33, 58, 79, 91, 115, 191-199, 276, 284, 299
Infrastructure Australia 40, 171, 172, 295
Infrastructure Canada 295
Infrastructure Consortium for Africa 140
Infrastructure Crisis Facility 86
Infrastructure Crisis Facility 86
Infrastructure funds 114-118
Infrastructure Ontario 59
Infrastructure Partnerships Australia 140, 241
In-house delivery 311
Innisfree 115, 129, 186

Inverness Airport 310
Innovation 21, 75, 253
Insurance companies 119
Integration of Regional Infrastructure in South America 179
Integrator model 207
Inter-Governmental Panel on Climate Change 22
International Centre for the Settlement of Investment Disputes 272
International Chamber of Commerce 140
International Finance Corporation 30, 83, 85, 180, 272
International Financial Reporting Standard 257
International Financial Services London 123
International Monetary Fund 19, 22, 35, 40, 74, 82, 89, 140, 306
Investment returns 92
Iran 28, 174
Ireland 74, 98, 121, 124, 143, 154-157, 216, 225
Irish Congress of Trade Unions 157
Italy 57, 117, 143
Japan 21, 26, 57, 120, 123, 131
Japan Airport Terminal Company 125
Jarvis 154, 189
Jersey 27, 110, 120
Jerusalem 42
John Laing PLC 126, 167, 189, 190
Joint Assistance in Supporting Projects in European Regions 144
Joint European Support for Sustainable Investment in City Areas 144
Joint investment 295
Joint Venture Company 47, 270, 279, 307, 310

JP Morgan 110, 128, 139, 160, 162
Kazakhstan 28
Kentucky 271
Keynesian economic model 65
KfW Bankengruppe 106
Kohlberg Kravis Roberts 130
KPMG 13
Korea 25, 97, 252
Kuwait 28, 121, 269
Kuwait Investment Office 120, 265
Kyrgyzstan 28
Land Securities Trillium 190, 276
Lane Cove Tunnel 174
Laos 176
Latin America 51, 53, 117, 135, 144, 146, 209, 218, 230, 231, 278
Leeds 55
Leighton Holdings 132-133, 173
Liberalisation 32
Lisbon strategy 143
Listed infrastructure fund 98, 114
Lloyds TSB 37, 128
Local Asset Backed Vehicle 298
Local Education Partnership 71, 75, 152, 208, 309
Local Government Services Market 97
Local Improvement Finance Trust 63, 97, 129, 151, 208, 270
Local Partnerships 153
Local Strategic Partnership 68
London 136
London Borough of Haringey 243, 270
London Underground 150, 183
Los Angeles 166
Low carbon economy 13, 285
M6 toll road 55, 188
M25 highway 87
Maastricht Treaty 35, 76
Macquarie Bank 27, 55, 58, 86, 92, 110, 115, 123, 124, 125, 126, 127, 129, 130-132, 171, 172, 175, 179,

184, 189, 266, 300
Macquarie Infrastructure Group 93, 113, 124, 164, 165
Macquarie model 99, 123
Madeira Project 177
Malaysia 97, 145
Manchester 55
Manor Care 122
Mapeley 110
Market mechanisms 68
Marketisation 14, 22, 67, 70, 207, 301, 325
Massachusetts Infrastructure Investment Coalition 62
Mega-projects 42
Megacities 23, 25-26, 95
Megaregions 22-23
Melbourne 240
Merrill Lynch 132
Metronet 223, 249
Mexico 24, 57, 147, 148, 149, 218
Middlesbrough 54, 275
Middle East 28, 98, 112, 144, 215
Millennium Development Goals 29, 81
Ministry of Defence Estate in London 214
Minnesota 273
Mixed economy 77, 78
Monoline insurance 100
Morgan Stanley 98, 115, 129, 168, 295
Mott MacDonald 235, 241
Mouchel 138, 275
Mumbai 178
Multilateral agreements 88, 305
Multilateral Investment Guarantee Agency 30, 83, 85, 272
Multipliers 61
Mutual and managed funds 119
Myanmar 176
Namibia 28
Nanotechnology 31

National Association of State Budget Officers 166
National Asset Management Agency 121, 293
National Audit Office 108, 153, 185, 192, 235, 244, 256
National Council for Public Private Partnerships 141
National Express 221
National Health Service 61, 78
National PPP Forum for Australia 141
National Surface Transportation Policy and Revenue Study Commission 159
Neoliberalism 66-83, 87
Netherlands 123, 144
Network industries 13, 40
Network Rail 116, 220
Newcastle City Council 54, 152, 243
Newcastle United 107
New Brunswick 167
New energy order 27
New Jersey 161, 267
New Jersey Turnpike 163
New Labour 134
New Orleans 20, 90
New South Wales 171, 173, 275, 317
New York 110, 136, 267
New York Attorney General 132
New York State Commission on Asset Maximisation 166
New Zealand 221, 222
Niger 28
Nigeria 149
Non-Profit Distributing Organisation 301
Norfolk & Norwich Hospital 187
North East England 54
Northern Rock 110
Northern Way 55
Northumberland 52
North America 91, 98, 114, 231

North American Free Trade Agreement 320
North Atlantic Treaty Organisation 28
North Texas Tollway Authority 165, 299
Norway 121, 305
Norwegian Forum for Environment and Development 230
Norwegian Union of Municipal and General Employees 80
Nottingham City Council 294
Nova Scotia 167
Off balance sheet 15, 59, 71, 75, 256, 303
Official Development Assistance 55
Offshoring 294
Ohio Turnpike 259
Oil and gas 117
Oklahoma 127, 260
Oldham 136
Ontario 167, 247, 248
Ontario Municipal Employees Retirement System 27, 99, 120, 123, 125, 168
Ontario Teachers Pension Plan 27, 99, 168
Options appraisal 77, 326
Organisation for Economic Co-operation and Development 23, 29, 31, 33, 52, 56, 58, 65, 69-70, 81, 84, 123, 243, 277, 290, 293, 306, 314, 320
Organising 324-326
Osprey Acquisitions 99
P & O Steam Navigation 122
Pakistan 28, 176
Panama Canal 26
Paraguay 148
Paris 136
Parking 161, 258, 292
Partnership 22, 42, 49, 76, 261
Partnerships British Columbia 59, 237

PartnershipsUK 89, 101, 103, 151, 260, 301
Partnerships Victoria 237, 317
Pension funds 74, 119, 123-125, 296
Pennsylvania 261
Pennsylvania Turnpike 37, 163
Peru 88, 148, 180, 278
Personalisation 67
Philadelphia 262
Philippines 145
Poland 144, 226
Political Economy Research Institute 56, 62
Porterbrook Leasing Ltd 115
Ports 23, 24, 122, 159, 175, 218
Portugal 115, 143, 213
Poverty reduction 81, 277
Power shifts 31-33, 41
PPP Forum 141
PricewaterhouseCoopers 139, 214, 304
Prisons 148, 154, 260-261, 273, 278-279
Private debt 289
Private equity funds 91, 109, 118, 119, 130-131, 304
Private finance 64
Private Finance Initiative 36, 72
Private Investment Commission 52
Private sector investment 55, 66, 91, 146
Private sector strategy 281
Private towns 215
Privatisation 15, 17, 32, 42, 67-70, 81, 79, 89, 99, 102-103, 143, 148, 167, 209, 217, 274, 325
Procurement 77, 309, 325
Prudential 120
Productivity 51
Profit from equity sales 200
Progressive public service renewal 308
Project Delivery Organisation 210

Property partnership 48
Pro-poor PPPs 33, 83
Prudential 96
Public benefit 278
Public expenditure 15, 290, 293
Public goods 39, 79
Public health 70, 312
Public infrastructure 13-17, 20, 40-44, 54, 72, 79, 92
Public Infrastructure Investment Evaluation Framework 315
Public Interest Template 317
Public investment 284-302, 311, 329
Public management 311, 312
Public Private Infrastructure Advisory Facility 37, 38, 86, 105, 146
Public-Private Partnerships 13-18, 55, 71
   delays 34, 35, 147
   equity 188-199
   models 45, 44, 93, 135, 206
   rate of return 151, 186, 252, 256
   terminated projects 212-230
Public-Public Partnership 81, 299
Public sector capability 280, 312
Public sector capital spending 52, 54
Public Sector Comparator 75, 97, 167, 235-252, 278
Public sector debt 15, 33, 101, 289
Public service industry 136
Public value 236
Qatar 28
Quality of life 53
Quality of service 259-263, 311
Queensland 171
Rail privatisation 115, 143, 145, 220, 259
Railtrack 116, 220
Rapid transit 62, 176, 181
Rating agency 100
Rationalisation 74
Real estate 210

Real Estate Investment Trust 48, 119, 210
Redcar & Cleveland 54
Refinancing 16, 69, 102, 111, 118, 183-190
Regeneration 75, 282
Regional Business Centre 274
Regulation 313
Restructuring the state 68
Revenue bonds 294
Risk 16, 77, 101, 105, 106, 243-252, 311
RiskMetrics 110
Roads 143, 145
Road King Infrastructure 175
Rolling Stock Companies 113
Royal Bank of Scotland 37, 84, 115, 128
Russia 27, 28, 59, 121, 145, 169-171
Russian Bank for Development 170
St Michaels Estate 156
St Petersburg 170, 171
Sao Paulo Metro 180
Saudi Arabia 28, 57, 121, 119
Savings claims 71
Schools 155, 248, 261
Secondary market 16, 99, 183, 199, 257
Secondary Market Infrastructure Fund 189, 203, 202
Scotland 275, 297, 310
Secrecy 207
Securitisation 18, 102, 106, 108, 304
Semperian PPP Investments Partners 189, 276
Serco Institute 153
Service Employees International Union 122
Shanghai 174
Shared services 271
Sheffield 55
Sheffield City Council 77, 213
Shock doctrine 89

Singapore 99, 120, 121, 135
Skanska 138, 300
Skye Toll Bridge 223, 310
Social infrastructure 39
Social justice 33, 70, 272
Social needs 70
Social private partnerships 214
Societe des Autoroutes du Nord ct de l'Est de la France 153
Societe Generale 189
Somerset County Council 136, 267, 280
South Africa 28, 57, 97, 137, 181-182, 237
South America 112
South Asia 55, 147, 215
South Australia 172
South East Asia 57
South Korea 57, 95
South London Healthcare 255
South Tyneside 54
Southwest One 267, 280
Sovereign Wealth Funds 96, 107, 116, 118-123
Spain 25, 57, 97, 113, 134, 143, 247
Special Purpose Vehicle 46, 66, 71, 75, 99, 244, 248, 261, 262
Stagecoach 115, 175
Standard and Poor's Global Infrastructure Index 93, 92
Stapled 110
State subsidies 250, 267
Statistics Canada 40
Stichting Pensioenfonds ABP 124
Strategic alliances 330
Strategic Estate Development Vehicle 44, 214
Strategic Infrastructure Partnership 211
Strategic partnerships 79, 99
Strategic planning 309
Strategic Service-delivery Partnerships 13, 47, 59, 63, 75, 78, 101, 150, 212, 249, 262, 265, 270, 274
Street lighting 239
Stress Test 317-319
Sub-Saharan Africa 82, 144, 215
Sudan 149
Suez 176
Sustainable development 70, 286
Sydney 125, 136, 173, 242
Synthetic securitisation 106
Sweden 144, 213
Switzerland 144, 296
Taunton Deane District Council 267, 280
Tax concessions 249
Tax havens 110, 112-113, 294
Tax Justice Network 294
Tax regulations 290
Taxes 290
Teeside Pension Fund 55
Telecommunications 134, 145, 147, 215, 218
Tenaska Capital Management 115, 120
Terminated projects 212-230
Texas 127, 160, 271
Texas State Highway 299
Thames Water 97
Three Gorges Dam 176
Thornton Hall 37, 156, 212
Toll roads 92, 113, 117, 148, 151, 159, 168, 173, 180, 181,188, 218, 240, 242
Toronto 136
Toronto 407 Express Toll Route 168
Toronto City Council 169
Toronto Hydro 169
Toronto Parking Authority 169,
Trade union involvement 269, 314
Transaction costs 249
Transatlantic Business Dialogue 140
Trans-European Transport Network 27
Transfield Infrastructure 174
Transformation 64, 247

Transnational corporations 137-139
Transparency 291
Transportation Infrastructure Finance and Innovation Act 1998 159
Trans Texas Corridor 27, 127
Transport 134, 215
Transport for London 229
Trident 298
Troubled Asset Relief Program 38
Tube Lines 116
Turkey 57, 145
Turkmenistan 28
Twin track strategy 321-323
Tyne and Wear 54
Tyne and Wear Pension Fund 54
UBS 121, 128
Unified Energy 170,
UNISON 267-268, 280, 299
United Arab Emirates 28, 121, 122
United Kingdom 29, 38, 46, 55, 57, 74, 76, 79, 88, 96, 115, 117, 123, 134, 136, 143, 149-153, 216, 219, 225, 226, 256, 258, 277, 297, 303
UK Trade and Investment 135
United Nations 49, 88, 306
United Nations Conference on Trade and Development 134, 136
United Nations Development Programme 30
United Nations Economic and Social Commission for Asia and the Pacific 88
United Nations Millennium Declaration 39
United States 23, 25, 28, 29, 31, 41, 54, 59, 61, 88, 91, 106, 117, 120, 120, 132, 147, 158-167, 226-227
Universities Superannuation Fund 124
Unlisted infrastructure fund 98, 111, 116
Unsolicited bids 161
User charges 300
User involvement 314

Utilities 115
Uzbekistan 28
Value for money 74, 77, 207, 235-252, 276, 282
Venezuela 148, 222
Veolia 124, 176, 209, 273
Victoria 169
Victoria Supreme Court 133
Vietnam 23
Vinci 193, 214
Virginia 160, 263
Washington DC 261
Waste 273
Water crisis 29-30
Water investment 27, 41, 62, 83, 117, 143, 145, 158, 176, 215, 231-234, 259
Welfare state infrastructure 42
West Midlands 55, 188
West Midlands Pension Fund 124
Whitehall funds 210
Whole life costs 74
Whole service concept 213
Wisconsin 273
Worker/user plans 323-324
World Bank 13, 17, 22, 30, 40, 54, 57, 64, 82-83, 86, 89, 103, 140, 234, 272, 306, 320
World Trade Organisation 14, 32, 306, 325
Workplace Parking Levy 294
Wrapped bond market 101
WS Atkins 219
Yangtze River 176

Dexter Whitfield

Dexter Whitfield is Director of European Services Strategy Unit (continuing the work of the Centre for Public Services founded in 1973) and is Adjunct Associate Professor, Australian Institute for Social Research, University of Adelaide. He has carried out extensive research and policy analysis of regional/city economies and public sector provision, jobs and employment strategies, impact assessment and evaluation, marketisation and privatisation, modernisation and public management (www.european-services-strategy.org.uk).

He has undertaken commissioned work for a wide range of public sector organisations, local authorities and agencies and worked extensively with trade unions in the UK at branch, regional and national levels, and internationally. He has advised many tenants and community organisations on housing, planning and regeneration policies.

Dexter is the author of New Labour's Attack on Public Services: Modernisation by Marketisation (2006), Public Services or Corporate Welfare: The Future of the Nation State in the Global Economy (2001), The Welfare State: Privatisation, Deregulation & Commercialisation (1992) and Making it Public: Evidence and Action against Privatisation (1983). He was one of the founding members of Community Action Magazine (1972-1995) and Public Service Action (1983-1998). He has published many articles in journals and delivered papers and advised public bodies and trade unions in Europe, US, Canada, Australia and New Zealand.

New Labour's Attack on Public Services
by Dexter Whitfield

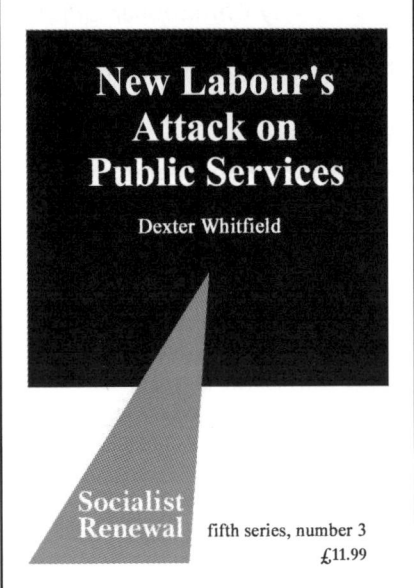

New Labour has created markets in public services on an unprecedented scale. Education, health and social care, children's services, housing, planning and regeneration, the criminal justice system and the welfare state are all being marketised.

Privatisation inevitably follows marketisation, eroding democratic accountability and embedding business interests. The impact will be far reaching. Any benefits in terms of economic, social and sustainable development that are gained through regional strategies and city regions could evaporate if market forces are allowed to run rampant across the public sector.

Alternative policies and strategies must build on the support for democratic governance, social justice and the welfare state. As this book makes clear, action by alliances of trade unions, community and civil society organisations is urgently required.

Spokesman Books, Russell House, Bulwell Lane, Nottingham, NG6 0BT
Email: elfeuro@compuserve.com | Tel: 0115 970 8381 | Fax: 0115 942 0433
www.spokesmanbooks.com